the

ULTIMATE GUIDE
TO HOMESCHOOLING

Debra Bell

apologiaPress™
RESOURCES FOR THE HEART AND MIND

the ULTIMATE GUIDE to HOMESCHOOLING

published by ApologiaPress,
a division of Apologia Educational Ministries, Inc.
1106 Meridian Plaza, Suite 220 • Anderson, IN 46016 • www.apologia.com

© 2009 by Debra Bell
International Standard Book Number: 978-1-932012-98-9

Book and Cover Design: Kim Williams

Printed by Courier, Inc., Kendallville, IN
First printing: November 2009

Diligent effort has been made to verify the accuracy of e-mail and Internet
addresses, website links, and other sources provided within this volume. Given the rapid changes
that can occur in electronic media, however, no guarantee can be made that these addresses
remain correct following publication. If you can provide updated source information please contact
the author through one of the means listed on the final page of the book.

**To my dad and mom,
Bill and Jean Joseph,**
educators who always did what was in their
power to do to help kids. I know this isn't exactly what
you envisioned when you told me to teach, but you've
both been good sports about it.

And to Kermit,
who knows me better than anyone else and still
agrees to live with me. What a feat! I can't imagine a
better husband or father for our kids.
I love you.

CONTENTS

Part 3: Organization and Planning

Part 4: Preventing Burnout

Part 5: What to Teach—When and How

Part 6: Homeschooling Teens

Part 7: Computers in the Homeschool

Part 8: Creative Solutions

Part 9: Measuring Your Success

Part 10: Resource Guide

Notes

Index

Contact the Author

FOREWORD

Editor's Note: Michael Farris is chancellor of Patrick Henry College and founder of the Home School Legal Defense Association. He was named one of the Top 100 Faces in Education of the 20th Century by Education Week *magazine. Farris has argued constitutional cases in the United States Supreme Court, six U.S. Circuit Courts of Appeal, and the appellate courts of twelve different states. Michael and Vickie Farris have been married since 1971 and have ten children.*

Debra Bell's *The Ultimate Guide to Homeschooling* is a wonderful tool for veteran homeschoolers as well as those who are thinking about teaching their own kids at home. I have been involved with homeschooling a long time now, since 1982, but the basic needs of homeschooling parents (especially moms, who do most of the work) haven't changed: They need information, they need help, and they need encouragement. Debra's book ably meets all three of these needs. *The Ultimate Guide* is incredibly easy to use and is immensely practical, which means it passes Mike Farris's Official Number One Rule in Homeschooling: *If it ain't easy for Mom to use, throw it out.*

If you want information on choosing curriculum, you'll find it here. If you want to learn how to use the Internet to help you homeschool, you'll find what you need here. If you want a guide to the best organizations, it's here. Or if you just need a few good ideas to help you solve a problem you've encountered, those are here as well.

Homeschoolers through the years have taken a lot of heat from the educational establishment. Many of us have also met with an initial lack of support and even hostility from friends, in-laws, and neighbors who don't understand our choice to homeschool. One of the things I most appreciate about Debra's book is the spiritual underpinning it brings to the table. Her Christ-centered approach will enable you to not only stand firm if ever challenged by authorities or loved ones, but her faith-filled advice will also keep you from reacting with fear, discouragement, or negativity.

For my part, let me tell you that homeschooling is worth all the effort that Debra realistically describes in these pages. We have seven grown children and eleven grandchildren—so far. We will be homeschooling our three younger children until approximately 2016, but already we have tasted the fruits of victory that come with bringing a child to maturity. While there are many tools to make homeschooling easier—and this book is certainly one of the best—it remains hard work. But the harvest you will reap is worth every sacrifice, every effort, and every hour you invest.

Michael Farris

Acknowledgments

Once again, I must thank our four children—Gabe, Mike, Kayte, and Kristen—for your enduring patience through the many revisions of this book and also for your willingness to share our homeschool adventure with just a few other folks. The amazing grace of God abounds in each one of your lives, and for this your father and I are forever grateful.

My deepest thanks and respect to Jay Wile and Davis and Rachael Carman for their faith and endurance in seeing me through the process that made the tenth-anniversary edition possible, and to my editor, Zan Tyler, for being a good friend and undaunted source of encouragement. I'm grateful to be locking arms with you.

Special thanks to Joanna Breault, who provided a wealth of editorial suggestions and directed me to many new homeschooling resources that I'm now happy to recommend to my readers. I hope this is the first of many future collaborations.

My deep respect goes to my support team: The heroic moms and dads of south central Pennsylvania with whom we shared our homeschool journey. You have raised some of the most engaging and appreciative kids I know. It has been a privilege to share the adventure with you.

And finally, inexpressible love and affection to my church family at Living Hope Church, Harrisburg, Pennsylvania, where we have gratefully been planted all these years. To our pastor, Ken Mellinger, and his joy-filled wife, Beth; to Gary and Kathy Teaman; and to our dear, dear friends who make up our local expression of the body of Christ. Thank you for the selfless investment each of you has made in our family's life over and over again. Thank you for living your lives at the foot of the cross. May we never move from that position of grace.

TIPS FOR USING THIS BOOK

Icons

These graphics alert you to important stuff you may want to know:

Suggested Reading
For the self-educating do-it-yourselfer. If you want to know more about the subject being discussed, here's suggested reading to get you started.

Websites
You'll find what you're looking for at this website.

From the Bell Files
From the Bell files—stories now from yesteryear, but still good enough to keep you from nodding off, I trust.

Voices of Experience
I thought you'd like to read more than just my opinion for four hundred-odd pages, so I got my friends and acquaintances around the country to chip in with their experiences as well.

Buying & Resource Information
Here's where you can buy or find more information about recommended resources. We've given preferences to those suppliers with websites or toll-free numbers.

Resource Guide

At the end of the book, this one-stop reference guide will get you plugged in to the homeschool community. Only the best organizations, suppliers, products, competitions, and other resources have been included here, and they're all organized for you in one convenient place.

Companion Site

A companion site for this book can be found at:
www.apologia.com/bookextras. The password is UltimateGuide.

INTRODUCTION

Detours Ahead!

I am reputed to have a terrible sense of direction. I maintain, however, it is a matter of perspective. Because of this quirk in my synapses, my children have unintentionally visited New Jersey and Ohio when we were aiming for someplace here in our home state of Pennsylvania. Others might have been frustrated that their intended destination had been delayed. But we chose to enjoy the unexpected pleasure of visiting a state we'd never been through before—even if it wasn't Hawaii.

The latter is my approach to life and to homeschooling.

Both have been filled with unexpected detours and unintended delays—often caused by my own human failings. Praise be to God and the unfathomable riches of His grace—the foundation upon which I have purposed to build my life! I'm not surprised or discouraged by these errors. I know my Redeemer lives, and He is able to "undo" exceedingly and abundantly beyond all that I can ask or imagine, to paraphrase the apostle Paul.

A Long and Winding Road

If you are currently homeschooling or intending to homeschool your kids, then start with these givens: You're going to make mistakes. You're going to change your mind about resources and direction. Some days you'll get frustrated, feel like quitting, and wonder if all the effort is making any difference at all. In fact, all the evidence before you may suggest you've only made things worse!

The intent of this book is to help you minimize those moments. This is a "live-from-the-trenches" report, including:

- lots of stories
- practical tips
- concrete strategies
- recommended resources
- and more

The Ultimate Destination

But that's not the foundation for successful homeschooling, nor is it the source of joy that will keep you motivated. Those are only found in the grace of God.

So add one more thing to that list of givens: God doesn't expect you to get it right the first time. He wants you to enjoy the process—wrong turns and all.

Why? Because our only destination in life is really a journey of discovery—a discovery of who He truly is: merciful and sovereign over all.

> "What we call *the process* God calls *the end*."
> —*Oswald Chambers*

A Graceful Finish

This is my prayer: May God's grace permeate these pages and my words. While I'd like you to think I've got it all together here, I know that dishonesty does nothing to help you successfully homeschool your children. All I'd have to do to dispel that myth is describe what my house looks like right now. Here it is algebraically:

$$\text{wildest imagination}^{10} = x$$

This book is merely a distillation of our homeschooling adventure, an adventure I can honestly say has been a true journey of joy thus far. In these pages you'll find the successes and all the picture-perfect moments, but you'll also see the misfires and wrong turns, the limitations of our abilities, and the consequences of our failings. Above all, I pray you'll see throughout this book a testimony of the redeeming grace of God, which is equally available to all (even to *your* family) and is the *only* place to start and end the journey of life—and homeschooling.

Meet the Husband and Kids

My intention in this book is to intersperse all kinds of impressive research, profound wisdom, and compelling arguments for homeschooling with vignettes from the real lives of homeschool families. Since my own kids and hubby have signed off on being featured in many of these tales, I'll take a few moments to introduce everyone to you now and to update their vital statistics:

Kermit: In past editions, I've identified my wonderful husband as everyone's favorite playmate (obviously the elementary years); last edition he had become everyone's favorite lender (teenagers on board!). Today he is the wise counselor to our four grown children. He's still doing something with computers to bring home the bacon, and together we look forward to a second generation of progeny to shepherd about.

Gabe: Along with his identical twin, Gabe graduated from homeschooling in 2001. In 2005, he graduated from Indiana University of Pennsylvania's honors college with degrees in finance and economics. In between, he also managed to see much of the world through studying abroad three times and backpacking through more than twenty countries. He completed several internships in public policy in high school and college, and today works in business-to-business sales. He currently enjoys rehabbing his home in the city, investing time in the youth of our church and saving up for whatever comes next.

Mike: Mike attended the same university and honors program as his brother (but did not room with him) and completed his education in international business in three and a half years. He spent extended periods of time in South Africa, Thailand, France, and Bangladesh and also traveled to many places in between. In some cases, he was studying at foreign universities; but in others, he worked voluntarily with children affected by AIDS. Today he is a sales manager, and along with his wife, Destiny, is also saving up for whatever comes next. Destiny had an eclectic education (you name it, she did it) and today is an English teacher in an urban setting.

Kayte (aka Kathryn): Kayte was a Presidential Scholar at the University of Pittsburgh and graduated in 2007 with degrees in mathematics and French and a minor in Arabic. Not to be outdone by her globe-trekking brothers, Kayte circumnavigated the globe on Semester-at-Sea (semesteratsea.com) and also studied in Provence, France, and in Cairo, Egypt. Her capstone adventure was finding the mountainous village in northern Lebanon my grandparents emigrated from in 1908. She also found relatives of ours still living there, with whom she conversed in Arabic and French. (They said not to wander around northern Lebanon like that again!) Today she is completing two years of service with Teach for America as an urban math teacher and is a graduate student at the University of Pennsylvania.

Kristen: Kris is currently a junior at a state university, also preparing to work in an urban setting as an elementary teacher. She has taken summer classes, online classes, and extra-credit loads in an effort to finish her degree swiftly and frugally (check her status on Facebook if you want to guess why). Kristen has been a source of encouragement for many a homeschool mom—she read late and overcame many challenges to become the dean's list student she is today. She put her faith in God for her academic success, and He met her with generosity. Her primary reason for going into education is to help kids who struggle to learn.

Supporting Cast

Beyond my own family's experience, I draw heavily upon the lives of my dear friends who are great sports about figuring unadulterated into my tale. Homeschooling would have never been quite as rich an experience if we had not had a large homeschool and church community to share the journey with.

In particular, Cindy McKeown and Marie Gamon have been my mentors throughout this adventure. Both have fulfilled the role of a Titus 2 woman in my life, encouraging me first in my marriage, and then generously sharing with me the rewards and challenges of homeschooling as I followed them doggedly down the road. When they tackled elementary school, I stuck close at their heels with my younger kids. Then, with fear and trepidation, I went over the cliff of high school only because they were still determinedly blazing a trail up ahead.

Currently, Cindy and Marie are retired from homeschooling (or on hiatus until the first grandchildren come along). But Marie continues to teach art classes to the homeschool community, and Cindy is ever available as many of us now navigate our children through the post–high school years.

Just to help you keep things somewhat straight, here is a brief rundown of the three homeschool co-ops we participated in during our homeschooling years:

Learning Center Homeschool Co-op

This bimonthly co-op was started back in 1987 by my pastor's wife, Beth Mellinger. I joined in 1988 with my 5-year-old twins and only retired from leadership in 2003 and involvement in 2004. It is still going strong today with an average of thirty families participating every year. Here is where my children made many of their fondest homeschool memories—the Learning Center has provided choir, physical education, art, drama, cooking classes, Geo Bee, the Book-it program, field trips, service projects, and an endless list of other special activities over the years.

CHESS (Creative Home Educators Support Services)

Founded by Cindy McKeown in 1996, CHESS is a hybrid of homeschool and private school. CHESS meets once a week in a former Christian school building and provides core classes for junior high and high school students. I am one of six teachers providing English courses, while other qualified homeschooling parents teach the sciences with labs, math, Spanish, computers, and art. We serve more than two hundred students at CHESS, and this is the secret to how I got through high school with my kids.

Encore! Home School Productions

When my daughter Kayte and her friends were about to enter high school, they called a meeting of their mothers. Here they informed us that they weren't going to give us grief about homeschooling them through high school (as some of their brothers had), but the one thing they wanted was a "real" drama program, with productions on scale with what they might get to be a part of at the local high school. This seemed a good deal for avoiding grief, so we hired a director from the local community theater group and began holding acting classes, taking bus trips to New York City to see Broadway shows and putting on an end-of-the-year production. Shortly our drama troupe became so large we needed to set it up as its own nonprofit organization. By the time Kristen was in high school, we started tackling full-scale musicals. I've stayed involved even though all my kids are now graduated because I love musical theater. And because I'm just a hanger-on at this point, I can tell you that the team of homeschool moms who've taken over directing and staging these shows has reached the semi-professional level.

You can read more about setting up co-ops in Chapter 18. I only take space here to highlight our experiences because this kind of networking in the homeschool community is happening across the United States, and you'll certainly want to get plugged in wherever your locale.

The Fruit

"I would never homeschool my kids." —Debby Bell, 1980

Thirty years ago, when the first woman at our church began to homeschool, I wrote her off as being a bit eccentric (she also had her babies at home and did once-a-month cooking).

But when, the following year, my two closest friends, Cindy McKeown and Marie Gamon, likewise withdrew their children from a private school and took up homeschooling, I was on my knees in a panic, begging, "Oh, please, please, Lord, don't let this be a trend! Let this be another silly, short-lived fad Christians get suckered into, like prayer plants!"

I had just given birth to twins (in a hospital, with drugs), and my goal in life was to survive till they were five and I could send them to school. (I was also hoping to comb my hair and take a shower then.) Having just finished the graduate work necessary for my permanent teaching certification as well, I took offense at my friends' boldness to undertake my profession—without degrees!

But fruit is fruit and deserves an honest examination. I quelled my panic and waited for the results.

"Congratulations, Mrs. Bell! Your Test Is Positive"

Well, the results came in, and I couldn't argue with the evidence: Cindy's and Marie's kids loved to learn, they scored well on the standardized tests I gave them over the years, and they were consistently motivated to do their best in their studies.

Further, these kids loved the Lord, were kind to their younger siblings, enjoyed and respected their parents, and were funny and fascinating to know.

Cindy's and Marie's kids had no difficulty gaining entrance to their colleges of choice, and today all have graduated and are busy establishing successful careers in their chosen professions. They are all fascinating to talk with, and each continues along a path of lifelong learning.

Guess Who Signs Up

In short, by the time my twins, Mike and Gabe, were five, I had concluded that Cindy's and Marie's kids were the way I wanted my own to turn out—and I had to admit that homeschooling was a major contributor. (I'd also figured out how to work showering into the schedule as well.)

All these years later, my enthusiasm has not been dampened.

Guess Who Opens a Recruitment Office

I have seen the positive results not only in my own children but also in hundreds of students I've worked with since 1988.[1] Among those students are National Merit scholars, winners of national and international competitions, teens who have started and established their own businesses before leaving high school, and those who have distinguished themselves at college.

But homeschooling is not just a forum for intellectually talented kids to achieve their fullest. I've seen equal success with kids otherwise labeled delayed or learning disabled, as well as with those who are wired to learn differently.

It's All in the Family

Ultimately, though, my greatest enthusiasm comes from observing the quality of family life I see among homeschoolers. It is a powerful opportunity to integrate our children's spiritual, intellectual, and character development in a natural and nurturing setting. It's a proactive stand against a disintegrating culture that splinters families apart and exalts self-absorbed individualism.

Despite my reluctant beginnings, homeschooling has become my *joie de vivre.* I was not only there the day each of my children walked, but I was also there the day each began to read. Together we've spent the day learning triangular navigation while sailing the Chesapeake Bay. Together we've explored the battlefields of the Revolutionary and Civil wars. And together we've shared the books that color their childhood: *The Cay, Shiloh, The Giver, To Kill a Mockingbird,* and others.

It is the fabric of our family life. We enjoy learning. We enjoy each other. I don't have perfect kids, and I certainly am a very imperfect mom, but I believe homeschooling has allowed Kermit and me to maximize the time we have to prepare our kids for adulthood. I'm grateful for that and want to add my voice of encouragement to others who consider traveling this road.

A Blessing, Not a Cross

If God is calling your family to homeschool, it's not a cross to bear—it's a manifold blessing that I look forward to helping you realize.

The Big Picture

Obviously, homeschooling can no longer be viewed as a short-lived fad. The U.S. Department of Education reported 1.5 million schoolchildren as being homeschooled in 2007. In a more detailed analysis, Dr. Brian Ray, director for the National Home Education Research Institute, projects between 1.7 million and 2.1 million children in K–12 as being homeschooled currently.[2] And researchers have found steady growth in the number of homeschoolers—between 7 percent and 15 percent annually since this guide was first published in 1997.

That has certainly proven true here in Pennsylvania. Last year, there were 23,000 registered homeschoolers in our state (and we do not have to report until our kids are eight), nearly 60,000 registered in Florida, more than 90,000 in Texas; and a reported 166,000 in California–one reason why everyone, including most school officials, wanted to overturn the egregious Court of Appeals ruling that homeschooling was illegal. The numbers are growing everywhere, including internationally.[1] In his 2007 best-seller *Microtrends*, political strategist Mark Penn named homeschooling one of the "small forces behind tomorrow's big changes."

Why is this happening?

Techno-Revolution Meets Parental Choice

The growing homeschooling movement may be fueled by the collapse of our country's Judeo-Christian underpinnings, placing conservative and Christian families increasingly at odds with our culture. Also, the bureaucratic quagmire of our public schools as well as the agenda of the National Education Association leave parental concerns far down the list of considerations. Recent economic upheavals have also led to an exodus from private schools.

While these and other factors have provided the motivation for many families to exit the system, the technological revolution is providing the means. Online classes, university-size libraries compressed to a couple of CD-ROMs, intuitive software, and Internet connections to the far corners of the world have opened up new vistas of learning—and the homeschool community is among the first in line at these doors.

Even for those still plodding through life without high-speed access, the proliferation of video courses, DVDs, satellite schools, and hybrid organizations (like CHESS) that combine home and private schooling all enable an ever-increasing number of families to believe they can undertake home education without having to shoulder the responsibility alone.

While full-time homeschooling may never become mainstream, it is the radical edge of the parental-choice movement, which, coupled with the technological revolution, will eventually force our mass-production approach to education to give way to one that is individualized, flexible, and respectful of the diverse needs of families.

There's Something Happenin' Here

In the spiritual realm, I believe something far more profound is at work. While I never want to be misunderstood as saying that homeschooling is the only appropriate choice for Christians, I do believe it is an example of the creative solutions God can be counted on to supply when we feel outmaneuvered by cultural forces. Homeschooling is a defense against the relentless and pernicious assault upon traditional family life. More than that, it is a training ground from which future redemptive leadership can come forth.

School violence, drug abuse, and sexual amorality can overwhelm many of us with fear for our kids. Homeschooling is a tactical step to insulate them from these harsher realities. But that's not the whole picture.

Converging Forces

God is more than protecting; He is preparing. At its fullest potential, homeschooling affords us the concentrated time we need to cultivate our children's talents and hone their skills, plus instill in them a passion for impacting their generation with the gospel.

Meditate on the potential of this synergy, then read Thomas Friedman's book *The World Is Flat: A Brief History of the Twenty-First Century, 3.0* and see what future opportunities the technological revolution will make possible. Just as the Roman roads and Gutenberg's printing press facilitated the spread of the Christian message, so will the information superhighway enable the good news of Christ's reconciliation of God and man to spread to the far corners of the world.

As I meditate on the future intersection of these vastly different forces, I feel certain that God's intent in calling our family to home educate is a small part of His compassionate response to the profane times in which we live.

Our Pioneer Days Are Over

Thirty years ago this would have been a thin book. The choices and opportunities for homeschoolers were few and far between. Pulling together a support group might have meant traveling a couple of hours to find the nearest homeschooling neighbor. Curriculum sources were limited to a few Christian school suppliers. And national organizations could be counted on one hand. But our pioneer days are over.

Warning! Information Overload Ahead

The problem now is too much choice: What curriculum do I buy? Which support group do I join? What educational philosophy should I adopt? Without direction, you'll soon be trapped in a maze of confusion.

That's the purpose of this book—to give you a framework for your decision making.

Right This Way

This is your access guide, a navigational chart to all the best destinations and opportunities you won't want to miss, as well as all the pitfalls and danger points you need to avoid to realize the full potential that home education offers. If you're game, then come on board. The first leg of the journey's about to begin.

Bon voyage! Toodle-oo! It's time to leave the dock.

CHALLENGES　TIME

PART I

HOMESCHOOLING: IS IT FOR YOU?

ADVANTAGES

SINGLE PARENTS

IN THIS SECTION

Special Needs　Success

CHAPTER I
Determining Your Destination

How do you decide which educational choice is right for your family? It all depends on where you're headed.

Working backward is a nifty math strategy my kids have learned to use, and I find it's a pretty useful approach to life as well. Therefore, your first step is to decide where you want to be when you complete your last step in the homeschooling journey. In other words, step one is to determine your destination.

Where Are You Going?

Where's your family headed? What goals do you desire to see your children reach while they are under your care?

If you haven't thought this out before, now's the time to do so. This little exercise will become an important reference point when you lose your focus in the future. It will also give you confidence that you have made a wise (logical and prayerful) decision and not a foolish (whimsical and presumptuous) one. Then you'll have the faith you need to press through the tough times (which are guaranteed to come).

Prayerfully consider the goals you desire your children to reach while they're under your care. Write them down. Share them with your kids.

Here's the list Kermit and I made a number of years ago:

Targets We Are Aiming to Hit While Our Children Are Under Our Care

❶ We want our children to love to learn.

❷ We want our children to have a marketable set of skills.

❸ We want our children to accurately understand the Christian faith and enjoy a vital relationship with the Lord.

❹ We want our children to articulate with integrity the Christian faith to a lost and dying world in a way that is both culturally relevant and persuasive.

We certainly had other goals, values, and interests that were very important to us, but these were the biggies. These made the emphasis in our home just a bit different from the emphasis in another family's home.

When it came time, then, to decide how to school our kids, we looked at all the realistic options available to us:

- Homeschooling
- Local public school
- Private schools in our area

We listed the advantages and disadvantages of each in terms of achieving our family goals. Then we chose the one we found to be the best fit for reaching them.

Over the years, as our children grew, we re-evaluated our targets and revisited our options. We ended up home educating all four of our kids K-12, but we were indeed open to God having different plans for each of them.

Here are other targets gleaned from families I know and admire for the quality of their family life:

- Spiritual growth
- Community or civic involvement
- Preparation for missions
- Friendship evangelism
- Academic excellence
- Hospitality
- Classical education[1]
- Leadership
- Vocational training
- Urban or social outreach
- Service in the church
- Communication skills
- Musical or athletic endeavors

These targets were specified by families with children in public, private, and home schools. (Many of them exercised more than one option over the years to best facilitate each child's growth.) But in all cases, first determining the family's unique goals helped them discern their best schooling choice.

A Vision Corrals Our Impulses

This short list served me well over the years. One of my favorite proverbs says, "Where there is no vision . . . the people perish" (Proverbs 29:18, AMP). The New American

Standard version says, "Where there is no vision, the people are unrestrained."

Do you know what it is to be unrestrained? I do.

When I don't have a clearly delineated vision guiding my decision making, my life becomes chaotic. I waste time looking at all my options and heading down paths with no destination in mind. I meander aimlessly and accomplish nothing. I become "double-minded" and "unstable in all my ways" (James 1:8), rethinking decisions over and over again and growing weary and discouraged.

The goals I've listed corralled me during my homeschooling years. They were the parameters I needed for assessing my options, and not just which educational choice to pick, but also:

- What curriculum to follow
- What courses to teach
- What activities to engage in

A Vision Fuels Our Motivation

Further, these goals got me refocused when I was discouraged by the day-to-day grind. They were the source of my motivation. I would have skipped labor during the birth of my children if there had been a way (I asked), but I chose to go through it time and again because I had a vision of the joy at the end of the journey.

The same holds true in choosing to homeschool (some parallels to labor can be drawn, I must admit). But the picture I envisioned of my children grown, loving to learn, and serving the Lord from the sincerity of their hearts fueled my motivation. And that energized me daily to do what I could to make that vision a reality.

Okay, One More Time, Class

Have you written down your destination yet? You can't skip this part and hope to succeed. This isn't a self-help strategy; it's a biblical principle.

Throughout history, God has consistently given a vision to His people: the promise of a coming Messiah, the hope of Christ's return, our future perfection in Christ—the list goes on. Why? So we will continue to be motivated and disciplined to press on.

> WHEN I DON'T HAVE A CLEARLY DELINEATED VISION GUIDING MY DECISION MAKING, MY LIFE BECOMES CHAOTIC.

Consider this wisdom:

> Record the vision
> And inscribe it on tablets,
> *That the one who reads it may run.*
> —Habakkuk 2:2 (emphasis mine)

> Run in such a way that you may win. . . .
> Therefore I run in such a way, *as not without aim:*
> I box in such a way, *as not beating the air.*
> — First Corinthians 9:24, 26 (emphasis mine)

I can't emphasize enough the importance of a family vision to guide you through the parenting years. I'll be bringing it up again. I can't let you finish this book without reminding you quite a few times about the benefits of a guiding vision for your family life.

That's another useful teaching strategy—repetition.

CHAPTER 2
The Advantages of Homeschooling

Here Comes the Sales Pitch!

Okay, here's the pitch—my best sales job on why you should homeschool. Keep in mind I was voted most outstanding cheerleader in high school, and I've been rooting for my team—whatever team that's been—ever since. However, this isn't a snow job. It's an exercise in conviction building, an important ingredient of a successful homeschool.

I want to provide you with well-formed, rock-solid reasons for choosing the road less traveled (although it's getting busier every day). Your kids need to know these reasons as well, and your mother-in-law does too, I'm sure. Besides, during the difficult times you will draw faith from reviewing these reasons and be ready to make a persuasive defense should the media come calling.

Now, to be honest, after we've covered the major rewards I'll also list the drawbacks you need to consider as well. Then, like the wise man Luke described (see Luke 14:28 ff.), you can sit down and count the cost before undertaking the task.

Now, onward. Here's what we saw that tipped the scale in favor of home educating our brood:

Advantage #1:
Transference of Our Family Values

Passing on our faith and our values to our children is our sacred trust. As someone who takes a pretty lighthearted approach to life, nothing sobers me more than the weight of this responsibility. Kermit and I endeavor to make all our parenting decisions in light of the impact our choices will have on our children's budding relationship with the Lord.

I found it ironic that when we finally reached the high school years of our sons' lives, instead of being consumed by the academic demands of the curriculum (as I thought I would be), I was more focused on their spiritual development—giving this far more weight in our decision making than any academic considerations.

Academics Are Ephemeral

Worst-case scenario: Our children don't understand physics, calculus, or Shakespeare or speak French as we would like them to by the time they leave home. What has been lost? Nothing of eternal value—nothing that can't be picked up later.

But if we don't ardently pursue the cultivation of their relationship with the Lord, what has been sacrificed? An opportunity we as parents will never have again. Their hearts are malleable; their minds are impressionable. I wanted the best shot I had to demonstrate to our kids the importance and impact of the faith that unites Kermit and me.

Maximum-Strength Parenting

Homeschooling maximizes parental influence and lengthens that window of opportunity. It also gives us the greatest control over who else will influence our kids and shape their beliefs.

The studies cited in *What Works: Research About Teaching and Learning* (U.S. Department of Education)[1] found that values are most likely transferred when taught in an environment that supports them. Parents, teachers, and peer groups must all validate the beliefs being espoused.

If we teach our children that sex outside the commitment of marriage is wrong, that parents have the right and responsibility before God to hold authority in their lives, or that the Bible is inerrant and absolute, but we simultaneously place them in an environment every day that does not support these beliefs, we've seriously eroded the chances that these values will be embraced.

The homeschool community is certainly not a monolith of Christian virtue, but it was effortless for us to find peers and other adults who also embraced the values we treasured and sought to impart. And we were able to surround our children with them.

Positive Peer Pressure

I was most grateful for the influence on my children of older teens, like Cindy's and Marie's kids, who only grew bolder in their faith during these typically turbulent years and were not ashamed to seek out their parents' counsel or publicly express respect for them.

I choked back emotion during one of my first sessions with a senior high composition class at Creative Home Educators' Support Services (CHESS) the first year I taught there. I had

> HOMESCHOOLING MAXIMIZES PARENTAL INFLUENCE AND LENGTHENS THAT WINDOW OF OPPORTUNITY.

twenty-one students, ages fifteen through seventeen. In getting acquainted, I found two-thirds of them had already been on cross-cultural or overseas mission trips. I was moved by the ease with which many of them shared their faith as well as their desire to give themselves wholeheartedly to God's will for their lives. They spoke earnestly and openly even though most of them had never met before.

I've been teaching kids for years in a variety of settings. This kind of candid discussion is pretty unusual—in my experience at least. I'm humbled that God has given me the opportunity to work with kids with such mature focus.

The Apron Strings Must Be Cut

There certainly will come a time when we, as parents, must pass the baton and watch our children run their leg of the journey alone. For Kermit and me, parenting was all about preparing our kids to make an impact in their generation. We aren't isolationists here. It's God's intention that our children integrate their lives with others outside our system of belief. But before they go, they need a faith that's rooted and mature, not one that will quickly shrivel in the face of opposition. So how do we best prepare them?

I think of the concentrated and intensive training of an Olympic contender who sets aside all other distractions, and I see a correlation to the opportunity that homeschooling gives parents to coach their kids in the fundamentals of our faith.

Homeschooling does not guarantee a child's salvation; only the grace of God does. But it's an option with impressive results.

If you have an authentic, active faith to pass on, if your life's been changed by the power of the gospel, if your home is a model of commitment and love, then homeschooling may just be the strategy to best show your kids what God has done in your life.

Advantage #2: Character First

Closely tied to passing on our faith is our responsibility as parents to shape our children's character. It wasn't until I met Christians in college whose lives were consistent with the faith they espoused that I took a serious look at the claims of Christ.

The integrity of our character is what counts with unbelievers. It's what counts with God as well. Without it, we bring shame to the

> **CLOSELY TIED TO PASSING ON OUR FAITH IS OUR RESPONSIBILITY AS PARENTS TO SHAPE OUR CHILDREN'S CHARACTER.**

gospel of Christ.

I love to learn. I love intellectual pursuit. That bias will certainly bleed through these pages. I want to foster in my children the pleasure that comes from academic achievement. But—and that's a big "but"—character is paramount. When our kids ultimately stand before the throne of grace, they won't be bringing their transcripts and SAT scores with them. It will be their hearts the Lord examines.

Homeschooling gives us the potential to stay on top of the condition of our children's hearts daily. Within the dynamics of one-on-one instruction, we are acutely aware of the bad attitudes or actions that erupt. And we can close our books and deal with the more important issues at hand.

There are many advantages to the classes offered at CHESS family school, but this is not one of them. In the context of a classroom, I didn't have close examination of my children's lives or the time to stop and deal with the character issues that arose.

Homeschooling did give me that time. I needed to make sure I seized the opportunity.

Advantage #3:
A Tailor-Made Education

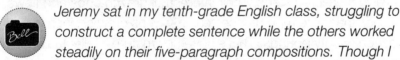 *Jeremy sat in my tenth-grade English class, struggling to construct a complete sentence while the others worked steadily on their five-paragraph compositions. Though I gave him far more attention than the rest, I couldn't do the one thing he needed most, the only thing that would have enabled him to eventually construct a five-paragraph composition with ease—slow down the curriculum. Jeremy needed to start at his level of success and move forward only as he mastered the necessary skills. But in fairness to the others, I couldn't wait for Jeremy. His confidence and mastery of the English language continued to languish. Later that year he dropped out.*

Lisa, on the other hand, stared out the window. Her five paragraphs had been effortlessly produced in the first ten minutes of the allotted time. The previous week she had shown me a remarkable short story she had written outside of class. She was, of course, identified as gifted. That entitled her to a forty-minute "pullout program" once a week. She wasn't particularly interested in the focus

of that class, and she especially resented being required to make up any assignments missed while attending it. Eventually she convinced her parents to pull her out of the gifted track. And despite my scintillating personality, she sat in my English class, bored and underchallenged.

An Inner Timetable

Children are unique. They aren't computers that can be programmed or synchronized. Each one has an inner timetable designed by God that should be honored. Some babies walk at nine months, some at sixteen. Some kids read at four, some at ten. As adults, these early differences are usually indistinguishable.

Schools place kids on an artificial timetable. If you're seven, it's time to read. If you don't, you're labeled "delayed." Fifth grade, first semester: time to memorize the state capitals.

We've created a linear and arbitrary scope and sequence, and we expect kids to fall in sync with it.

The Ebb and Flow of Growth

But kids are not machines, or blank slates, as behavioral psychologist B.F. Skinner thought. They don't learn in sequential, evenly measured steps. Their intellectual growth ebbs and flows. In less than nine months one year, my twins grew six inches and put on twenty pounds. That's how they mature intellectually as well—swinging between stages of dormancy and growth. In a six-week period, my daughter Kayte jumped directly from struggling with her easiest readers to The Boxcar Children chapter books, skipping all the levels in between. Suddenly everything clicked for her. And I didn't hold her back by insisting she continue to work through her reading program in a systematic, sequential fashion. I capitalized on the growth spurt.

Readiness

Before your child is going to read *War and Peace*, solve a problem algebraically, or write a ten-page research paper successfully, he must master the prior skills necessary. Homeschooling gives you the opportunity to start your studies in every subject at the level of your child's success without labeling him "delayed" or "accelerated," as if there were a scientific standard we are measuring his progress against.

There needn't be any sense of falling behind or rushing to catch up. Your scope and sequence are cued to your child.

Interests-Based Learning

At age eight, Gabe became fascinated with flight. I didn't say, "Well, be patient there, buddy; in fifth grade your science text will cover the physics of flight." No, we capitalized on the opportunity to study something *when he was motivated to learn about it.* We checked out a stack of books at the library. We designed paper airplanes and recorded their flight. Kermit bought Estes rockets and set up a launch pad in the backyard (attracting all kinds of additional students). And a pilot at Kermit's office answered Gabe's questions. In third grade, this kid knew more about the physics of flight than most high school graduates.

And it's a good thing we captured the moment: By the time Gabe was in fifth grade, his interests had turned to rocks.

Immediate Feedback

My goal as an English teacher was to return all compositions within five days. I had to really forge ahead to wade through thirty-five compositions, but even so, most teenagers' lives were eons beyond that assignment in a week's time. My comments went largely unnoticed. And the grade was already recorded. What difference did my feedback make anyway?

The best time to capitalize upon mistakes is when they are made, not two weeks later when the test is returned.

As soon as my own kids got headed down the wrong track, I adjusted their thinking. When Kristen forgot to carry her tens to the next column, I caught her error before she completed the entire page incorrectly and reinforced her mistakes.

And we don't have to settle for just a passing grade. We can continue to work with the assignment until it's right.

I circled the wrong answers on my children's math tests and had them rework the problems. My sons self-checked and self-corrected their algebra. Then they explained the errors they discovered to me.

In our house, mistakes are powerful teaching tools, not at all a measurement of failure.

Shifting Gears

Home education allows you to change immediately to better methods and materials. If what you're doing isn't working, stop and adjust. You don't have to wait for board approval or acquisition of funds (well, maybe).

One must navigate a ream of red tape to change course in a traditional setting. In the early 1970s the latest educational fad was mini-courses. English 10, 11, and 12 were replaced with scores of electives such as science fiction, media production, and independent reading. For my father, the director of guidance at a public high school, it was a scheduling nightmare. And very quickly, the research began to prove this idea a resounding failure. The program was too splintered, and kids were missing basic skills in composition and literature. My own husband graduated from high school without ever reading one of Shakespeare's plays (a deficit that causes me far greater concern than it ever has him). It took more than a decade to weed mini-courses out of the schedule.

The first reading program I tried with the twins spent far too much time on phonetics drills and far too little time on real reading. They were rapidly getting discouraged. I analyzed the problem, sold the program, and switched to a whole-language approach in less than a week. (Lest you are concerned, intensive phonetics is just what the woman I sold it to was looking for, and real books were what my kids craved.)

> **IF WHAT YOU'RE DOING ISN'T WORKING, STOP AND ADJUST.**

I Prefer a Custom Fit

No other option offers you the opportunity to customize your child's education to fit her readiness, interests, and abilities. Modifications are easy. Feedback is immediate. Results: Kid reaches her maximum potential. Kid loves to learn.

Advantage #4: Academic Excellence

For myriad reasons, academic standards in our educational system have plummeted. Despite recent reports of modest gains, American students still lag far behind their European and Asian counterparts.

Twenty-five years after *A Nation at Risk* and five years of the nationwide mandates of No Child Left Behind, The Hoover Institute's Koret Task Force yearly concludes little has changed. Charles Sykes, a respected education journalist, reports these findings in his book *Dumbing Down Our Kids: Why American Children Feel Good About Themselves But Can't Read, Write, Or Add:*

- More than a decade after *A Nation at Risk* drew attention to the nation's educational mediocrity, the reading proficiency of nine- and thirteen-year-olds has declined even further.[2]

- Although the United States is among the countries expending the highest proportion of their gross national product on education, our elementary school and secondary school students *never place above the median* in comparative studies (with Asian and European students) of academic achievement.[3]

- The National Education Commission on Time and Learning found that most American students spend only about 41 percent of their school day on basic academics.[4]

- American students spend only 1,460 hours on subjects like math, science, and history during their four years of high school. Meanwhile, their counterparts in Japan spend 3,170 hours on basic subjects, students in France spend 3,280 hours on academics, and students in Germany, 3,528 hours studying such subjects—nearly three times the hours devoted to those core subjects in American schools.[5]

- According to the National Research Council, *average* students in other industrialized countries are as proficient in mathematics as America's *best* students. Further, when the very best American students—the top one percent—are measured against the best students of other countries, America's best and brightest finish at the bottom.[6]

Though critics argue that compulsory-attendance laws, working mothers, and the impact of television in this country explain the scores, Sykes points out these fallacies: Compulsory education for elementary school is worldwide, and the same discrepancies still show up at that level in student achievement. In many countries, a greater number of women are working outside the home than in the United States, and believe it or not, Japanese students on average watch more television daily than their American counterparts.[7]

Where's the Curriculum?

Sykes's book and others like it (see also *The Closing of the American Mind* by Alan Bloom and *Cultural Literacy* by E. D. Hirsch Jr.) contend that our failure is rooted in the loss of a core curriculum. While European and Asian school systems focus heavily on academics and leave other arenas to the province of the family, American schools are saddled with politically correct agendas; faddish, untested reforms; and responsibility for salvaging societal problems:

> Schools have been asked to assume (and have asked to assume) extraordinary burdens; they are expected not to merely educate children but to deal with and help resolve society's race problems, to eradicate poverty, to be on the front lines of economic competitiveness, environmentalism, AIDS, multiculturalism, child abuse, drug addiction, and sexual harassment, to mediate our ambivalence about family life and sexuality, and to provide children with a moral compass.[8]

No wonder many teachers complain that they don't have time to teach!

Homeschooling streamlines the educational process. High standards of academic excellence, accelerated learning, and a return to core studies in math, science, history, and literature are quickly and easily facilitated.

Full Exploration and Mastery

Homeschooling allows time for full exploration and mastery of the material. It's not once over lightly and quickly forgotten: *Okay class, it's second semester, seventh grade, time for our two-week study of the Roman Empire.* That was it, never to be mentioned again. *Okay kids, that was your chance to try that chemistry experiment. Sorry it didn't work for most of you, but the supplies have been consumed. Next week we move on to electrolysis. We have to complete this textbook by the end of the year.*

Bell

One summer, Gabe took a writing workshop through a local "College for Kids" program. It was his first experience in a traditional setting, and his comments during the week were insightful. He worked hurriedly one evening to complete the next day's assignment.

"You know, Mom," he said, "I know now why kids don't do their best in school. I'm just writing this poem to get it done. I don't have enough time to make it good, and I wasn't really interested in the topic in the first place."

When we rush kids through material, it is lost. That's why there is so much repetition in textbooks year after year. But even that redundancy often fails to lodge the material in a child's brain. If we do not s-l-o-w down the program to allow kids to delve deeply into the material and interact with it in a variety of contexts, it cannot be transferred from short-term to long-term memory.

Smarting Us Up

Homeschooling affords you the time you need to set and achieve high academic standards. No grading on a curve is necessary. Set an objective standard and measure your child's success against that. If he doesn't hit the mark, reward his improvement and set a goal to come closer next time. With time on your side, you need not feel any pressure to lower the bar.

Many families introduce concepts to their kids years earlier than is traditionally accepted in a standard curriculum. And it's not that these kids are unusually bright—it has more to do with their personal drive and their parents' high expectations for their children's achievement.

> **HOMESCHOOLING AFFORDS YOU THE TIME YOU NEED TO SET AND ACHIEVE HIGH ACADEMIC STANDARDS.**

Care to hazard a guess as to the sources of each of these vocabulary lists?

List 1	List 2
aggression	inimitable
divergent	epistolary
prestigious	assailed
bizarre	invidious
cogent	assiduous
propagate	appendages
ambiguous	sagacity
exonerated	pecuniary

List 1 Source

SAT I (revised)
Practice Test

List 2 Source

Fourth-grade *McGuffey Reader,* in use during the late 1800s (after compulsory education was mandated). An 1897 fifth-grade reader we purchased at a library sale includes the same literary selections I studied in my undergraduate American literature courses.

Authentic Experiences

Homeschooling also affords the opportunity to involve your kids with material and activities that are relevant and applicable to real life. Parents have full control of the content; we can use that advantage to our kids' benefit.

Homeschooling is far more than "school at home." If you only re-create an institutionalized setting around your kitchen table, you've lost much of the opportunity homeschooling affords.

Do you remember wondering in school, *When will I ever use this?* or *Why do I need to know this?* Do you ever ask those questions when you must acquire new skills or knowledge for a job? No. That's because you are learning material in the context in which it is used. The immediate relevance to the tasks at hand is obvious. And we are motivated to learn because the learning is purposeful.

Many homeschoolers believe they must follow a state-prescribed scope and sequence. But while many state laws dictate the subjects that must be studied, none dictate the content or the methods. So visits to workplaces, historic sites, laboratories, musical performances, and dramatic productions; long-term, purposeful projects; apprenticeships; interviews with those in the field of study; and a spontaneous response to opportunities that arise can all be done as frequently as you wish.

As a classroom teacher, I took one field trip a year. The paperwork required, the sheer size of the group, and the students' attitudes that this was more a release from confinement than a learning adventure made it an exhausting effort.

But arranging the same kind of opportunity for just my four kids was a frequent occurrence.

Welcome to the Twenty-First Century

We're in the midst of a technological revolution that will dramatically change every aspect of our lives. Our kids need to be equipped now to participate in the future. The job market of tomorrow is a lush opportunity for creative, independent thinkers with well-honed problem-solving skills and an entrepreneurial drive.

"Time on task," my father, a retired school guidance counselor, always says (and research consistently shows), is the only thing that determines kids' proficiency in a skill. Want better writers? They need to write, not to fill out worksheets, answer quick true-and-false tests, or do grammar exercises. The more they write, the better their writing skills. Want readers? Give them time to read, not crowd the schedule with special assemblies and then load them up with so much homework that reading a book for pleasure or enlightenment is out of the question. (A consistent comment I hear from parents whose home-educated kids have transitioned to a traditional setting is that they no longer have time to read!)

You want your kids to be prepared for the job market of the future, no matter how it shakes out? Then here's the short list of necessary proficiencies:

- Research
- Communication
- Technology

If you will merely design a program that gives your kids lots of opportunities to hone these skills, they will be equipped to compete.

Advantage #5: Nurturing Environment

I'll Take Hothouse Tomatoes

Today's kids enter the rat race at the earliest possible moment. Infant day care, highly structured preschools, and daily schedules beginning early in the morning and ending late at night are far too common. Dr. David Elkind, a highly respected child psychologist at

Tufts University, has authored a number of disturbing books drawn from his practice.

He noted adult diseases appearing in children at earlier and earlier ages including heart disease, hypertension, mental illnesses, eating disorders, and suicide. He has concluded that the hurried, harried lifestyle we've created is the root cause.

Tightly packed schedules and overly structured lives leave kids with no personal space, no control, and no time. Gone are the lazy, carefree days of childhood spent on a backyard tire swing or scouring the creeks for crayfish.

Some onlookers think homeschooling is time-consuming, but kids in a traditional setting often complete two hours of homework most evenings after spending up to seven hours in school each day and then riding up to an hour on a bus to get home. Crammed into this already tight schedule are ballet lessons, sports, and church activities. To top it off, vacations must be taken at the height of vacation season with 2 million other families. (Give me the beach in September—*that's* a vacation.)

Change agents crying for a longer school year, more hours in every day, and more homework are only inviting further disaster into children's lives, I believe. What attracted me to homeschooling was the opportunity to recapture childhood for my kids. After reading Dr. Elkind's *The Hurried Child,* I vowed not to let the forces of our culture's whirlwind lifestyle drag us into its vortex. I want a childhood for our kids that allows lots of time for play in the backyard, rainy afternoons in a cozy chair with a book, and building secret hideouts in the woods.

 For details about Dr. Elkind's research and his suggestions for rearing relaxed, well-adjusted children, see his books *The Hurried Child: Growing Up Too Fast Too Soon* and *The Power of Play: How Spontaneous, Imaginative Activities Lead to Happier, Healthier Children.*

Confident to Learn

Homeschooling has also given us the safeguards to protect our children's self-esteem and confidence to learn. Comparison is a natural inclination of children. But for the ones who lag behind or don't fit into the constantly changing standards of peer acceptance, a belief in their own inabilities quickly becomes a downward spiral.

> **WHAT ATTRACTED ME TO HOMESCHOOLING WAS THE OPPORTUNITY TO RECAPTURE CHILDHOOD FOR MY KIDS.**

And without faith in themselves, kids just don't do well in their stud-ies—or in life.

I'm sure you've collected labels about your own abilities to learn: "I'm smart," "I'm dumb," "I don't do well on tests," "I can't speak in front of a group," "I'm good at math," etc. Aren't these labels rooted in your own school experience? And don't we then set limits for ourselves because of them?

I know otherwise rational adults who have had successful careers, recognized leadership in the community, financial security, even high grades in college and graduate school, who still view themselves as "unintelligent" because of the standardized tests they took in grade school.

Labels are extraordinarily powerful, especially on young children. As adults, we have the maturity to keep others' categorical statements about us in perspective. But it's different for kids. The comments of adults and peers in their lives will have a profound impact upon their self-image.

Cindy McKeown's son Joey showed impressive drive in high school. In ninth grade he read Stephen Covey's book *The Seven Habits of Highly Effective People* and set about getting organized. He got a job and used his wages to purchase Covey's expensive organizer. He then scripted out his goals for his high school years. Among many other ventures, he interned at Penn-sylvania Family Institute, a pro-family watchdog in our state capital. He was a recognized leader among his peers and scored quite high on his college entrance exams and Advanced Placement tests. To conclude his senior year of high school, he backpacked through Europe and then attended a "great books" college[8] on the West Coast.

But in grade school, Joey had read late and lagged behind his peers in many areas. He had difficulty with math and didn't test particularly well. Cindy used many nontraditional strategies with Joey all through elementary school to give him a basis for abstract thinking. But above all, she didn't rush him or suggest he was lazy and falling behind. Her family doctor, who was not particularly pro-homeschooling, told her it was wise of her to home educate Joey. He predicted that in a traditional setting Joey would quickly get lost in the shuffle.

While Cindy and her husband, Cliff, once worried privately that they might not be pushing their laid-back son enough, their current concern is whether they should try to restrain his boundless energy and ambitious goals.

I tell Joey's story only because he is not unusual. Had I the space, I could tell you of numerous children I have observed closely from grade school to graduation who proved that early test scores are not certain predictors of later achievement.

I wonder if the growth I have seen in these kids would have been possible had they been labeled "delayed" and assigned to a low-ability group in grade school. And what would the comments of their peers have done to their confidence to learn?

Advantage #6: Flexibility and Choice

If you asked my sons, Mike and Gabe, what they enjoyed most about homeschooling, their answers would fall under this advantage. They loved the freedom to pursue their own interests, to control their time, to stay up late reading, to not be bogged down with homework after supper, to choose and change the direction of their education.

We spent two years on Colonial American history because we wanted to. Mike and Gabe started algebra in sixth grade because they were ready. Kayte read *The Adventures of Huckleberry Finn,* unabridged, in fourth. We could stay up late to catch a meteor shower or the final game of the World Series and then sleep in. When the Concorde, the world's fastest jet, landed at Harrisburg International Airport, word spread like wildfire through the homeschool phone chains—moms declared a field trip and drove their kids over to watch it take off.

One morning the papers ran a story on Mel Fisher, the man whose family had recovered the sunken treasure of the Spanish galleon *Atocha*. Mr. Fisher was appearing in Harrisburg that day with $2 million worth of recovered treasure to sell. We had just watched the *Reading Rainbow* segment on the Atocha and had read a book about it together. We put away our work, headed to Harrisburg, and had one of the most educational days of the year. Since mine were the only kids in the store (everyone else was there to consider buying this stuff), we got a lot of attention. Mr. Fisher was fascinated by our mode of education and the knowledge the kids demonstrated about his ten-year search. He allowed them each to handle gold bullion, emeralds, and pieces of eight.

No other option can give you the flexibility you need to seize these opportunities.

Before You Sign, Read the Fine Print

While these are a few of the benefits we've found, it's important you know they aren't guaranteed. Homeschooling affords us some wonderful opportunities to shape our children's lives and to tailor their education to their unique specifications. But that doesn't mean it isn't without its drawbacks. Homeschooling is and always will be a trade-off.

It's time to count the cost before making that final decision.

> **HOMESCHOOLING IS AND ALWAYS WILL BE A TRADE-OFF.**

CHAPTER 3
The Challenges of Homeschooling

When I was nine I got braces. The dental assistant who put the plaster of Paris in my mouth to make the mold said, "This is going to taste great—just like oatmeal." Well, I loved oatmeal as a kid, and I eagerly bit down on the mush she had scooped into my mouth. To this day I remember my disillusionment and astonishment that she had lied to me. (I believe that woman later wrote the book *Childbirth Without Pain*.)

And that is why I'm going to tell you the downside of homeschooling: I don't want any angry letters accusing me of an inflated sales pitch.

If you don't take the time to sit down and count the cost, as well as to lay a solid foundation in the grace of God before you begin to homeschool, you'll spend much of your time dealing with double-mindedness instead of seizing the opportunity at hand.

Frustration, discouragement, ambivalence: These are common emotions you will live with if you choose to homeschool. My friend Peggy calls homeschooling "the crucible of my life." It not only constantly brings to the surface her children's character flaws but her own as well. And she can't put off dealing with them.

It's very common for the conversations in the mothers lounge at the Learning Center homeschool co-op to center on the challenges and discouragement of homeschooling. Not only do our children need these bimonthly group experiences, but we moms also need the support and re-envisioning that come from upholding one another.

Some of the difficulties I want to address can be minimized with the strategies presented in this book. But others are inherent in the choice and must be weighed before you decide.

> **NO MATTER HOW YOU APPROACH IT, HOMESCHOOLING IS A TREMENDOUS INVESTMENT OF TIME AND ENERGY.**

The Cost to the Homeschooling Parent

Challenge #1: Time

No matter how you approach it, homeschooling is a

tremendous investment of time and energy. It's not another interest to fit into an already busy schedule; it's a way of life.

Other Demands on Our Time

Other family members may have needs that require a competing time commitment. Perhaps you are caring for an elderly parent or a child with special needs. Perhaps you are working and do not have the option of quitting or scaling back your hours. In these situations, you may not have the time to give to homeschooling that it requires.

My friend Barb was deeply committed to the principles of homeschooling. However, her third child, Anna, had some learning delays, and she needed a lot of one-on-one attention in order to move forward. The time Barb was investing in Anna was leaving her older children without enough direction. After a particularly dissatisfying homeschooling year (when her oldest son, Adam, had most of his schoolwork "artistically" rearranged by Anna), Barb and her husband, Steve, reluctantly visited a publicly funded intermediate unit classroom that served their public school district —and were pleasantly surprised. The teacher was supportive of Barb's commitment to homeschooling and agreed to a unique arrangement. Barb continued to work with Anna at home, but having Anna enrolled for several days a week in their therapy program gave Barb the time she needed for her other kids as well.

On the other hand, another friend with a special-needs child chose in the end to enroll her two older children in school as part of the solution to the time commitment her youngest daughter needed.

Even without extenuating circumstances, homeschooling is primarily a time commitment. The time you might have given to a career or ministry gets diverted here. For women who have worked solely at home or who have children that have not yet been to school, the transition to homeschooling is usually not as big an adjustment as it is for those who must leave the work force or pull their children out of a traditional setting. If you are in the latter situation, then you need to be realistic about the adjustment and sense of restraint that the transition to homeschooling will bring into your life.

Prep Time

While the actual time devoted to homeschooling your kids is far less than the time they would spend in school each day, you still have lots to do to prepare for that instructional time. To maximize the opportunities homeschooling affords, you need to be self educating and constantly fine-tuning your program. In later chapters I'll give you strategies for raising an independent learner as well as motivating the reluctant one. But in the end, kids can't teach themselves. You need to provide daily accountability, direction, and tutoring.

My first year as a classroom teacher was very difficult because I had to create the courses I was teaching. But the following years were much less time-consuming because I often taught the same courses over again. That's not true in homeschooling. Every year there's a different schedule. Every year there's new coursework to oversee. And even though Kayte and Kristen followed behind the boys, tailoring the program to their needs and interests enabled me to do a lot of new things with them as well.

Depending upon our temperaments, never having a break from the kids or time to ourselves can be a difficult demand. I don't think homeschooling needs to be as restrictive as many people imagine in order to be successful. But the amount of time you can carve away from your responsibilities is certainly limited, and we have to be creative about finding moments of relaxation.

Once I spent a few days with a college roommate whose two children were doing well in public school. She hadn't yet returned to the work force, and her weekly schedule included aerobics classes, women's Bible study, and lunch with friends. Her house was neat as a pin and beautifully decorated. I returned home grumpy and envious.

I find I need to keep blinders on to maintain my contentment in homeschooling. Once my children were older, I really did enjoy their company and didn't think much about the limits of my life. But when they were little, it didn't come quite so naturally—not by a long shot! I needed to stay fixed on the conviction that this was God's will for my life and that He had designed the limits of my freedom, not just for my children's good but for my own good as well. I couldn't let myself look at the "freedom" I thought other women had and grow resentful. But that's not always easy.

> DEPENDING UPON OUR TEMPERAMENTS, NEVER HAVING A BREAK FROM THE KIDS OR TIME TO OURSELVES CAN BE A DIFFICULT DEMAND.

A Question That Needs an Honest Answer

Before you choose to homeschool, answer these questions:

- Am I able and willing to devote the time necessary to do this right?
- Will I have enthusiasm for teaching my children and be dedicated to seeking out opportunities and strategies for maximizing this opportunity?

If your answer to either question is no, your children will probably be better served in a classroom setting with a teacher who is enthused about teaching and creative in his or her approach.

Many parents who want the benefits of an environment that reflects their value system, but can't give the time necessary to teach the academics, invest their energy in setting up a private school for their kids. Classical schools, charter schools, parent-run schools, and hybrids of private schools and homeschooling like Creative Home Educators' Support Services (CHESS) are springing up all over the country. And in some places, it's still possible for parents to have a positive impact on their public schools through involvement in parent organizations or booster clubs or by serving on their school board.

Challenge #2: Unrealistic Expectations

When we make the choice to homeschool, it's with the expectation of results commensurate with the sacrifices we are about to make. Or at the very least, we want enough evidence to prove our skeptics wrong. And we want it soon.

Many of us enter homeschooling anticipating immediate success. A spouse or relative may be adding pressure to that anticipation as well. With all the glowing reports of individual students' successes, it's very easy to set unrealistic expectations for ourselves and for our children.

I think the homeschool moms of the Learning Center homeschool co-op are the absolute cream of the crop. They are creative, diligent, and fervent in their faith. One year, as we gathered to open our school year with prayer, I was surprised to

> MANY OF US ENTER HOMESCHOOLING ANTICIPATING IMMEDIATE SUCCESS.

hear how discouraged and wrought with guilt most of the moms were. They were very conscious of all they were not getting done in their homes and homeschools. They were worried that they were not doing something right with one or more of their kids. And they were sure they were the only one failing in this way. By the time it was my turn to share, I was feeling very guilty about not feeling guilty! And by golly, I then found it easy to make a list of all I was falling short on as well.

From my travels I've heard the same angst in many, many mothers' voices.

There Are Always Trade-Offs

Homeschooling is a trade-off. There are always going to be things that are either not done or not done well. Howard Richman, a homeschool evaluator and researcher in Pennsylvania, evaluates more than 500 homeschooled children every year. His cumulative research is very impressive—high SAT scores, high achievement scores, post-graduate success. But in his analysis of individual homeschool programs, he consistently sees strengths and weaknesses in every home. We do some things very well (usually homeschoolers raise very literate kids), but sacrifice time in other areas to do so.

I minimized the impact of my weaknesses by involving my children in many cooperative learning experiences where they had other teachers who offset my shortcomings. But time restraints still prevented us from doing everything as well as I could envision. I had to be at peace with the gap between the ideal and the reality.

Homeschooling Is Not a Cure-All

Another frequent assumption is that homeschooling will remove our children's character flaws, rescue them from academic failure, or miraculously cure family problems. But the converse is true: Homeschooling can exacerbate these situations. These issues typically must be addressed at a more fundamental level. Homeschooling is an educational choice, not essentially a biblical solution for a fractured family life.

At the end of Part 1 of this book, I ask you to evaluate the health of your family relationships before beginning to

> THERE ARE ALWAYS GOING TO BE THINGS THAT ARE EITHER NOT DONE OR NOT DONE WELL.

homeschool. It's important that you have a realistic picture here and that you have a plan for dealing with these weaknesses if you want to minimize, not maximize, the stress that homeschooling can bring.

I have seen numerous families undertake homeschooling as a last-ditch effort to prevent a rebellious teenager from dropping out of school. Unfortunately the issues that led to this impasse sprouted long ago. Homeschooling may be a good option for cutting off negative influences that aggravate the situation, but "tough love" and biblical counseling are more likely to make the real difference in this child's life. See page 69 for recommended parenting books to encourage you in this area.

Fruit Takes Time, Faith, and Effort

When you consider homeschooling, you must recognize that the fruit you hope to realize will likely take longer and be harder to grow than you anticipate. In many cases you must merely live in faith for the future results. I watched Cindy spend most of her homeschooling years with Nate, her oldest, very ambivalent about the choice she had made. Then, shortly after his freshman year of college, Nate told his parents how grateful he was to have been homeschooled and how well prepared he felt he had been for college life. It's hard to quantify how much his comments meant to Cindy or how challenging it had been to wait to hear them.

Challenge #3: Limits on Your Family's Impact

Homeschooling can limit your family's impact and outreach in your community. School is a natural vehicle for getting to know other families and opening opportunities to share our faith and lives. Christian teachers, students, and parents whose character squares with the values they espouse can make a real difference in other children's lives and better their schools and community through their service.

For ten years, Kermit and I served on the board of a pregnancy care center we founded. Today this center operates four offices and reaches thousands of women annually. We loved being a part of a ministry that's making a tangible difference, coupling the gospel with meeting legitimate needs in our community. And we loved the people we labored with. Stepping down from active involvement there was one of the most difficult decisions I've had to make. But it was necessary if I was going to homeschool my children with integrity.

The center has likewise lost many volunteers because they have chosen to homeschool their children. It has created a dilemma that has been difficult to resolve.

A Source of Tension

Churches can feel this same tension. Many needs that were once met by the women of the church now go unmet because moms are re-entering the work force or homeschooling.

It has become a sore point in the church. It's a challenge not to become critical of the homeschool movement when the obvious impact these strong Christian families could be having is shifted away from legitimate needs.

Creative Solutions

This is a drawback I believe can be minimized. I know many homeschool families with older children that have found ways to reach out to others as part of their homeschool programs. The flexibility that homeschooling affords makes short-term mission trips a real possibility. Our co-op has done a number of service projects and put on an after-school program at the city mission. It's not always easy to facilitate these opportunities, but homeschool families who make outreach a priority find creative ways to serve in their churches and communities.

The Cost to the Homeschooled Child

It's hard to beat the one-on-one instruction homeschooling can provide for a child. But even with all its benefits, I find there are some drawbacks for our children that need to be considered, especially as they grow older.

Challenge #1: Limits of the Teacher

Our children will benefit from our strengths and be limited by our weaknesses if we do not offset them. My kids are fluid writers. Gabe was published and paid twice in elementary school. In fifth grade he and Mike generated more than twenty thousand original words for school assignments. Kayte routinely wrote ten-page stories. They all read avidly and seized any opportunity for public speaking, just like their mother. Obviously they benefited from the strength of my background. But they suffered from my limits as well.

Kayte attended her first Young Writers' Institute with Christian author Sigmund Brouwer in third grade. I was watching the children complete an assignment for Sigmund when I noticed all the other children (thirty-four of them to be exact) were composing their stories in cursive. Kayte was laboriously printing hers. I suddenly realized I had completely forgotten to teach my daughter cursive handwriting! It just never entered my brain. I was almost hyperventilating over the panic attack that ensued—if I could forget cursive, what other venal or mortal oversight was I capable of? Would my daughter ever recover? What doors were now swinging shut because of her mother's incompetence?

Of course I had overreacted, and Kayte survived. Handwriting isn't a life-and-death skill, but this experience illustrated for me the impact the limits of my abilities or initiative can have on my children.

We Need Others' Involvement

I disagree with homeschooling families that choose to isolate their kids. It's not healthy, and the children will not have the opportunity to hone their skills and character if they never rub shoulders with others with different strengths and weaknesses.

A church is not healthy without every member contributing his or her gifts and talents to church life. A homeschool isn't healthy either if we misconstrue Scripture to mean parents are to be the only influence or teachers in our children's lives.

It is so important that we recognize our limitations and seek out opportunities for our kids to offset those limitations.

Challenge #2: Lack of Recognition

Many of the homeschooled kids I've evaluated have had tremendous academic and artistic achievements, but often these accomplishments go unrecognized. While the local papers feature pictures of school happenings and recognition of individual students, the homeschool community is mostly overlooked

> OUR CHILDREN WILL BENEFIT FROM OUR STRENGTHS AND BE LIMITED BY OUR WEAKNESSES IF WE DO NOT OFFSET THEM.

Several of the homeschooled students I've worked with have now transitioned into a public high school and have done exceptionally well. It is gratifying for me to see all the awards they've garnered. Frankly, they've found the accolades pretty motivational too.

Appropriate recognition is an important source of motivation for adults and children. And local homeschool communities are beginning to find creative ways to recognize the accomplishments of students—awards banquets, exhibits at conventions, juried science and history fairs, graduation ceremonies. I'd like to see us go further by inviting the local media to these events. The local newspaper is not purposefully overlooking the homeschooled kids; it just doesn't have a clue as to what we are doing. It's our job to educate them.

Challenge #3: Lack of Competition

I've changed my views on competition over the years, and it's come from observing my identical twin sons. I've had to conclude that the natural competitiveness between them has been to their benefit.

When the first one began to read, the other was motivated to work harder at his own reading. When Michael worked ahead in algebra, Gabe complained but buckled down and caught up. When one could beat the other racing or throwing a ball, the other worked harder to exceed the standard. Once he did, then his brother stretched himself even further to surpass his twin's accomplishments once again.

Now, before you imagine a cutthroat environment at our house, let me assure you they didn't risk their relationship over this. They are best friends and agreed on their own never to compete against each other publicly. (For example, rather than wrestle each other in a tournament, they would ask the referee to flip a coin to determine the winner.)

Competition can be an important motivational tool, especially for older students. I've worked with quite a few families who found that a traditional setting was better suited for their teenagers (usually boys) because they needed an element of competition to be motivated to learn.

COMPETITION CAN BE AN IMPORTANT MOTIVATIONAL TOOL, ESPECIALLY FOR OLDER STUDENTS.

The CHESS classes Cindy McKeown organized have demonstrated to me the benefits of competition in a carefully controlled environment. In this setting, the kids admire the students who do their best. My kids invested a lot more time on assignments for their classes there than on assignments they did at home because they knew their projects were going to be displayed alongside those produced by their peers. They didn't want to be embarrassed.

Challenge #4: Lack of Accountability

In many places it is easy to home educate without much outside accountability or government regulation. I'm not advocating tougher laws, but I do see a drawback that can work against our children's best interests if we allow it to.

Real change or progress in life is difficult to bring about without some level of accountability. That's why the Bible says, "Confess your sins to one another" (James 5:16), and it's why accountability groups like Weight Watchers and Alcoholics Anonymous work.

I have found that where I lack accountability, I typically lack discipline. While I'd like to see the homeschool law in Pennsylvania streamlined, I know the annual review of our program helped me complete what I committed to do each year. I gained valuable insights from my evaluator (chosen by my husband and me, not the state), and my kids really looked forward to sharing their schoolwork with her each June. The families I evaluated also commented often on the helpfulness of an outside review.

> **WITHOUT SOME KIND OF ACCOUNTABILITY, IT IS EASY TO SLIDE YEAR AFTER YEAR TOWARD AN UNDISCIPLINED LIFESTYLE.**

Without some kind of accountability, it is easy to slide year after year toward an undisciplined lifestyle. Are our kids learning to meet deadlines and to complete a course of study, sticking to it even when they are tired or disinterested in the material? A traditional setting does provide this framework. I personally find that framework too restrictive, but some framework is still beneficial.

If you home educate in a state where little accountability is required, consider building accountability into your program. Deadlines, goals for the year in the core subject areas, and an annual day of sharing your work with others in your homeschool support group (especially for your older students) can only improve your program. We want our kids to cultivate a disciplined lifestyle, and that doesn't come from doing only those things they feel like doing.

Challenge #5: Exclusion from Scholastic Sports

Almost any opportunity available to conventionally schooled students is now open to kids who are homeschooled—except for scholastic sports. Academic competitions—such as Knowledge Open, ThinkQuest, MathCounts, and Odyssey of the Mind— have adjusted their requirements to accept homeschoolers. Extracurricular activities in music, drama, dance, etc., can all be found at a competitive level outside of your local school district. But the athletic competition that will open doors to college-level play or scholarships often is not. And this has been a frequent reason for homeschooled students to enroll in a traditional setting.

A Confession

For some of you, a passionate devotion to competitive sports is hard to comprehend. Kermit and I did not set out to raise athletes. It doesn't rank high on our list of targets in and of itself. We saw our recreation league's sports program as an arena for integrating our lives with those in our community (see Target #4, page 12). So we innocently signed our sons up for T-ball when they were five. One thing led to another, and before I knew it I'd spent equivalent to a year of my life watching Mike and Gabe play baseball and my daughters play softball—and that was just in the summer.

To say I was worried about what we were going to do when my sons no longer had access to competitive sports is an understatement. My daughters played on homeschool volleyball teams and basketball teams. Those were pretty easy to pull together, but Mike and Gabe wrestled and played football. I like a challenge, but there was no way I was going to pull together a homeschooled wrestling team and then find a league to play in.

So, two years before their teams were scheduled to come under the jurisdiction of the school district, I started a dialogue with my school board. In the end they extended to the homeschool community not only access to sports but also access to all extracurricular activities and secondary classes.

This is currently a hot issue in the homeschool community. Some states have already legislated access to scholastic sports for homeschoolers, and around the country many homeschool families have a cooperative relationship with their school district. But those open doors have all come about through hard work.

At the same time, the homeschool community has continued its end run around the Old Guard and has been setting up alternative leagues around the country. Though still in the early stages, in some leagues, the homeschool teams are then going head-to-head with the public and private school teams and holding their own. College scouts are picking up homeschooled graduates directly from these leagues, and I believe it is only a matter of time until it will not be necessary to gain access to public school teams in order to earn those college scholarships.

In homeschooling you don't waste time. That was an extreme adjustment for me in public school. For example, at home I could combine subjects; a science report could count for English and science. In public school you have to do a lot more to demonstrate your understanding of a subject—in homeschooling your mom knows what you know. We have to take a lot of quizzes just so the teacher can determine if we read the assignment. In homeschooling you can work more efficiently—you don't have twenty minutes for homeroom. Also, at school at least ten minutes of every class is taken up just getting kids in order. I find the other kids very distracting.

In homeschooling I could pursue my own interests. If I saw something on TV that interested me, I could go and find out more about it. After I saw the movie Apollo 13, *I got real interested in space, but it was not what we were studying in science at school.*

The advantage of public school, though, is the teachers are specialized in their area. I really like that I can talk to my science teacher. He knows so much. I think I am pushed harder in school. I have deadlines to meet. That has helped me to learn that the world functions in an orderly fashion. I've also learned how to speak in front of a large group. I have to do that a lot. I think school has given me more special opportunities. This year we had a Civil War re-enactment, and another time a Holocaust survivor came and spoke, and sports—I couldn't have played organized football at home.

—Joel Martin, at age fourteen
(homeschooled through seventh grade, then
valedictorian of his graduating class, and later a
graduate student at Harvard)

CHAPTER 4
Do I Have Time to Homeschool?

A woman called my friend Cherrie Moore at her homeschool supply store in Virginia Beach. "I'm going to homeschool my daughter," she said. "Tell me what I need to buy for a third grader."

"Well," Cherrie replied, "it's not as easy as that. I would need some more information: What's your daughter's learning style? What goals do you have? What philosophy of education are you building upon?"

"I don't have time for all that," the woman answered. "Just tell me what I need to buy."

"If you don't have time for that," Cheri countered, "you don't have time to homeschool."

How much time does it take to homeschool? The answer has a number of contributing factors.

Getting Started

Your first year will be your hardest, Marie Gamon told me.

I didn't see how that was possible, considering we were just talking kindergarten here and not high school physics. But she was right, all because I had a lot to learn and needed to commit the time to that.

Preparing to begin homeschooling is your biggest time commitment and one you must make if you are serious about doing a responsible job. If you don't have time to clear your schedule for a season and focus on educating yourself, then please don't undertake the education of your children.

A responsible parent will do several of the following *prior* to starting to homeschool:

> **YOUR FIRST YEAR WILL BE YOUR HARDEST.**

- Read lots of books related to homeschooling and educating children. My list:

Beyond Survival: A Guide to Abundant-Life Homeschooling, Diana Waring

A Charlotte Mason Companion, Karen Andreola

Educating the WholeHearted Child, Clay and Sally Clarkson

Einstein Never Used Flash Cards: How Our Children Really Learn—And Why They Need to Play More and Memorize Less, Karthy Hirsh-Pasek and Roberta Michnick Golinkoff

For the Children's Sake, Susan Schaeffer Macaulay

Help for the Harried Homeschooler: A Practical Guide to Balancing Your Child's Education with the Rest of Your Life, Christine Field

- Attend a homeschooling seminar on getting started.
- Attend a state convention and curriculum fair.
- Spend the day with a homeschooling family or co-op.
- Attend a support group meeting.
- Write to request a variety of catalogs from homeschool suppliers.
- Tool around the Internet. These sites will get you started:

Home School Legal Defense Association (www.hslda.org, www.youcanhomeschool.org)

About: Homeschooling (www.homeschooling.about.com)

A to Z Home's Cool Homeschooling (This is one of the oldest sites on the Web, run by feisty Ann Zeise, who nimbly manages to serve the broad horizons of the homeschool community with well-researched and up-to-date information—homeschooling.gomilpitas.com)

- Subscribe to a state newsletter and other homeschool magazines and newsletters. My list:

Homeschooling Today, Steve Murphy, publisher (www.homeschooltoday.com)

The Old Schoolhouse, Paul and Gena Suarez, publishers (www.thehomeschoolmagazine.com)

Practical Homeschooling, Mary Pride, publisher (www.home-school.com)

You Have to Be a Reader

Here's a sample of my reading list from the summer prior to the twins beginning school (most of these are out of print but may be available through your public library):

How to Tutor, Samuel Blumenfeld

A Nation at Risk: *The Imperative for Educational Reform*, The National Commission on Excellence in Education)

The New Illiterates, Samuel Blumenfeld

Parents' Guide to Raising Children Who Love to Learn, Children's Television Workshop

Teach Your Own, John Holt and Pat Farenga

If you don't have time to read, you don't have time to homeschool. Just to drive home this point, here's a sample of Cindy McKeown's reading list from one summer (after twelve years of homeschooling):

The Art of Thinking, Vincent Ruggiero

The Creative Mind, Margaret A. Boden

Killing the Spirit, Page Smith

Raising Self-Reliant Children in a Self-Indulgent World, H. Stephen Glenn and Jane Nelson, Ed.D.

The 7 Habits of Highly Effective People, Stephen Covey

Time Management for Unmanageable People, Ann McGee-Cooper (this book helped Cindy get her kids organized)

Toxic Psychiatry, Peter Breggin

> **IF YOU DON'T HAVE TIME TO READ, YOU DON'T HAVE TIME TO HOMESCHOOL.**

Cindy also enjoyed reading a healthy dose of P.G. Wodehouse and Dorothy Sayers. She considers these her "stress-busters."

Point: If you're not self-educating, how will you reproduce that in your kids? If you don't have the time to prepare to homeschool, how will you have the time to homeschool?

A Typical School Day

 Most homeschoolers will tell you there isn't such a thing as a "typical" day. Nancy Lande has compiled a charming collection of "A Day at Our House" anecdotes in her book *Homeschooling: A Patchwork of Days*, as has Rhonda Barfield in *Real-Life Homeschooling: The Stories of Twenty-One Families Who Teach Their Children at Home*, just to illustrate this point.

It's a Lifestyle

Homeschooling is better described as a lifestyle—a complete integration of family life and learning. When school starts and stops is a nebulous line at best in most homes. Does going to the library after supper count? Or how about slowing down the car to watch a pair of whooping cranes alight beside a stream? Reading together at bedtime? Watching a Ken Burns documentary on the history of baseball? Staying up late to see a meteor shower?

Could You Be More Specific, Please?

That may sound lyrical and enticing, but that doesn't help you make a decision, does it? What you really want to know is, *How much time—max—must I carve out of my schedule to devote solely to teaching a child to read, helping with assignments, organizing science experiments, grading papers, going to the library, testing, completing a textbook, and so forth?*

Here's a rough generalization of school life, time-wise, for you number-crunchers. But you've missed the point if you don't grab the binoculars when a downy woodpecker shows up after regular school hours.

> HOMESCHOOLING IS BETTER DESCRIBED AS A LIFESTYLE—A COMPLETE INTEGRATION OF FAMILY LIFE AND LEARNING.

- The hard-core work of **kindergarten** can be compressed into a thirty-minute daily schedule.

- **First through third grade:** one to two hours of structured learning each day.

- **Fourth and fifth grades:** three to four hours.

- **Sixth grade and up:** Somewhere between sixth grade and eighth grade, many kids move away from hands-on, concrete learning (which takes a lot more time for Mom to set up) and begin to acquire the majority of their content knowledge from their own independent reading. Projects, field trips, and othe concrete methods are still an important component, but if you've done your job well, the kids are now initiating these learning activities without much oversight from you.

- **Middle school and beyond:** For the serious student, these years begin early in the morning and end around mid-afternoon. My teens' math lessons easily took sixty to ninety minutes a day. They practiced their music a minimum of thirty minutes and read more than two hours as well as completed writing and research projects. They also did chores and apprenticed at our family business.

My supervision was pretty minimal. All four of my kids were setting their own goals by high school or completing courses outside the home: college classes, online coursework, or through CHESS. I would troubleshoot where necessary or meet with them for scheduled tutorials they had requested. I invested a lot more time of direct instruction during the elementary years.

Time's Up! We Must Call for Your Answer

So do you have the time to homeschool? The answer probably lies within the context of this larger question: How much other stuff is on your list of responsibilities that cannot be integrated into your homeschool life? A job outside the home? An elderly parent who needs constant care? Ministry responsibilities that don't include your kids? The most successful homeschools have a pretty short list in this regard.

CHAPTER 5
Single Parents, Special Needs, Careers, and Other FAQs

FAQ #1: What If I'm a Single Parent?

A growing number of single parents are making homeschooling work for their families, but it is not an easy task to accomplish. It requires a great deal of resourcefulness and initiative.

The Issue Is Work

The greatest tension exists when the homeschooling parent must work to support the family. It can succeed when the single parent works at home, works part-time, or has flex hours. It doesn't work when the children—including teenagers—are left alone during the school day or when a full-time job outside the home is necessary. In the latter situation, there just is not enough accountability or adult involvement with the kids.[1] I strongly believe in training our kids to be independent learners, but they still need the adults in their lives to be available and focused on their learning.

 Ruth is a single mom I greatly admire. She homeschooled one of her daughters, Amy, for several years solely because Amy pleaded with her to do so.

Ruth had a network of support that was a crucial component of her success. Her employer allowed Amy to come to work with Ruth and make use of an empty office. Amy also took most of her core classes through CHESS as well as enrichment classes at the Learning Center homeschool co-op. The number of subjects Ruth needed to cover with Amy on her own was minimal. They also had a computer and access to software and other self-instructional materials for Amy to use. Don't get the impression that Ruth was living on a comfortable income to do this, either—she was not. She sacrificed dearly to get creative resources, often used, in her children's hands.

Despite the wide array of opportunities and support available to her, Ruth was very thoughtful about this decision. She already found the responsibility of being a single parent pretty overwhelming. Homeschooling did not reduce that feeling.

On the plus side, Ruth loves to learn, has always supplemented her kids' education a lot at home, and was very attracted to the homeschool community she had come to know through her church. And she found an unexpected camaraderie among homeschoolers that she had little time for before. She's also enjoyed a great deal of support for her effort. For a single parent, many things leaned her way. And Amy, who was always a highly motivated student, prospered through homeschooling.

FAQ #2:
What If I Have a
Special-Needs Child?

No matter what area of difficulty your child faces, an individualized program and one-on-one instruction create the optimum learning environment. I have seen great success— actually remarkable improvement—with children challenged with a wide array of disabilities.

A study by Dr. Steven Duvall compared learning-disabled students in public school special-education programs and those who were home educated. Higher rates of "time on task" and greater academic gains were made by homeschooled students. Dr. Duvall concluded, "Parents, even without special education training, provided powerful instructional environments at home."[2]

The Success Factor

The common factors in these successful situations are:

- Parents who self-educate about the specific challenge their child is facing.
- Support from a network of resource people in the community. Some of these are professionally qualified; others are simply warm, nurturing individuals from within the church or homeschool community.

Here are recommended sources of support for parents who are homeschooling special-needs children:

Almaden Valley Christian School
Sharon Hensley
16465 Carlson Drive
Morgan Hill, CA 95037
408-776-6691
www.almadenvalleychristianschool.com
Book, information packet, program planning

Child Diagnostics
Dianne Craft, MA, CNHP
6562 S. Cook Court
Littleton, CO 80121
www.diannecraft.com
Seminars, private consultations

Home School Legal Defense Association
P.O. Box 3000
Purcellville, VA 20134-9000
540-338-5600
www.hslda.org
Struggling learners section of website, qualified
special-needs coordinators

NATHHAN (National Challenged Homeschoolers
Associated Network)
P.O. Box 310
Moyie Springs, ID 83845
208-267-6246
www.nathhan.com
Newsletter, referrals, resources, etc.

Dr. Joe Sutton
Exceptional Diagnostics
5 Jericho Court
Simpsonville, SC 29681
864-967-4729
www.edtesting.com
Diagnostic testing

Timberdoodle Autism Center
timberdoodleautismcenter.com
(In recent years, the family operating this long-established
homeschool supply company has cared for an autistic child.
The site includes a blog, product reviews, and other excellent
information for those homeschooling an autistic child.)

And here are the best books I've found on the subject of
special needs:

*Homeschooling the Challenging Child: A Practical
Guide,* Christine Field

Home Schooling Children with Special Needs, Sharon
Hensley

*In Their Own Way: Discovering and Encouraging Your
Child's Multiple Intelligences,* Thomas Armstrong

Learning in Spite of Labels and other titles, Joyce Herzog

Testing

If you suspect that your child has a learning disability, the staff
at NATHHAN recommends you use a private testing service,
such as Dr. Sutton's. NATHHAN can help you find a certified test
administrator in your region as well as connect you to families that
homeschool children who are challenged in the same area as yours.

Public Services

You may wish to avail yourself of public school services that
are free of charge, but don't walk into the situation naively. Be
prepared to speak intelligently about your child's needs and
communicate graciously but clearly your intent to take an active
role in the decision-making process. I've known a number of
parents whose children were identified as special-needs through
the local school system, and they had a difficult time retaining
control of the situation. There's a lot of money flowing into the
special-needs end of public education, and this is a built-in
incentive to get as many kids as possible into the system.

Be Advised Before You Sign

If you wish to leave open your option to homeschool your special-needs child, then you should seek advice from the Home School Legal Defense Association (page 224) before you sign any papers indicating your agreement with the diagnosis of your child. In a number of states, the formal identification of a child as handicapped or special-needs places him or her under separate legal regulations. This will then give you access to publicly funded services, but it can also make you legally bound to requirements you may wish to avoid.

FAQ #3. What About My Career?

Something has to give—you can't do it all. Believe me, if that were possible, I would have figured out how because I love to do anything and everything. Saying no is my biggest challenge; keeping things simple is a close second.

If you choose to homeschool, it has to be far higher on your list of priorities than your career. Ideally, the main teaching parent is not working outside the home, especially when the children are younger. But as that is often not the case, here's the way I have seen the two mix successfully.

Home Is Where the Work Is

Entrepreneurialism runs deep throughout the homeschool community. The same philosophical underpinnings that support home education have also led many to take charge of their careers. And as with education, technology is making it possible to base our work lives at home.

A home-based career can integrate well with your child's education. Choose one that has inherent educational value: Wendy is a single mother who works for her extended family's geranium nursery that specializes in scientific research, with clients around the world. While acknowledging it hasn't been easy, Wendy is enthusiastic about the fascinating business and research opportunities her children have been able to have.

During the years they homeschooled their seven children, Stephen and Naomi Strunk also owned a homeschool supply business. Each child has had responsibilities in the business over

> IF YOU CHOOSE TO HOMESCHOOL, IT HAS TO BE FAR HIGHER ON YOUR LIST OF PRIORITIES THAN YOUR CAREER.

the years. Amanda, the eldest daughter, worked hand in hand in overseeing daily operations with Naomi until leaving home. While in high school, Elizabeth was in charge of all billing and graphic design; and Hannah, the second oldest, handled all sales. At age eleven, Lydia began clerking at smaller events, pricing inventory, and handling phone calls. Ezra and Benjamin began processing inventory while still in elementary school, and even Suzanna, who has Down syndrome, was involved with mailings and labeling.

Look for similar opportunities that will enable your children to be integrally involved with the business while acquiring a marketable skill and a specialized knowledge base. I know homeschooling families that have mixed education and occupation in the following areas: construction, horticulture, bulk-food co-ops, bread making, private practice of medicine and psychology, writing, computer consulting, homeschool supplies, private instruction in music and art, animal breeding, and legal services.

> IN 2004, TWENTY MILLION AMERICANS WERE WORKING FROM HOME FOR AT LEAST SOME PORTION OF THEIR JOB.

Since I first wrote this book ten years ago, working at home has mushroomed. In 2004, twenty million Americans were working from home for at least some portion of their job; that's close to one in six workers. And the higher your educational attainment, the more likely you are to spend a portion of your work hours telecommuting. (This ups the value of a college education in my book—many of us can raise our families and still bring in part-time income without leaving home.) In recent years, Kermit has been freed up by the rise in technology to work from home at his discretion, which has made him much more available to our kids and to his parents, and both of my sons are able to do a portion of their jobs from home, as are many men in our church.

All this bodes well for the future growth of homeschooling, as the issue of loss of income is increasingly minimized. So, what follows is a few of the key authors who've been focused on home-based business the longest; but you will also be able to find books online that are targeted to working at home in a specific industry because the readership is now there to support that:

 The E Myth Revisited: Why Most Small Businesses Don't Work and What to Do About It, Michael Gerber

Homemade Money: Bringing in the Bucks, Barbara Brabec

Homemade Money: Starting Smart, Barbara Brabec

I Love My Life: A Mom's Guide to Working from Home, Kristie Tamsevicius (kristiet.com)

The Stay-at-Home Mom's Guide to Making Money from Home, Revised Second Edition: Choosing the Business That's Right for You Using the Skills and Interests You Already Have, Liz Folger

FAQ #4:
Can I Teach More Than One Child at Once?

Yes, you can teach more than one child at a time, but it's like juggling. It will take a bit of practice to keep all the balls rotating in the air. There are a couple of basic strategies to employ to manage this feat:

> **YES, YOU CAN TEACH MORE THAN ONE CHILD AT A TIME, BUT IT'S LIKE JUGGLING.**

1. Choose multilevel resources that enable you to present the same subject to all or several of your kids at once. My children are five years apart in age. I could group Kayte and the boys together for quite a few activities or let Mike and Gabe work independently and group Kayte and Kristen. The subjects we most frequently combined were history, art, science, and English.

   Cindy McKeown and Marie Gamon grouped their kids together for lots of subjects throughout the years. Marie taught art to the younger children while Cindy had the older ones for science next door. Even though there was a span of four years between Marie's oldest teen and Cindy's youngest teen, they were able to have the four of them do the same science and use the same math tutor simultaneously. Once we get the idea out of our heads that there is a linear progression of subject matter we must follow, we are free to do biology one year with kids in ninth through twelfth grades or Colonial American history with children in second through fifth.

2. You'll need to devote time weekly to scripting out a schedule for all your children. You'll read aloud with older kids while your baby is napping; you'll help a little one work on letter recognition while your school-age children use the computer. If all your kids are young, you will probably need to think in twenty-minute segments; and you may need to select resources such as software solutions or video instruction to keep all your children learning while you are giving one-on-one time to another child.

3. Recognize that your job is not so much to teach your children as it is to facilitate educational opportunities and undergird their independent learning. In high school, Mike, Gabe, and Kayte functioned fairly independently while I worked one-on-one with Kristen. My older three checked in with me on an "as needed" basis, and I held them accountable to accomplish their weekly goals by reviewing their completed work.

As you read through the practical tips that follow, you should get a clearer picture of homeschool life. As I told the perplexed folks who frequently asked me how I did this, homeschooling is more like tutoring than teaching. If you have a picture in your mind of your children sitting in desks with you at the front of the class presenting all the lessons in lecture form, we've got to tune you to another station.

 Help for the Harried Homeschooler, Christine Field

> **RECOGNIZE THAT YOUR JOB IS NOT SO MUCH TO TEACH YOUR CHILDREN AS IT IS TO FACILITATE EDUCATIONAL OPPORTUNITIES AND UNDERGIRD THEIR INDEPENDENT LEARNING.**

FAQ #5: But What About Socialization?

Of course, this section wouldn't be complete without addressing the top FAQ posed to homeschoolers. Some folks seem to expect our kids to be as clueless in social situations as the Beverly Hillbillies. But if you spend even a little bit of time among homeschoolers, you'll realize this is a nonissue.

First, let's define our terms. Make a list of what you mean by *socialization*. Here's mine:

- Works cooperatively with other people, including those from different backgrounds and beliefs.
- Not socially awkward in group situations.
- Works out differences with others.
- Understands appropriate behavior in social situations.

Now let me ask you this: Where did you learn appropriate social behavior? School? Where did you learn to appreciate folks who dress differently, act differently, think differently? School? Where did you learn proper etiquette? The high school cafeteria? Get the point?

Homeschooled kids can learn in a much broader context of social experiences than they would in school. Typically it is an age-integrated environment. They are frequently in group settings with adults, senior citizens, toddlers, and peers. There is none of this silliness about sixth graders not talking to fifth graders or big brothers not talking to younger sisters. There is no pecking order to fall in line with or acceptance measured by the clothes you wear or the dares you take.

Growing up, my kids often found the social mores of their public school friends very perplexing. On one baseball team the twelve-year-olds relegated the eleven-year-olds to the end of the bench the entire season. One friend was astonished when Mike acknowledged his sister as she walked by him at the community pool. Once some players thought the backfield should shave their heads prior to an important game. Gabe, the quarterback, couldn't figure out what strategic advantage this would give them. He left his hair intact.

Here's one anecdote from a mom who began homeschooling reluctantly after watching her bright son lose his vitality in a private school setting:

Jeffrey was excelling academically in a Christian school but hurting in his heart. The cruel comments from classmates, being picked last for a sports team, and never feeling accepted by his peers were daily happenings. Every night John and I prayed with him, encouraged him, and told him he is special, but every day he came home defeated. Despite many misconceptions about homeschooling, we began praying for wisdom.

Two years later we began homeschooling and joined the Learning Center homeschool co-op. We were received with open arms and hearts. Jeffrey now felt comfortable with friends of all ages. Maybe homeschoolers are so accepting of children who are a "little different" because they are a minority themselves. The good news is that Jeffrey is more secure and happy with who God has made him.

I see homeschooling as an environment to give my children wings. We were paying for Jeffrey to receive a wonderful education, but he could never reach his full potential when he felt so worthless.

— Beverly, mother of three

This is the kind of basic human decency I can count on finding among our homeschool community, and that, to me, is the essence of what is typically meant by socialization.

But you don't have to take my word for it . . .

Research Conclusions

Research focused on the social and emotional adjustment of home-educated children has indicated that they have:

- Significantly lower problem-behavior scores than their conventionally educated agemates (Shyers, 1992)

- Higher self-concepts than age-mates in public school (Shyers, 1992, and Taylor, 1986)

- Social and emotional adjustment comparable to private-schooled age-mates, while being less peer dependent (Delahooke, 1986)

- Just as much involved in out-of-school and extracurricular activities that predict leadership in adulthood as those in a comparison private school (comprised of students more involved than those in public schools) (Montgomery, 1989)[3]

FAQ #6.
But Am I Qualified to
Teach My Children?

Maybe you're with me so far, but you've got one hang-up: You seriously doubt your ability to teach your own children. After all, you didn't do so well in school yourself. Or perhaps you're so highly educated you think of teaching as an exacting science, like medicine.

Teaching Is an Acquired Skill

But teaching is an art, not a science. If you love your kids and are motivated to help them learn, you can acquire the skills you need.

Ask the best teachers you know what factor they most credit with their success. It won't be their degree or certification; it will be their on-the-job training.

> **IF YOU LOVE YOUR KIDS AND ARE MOTIVATED TO HELP THEM LEARN, YOU CAN ACQUIRE THE SKILLS YOU NEED.**

- The large body of research that exists shows little empirical evidence that teacher certification impacts student outcomes. Private school students routinely outscore public-educated counterparts on standardized achievement tests, and teachers without certification are prevalent in private schools.

- All researched comparisons of homeschooled students' achievement scores show significantly above-average achievement as a group. In 1995, Riverside Publishing Company announced that of the sixteen thousand home-educated students tested with the Iowa Test of Basic Skills, the mean score in reading was in the 77th percentile and in mathematics was in the 73rd percentile.

Of the thirty moms in the Learning Center homeschool co-op, I was the only certified teacher; three others have degrees in education. But you wouldn't be able to pick us out based on an observation of the classes taught. The moms at the Learning Center, like so many other homeschooling moms I know, are not hindered by their lack of professional training. These are *their* kids they are teaching, and they are highly motivated to do their best.

The homeschool parents I know are continuously reading, networking, and weighing different strategies for becoming better teachers. It's the most stimulating professional environment I've been in.

If You've Potty Trained, You're Qualified

Any child you've potty trained, you can certainly teach to read. And any child you've taught to read, you can certainly teach to learn on his own. And once you've taught a child to learn on his own, your job is just to facilitate that learning: scouring out resources, experiences, mentors, etc. that will support the child's own endeavors.

This is not to say without qualification that all parents are their children's best teacher. There are certain prerequisites that have been proven to make a difference.

Let's look now at the real recipe for success in homeschooling.

> **ANY CHILD YOU'VE POTTY TRAINED, YOU CAN CERTAINLY TEACH TO READ.**

CHAPTER 6
Six Ingredients of a Successful Homeschool

Marlene is unexpectedly pregnant—again. Today she's having a hard time getting started. From the bed, she listens to Timmy and James arguing in the kitchen. In the background, the television blares. She rolls over and sighs deeply. She hears the school bus pull up to the corner and swing open its doors. What she'd give to have her kids on it—especially the two-year-old. But no such luck. Marlene's homeschooling.

She can tell you a spiritualized story of how she arrived at this decision, but the bottom line is that her pastor homeschools and she is eager for his respect.

Allen, her husband, left early this morning. He's out looking for work. It's a second marriage for both of them, and in the past seven years, he's been unemployed three times. Just not much of a market anymore for printers. He really didn't want Marlene to homeschool; he wanted her to get a job. But that wasn't in her theology.

Her oldest, Robby, sticks his head in the room. He's a bright kid. He likes to read and to play soccer. "Uh, Mom, what should I be doing for school?"

Marlene has borrowed books for the year from her school district. And she found some workbooks and readers at the library sale, all for five dollars. She tells a great story of how the Holy Spirit guided her to this overlooked pile of material.

"Can't you just read the next chapters in science till I get up?" Her voice has an edge.

"That science book is really boring, Mom. I was wondering if I could finish the woodworking project Dad and I started."

"Rob, you know you aren't allowed to handle the tools alone. Listen, get Timmy and James breakfast while I get dressed."

Sometime after nine, Marlene makes an appearance. Robby, seated at the table, is just beginning to find his place in the science book. James and Timmy are watching television.

The phone rings. Marlene's voice brightens as she talks to a young mother from church. Her friend is having problems with a toddler, and Marlene is full of advice.

Robby stares at the pages of his textbook and intermittently checks the clock. The little guys spill into the kitchen. Marlene periodically covers the phone and tells them to be quiet. Each time, her voice raises another notch.

Timmy has a fork. He aims for James but misses and sticks his mother. Marlene screams. She manages to hang up the phone before she vents her anger on everyone in sight.

Robby sighs, picks up his books, and heads for his bedroom.

After lunch, Marlene leaves for a weekly Bible study, and Robby's left in charge. At four o'clock, Robby thinks of his friends at school just heading out to the soccer fields. He misses the team, and he misses his friends. He misses English class. He even misses grouchy Mr. Whittler who gave him in-school suspension last year. He sure wishes God hadn't told his mom to homeschool.

Recipe for Success

It's been my experience that families who elect to home educate meet with varying degrees of success. But that success has little to do with teaching certificates or college degrees. Rather, it has a lot to do with Christian character.

This recipe for success is not meant to discourage you. If your family is unable to meet one of these prerequisites but is willing to seek change, you're on the right road.

If you can't or won't add one of these ingredients to your homeschool, it still may be the best option you have. But, honestly, you will not be able to give your children the education they deserve, and you are going to be frustrated and stressed.

Is She Happy?

Probably the *key factor* in those homes that have happy, motivated children who are achieving at the level of their potential is *Mom's attitude*. Is she happy? Are we having fun yet? Does she enjoy homeschooling and maintain relatively consistent enthusiasm? Or does she have a pinched look on her face most of the time?

Here are the factors I find affect her outlook.

Ingredient #1:
Family Relationships Are Healthy

Common Vision

Start with your spouse. Do the two of you have a common vision and goals? If you applied the principles of chapter 1 to your marriage, would your list of targets have any overlap?

When Kermit and I first married, we were still two very independent people with divergent plans for our lives. Our views on money, church, a woman's role, and the proper way to fold a towel (just to name the biggies) were often at odds. Now, over two decades later, by the grace of God (and what can feel like sheer force of will), we're both headed in the same direction and very happy to be doing so. How that happened is another story, and I know many of you can relate to that scenario. (Towels should be folded in thirds and stacked with the folded side out, by the way.)

It is very typical for one partner to have more of a vision for homeschooling than the other at first. It can take time to balance this out. But here are the necessary components in marriage for surviving the rocky first years of homeschooling:

1. Quick Resolution of Conflict

You resolve conflict quickly. Notice, I didn't say you don't have any conflict. The crux is, you know *how* to resolve it. In our house that means not letting issues fester, demonstrating humility and forgiveness, communicating constructively, and asking for outside help from spiritually mature friends when necessary.

2. Dad's Attitude

Dad is supportive of homeschooling. I believe this factor, much more than Dad's direct involvement in homeschooling, determines success.

The worst thing a husband can say to his wife is, "All right, I'll give you a year, and we'll see how you do." It is very unfair to put this kind of pressure on your wife. The first year of homeschooling is the toughest. In the best of situations, there are going to be

> IT IS VERY TYPICAL FOR ONE PARTNER TO HAVE MORE OF A VISION FOR HOMESCHOOLING THAN THE OTHER AT FIRST.

mistakes, discouragement, and self-doubt throughout. To add to that the stress of having to get this right the first time or she's pulled from the game is a setup for failure from the start.

3. Mom's Attitude

Wives, on the other hand, need to be realistic about their husbands' involvement. I've attended seminars and read books where the father's role in homeschooling is presented as something akin to the school principal: Dad should be directly involved in setting curriculum, reviewing work, and spending time daily instructing his children. As I look around the auditorium where this is being said, I see the fathers slowly sinking down in their seats under the pressure of one more thing on their plates.

It Looks Different at Every House

When our kids were younger, Kermit read aloud to them nearly every day and looked at their daily work. It was easy to use vacation days for special things. But by the time our kids hit the teen years, his responsibilities on the job had expanded and his work week became much longer. He could troubleshoot difficulties that arose, but a weekly update was really the best way for us to manage his limited schedule.

One day, I realized I knew countless home-educating families in the same situation. I'm grateful Kermit is gainfully employed. I'm happy that the free time he did have was devoted to his kids. But he wanted to play ball or take the girls on a field trip, not review papers or teach a course, when he had free time to give.

And he has always been willing to take over responsibilities at home so I can get away to plan or just have a break.

Some fathers do teach, but it's because they have an interest, not an obligation. Marie's husband, John, taught science to his kids. He had a lab set up in the basement. Pickling there were fetal pigs and cows' eyes. He loved it. I know several homes where the father is the primary teacher. And I've seen many fathers' involvement increase as the kids enter their teen years. In general, they seem more comfortable with the material at that level. The point is that there's a principle, not a pattern that must be adhered to.

> SOME FATHERS DO TEACH, BUT IT'S BECAUSE THEY HAVE AN INTEREST, NOT AN OBLIGATION.

It's a Joint Decision

Homeschooling needs to be a joint decision. Both spouses should be able to say, "We're going to try this for a year and give it our best shot. Then we'll re-evaluate the situation." During the year, Dad should be committed to tangibly encouraging and supporting his wife.

Predetermine Responsibilities

Talk through with your spouse what responsibilities each of you will assume to contribute to the integrity and success of your homeschool. The job description for both of you will shift and change over the years, so don't expect this to be a once-and-done discussion.

If the primary teacher—usually Mom—starts showing signs of stress and exhaustion during the year, it's a good bet the other partner needs to either provide some R&R (a weekend away works wonders) or shift some responsibility onto his or her plate for a season.

Here is a book you will find encouraging and faith-building, especially in the midst of the demands of homeschooling:

 When Sinners Say "I Do": Discovering the Power of the Gospel for Marriage, Dave Harvey

Check Out the Kids

After assessing your marriage, be honest about your relationship with each of your children.

Kids need two things in order to learn well:

- A secure environment, free from stress and fear
- Praise and encouragement from someone they trust

Is your child motivated by your praise and still interested in your approval? Do you have an effective plan for dealing with discipline problems?

Say It Again, Sam

If you have a strong-willed child or a rocky relationship with your spouse, homeschooling is only going to accentuate these problems, not solve them. I know too many families that thought

HOMESCHOOLING NEEDS TO BE A JOINT DECISION.

homeschooling was the solution. It isn't. These problems must be worked on at a deeper, more fundamental level. In some cases, you need outside help.

Meaningful Church Involvement

I am very grateful to be involved in a church where the pastoral staff and small-group leaders are available to constructively guide us through the challenges of marriage and parenting. I cannot overemphasize how crucial a role this has played in the success of our family life. I credit that support with the fruit in my children and my marriage.

Marlene eventually put her children back in a private school, and she and her husband sought pastoral help for their marriage. Today their home is much stabler. Robby returned to playing soccer, and his confidence in God's loving care in his life has grown.

If you need sound advice in the parenting realm, these books that have had the greatest impact in our home:

Educating the WholeHearted Child, Clay and Sally Clarkson

Our 24 Family Ways, Clay Clarkson

The Heart of Anger: Practical Help for the Prevention and Cure of Anger in Children, Lou Priolo

Shepherding a Child's Heart, Tedd Tripp

Ingredient #2: Your Home Is Educationally Stimulating

A quick tour of my home tells people a lot about me. I'm not very committed to laundry or dusting or even interior decorating. But my commitment to reading and learning, I hope, is evident. Books, magazines, projects, computers, music, etc. dominate the landscape. There are bookshelves in every room.

My downfall is any bookstore. My husband and I have a sick, co-dependent relationship. He's not to be trusted near one either. Our family business was really an elaborate scheme I hatched to make sure I could get books any time I craved one. My heart sinks if the UPS truck passes my house without stopping. My library fines are so hefty they've mentioned naming me a major donor. Our kids are infected as well.

If your home does not reflect your commitment to education, your kids will clearly get the message that it isn't important. Your kids deserve to be taught by someone who loves to learn.

Is school time a pressured thing you rush to get through? Have you committed the finances to provide educational materials? I know what it is to live on a restricted budget. But I am committed to buying the best material I can afford.

When a parent's initial question is, "How cheaply can this be done?" I know his or her kids are going to be shortchanged.

I know many, many families who are homeschooling on a limited budget, but the best of these are getting to the library regularly, setting aside funds for the used-curriculum sale, and praying in faith for the provisions to come in. There is serious personal sacrifice going on to see that the kids have access to quality materials.

> **YOUR KIDS DESERVE TO BE TAUGHT BY SOMEONE WHO LOVES TO LEARN.**

Ingredient #3:
You Have a Biblical Conviction That God Has Called You to Homeschool

Our initial decision to home educate has to be more substantive than, "Gee, that's a neat idea. I think I'll try that," or acquiescence to the subtle pressure (real or perceived) that it is more "spiritual" to homeschool.

Our conviction must be borne out of prayer, study of God's Word, and godly counsel. It is imperative that we take the time we need to hear God personally. These convictions are the foundation for appropriating the faith and grace we need to complete the task. Otherwise, when discouragement and disillusionment hit, we will dig a deeper hole by questioning if we should be doing this in the first place. Constant doubts such as *Am I really the best teacher for my children? Am I cheating them out of fun and opportunities? Is this going to be worth it in the end?* will wear us out.

The writer of James said a double-minded man is unstable in all his ways. Without this bedrock of faith that God said, "Do it!" we're in for some rough seas. Firmly rooted convictions will be the source of endurance for the course.

 Read Chris Klicka's book *The Heart of Home Schooling: Teaching and Living What Really Matters* if you want a persuasive, biblical argument to help you build convictions about homeschooling.

Ingredient #4: You Have Initiative and Discipline

To homeschool successfully, we don't need degrees or loads of creativity and talent, but we do need some measure of maturity in our character. We need "get up and go" and the ability to restrain ourselves when discipline is required.

There's a Learning Curve

If you are new to homeschooling, then the hard part is now. You have to invest a lot of time in reading, preparing, figuring out what methods work best, and learning to manage your time.

Every new venture requires an initial outlay of time and training. I could not live without a computer. It is such a timesaver. But I spent hours reading, being frustrated, crying "Honey, help!" and learning in order to reap those benefits.

Just Say No

We need to be able to say no to other opportunities and be at peace when others don't understand why we do. Two things I've had to discipline myself to do are to go to bed on time and not answer the phone. I return the calls I can in the afternoon. Some I just can't respond to. Sometimes people are angry and disappointed with me, but there's peace in our day now.

Hobbies, friendships, ministries, jobs—many things may have to be sacrificed in order to homeschool with integrity. It all comes back to this vision that provides us with parameters for evaluating all the choices before us. Homeschooling successfully requires us to take radical control of our schedules. If you don't, you'll never hit the target.

> WE NEED "GET UP AND GO" AND THE ABILITY TO RESTRAIN OURSELVES WHEN DISCIPLINE IS REQUIRED.

Here's a recommended resource to help you do this:

 Shopping For Time: How to Do It All and NOT Be Overwhelmed, Carolyn Mahaney

Ingredient #5:
A Support System Is Available to You

Your support system may be formal or informal, but it needs to be made up of tangible people, not a state newsletter or a homeschooling magazine. You need folks standing with you and committed to helping you through. The more multilayered this support system is, the quicker you will surmount discouragement.

I am blessed beyond measure that my church, my relatives, and my friends support the choice we've made and are available to pick me up when I am down.

My network has not always been so thick—neither my parents nor my in-laws supported our choice at first. My friends were threatened by our decision. And I've talked to many homeschool families that have been isolated in their churches or even outrightly opposed by the leadership.

You need support. Get out of bad situations if you can. Find a church that is standing with families who make this choice, and find friends who homeschool. I guess you have to keep your relatives, but I've seen lots of grandparents change their minds once they see the fruit in their grandkids' lives. (They are only reacting out of love and concern, so don't be too hard on them.)

Some folks are going to call you a separatist, but your first priority when starting out is to lay a firm foundation. Get your house in order first. In the early years we immersed ourselves in the homeschool community. We talked about it nonstop and felt most attracted to others with our perspective. It was a necessary season of our life. It demanded our intense focus.

Eventually, our lives were much more balanced. Our family had many close friends who did not homeschool. We had other circles of interest we moved in. But we could only do this and remain effective at home because a solid foundation of support was in place first.

Ingredient #6:
You Are Willing to Seek Help

Homeschooling should not be done in isolation. It's not healthy for you or for your children. Without the input of others, you won't have a balanced perspective of things. Even though I had a teaching certificate and a lot of experience working with kids, I still needed and pursued the input of others. I went to seminars, I read books, and I talked to parents further down the road than we were.

HOMESCHOOLING SHOULD NOT BE DONE IN ISOLATION.

If you are a learner, you will always be looking and listening for better ways to fine-tune your program.

When you are discouraged or unmotivated, humble yourself and talk to someone with strengths in your area of weakness. The Bible says if we don't solicit the wise counsel of others, we are proud, and God will oppose our ways. Find a mature Christian woman who is obviously succeeding with her children and ask her advice. Be willing to serve her in return for her time. Annually attend seminars, listen to CDs, and read books—all with an attitude to learn. This is the fastest way to become qualified to teach your children.

CHAPTER 7
But I Don't Want to Homeschool!

Okay, maybe after all this, we've gotten to the bottom of things. You really don't want to homeschool, but you're reading this book because you have this niggling feeling that maybe you *should*. Let me see if I can help you out there as well.

I didn't want to homeschool. I was pretty career-minded. I was willing to stay home with my kids until they were school age (and felt pretty smug about it), but then I was planning to get back to my real life.

I'll tell you something else. I didn't want to become a Christian either. A campus missionary presented the gospel to me in a compelling, rational manner (à la Josh McDowell). I realized it was true—I was a sinner and needed a Savior—but I sure didn't want to give up the lifestyle I was leading. What did I do? I knew it would be foolish of me not to become a Christian, but I certainly wasn't as happy about it as all the other folks in the room were. Talk about hubris!

But for the compelling grace of God in my life, I might have tragically let my feelings be my guide—and modern society certainly supports that kind of emotion-based decision making.

How do I "feel" about being a Christian now? The joy is inexpressible. How do I "feel" about homeschooling? Well, I *could* describe that. Most days I loved it. Some days, I sure didn't. But I was there the day each one of my children learned to read, I was there the day Kayte piloted a Pungy Schooner into port, and I was there the day we all sat in the living room listening to the closing chapter of *The Cay* on tape, our eyes glistening. And nothing beats the satisfaction I found in seeing all four of my kids with their noses in a book.

Right at the beginning of recorded history, God gives us a very important principle for living. He challenges Cain: "Why has your countenance fallen? If you do well, will not your countenance be lifted up?" (Genesis 4:6). Paraphrased, the point is this: If we do what is right, our feelings will change. The Bible's way is not "feel your way to a new way of acting" but rather "act your way to a new way of feeling."

God's ways are not burdensome. He said, "Blessed are those who hear my commands and obey them" (Luke 11:28). We have a promise that obedience brings joy. But first things first: Forget about how you are feeling about homeschooling. Concentrate on determining God's will for your kids' lives (and feelings are not where we check to discern this), then draw faith from His promise that obedience to Him will produce joy in your life. We often look at the future calling God may have for us and imagine ourselves miserably obeying. That indicates a faulty view of who God is.

So exercise faith and draw hope from the promises of His Word.

 I was recently asked if I liked homeschooling my four children. My usual response would have been, "Yes, it's great!"

But in recent years our oldest son has become a teenager, and I've come to admit to myself that no, I really don't like homeschooling my four children very much. Over the past decade I've taught three, almost four kids how to read; confronted innumerable personal weaknesses and sinful behavior in my children and myself; failed countless times to do what I planned in a school year; viewed good and bad test scores; and been discouraged and overwhelmed more times than I like to remember.

So my answer this time was, "Well . . . I like the fruit." I love what I am seeing in my children, especially my fourteen-year-old son. We simply do not have the same struggles that other parents of teens I know have, and I'm convinced that the reason is that my son is not being socialized and civilized by his peers.

I recently drove Stephen to a student meeting at our local college. When we got there, I nearly asked him if he wanted me to go in with him but quickly decided against it. I thought he would object. But when he mentioned that he was unsure where to go, I volunteered to go with him.

"If you don't mind . . ." I said.

"No, I don't mind," he said sincerely.

I realized that he had no clue that boys his age don't like to be seen with their mothers, especially when meeting a college friend.

I love homeschooling because of episodes like this one that confirm to me we're on the right path for our family. I don't like the process much at all. I can talk big with my homeschooling friends, but when it comes right down to it, there are many days when I feel like a total failure. But I see things in my children that great schools and great programs could never produce, and I'm encouraged to keep going. I can't quit now. I'm not willing to give up what we've gained.

I don't expect that it will be clear sailing the whole way to adulthood. I can't do what only the Holy Spirit can do. But I can at least work hard in the garden He's given me to tend; I can keep the fence mended and the gate fixed and try to preserve the fruit we've already harvested. Do I like homeschooling? No, not really; but I love the fruit!

— Kristi, mother of four

FAMILY WORKSHEET

Homeschooling: Is It for Your Family?

Here's the exit interview before we close out Part 1. Use it as a tool to help you and your spouse make a wise decision about homeschooling.

1. Evaluate your relationship with your spouse.

○ **Excellent**: You have a common vision and goals, and are able to move quickly to resolve conflicts that arise.

○ **Good**: You communicate well about your differences in vision and goals. You seek out wise counsel to resolve conflicts when necessary.

○ **Fair**: You are both Christians. You eventually make peace about your differences. You rarely lose control of your emotions when you experience conflict. You do not seek help in resolving conflict.

○ **Poor**: You disagree strongly about your vision and goals. You have a great deal of conflict, and you resolve it in a destructive way.

2. Evaluate your relationship with each of your children.

○ **Excellent**: This child is highly motivated by your praise and has a strong desire to obey his or her parents.

○ **Good**: This child can be motivated by your praise, and you are making steady progress in his or her willingness to obey you.

○ **Fair**: This child is challenging, and you are often overwhelmed by him or her. You and your spouse do not have an agreed-upon plan for training the child. You do believe that God can sustain you.

○ **Poor**: This child is wearing the pants, and you gave up long ago. You feel like a failure as a parent. You aren't getting help, and you have no hope that things are going to change.

77

3. Evaluate the atmosphere in your home. Check all that apply.

Positive	Negative
◯ peaceful	◯ stressful
◯ secure	◯ insecure
◯ fun	◯ somber
◯ hospitable	◯ isolated
◯ spontaneous	◯ rigid
◯ stable	◯ unstable
◯ organized	◯ chaotic
◯ encouraging	◯ discouraging

4. List all other responsibilities and commitments you and your spouse have beyond maintaining your home and caring for your children.

EMPLOYMENT

CHURCH

VOLUNTEERING

HOBBIES

5. What plans do you have for limiting other responsibilities and commitments in order to homeschool with integrity?

6. Evaluate your home as an educationally stimulating environment.

a. How often do you use the library? _____

b. How many hours a week is your television on? _____

c. How many books are in your home? _____

d. What types of presents do you usually buy your children?

_____

e. What magazines do you subscribe to? _____

_____

f. What interests do you share with your children? _____

_____

g. What kinds of topics do you discuss as a family? _____

_____

h. Are pencils, paper, and art supplies readily available? ___

i. Do your children have an adequate place to play outside?

_____

7. Can you commit a minimum of five hundred dollars per year to home educating?

8. Rate yourself on initiative by asking yourself these questions and circling one of the words that follow. Are you a learner? How many books a year do you read on a subject of interest? Do you enjoy tackling new projects?

    Excellent   Very Good   Good   Fair   Poor

9. Rate yourself on discipline. Do you finish a job? Can you set goals and achieve them? Do you get up and go to bed on time? Do you fulfill your obligations?

    Excellent   Very Good   Good   Fair   Poor

10. What are your reasons for homeschooling?
Is this a biblical conviction?

11. How supportive of homeschooling is the father?

◯Very supportive ◯Supportive ◯Neutral ◯Not supportive

12. What role will the father be able to play in
your homeschool?

13. What support system is available to you? Does
it include your spouse? Your family? Your church?
A homeschool support group? A friendly teacher? A
Christian school? A library? An educational consultant?

14. Are you willing to go to seminars, attend support
group meetings, read books, etc., in order to always
be improving your teaching skills and your homeschool?

15. Evaluate your willingness to seek help.

◯ I readily seek help from others who have a strength in
the area I am struggling with.

◯ On occasion I do seek outside help if things get
pretty bad.

◯ I prefer to make things work on my own.

16. Having prayerfully weighed the cost of
homeschooling, are you prepared to commit
yourself to home educating for one year before
reevaluating your decision?

PART 2

CHOOSING A CURRICULUM

Learning Style

Money

The Library

Decisions

CHAPTER 8
How Do I Decide?

Just tell me *what* to buy! That's the $64,000 question. It used to be pretty simple (and pretty dull). Twenty years ago there wasn't much curricula to choose from. You just ordered textbooks from a school supplier who was willing to sell to homeschoolers, sometimes disguising your homeschool with a school-sounding name in order to do so.

Every time I ordered from one publisher, I endured the sales rep telling me why she did not approve of homeschoolers and what a passing fad it was.

You're a Niche Market

Today, homeschool conventions attract thousands of parents and hundreds of vendors. Some of the most traditional suppliers have added *"Great for homeschooling!"* to their splashy ads. Companies like Scholastic have hired a homeschooling consultant to help them better target their products. Homeschooling has become a hot niche market, and lots of businesses want your dollars. Homeschoolers spend between $600 million and $1 billion annually on educational supplies.

This all adds up to choice—lots of it. Not only are there scores of printed materials to help you teach every subject area, but there are software and video programs to consider as well.

All this is good news (even if you find it overwhelming). You have the opportunity to design a program that uniquely fits your child and your family. It's individualized, not institutionalized learning. And that allows you to produce kids who can learn at their fullest potential and enjoy it.

> **NOT ONLY ARE THERE SCORES OF PRINTED MATERIALS TO HELP YOU TEACH EVERY SUBJECT AREA, BUT THERE ARE SOFTWARE AND VIDEO PROGRAMS TO CONSIDER AS WELL.**

Prepackaged Programs

You can save yourself a lot of time wading through all these choices by settling on a traditional curriculum designed for

Christian or public school use. This way you get all the material you could ever possibly want for every school subject. And no one says you have to buy it all. Another option is to purchase just a portion of a program for the subjects you feel most insecure handling alone.

Here are the advantages of prepackaged curricula:

❶ The work's been done for you. The teacher's manuals lay out daily lessons and assignments. Textbooks and workbooks contain all the reading material and paperwork the student needs to complete for the year. You save time planning and organizing.

❷ You have greater peace of mind. A common concern of parents is forgetting something. If you use a complete line from one supplier year after year, you know they've seen to it that nothing is left out.

❸ If you think your child may return to a traditional setting, you've followed the standard scope and sequence.

❹ The material is covered in a logical fashion.

Many of us feel most comfortable choosing this option when we begin to homeschool. We want to keep things simple until we get our feet wet. Taking responsibility for designing our own program can just be too drastic a step to add to the first years of homeschooling. Textbooks, workbooks, and teacher's manuals look familiar and make sense. They give us a framework to follow, and that feels secure.

Given my bottom-line indicator of a successful homeschool (Mom is happy), this may be reason enough to choose a traditional program at first.

> **MANY OF US WANT TO KEEP THINGS SIMPLE UNTIL WE GET OUR FEET WET.**

I Recommend

Now in a minute I'm going to reveal my true colors on this subject, so you may want to find a less biased source of advice. But for what it is worth, if I were going to use traditional materials in my program, I would look at the curricula from Bob Jones University Press first.

What I Like about Bob Jones University

Whereas I may part company with BJU on some of their practices and theological distinctions, I can commend them for valuing academic excellence and the arts. (BJU has a fabulous religious art collection on campus and a world-renowned drama and music department.) Secondly, the school has an outstanding group of professors and education researchers writing its curricula. And these folks are frequently available to talk with you by phone or at the curriculum fairs around the country. Further, most of the BJU material has been recently revised to include higher-level thinking and assignments that require the student to interact with the material on a more thoughtful level.

The teacher's manuals are especially well done. Marie Gamon used much of the BJU program, and she had her children use the teacher's text for the higher-level courses instead of the student's. This way they get the information BJU has provided for the classroom lectures.

Here is BJU's address as well as the sources of additional traditional materials that are popular among homeschoolers:

Bob Jones University Press
Greenville, SC 29614-0062
800-845-5731
800-525-8398 fax
www.bjup.com

A Beka Book Publications
Box 19100
Pensacola, FL 32523-9100
877-223-5226
www.abeka.com

Alpha Omega Publications
804 N. Second Ave. E.
Rock Rapids, IA 51246
800-622-3070
www.aop.com

Christian Liberty Press
502 W. Euclid Ave.
Arlington Heights, IL 60004
847-259-4444
www.christianlibertypress.com

Modern Curriculum Press
Pearson Learning Group
800-526-9907
www.pearsonschool.com
This website can be difficult to navigate. You can also find these materials at www.amazon.com.

Grade Levels Vary

You will find there is little standardization about grade levels among textbook suppliers. Some material is very academically accelerated (A Beka, for instance), and some is academically delayed. (If it is inexpensive, cheaply produced, and requires students to only fill in the blanks, it's suspect.)

Lay grade-level material from several companies side by side before making your purchase. This will make it easier for you to see the differences. (You can do this at your state curriculum fair; or most companies have sample PDFs online to download for comparison sake.

> **LAY GRADE-LEVEL MATERIAL FROM SEVERAL COMPANIES SIDE BY SIDE BEFORE MAKING YOUR PURCHASE.**

Make Your Own Curriculum

Quick, name your favorite textbook from school. How about your favorite worksheet? Drawing a blank? Why am I not surprised?

Well, how about your favorite books from childhood? (*Little Women, Huckleberry Finn, To Kill a Mockingbird . . .* what's on your list?) Or your favorite projects? (A short story in fourth, my leaf collection in fifth, a relief map of Egypt in seventh.) Wouldn't you prefer to draw these last two questions in a game of Outburst?

If we can't even remember the textbooks and worksheets of childhood, how much better can we remember what we learned from them?

I still remember where the Nile River flows through Egypt, the placement of the pyramids, the elaborate irrigation system of that ancient civilization. And I can identify quite a few trees by their leaves. I still have that short story locked in a trunk of mementos, but I seem to have misplaced those worksheets.

So how come we're using textbooks to teach? And am I about to suggest you skip these lovely childhood treasures in your home-education program? And if that is where I'm headed, what in the world would you replace them with?

The Truth About Textbooks

Textbooks are our answer to how to package a wealth of information for mass distribution. We've got to teach everyone the same thing so we can administer a standardized test to compare students' achievement at the end. This keeps everyone inching along that linear (and arbitrary) scope and sequence I mentioned in chapter 2.

We don't have time to individualize the curriculum to suit each child's needs, interests, and learning style. And we certainly don't have the time to do individual assessment of each kid. Thus the birth of the testing industry.

Besides that, the foremost concern I had as a classroom teacher was crowd control. How do I keep all these kids busy and out of trouble for the next forty minutes? Standardization is the key. *Everyone turn to page 41 of your textbook. Everyone fill out this worksheet for class tomorrow.*

Institutionalized Versus Individualized Methods

Look at the chart on the next page. This is a comparison of traditional teaching methods that we endure in many classrooms and the individualized methods you now have available to you in home education. Which one looks more inviting, motivating, and effective?

Institutionalized	Individualized
Grades	Mastery
Standardized tests	Evaluation of all work
Sitting at desks/raising hands	Freedom to move and contribute
Textbooks, workbooks, worksheets	Children's literature Long-term projects
Segmented subjects	Integrated learning
Sequential learning	Teachable moments
Component teaching	Using in context
Scope and sequence	Readiness and interests
State-mandated objectives	God-given directives

The model on the left has already fallen out of favor in many innovative classrooms because the benefit of an individualized program, or at least one that is more hands-on and creative, is substantially supported by research. Unfortunately, this market trend has caused some suppliers to pursue the homeschool market as a naive dumping ground for their outdated product.

What in the World Do I Use, Then?

So if I'm suggesting you abandon the standard grade-level curriculum route, with what do I suggest you replace it? Any number of inviting, creative, and inexpensive resources are available from homeschool suppliers and, better yet, from your local public library. You just have to take the time to pull it together.

Here's how to decide exactly what you are looking for and then where to find it.

It's That Vision Thing Again

Remember? You need a framework for making decisions. It's time to march off to your state curriculum fair or sit down with your pile of homeschool supply catalogs (see the Resource Guide for sources) with the list of targets you're aiming to hit firmly in hand.

YOU NEED A FRAMEWORK FOR MAKING DECISIONS.

87

When you lay your four targets alongside all the choices you have, you can quickly weed out a whole lot of options:

- This resource is so boring and uninviting, it does nothing to cultivate a love for learning in my kid. How the author managed to stay awake throughout its development is beyond me. In the incinerator!

- This resource covers material that is no longer relevant to the changing job market or takes precious time away from those areas of the curriculum that are. I don't have time for this subject. To the recycling bin!

- The worldview inherent in this product inaccurately represents the Christian faith I wish to transfer to my kids. (This is not to say we did not use material from secular publishers; we did. I'm much more likely to pass up resources with shoddy theology or a propaganda purpose.) Down the disposal!

- This item is counterproductive to equipping my kids to impact their generation with the gospel (judgmental attitude toward unbelievers, an isolationist or ethnocentric view). Not on our list!

WEED OUT THE "NOT-ON-YOUR-LIFE" PRODUCTS BASED ON YOUR VISION FOR YOUR FAMILY LIFE.

Now that you've weeded out the "not-on-your-life" products based on your vision for your family life, you still have lots of stuff left to consider. Here's the next terminator of choices. Hone your list down to resources that match these three:

1 Your child: his or her interests, learning style, and level of mastery.

2 You: your time constraints, other responsibilities to consider, and preferred teaching style.

3 Budget: unfortunately.

Mom Counts, Too

Let's talk about the teacher before we look at choosing curriculum to fit your child and budget. As I've mentioned, a successful homeschool condenses down to Mom being happy.

If you don't ultimately choose resources and curricula you enjoy or feel comfortable with, you'll find that homeschooling quickly becomes drudgery. We want to keep that spring in your step.

Even though you've cleared your schedule of all non-essential responsibilities, there's still plenty that needs to get done—new babies, other children, church, or part-time work can all be on your list.

What's the Big Picture of Your Life?

When you look at potential curricula, keep the big picture in mind. Having an active toddler in the house seriously limits not only the types of resources you purchase but also the amount of direct teaching time you can put in. Video courses or software programs that cover subjects like algebra might be the solution for older kids during those years. Math curricula that require you to present the lesson will probably not work if you have four other children to teach at different grade levels. You also have to take into account your preferred teaching style (you should be able to recognize this when we look at learning styles).

I liked to pull resources together to create my own curriculum. Following someone else's program took a lot of the fun out of it for me. But other women hate the pressure of doing things this way. It saps them of energy. They are much better off finding an inviting, complete program that fits their kids without the responsibility of deciding what to do.

Profile Your Child
Areas of Interest

Now let's look at each child you'll be teaching.

What are his or her areas of interest? You'll want to integrate these into the curriculum wherever possible, especially at points where some extra motivation is needed. If he loves baseball and can't sit still to read, then a series of sports biographies and fiction by Matt Christopher is what you'll use. If she loves cooking and helping you run the home but can't make sense of the arithmetic problems on the paper, you'll use couponing, budgeting, *Grocery Cart Math*, and other household responsibilities to reinforce your math program.

LET'S TALK ABOUT THE TEACHER BEFORE WE LOOK AT CHOOSING CURRICULUM TO FIT YOUR CHILD AND BUDGET.

89

Levels of Mastery

Curricula can be divided into two categories: skill areas and content areas.

Is This a Content Area...?

American history, biology, and classical literature are content areas. Your job is to choose *creative* and *motivating* resources that help your kids *acquire a base of knowledge* in these subjects. This can happen through a variety of methods and does not need to be learned in a sequential, systematic style (random and chaotic is also an option).

Or a Skill Area?

Skill areas, on the other hand, are subjects like handwriting, arithmetic, composition, spelling, and reading. Most kids (emphasis on *most*, not *all*) more easily acquire these when presented in a *sequential, systematic fashion* with lots of *practice in a variety of different contexts*.

Example: Reading

- Daily, systematic, phonics-based reading program
- Reading real books, not just basals (readers with a controlled vocabulary)
- Playing word games with magnetic letters and other concrete models
- Composing a story on a computer and other creative projects that require the use of words (cards, signs, original stories, etc.)
- Reading road signs, cereal boxes, directions, and other contexts from daily life
- Being read to daily

Start at the Child's Level of Success

You'll want to determine each child's level of mastery in key skill areas. That's where you start—regardless of his or her grade.

This will be disconcerting for those of you with kids you think of as being delayed. Lots of us undertake homeschooling as a means of bringing our kids up to snuff. That's not a bad goal;

I want to encourage academic excellence. But the quickest method is to start the curriculum at your child's level of success in each skill area. And that pretty much shoots the idea of buying the complete line of third-grade materials from A Beka for your eight-year-old.

Think this through with me. Say you had never learned to drive (which may be true for some of us, even if we do have a license). How successful would you be if your instructor started with parallel parking when you can't even start the car? How frustrated would you be if he insisted you start there because the course manual says students your age should be ready to parallel park? What is the fastest and most motivational route to pursue? When you can't even start the car, you aren't going to parallel-park, are you?

As long as your ten-year-old cannot recall the sounds of the short vowels or how to blend triple consonants, he isn't going to understand his fifth-grade reader, no matter how much labor you invest. In fact, the opposite results occur. The kid is further demoralized by his failure. There won't be any aspect of reading he feels successful about, and he'll soon find ways to avoid it altogether. The good news is that age-appropriate materials are available, such as the tutoring kit Winning (Sing, Spell, Read and Write), to use with a ten-year-old boy who cannot blend triple consonants.

What can the child already do well? Is his cursive handwriting legible and uniform? No need to keep that on the schedule, even if there are two more levels in the series you are using. Can he consistently carry when adding double-digit numbers but often get confused when borrowing to solve a subtraction problem? His math program should give him plenty of practice with borrowing and move him into triple-digit addition and higher.

It will probably be easier for you to determine levels of mastery in your preschoolers than in an older child you may be pulling out of a traditional setting.

Placement Test Services

If you have a college degree, you can order the Iowa Test of Basic Skills from Bob Jones University and administer it to your child. The scoring report you receive back will give you a skill-by-skill analysis of your child's performance. This can then be used to determine what skills either need to be reinforced or have been mastered. (I explain how to read this report—called a criterion-skills analysis—in chapter 35.)

Here are two sources of placement tests that do not require the parent to have a college degree:

Hewitt Homeschooling Resources
P.O. Box 9, 2103 B Street
Washougal, WA 98671
800-890-4097
360-835-8697 fax
hewitthomeschooling.com

Seton Testing Services
1350 Progress Drive
Front Royal, VA 22630
800-542-1066
www.setontesting.com

Once you have a profile of each child's areas of interest and levels of mastery, next look for resources that teach to these areas using a method that honors each kid's preferred learning style. I'll show you how to determine that in just a moment.

This Process Eventually Becomes Intuitive

This process might seem a bit complicated at first. But it's really just a step-by-step analysis of what many parents can intuitively discern about their kids. Once you get comfortable homeschooling, you'll quickly recognize what resources will be successful and which ones just won't work. There's nothing like experience. But in the meantime, I want you to have the tools to begin a program that maximizes the advantages of homeschooling.

> ONCE YOU GET COMFORTABLE HOMESCHOOLING, YOU'LL QUICKLY RECOGNIZE WHAT RESOURCES WILL BE SUCCESSFUL AND WHICH ONES JUST WON'T WORK.

CHAPTER 9
Determining Your Child's Learning Style

Learning Styles

Some years ago, I set out to learn everything I could about learning styles. I ended up with a lot of academic research and clinical tests for figuring these out. Most of the material centered around the theory of learning modalities: auditory, visual, tactile, and kinesthetic. While I understand that research supports this theory, I found this information rather unhelpful. I couldn't determine which sense was dominant in myself, let alone in my own children. Do I learn better through hearing or seeing? Doing or touching? I still don't know.

Enter Dr. Golay

Then I came across the work of Dr. Keith Golay, an educational psychologist, and found it a breeze not only to recognize my own preferences but also to plug the scores of students I had taught into his model.

The difference is this: Dr. Golay's work is based upon the temperament theories of Dr. David Keirsey, who, in turn, is drawing upon the widely accepted Myers-Briggs Type Indicator test—i.e., we are looking at personality types and inferring learning preferences from these.[1]

It's easy to recognize your kid's style because we are looking at the readily observable characteristics on the surface of his life: Does he prefer to run and play or spend the afternoon alone in his room, holed up with a book? These are clues we can use in designing a suitable homeschool program.

Here's a quick overview of David Keirsey's personality types with Dr. Golay's extrapolations. (Don't let the Greek names throw you off. Keirsey's just paying homage to the ancient Greek philosophers who first observed generalizations we can make about temperaments.)

The Dionysian temperament: This fellow is fiercely independent and spontaneous. He lives in the "here and now"

> IT'S EASY TO RECOGNIZE YOUR KID'S STYLE BECAUSE WE ARE LOOKING AT THE READILY OBSERVABLE CHARACTERISTICS ON THE SURFACE OF HIS LIFE.

and derives self-worth from his ability to act swiftly with precision. Dr. Golay calls the Dionysian's learning style actual-spontaneous.

The Epimethean temperament: The strongest motivator in this personality type is duty. Her foremost concern is fulfilling her responsibilities. She does this by establishing, nurturing, and maintaining social order and organization in her life and community. The Epimethean does all things in moderation and is conservative and predictable. Dr. Golay calls the Epimethean's learning style actual-routine.

The Promethean temperament: The goal of the Promethean is to be competent. He does this by acquiring knowledge and exercising great patience and tenacity in delaying action until a rational, pragmatic, and carefully calculated conclusion can be drawn. He gives little credence to his emotions or desires. This is Dr. Golay's conceptual-specific learner.

The Apollonian temperament: For the Apollonian, life's goal is a quest for her unique identity and purpose. She is motivated to make a difference or leave her mark. The Apollonian is highly relational and gifted in leadership. Dr. Golay calls this the conceptual-global learner.

While I'm skeptical of Greek philosophy, I think there is a correlation between temperament theory and biblical teaching on spiritual gifts. The key to recognition is locked in our personality type. So I gave Dr. Golay's model consideration and have found it very helpful in our own program and in scores of others.[2]

The following books take a look at temperament theory from a Christian perspective:

> *Different Children, Different Needs: Understanding the Unique Personality of Your Child*, Charles F. Boyd

> *Wired That Way,* Marita Littauer.
> You may also be interested in Florence Littauer's original works (now out of print), which Marita is drawing upon.

Ground Rules

Here are a few parameters to keep in mind as we work through these profiles:

❶ This is not a scientific model. Don't panic if you can't

fit yourself or one of your children perfectly into one of the profiles.

Here is the principle: Use your child's personal preferences, the characteristics on the surface of his life, as clues to how he learns best. Use this empirical evidence when selecting resources and teaching methods.

I often ask parents what their child chooses to do in his spare time as a helpful clue to his learning style. Does she play alone or set out to find the neighborhood kids? Does he build with Legos or read a book? These all say something about how your kid is wired to learn.

2 Typically, learning styles do not solidify until age nine or ten. Almost all five-year-olds learn better when material is presented through hands-on experience.

So follow the principle above: Use your kid's characteristics as the indicators of his preferred method of learning. As he matures, be ready to adjust your methods to accommodate his preferences.

3 Within every learning style you will find children of varying intelligence, skill, and talents. These need to be factored into the program you design. And remember that one type of learner is not generally more intelligent than another. It can be easy to underestimate the intelligence of the active learner (Profile 1) and overestimate the intelligence of the focused learner (Profile 3). These are stereotypical assumptions, and we need to guard against them.

4 Finally, Dr. Golay believes that temperament governs behavior. As a Christian, I believe temperament influences behavior. We have a fallen nature. Through the power of the Cross we now have access to the grace of God, which enables us to overcome sin in our lives. Thus, an important distinction needs to be made: Each of the following learners has inherent character weaknesses. I am not encouraging you to accommodate these weaknesses, but rather to work to help your children overcome them through God's sanctifying grace available to all believers.

> **TYPICALLY, LEARNING STYLES DO NOT SOLIDIFY UNTIL AGE NINE OR TEN.**

The Actual-Spontaneous Learner

"I Dare You to Teach Me"

You've heard of *The Accidental Tourist*? Well, meet the Accidental Learner. It's never his intended purpose to acquire a useful knowledge base; it just sort of happens "accidentally" as he motors happily through life leaving a trail of broken parts in his wake. *Ouch! This stove is hot! Maybe I should figure out how to turn off those red lights before dismantling the burners. I think the same thing happened last time I did this.* This guy believes the world was meant to be taken apart, and he's the man for the job.

Dr. Golay calls this child the actual-spontaneous learner, or ASL. His learning is involuntary and, without training, is limited to a concrete level of thinking. He is impulsive, adventuresome, and better suited for the wild, wild West than today's confining world. Driving wagon trains, tracking gunslingers, blazing the Oregon Trail—that's the kind of mettle you find in this six-shooting, nerves-of-steel human bulldozer.

You want me to sit where? For how long? And fill out all these pages? Make me!

ASL's Indicators:
- impulsive
- autonomous
- distractable
- flexible
- short attention span
- risk taking
- constant motion thrives on variety and adventure
- competitive
- quick
- inventive
- outgoing
- defiant when boundaries are imposed

Some Strong Dislikes:
- structure
- reading or seatwork
- routine
- convention
- sitting still
- delayed gratification

Weaknesses:
- study skills
- long-range planning
- organization

An Overview

This kid is controlled by his impulses. Doing is his thing; forethought is not. He lives for the moment. Any learning that occurs is an unintentional byproduct of his actions. While it is not in the research, I'm sure there is a high correlation between the ASL and the kid with at least one broken bone by age eight.

The ASL does not grow up to teach in academia or contribute to analytical geometry. He wants to deal with the actual, concrete world and has little time for theories and abstractions.

Dr. Golay quotes Charles Lindbergh, a classic ASL, as saying he couldn't understand why anyone should "spend hours of life on formula, semicolons, and on crazy English." He could sit and concentrate for so long "and then, willy-nilly, my body stands up and walks away."[3]

It goes without saying that this guy is the least suited for the traditional classroom and formal learning experiences. He won't sit still for lectures, repetition, or drill. Material requiring concentration or seatwork quickly frustrates him. He does not organize or plan ahead. He cannot sustain a project or assignment over an extended period of time.

He wants to be unrestrained by structure, routine, or authority. He loves games and enjoys being in a group but is competitive and often takes charge. Other kids enjoy him for his antics and sense of fun. In a highly structured environment with strong authority, he can quickly become a behavior problem, causing disruptions and acting defiantly.

Here we have Dr. James Dobson's strong-willed child. Among teachers, psychologists, and exhausted parents, he is quickly labeled hyperactive and often medicated. Without consideration for this child's learning style, he is in danger of becoming a dropout.

That's the bad news.

> THIS LITTLE GUY IS JUST WHO YOU NEED TO GET THE JOB DONE WHEN THE SITUATION CALLS FOR QUICK WITS AND RESOURCEFULNESS.

Wait! There's Hope

Here's the good news. This little guy is just who you need to get the job done when the situation calls for quick wits and resourcefulness. He often has the ability to act swiftly with precision. He's Huck Finn improvising a plan that saves Jim's life, or Jim Lovell patching together an air filter that rescues the Apollo

13 mission.

He's Jacques Cousteau, Henry Ford, Wilbur Wright, and Daniel Boone, taking risks and opening up new frontiers. He's adept at manipulating, constructing, and performing. In an environment that allows for his interests, he excels in areas requiring invention, physical dexterity, resourcefulness, and courage. He will respond well to any subject presented in such a way that he is free to move and act.

Case in Point

As a teacher I had my share of ASLs in my classroom. These are not the children whose names and faces you forget! A group home for troubled boys was located in our district, and in my English classes I had several of these guys who had been labeled incorrigible by the court. I really had problems if I required excessive seatwork from them. They would become disruptive, put on a show, or get the other kids all keyed up. Each year, though, I taught a unit in which the class members videotaped a play they had produced. It took about five weeks of practicing, designing costumes, organizing the set, training the camera crew, editing, and then showing each production. This was always my most successful experience with my actual-spontaneous learners. They loved it, and I loved working with them on it. Unfortunately, it was a very noisy and confusing project, and we frequently got in trouble for disrupting other classes.

A conventional school setting is just not the place for an ASL to thrive. The order necessary and the constant distraction of a large group are just too much out of sync with the ASL's need for flexibility and limited stimulation.

Many parents who would not have otherwise considered homeschooling are now doing so because they have this type of learner in their home. Either out of pity for the classroom teacher or because they recognize their child was never wired to succeed in a traditional setting, they have undertaken his education, and I praise them for doing so.

More than any other child, this one needs to be homeschooled.

> **A CONVENTIONAL SCHOOL SETTING IS JUST NOT THE PLACE FOR AN ASL TO THRIVE.**

A Success Story

Our neighbor Anthony was a classic ASL. Until fourth grade

he was placed in a variety of school settings: public, private, and special classes for kids with learning disabilities. This kid was the Energizer Bunny. The same age but half the size of Mike and Gabe, he physically exhausted them. After a ten-mile bike hike, A.D., as he is affectionately called, would jump off and challenge them to basketball. We were the first family to invite him to spend the night—and I found out why. He was still going strong at eleven p.m., and by six the next morning, I peered bleary-eyed outside to see him zipping around on his bike, frustrated that he couldn't rouse Mike and Gabe from bed. I wondered if his parents had just had their first good night's rest since his birth.

Several years ago, A.D.'s parents came over to talk about homeschooling him. They were pretty unsure about undertaking this challenge, but it seemed like the only option left. A.D. was now spending an hour each way on a school bus to attend a Christian school that used a traditional curriculum and ran a very regimented program. He was coming home with two hours of homework every night. This was a nightmare for him and very demoralizing. He was falling further and further behind. But his behavior was so erratic and defiant, his folks were afraid they weren't up to the task. I wasn't very confident either.

Well, twelve years later, Anthony is a true success story. Since the 1997 edition of this book, A.D. has graduated from homeschooling and joined his father's heating and air conditioning business, where he gets to use his physical dexterity and resourcefulness to its maximum potential. Here's the back story: A.D.'s mom organized a lot of field trips in the beginning and relied heavily on a computer-based curriculum, which Anthony loved. She also gave him frequent breaks to go outside and run off pent-up energy. Most days he was able to stay focused until three p.m., when he was free to come over to our house and play with my boys. In high school, he started apprenticing with his father, and that's when A.D. really took wings. His skill levels in core competencies dramatically improved as a result of using what he had learned on the job.

Designing a Program for Your Actual-Spontaneous Learner

The first step in designing a program for your ASL is to accept him as God has made him. I am not asking you to acquiesce to his defiant nature or to give up on his character deficiencies. This kid needs strong parenting (see Clay and Sally Clarkson's *Educating the WholeHearted Child* and Tedd Tripp's *Shepherding a Child's Heart* for help). But I am asking you to stop wishing he would turn into someone else's child or be recast from another mold. The only way the ASL will ever be the kind of kid who can sit passively for hours doing seatwork and compliantly follow routine structure is if you break his spirit. And that is too high a cost for a little peace and quiet.

But don't despair. In most situations the behavior of your ASL will dramatically improve once an educational program is in place to accommodate how he learns. A lot of his frustration and defiance is rooted in years of being a square peg hammered relentlessly into a round hole.

He Needs Quiet

First, set up an environment that is quiet and clear of distractions—this will help him stay more focused on his schoolwork. Other kids, the phone, television, pets, etc. will all get him off task if they are within his range of vision. Once Mike and Gabe showed up on the basketball court outside his window, A.D. was unable to concentrate on his work. They had to agree to stay off the court until he was free to play.

He Needs to Move

Establish a daily routine that delays the activities and subjects he likes best until the afternoon as a reward for staying on task during the morning. Give him short breaks after each subject has been completed—this may be as frequently as every fifteen minutes for young ASLs. Let him do something physical at this time—go outside, exercise, do chores, etc.

And be tolerant of his need to move around, lie on the floor, or fidget when studying. This is the kid who taps his pencil or wiggles his feet. It may drive you nuts, but if you demand that he stop, all his energy will be focused on doing just that. He won't have anything left to concentrate on the material you want him to learn. Be flexible. Tolerate the non-essential stuff. Fight the battles that really matter.

> IN MOST SITUATIONS THE BEHAVIOR OF YOUR ASL WILL DRAMATICALLY IMPROVE ONCE AN EDUCATIONAL PROGRAM IS IN PLACE TO ACCOMMODATE HOW HE LEARNS.

He Needs Rewards

Set short, achievable goals and immediately reward good attitudes and acceptable work. Incentive charts, stickers, or a special treat can all be motivational. But don't expect him to be affected by delayed gratification—i.e., you'll buy him a bike for Christmas if he does well during the first semester. When the twins were in the elementary years, I'd let them run down to the corner store for a pack of baseball cards if they had accomplished their morning goals.

Don't Wimp Out

Even though he doesn't like it, this child needs strong leadership, a daily routine, and clear boundaries. A chaotic, random approach to teaching him will only exacerbate his impulsiveness. To keep his frustration level low, spice up the routine regularly with variety: field trips, special projects, cooperative classes. Introduce an element of competition where possible. A lot of computer software such as *Math Blaster* or websites such as www.iknowthat.com have a game-like format that rewards kids for improving their scores in skill areas.

Success by Increments

To improve his behavior and performance, set short goals starting at his level of success and incrementally increase these. If he can't stay on task for twenty math exercises, start with five. Then break and switch to reading. Then return to do five more math problems. Switch to another subject, and keep returning till the page for the day is done. After a week of success, extend the math exercises at one sitting to seven or eight. Repeat the steps above. Eventually he should be able to do the entire page in one sitting. The key is incremental steps toward the goal.

Don't avoid situations where your ASL must obey authority or cooperate. He needs to learn to control his impulses. Just expose him to these situations in short doses and gradually increase. When he becomes disruptive or takes charge in a group, isolate him. His desire to be with his peers should motivate him to control his behavior.

> SET SHORT, ACHIEVABLE GOALS AND IMMEDIATELY REWARD GOOD ATTITUDES AND ACCEPTABLE WORK.

Think Concrete

When looking at resources, choose as many as possible that are activity based. Your ASL needs to physically handle the material he's learning and be able to manipulate it in a variety of contexts to understand it. A reading program such as *Sing, Spell, Read and Write* is the only kind that has a chance of capturing his interest. It is multisensory and includes a measure of competition. Math manipulatives are absolutely essential (see the mathematics section in chapter 21 for details on manipulatives), as are physical demonstrations in science and history.

This learner needs help to think conceptually. Design concrete models to demonstrate abstractions: Use Styrofoam balls for a unit on the solar system, relief maps he can run his hands over for geography, pennies and dimes to explain decimals, a cherry pie to demonstrate fractions. He should have plenty of time to mess around with these, then, as a way of building a concrete base for higher-level thinking.

This route may seem too time consuming, but it is the shortest path to understanding in the end. A more traditional approach will only lead to frustration, resistance, and a loss of confidence on the part of your ASL. Without his motivation and cooperation, be prepared for daily battles over doing school.

Take a look at the KONOS curriculum or Amanda Bennett's Unit Studies as excellent examples of programs designed to enable this type of learner to thrive.

> WHEN LOOKING AT RESOURCES, CHOOSE AS MANY AS POSSIBLE THAT ARE ACTIVITY BASED.

Think Sports

One final suggestion: This learner frequently is gifted in areas that require physical dexterity, primarily athletics. I've seen many ASLs thrive in an organized sports program. This is an acceptable release of their energy, and it is often one place in which they can excel and feel good about their achievements. Sport gives them a much-needed focus in life, and it teaches them to control their impulsive behavior because they are highly motivated to play.

The Actual-Routine Learner
"Teacher, May I Help You?"

Whereas the ASL is every teacher's challenge, this learner is every teacher's joy. Here we have the cooperative child motivated by a desire to win the approval of her parents and teachers. She is responsible, studious, and nurturing. In a group of children, she is the one earnestly listening to the teacher or helping the ASL find his place on the page.

Dr. Golay calls her the actual-routine learner (ARL), and she does best in a quiet, well-organized, structured environment.

ARL's Indicators:
- compliant nature
- thoughtful
- helpful
- methodical
- likes routine, rules and tradition
- upset easily by changes
- seeks approval of others
- organized
- dependable and responsible

Some Strong Dislikes:
- large, chaotic groups
- change in schedule
- vague expectations
- open-ended assignments

Weaknesses:
- abstract thinking
- invention
- risk taking

An Overview

This learner is most concerned with understanding and meeting expectations. She will ask for clarification frequently in an effort to avoid making a mistake. Hearing lots of questions from the routine learner is a good indicator that she is stressed and insecure about the learning environment.

The actual-routine learner assimilates information by identifying and memorizing facts and procedures. She needs material presented in a sequential, step-by-step manner. She likes assignments with clearly defined instructions and expectations. She is most comfortable with traditional teaching methods: written assignments, repetition, drill, bookwork, workbook learning.

While she works hard to master subskills, her weakness is in seeing the big picture—understanding principles, concepts, and abstractions. She will do fine with her punctuation exercises in her language arts book but won't recognize when a semicolon is needed in her own writing. It will be important for you to design a program that will help her move to a higher level of understanding

> THIS LEARNER IS MOST CONCERNED WITH UNDERSTANDING AND MEETING EXPECTATIONS.

in her studies.

The actual-routine learner does not do well if she is expected to handle open-ended assignments or to choose her own activities. She does not like role-playing, estimating, predicting, or other exercises that require spontaneity, creativity, or extrapolation. To do an ARL in, just assign an impromptu speech.

She needs a learning environment with clear leadership and recognized rules. She respects authority and expects others to as well. She will quickly bring to your attention any rules infraction by others. *Teacher! Sammy's not doing what he's supposed to. Mom, you told Melissa to leave the baby alone, and she isn't obeying!*

If the routine or schedule changes, this learner becomes insecure and distressed.

In hindsight I can see now that my ARLs were distressed with me as a teacher. I love creativity and spontaneity. I used lots of open-ended assignments, grading more highly those students who used them as a springboard for their own creative ideas. As a teacher and as a homeschooler, my ultimate goal has always been to help children become independent learners. The ARL resists this more than any other type.

This is the kid who says, *"Just tell me what I need to do to get an A,"* or the homeschool mom who appeals, *"Just tell me exactly what I need to buy. All these choices are very overwhelming, and I'm afraid I'll make a mistake."*

We've Got One at Our House

My son, Mike, had strong ARL tendencies. He forced me to be more organized than I preferred. When we first started homeschooling, he wanted me to set up a schedule of classes and follow it every day. He especially wanted recess. Why? The neighborhood kids had told him that was the best part of school.

At ten a.m. each day he would head outside and swing for fifteen minutes. I found this very curious because this kid had long ago lost interest in the swing set. When I asked him why he was so hot on swinging, he said the neighbors had told him that's what you do at recess. He was determined to do his part to ensure our homeschool was legitimate.

Mike continued to amaze me with his incredible self-discipline and commitment to imposing order on our chaotic lifestyle. Mike was the first one up in the morning with a to-do list in hand. During his school years, he gave up on me and took matters into his own hands. He maintained the same daily schedule for most of high school: math first thing every morning. (He was frustrated when I asked him to work cooperatively with his brother, the later sleeper, because it messed up his schedule.)

In eighth grade, he created an exercise chart on the computer that incrementally increased every day. He went for months without missing his routine and was disconcerted when any kink interfered with it. For this reason he wasn't sure he wanted to go on a family vacation to Canada! In the end he smuggled his weights along in his suitcase. To this day, he maintains a rigorous physical workout. His goal is to run on all seven continents. So far, he's hit four.

Today Mike is a successful sales manager who continues to make lists and establish routines. Just the other day, his wife was teasing him about the twenty-two things he had listed on his weekend to-do list. He laughed, but quickly pointed out he had gotten through seventeen of them.

Designing a Program for Your Actual-Routine Learner

This learner needs well-organized, sequential lessons presented in incremental steps. Look for resources with clear directions and standards of evaluations. Make sure your expectations are clearly articulated as you launch into a subjectof study.

Materials developed for classroom use are easily adapted to this kind of learner. However, look over a sample lesson. How many concepts are presented per lesson? Does the math workbook jump around between concepts—i.e., are multiplication and division problems intermingled? This learner is the one who will have the most difficulty switching gears. She likes to travel the well-worn rut in the road.

Saxon Math and Explode the Code (EPS) are examples of the kind of resources the routine learner will be comfortable with. Each lesson has one clear goal, and the skills incrementally progress along a very linear scope and sequence.

Think Conceptually

The ARL will naturally divide big projects into smaller steps

> THIS LEARNER NEEDS WELL-ORGANIZED, SEQUENTIAL LESSONS PRESENTED IN INCREMENTAL STEPS.

and segment out subjects for study. This is an effective tool for accomplishing goals, but it's important to make sure your ARL doesn't lose sight of the larger picture. She may have memorized the dates of the Civil War battles, states of the Union and Confederacy, etc., but does she understand how economics, politics, scientific inventions, and religious movements converged to create this cataclysmic moment of our history?

Don't just settle for correct answers on a multiple-choice test; essay tests are a much better method for assessing the ARL's understanding of the larger concepts.

Move Her Toward Independence

Because this child is typically very compliant and satisfied with a steady dose of seatwork, it can be easy to not stretch her beyond her boundaries or place her in situations where she must learn to think creatively and take risks. This is a disservice in the end.

This child needs to be equipped to act when independence is given. She must learn to make decisions and act spontaneously. Otherwise, you end up with an adult who's rendered immobile by decision making. She needs to be equipped to handle new situations and evaluate choices with confidence. That only comes from repeated opportunities to do so.

Tap Her Creativity

Encourage your routine learner to invent and take risks. Reward her for creativity and trying new ventures: food, a sport, an academic competition, a creative story. Build open-ended assignments into your program. Teach her to handle these in a step-by-step fashion.

> **ENCOURAGE YOUR ROUTINE LEARNER TO INVENT AND TAKE RISKS.**

Case in Point

Once I asked a group of kids to take turns assuming the role of a character they invented on the spot. Some of the kids could slip into a role and fabricate a personality almost endlessly (we'll meet that kind of learner at the end of this discussion). But not my routine learners. They were frozen to the stage, stressed by a situation that had no wrong answers.

I joined one little girl who was near tears on the stage. Step by step, I took her through the process. "Is your character male or female?" I asked. "Give her a name. Tell us where she lives. What does she look like?" She relaxed as she found she could create answers to these simple questions and was pleased when she realized she had entertained the group for almost five minutes.

Use Her Nurturing Nature to Her Advantage

This learner has an innate drive to be helpful. Teaching other children is an effective strategy, then, with this learner. It will appeal to her nurturing nature and has the added plus of reinforcing her own learning in the areas she is presenting.

> **THIS LEARNER HAS THE INNATE DRIVE TO BE HELPFUL.**

The Conceptual-Specific Learner
"Frankly, Mother, I Prefer to Do It Myself"

Good news: This next student will learn despite you! Bad news: He's going to exhaust you with his intensity and questions.

This learner has an insatiable appetite for knowledge. He wants to be able to understand, explain, predict, and control realities. He seeks to understand principles and use them in structuring his cognitive and intellectual world. The absent-minded professor, Mr. Spock, and the mad scientist are all caricatures of this personality. Dr. Golay calls him the conceptual-specific learner (CSL), and he is not interested in isolated facts and information but in the theories and principles behind them.

CSL's Indicators:
- serious-minded
- inquisitive
- satisfied being alone
- focused interest
- prizes intellectual achievement
- strong powers of concentration
- collector (rocks, stamps, specimens)
- easily frustrated
- perfectionistic
- detail-oriented
- must be reminded to eat, change his clothes, comb his hair

Some Strong Dislikes:
- wasted time
- menial assignments

Weaknesses:
- social skills
- accepting his own limitations
- awareness of others' needs

An Overview

This learner loves problem solving, research, experimentation, and intellectual inquiry. He is a creative thinker and chooses scientific investigation as a leisure activity. He will focus on one task for long periods of time and can tune out all distractions.

One mom of a CSL I evaluated was perplexed by her son's habit of curling up for the evening with a volume of the *Encyclopedia Brittanica.*

A few years ago I read Bill Gates's book *The Road Ahead* and was struck by his intense focus and vision at an early age. At sixteen he and Paul Allen, eventual co-founders of Microsoft, were spending all their free time on computers, programming them to the edge of their abilities (this was back in the 1960s, when just booking computer time was a challenge). Gates dropped out of Harvard the day the first programmable microprocessor was released. He knew this seemingly insignificant announcement from Intel would revolutionize the computer industry, and he and Allen had predetermined to position themselves to capitalize on it. He was nineteen. Obviously Gates, now the richest man in the world, has more foresight than the rest of us.

This learner has a serious nature and is happy that way. He finds great self-satisfaction in his own achievements and doesn't need the approval from others that the ARL seeks.

His difficulties lie in accepting his own limitations. He becomes very distressed if he cannot succeed in solving a problem or attaining his goals. He will need your help and encouragement in keeping his shortcomings in perspective.

He will pay close attention to a teacher's presentation as long as it is not repetitious or routine. He becomes very frustrated with any hindrances to his own intellectual growth, such as being forced to work through material again that he has already mastered. He is often not a fluent writer and doesn't like to take the time to communicate what he already believes he understands.

This learner enjoys working independently or in a tutorial relationship with a competent teacher. But he does not do well in a situation where he must work with those not as interested in intellectual inquiry. I like to organize kids into cooperative groups. You can spot the conceptual-specific learners right away then—

> **THIS LEARNER ENJOYS WORKING INDEPENDENTLY IN A TUTORIAL RELATIONSHIP WITH A COMPETENT TEACHER.**

they are the kids still working alone.

These kids don't grow up to join organizations; they don't thrive in a business environment that emphasizes team building. These are the adults who tinker in the garage every weekend or work long hours in a research and development lab.

The CSL is very objective in his decision making and has a difficult time expressing emotion or understanding others' emotional responses. He typically relates to peers in an instructional, not personal, manner. For this reason he is often the odd man out socially. The CSL gravitates toward careers in the sciences, engineering, technology, mathematics, and research and development.

Case in Point

At one point in my teaching career, I developed and taught an honors English program for gifted and highly motivated students. George was a remarkably gifted student, but one who had little interest in my classes, which predominantly involved discussing in a subjective way the literature we were studying. What were the ideas and opinions the kids had formulated after reading a work? How did they see these ideas influencing their lives? Every day we would discuss such things, just for the sake of sharing our reactions. Well, this just wasn't for George and others like him. The CSL values facts and empirical knowledge, not knowledge that is personal in nature.

Probably the most rapport I ever had with George came when I asked him to teach me to play chess. (The reason I asked was that I was about to marry Kermit, who loves chess. This should have been a big clue . . . Guess what kind of learner I married!)

Designing a Program for Your Conceptual-Specific Learner

This student can be satisfied with materials created for classroom use, if you must go this route, but don't hand him inferior stuff. He doesn't need to be entertained; he needs to be challenged. Make sure the activities and assignments do more than just measure memorization of material.

> **HE DOESN'T NEED TO BE ENTERTAINED, BUT HE NEEDS TO BE CHALLENGED.**

Allow Acceleration

Don't hesitate to let him jump several levels in subject areas of great interest and strength. In many cases, a college textbook may be a better investment. My friend Susan's son, Jacob, was intensely focused in math and computer science. He scored a 5 on the Advanced Placement calculus exam in ninth grade and an 800 in mathematics on the SAT in tenth. (Those are perfect scores, folks!) He competed on the international level in mathematics and programming in high school. This was only possible because his parents let him work with advanced math years earlier than traditionally accepted. He was free to whiz through lessons or skip entire sections until he hit his level of competency.

> IN MANY CASES, A COLLEGE TEXTBOOK MAY BE A BETTER INVESTMENT.

And obviously his abilities in programming would never have come to the surface had he not had a computer.

Prepare to Spend Some Bucks

This is not, then, a cheap child to homeschool. He needs raw data and supplies for his investigations. You can save money by skipping the textbooks and using nonfiction from the library. Invest what you can in those items that best support his inquiry: lab equipment, computer (with Internet access), tools, etc. Don't even bother with resources for areas with no apparent difficulties.

Think Mentors

Most of the CSLs I have worked with have had mentors in their fields of interest. This has usually been a formalized relationship on the high school level. One student I evaluated, Scott, was mentored in computer science for several years by a man in our church who works in artificial intelligence research. The mentor even arranged for Scott to have a summer internship (usually reserved for college students) in the research and development department of his company.

Cindy McKeown's son Daniel has a focused interest in film production (he is now a professional cinematographer). She arranged for him to spend a summer working at a video production company in Washington, D.C. The apprenticeship solidified Daniel's determination to pursue this as a course of study in college and also gave him valuable experience that led to

III

other work experiences.

While a tutor may seem too big a step for an elementary student, participation in an organization or club for his area of interest is a way to cultivate informal mentoring. My sons' friend Christopher loves rocks. By fourth grade he had an extensive rock museum in his basement with everything neatly displayed and identified. He spent every dollar he earned on specimens and books about rocks. His parents were very perplexed by this fixation but supported his interest by taking Chris to rock and mineral shows and connecting him with local geologists.

Work on Interpersonal Skills

The CSL does need to hone his social skills. And as with other learners' weaknesses, this is best done in a step-by-step fashion. He needs to be made aware of his perceived insensitivity to others. Training in proper etiquette and polite conversation will help: "Here's how you show interest in others, son. Ask about their hobbies and family, etc." Then role-play a conversation.

Have your CSL serve in the children's program at church, babysit, or volunteer for a local ministry to thrust him into situations where he will need to cultivate his people skills and develop some empathy.

At Our House

Kermit has many CSL characteristics. He is pragmatic and objective in his decision making. In college, his friends called him "The Professor"—unlike the rest of us, he had come to study. He was usually either in class or in the library (two places I rarely visited; thus we did not meet till after graduation).

Like many men, he thinks that whenever I tell him I have a problem, I'm asking for a logical solution to it. Are you kidding? I enjoy the drama of my pain! I just want him to listen and empathize with my emotions. I've finally taught him to say, "I understand, Honey" on cue. He still jokingly parrots this phrase when I unload.

> **THE CSL DOES NEED TO HONE HIS SOCIAL SKILLS.**

The Conceptual-Global Learner
"Hey, Everybody, Look at Me!"

Have you been most curious to discover what kind of learner you are as you've been reading this section? That's a strong indication you'll fit this last profile.

Dr. Golay calls this final type the conceptual-global learner (CGL). She is first and foremost people-oriented. It is in her nature to look for the potential in others and to help bring out these possibilities. For this reason, she is often a leader who inspires others through her abilities to speak and write fluently. This learner loves group situations, especially when that group is her audience.

CGL's Indicators:
- creative
- early reader
- outgoing
- ambitious
- dramatic
- perceptive
- popular with adults and peers
- forgetful
- broad array of interests
- not competitive
- careless

Some Strong Dislikes:
- unresolved conflict
- dry lectures
- routine assignments
- not having choices

Weaknesses:
- study skills
- technical details
- organization
- spelling

An Overview

In contrast to the CSL's specific focus, this learner has a wide breadth of interests, often finding it difficult to narrow her pursuits to a few areas. This learner has the longest entry in the yearbook and keeps her parents hopping as they try to keep track of all the social engagements she has scheduled.

The CGL is visionary and thinks about the future, but unlike the focused learner who thinks about the possibilities of principles applied to, say, problem solving, the CGL focuses on the possibilities in people. She is fascinated by others' beliefs and attitudes: what they think, what they want, how they feel, how they respond.

She enjoys learning about ideas and values and tends to look at herself more subjectively than objectively. She is the student most interested in searching for the significance of things and personalizing their meaning. She is motivated to make a difference in the world, to search for her unique contribution to history.

She is creative and flexible but not detail-oriented or technical. Rather, this learner will act on hunches and impressions to form broad conclusions. This is the kid who takes a quick look at his or her math homework and says, "Oh, I know how to do this," then proceeds to fill out the whole thing incorrectly.

> ## SHE IS CREATIVE AND FLEXIBLE BUT NOT DETAIL-ORIENTED OR TECHNICAL.

CGLs are generally high achievers and do well academically. But they often set high standards for themselves. Their creations and work are an extension of themselves and are strongly tied to their sense of self-worth. Therefore, failure or rejection of their work is often interpreted as failure or rejection of themselves.

The CGL loves functioning in a group. She is a communicator and performer. She needs to be known, recognized, and acknowledged by others, especially her teacher. Yet she demands individuality and autonomy and the opportunity to act and express herself creatively.

She does not show the competitive nature of the ASL in a group. Friendship and cooperation are important to her. She empathizes strongly with others and does not do well in a competitive environment with uncontrolled ruthlessness and conflict. She is usually well liked and sought after by her peers, and enjoyed by adults.

The CSL typically gravitates toward the language arts, performing arts such as music and drama, psychology, counseling, the ministry, and social services.

The CGL's greatest area of academic weakness is in attention to details.

C'est Moi

It may be obvious by now that I am a conceptual-global learner. The inherent biases of my temperament will bleed through these pages: my passion for a guiding vision, my commitment to individualizing each child's program, and my belief that every student has a unique destiny we as parents should be set on discovering and cultivating.

Recognizing my learning style has made me a much better teacher for my children and my students at CHESS. I've made a lot of adjustments to my presentations because I'm conscious of the different kinds of learners in our family and in my classes.

Designing a Program for Your Global Learner

Dr. Golay recommends an individualized, personalized approach with this student. She will be interactive and enthusiastic as long as there is opportunity for her input and creative response. Thus, a discussion group will be more motivating than a lecture and a project more than a test.

Because of her interest in people, choose resources that focus on how individuals or people groups have been impacted by the areas of study. Study scientists behind the theories or how inventions changed people's lives. In history, biographies and historical fiction will have great appeal. *The Greenleaf Guide to Famous Men of . . .* (Greece, Rome, Middle Ages, etc.), *History Through Literature* unit studies, Tapestry of Grace, and Sonlight are the types of curricula that the CGL enjoys most.

For technical material, introduce the people behind the information. My kids have enjoyed *Mathematicians Are People, Too* by Luetta Reimer as well as biographies by Jeanne Bendick that give background information on inventors, scientists, and mathematicians.

Because she thinks globally, a unit-study approach that integrates subjects such as science, history, and literature around a common theme (Japanese culture, for example) will appeal to her interest in understanding how events, ideas, and inventions affect the people of that time and place.

Think Groups

Group activities are a must. And as you have probably gathered, we were certainly involved in our share. Kayte and Gabe are predominantly CGLs. They both thrive in the humanities.

Kayte was speaking in sentences at age two and reading avidly by age six. She was frequently chosen for the lead in the plays our co-op produced and was always organizing some kind of activity for the betterment of her friends.

Gabe's first response to a suggested activity was "Can we

> SHE WILL BE INTERACTIVE AND ENTHUSIASTIC AS LONG AS THERE IS OPPORTUNITY FOR HER INPUT AND CREATIVE RESPONSE.

invite some other kids to come along, Mom?" He spent days on his creative projects for CHESS and then forgot them at home the day they were due. (Mike, on the other hand, was a pain to live with while trying to complete a creative assignment but submitted it ahead of time—and also told Gabe where he had left his.)

Even though all my kids enjoyed our cooperative activities, these two (and their mom) both "light up" in a group situation.

Details, Details

This learner needs help in paying attention to details. She is forgetful and careless in her errors. I know I have this flaw, so I have taken steps to compensate for it. I always use a spell checker or a dictionary and an organizer to keep track of my commitments. My husband has pretty much given up on getting me to balance the checkbook, though.

Don't yell at your CGL for being a bit ditzy. Give her the strategies to compensate for her lack of attention to detail:

- Recognize her tendency to be careless.
- Re-read directions and write down assignments.
- Encourage her to have someone edit her work.
- Show her how to create organizational systems.

I've Got a Zillion Kids— I Can't Possibly Accommodate Them All in Every Area and Stay Sane!

That's right. Even those of us with fewer than a zillion cannot put together a program that is individualized to the fullest potential. It's a balancing act with trade-offs in every area. My husband is strongly conceptual-specific; Mike is a mix of that and the ARL; Gabe, Kayte, and I all approach material globally; and Kristen, though never hyperactive, was predominantly an actual-spontaneous learner. What an eclectic mix!

Our group activities appealed to everyone, but for different reasons. Gabe and Kayte enjoyed class discussions. Mike preferred teachers who were most organized. Kristen loved to socialize. The computer was an essential tool: Mike did research on the Internet. Gabe and Kayte wouldn't have done near as much writing without word processing. Kristen liked educational games.

By high school, all my kids had the freedom and responsibility to select their resources and set up their daily schedule. Other than the times we gathered for books we were reading aloud or projects we were completing together, Mike, Gabe, and Kayte achieved their weekly goals their way. I was the one who had to be most accommodating. For Mike's sake, I was more organized than I preferred to be, and because I was preparing my sons for future employment, I had to wade through my share of technical material of little interest to me personally.

Choose material for science that is hands-on for your actual-spontaneous learner, and then meet bimonthly with a unit study co-op to keep your global learner motivated. Buy a sequential reading program to use with all your kids if you are an ARL and need the security of a well-organized system.

The goal is to keep the family frustration level low and the motivation high. Have your children use the resources and subjects they find least appealing at the beginning of the day. Save the fun stuff for the afternoon as a motivator for keeping on task.

For more information about learning styles, here are the best sources:

> **THE GOAL IS TO KEEP THE FAMILY FRUSTRATION LEVEL LOW AND THE MOTIVATION HIGH.**

One Hundred Top Picks for Homeschool Curriculum: Choosing the Right Curriculum and Approach for Your Child's Learning Style, Cathy Duffy. An indispensable resource that evaluates curricula according to your child's learning type.

Discover Your Child's Learning Style, Mariaemma Willis and Victoria Hodson

Every Child Can Succeed, Cynthia Ulrich Tobias

In Their Own Way: Discovering and Encouraging Your Child's Multiple Intelligences, Thomas Armstrong

The Way They Learn: How to Discover and Teach to Your Child's Strengths, Cynthia Ulrich Tobias

The Last Hurdle

Now we know what kind of resources we're looking for to suit each of our children as well as what Mom, the teacher, needs to feel comfortable. But there's one more factor we've got to consider—the budgetary constraints we all must live with. I saw lots of resources I knew my kids would have loved and I would have found easy to use, but Kermit would have needed a third job for us to afford them. And he wasn't offering. We all have only so many homeschool dollars to commit. The next three chapters will help you make the most of them.

CHAPTER 10
Homeschooling on a Shoestring

First, let's clarify what kind of shoestring we are talking about here. If your kids are wearing Air Jordan Nikes with fifty-four-inch silver-tipped laces, you can skip this section. On the other hand, if your kids' shoelaces are held together with knots and retipped with candle wax, then I've got some advice you'll find helpful.

Time Is Money

Here's what you lose when economy drives the decision about which homeschool curriculum to buy: You trade time for money. Inexpensive resources leave a lot of work for the teacher. You get to prepare the lesson plans, make the games, cut out the shapes, and gather the materials (beans, buttons for counters, etc.).

When you buy software, textbooks, and expensive reading programs or video courses, you are paying for someone else's time. So don't just look at the price tag without answering, "Will I have the time to use this?"

I invested money where I didn't have the time and skimped on resources where I did. In my case, I very rarely bought composition or literature study aids. This was my forte and love. I enjoyed inventing writing exercises and discussion questions for our language arts program. But math was another story. I invested lots of dollars there: software programs, textbooks, testing materials, mathematical games, and videos. I felt very incompetent at this end of the curriculum and was willing to pay for someone else's planning and expertise.

Here are two examples of beginning reading programs at opposite ends of the price range. *Sing, Spell, Read and Write* retails for $275. For that you get master teacher Sue Dixon on DVD, plus workbooks, lesson plans, games, CDs, and readers—everything but the kitchen sink. Plus, all but the workbooks can be reused with your other children.

Or for $30 you can buy *Alpha-Phonics*, a reading program

designed by Samuel Blumenfeld that's condensed to one 168-page book. Until recently it did not have any support material other than a brief instructional paragraph for the tutor that accompanied each lesson. The phonics approach is excellent. (On page 236, I explain why.) But you will need to spend a lot of time finding readers for this program and developing practice work, games, and whatever else it takes to flesh out the lessons for your kids. I used *Alpha-Phonics* but switched to *Sing, Spell, Read and Write* when I realized I no longer had the time for all the preparation *Alpha-Phonics* required.

Think Multilevel and Reusable

Discounting full-time enrollment in an online school, the most expensive route you can choose is a grade-specific line of textbooks with support materials from a publisher that markets its products primarily to public schools (where your tax dollars are consumed by inflated prices).

Resources developed for individualized instruction or the homeschool community can often be used by more than one child and span a number of grade levels. This not only saves on your budget but also allows you the time-saving strategy of teaching several children using the same material.

The KONOS curriculum is an excellent example of this. It is a collection of unit studies appropriate for all elementary grades that uses children's literature and trade books (nonfiction) typically available at your local library. The reading is augmented with hands-on activities in all subject areas. You will get years of use from even one volume of KONOS. But the trade-off is time—you'll spend hours gathering resources and preparing activities. That's why the most successful use of KONOS I've seen has been among families that form a KONOS co-op and spread out the teaching load. (The new KONOS In-A-Box resources have been designed to be very user-friendly.)

Janice Van Cleave's science books are another fine example of a lot of bang for the buck. Books in her science exploration series, such as *Microscopes and Magnifying Lenses* and *Weather*, retail for $10.95 and were written for home use. Each book contains thirty experiments that can be pulled off with stuff around the house. They illustrate a central scientific principle and

> RESOURCES DEVELOPED FOR INDIVIDUALIZED INSTRUCTION OR THE HOMESCHOOL COMMUNITY CAN OFTEN BE USED BY MORE THAN ONE CHILD AND SPAN A NUMBER OF GRADE LEVELS.

121

work well for all grades through junior high. At the end of each lesson is a section marked "Check It Out" that poses a science question your older students can research at the library (or on the Internet). Using just *Janice Van Cleave's Molecules* and a few PBS videos, we met with another family for a weekly science lab that lasted most of the school year and included kids in third through seventh grades.

Shop Used

Many support groups hold an annual used-curriculum sale. CHESS holds one each spring as a fundraiser. This is scheduled right before our state convention to allow families to buy used items before shopping for new stuff two weeks later. And in some areas, you'll find a homeschool family running a used-curriculum supply business. You will find a list of used curriculum dealers in the Resource Guide.

You can also find used homeschool materials online; eBay, Half.com, Craig's List, and Amazon all have active marketplaces where you can pick up great deals on children's books, school supplies and popular homeschool curricula inexpensively. I have found I get my best return when I sell resources and books as soon as I am done using them. If I don't sell them within a short time period, then they go on my annual yard sale shelf in the garage. And when I advertise my yard sale in the circulars and on Craig's List, I put HOMESCHOOL SUPPLIES in all caps—that draws people.

To get you started, here are some of the best sites online, in addition to eBay and Amazon, to find used homeschool materials.

> **YOU CAN ALSO FIND USED HOMESCHOOL MATERIALS ONLINE.**

www.thebackpack.com
www.homeschoolclassifieds.com
www.vegsource.com/homeschool
www.usedhomeschoolcurriculum.com

Ask for Donations

Other sources of used materials include your local library, Christian or public schools, and colleges. Ask for paper from printers and newspapers. Be bold—call them up and ask if they have any materials they would be interested in selling or donating to your homeschool support group (more likely than to an individual). You'll be surprised how many will, especially if you are set up as a nonprofit.

Homeschool Discounters

As the homeschool movement has matured, so has the homeschool business community. We aren't a yuppie crowd, and most suppliers have found they need to offer a savings plan to their customers. Companies such as the Rainbow Resource Center and Christian Book Distributors have discounted pricing across the board, ranging from 5 percent to 20 percent. Others offer special pricing on sets. However, many discount suppliers have bitten the dust since the first publication of this book, so keep in mind that it is difficult to stay in business for long if the margins are too thin.

Too many homeschoolers I know have been stuck with cashed checks and unfulfilled orders. I've made a pointed effort to include in the Resource Guide only reputable suppliers who've been around long enough to have a proven track record in the homeschool community.

Rule of thumb: Do business with those companies you want to see stay in business, preferably those with whom you can have some personal contact.

> DO BUSINESS WITH THOSE COMPANIES YOU WANT TO SEE STAY IN BUSINESS, PREFERABLY THOSE WITH WHOM YOU CAN HAVE SOME PERSONAL CONTACT.

Other Strategies

1. Set up your homeschool co-op or support group as a nonprofit organization. Then you can solicit donations in goods and services from individuals and businesses. The first year our homeschool drama co-op did this, we increased our revenues by 20 percent, and it continued to grow from there.

2. Some publishers will sell at wholesale to homeschool co-ops that combine orders.

3. Scholastic Book Clubs are open to homeschoolers and offer children's literature at substantial discounts. Sam's Club and other buying clubs do not maintain consistent stock, but they do sell children's literature and school supplies at deep savings when available. Check out these businesses during

the back-to-school and Christmas seasons.

4. Pool your orders to qualify for bulk rates.

5. Split the purchase of big-ticket items with another family. Just work out the details for sharing these resources ahead of time. I purchased KONOS volume 1, and a friend purchased volume 2. After two years of use, we switched volumes. I also made this arrangement with others in purchasing Chalk Dust video math courses.

6. Buy items with a resale value among homeschoolers. Saxon Math, Apologia, and Bob Jones University textbooks can all be resold for close to two-thirds of their original purchase value. Keep these in mint condition to get the best price.

7. Attend annual library and book sales.

8. Take advantage of community programs and field trips that are low-cost. Many parks and historic sites offer free admission and also publish literature filled with lots of educational information.

9. Susan Richman, editor of the *Pennsylvania Homeschoolers* newsletter (well worth the subscription cost for homeschoolers anywhere), writes a regular column describing sources of free educational resources and opportunities.

10. Many businesses (e.g., OfficeMax, Barnes and Noble, Borders, Academic Superstore) that offer a teacher reward program or discount include homeschoolers with some form of identification.

11. The Internet is a cornucopia of educational materials that are free for the downloading. See chapter 28 for all the goodies.

12. Annenberg Media recently made all its high school and college-level video courses available free online. I used several of these for high school (and paid hundreds of dollars at the time). The content is current and reliable—the

hairdos and clothing will just appear out-of-date. Visit www.learner.org.

13. The best tip I have for the resourceful homeschooler is to *use the library*—and that's such a biggie, it warrants a chapter of its own.

Additional tips can be found in the following recommended resources:

Frugal Families: Making the Most of Your Hard-Earned Money, Jonni McCoy

Homeschool Your Child for Free: More Than 1400 Smart, Effective, and Practical Resources for Educating Your Family at Home, LauraMaery Gold and Joan M. Zielinski

Homeschooling on a Shoestring, Melissa Morgan and Judith Waite Allee

Miserly Moms, Jonni McCoy

CHAPTER 11
Using the Library

The local public library, one of the few institutions I do not mind supporting with my tax dollars, is the best, most creative friend of the resourceful homeschooler. Find the friendliest library in your area and travel there regularly. If it's a bit of a hike, turn it into a school day by organizing research projects to be completed there.

Interlibrary Loan

Most libraries now participate in an interlibrary loan program. This allows you to request books from any participating library in the United States. There is rarely a title, including Christian and obscure works, that I cannot find in some public or university library system in the country. I frequently use this option to review a book or resource I am thinking about buying. If your library does not have the title you are looking for, ask your librarian to help you submit an interlibrary loan request. Your library will then order the book for you from a library that has the book.

> **IF YOUR LIBRARY DOES NOT HAVE THE TITLE YOU ARE LOOKING FOR, ASK YOUR LIBRARIAN TO HELP YOU SUBMIT AN INTERLIBRARY LOAN REQUEST.**

Most Are Even Wired

I can also access my library's database via my computer at no charge. Here I can see how many overdue books I currently have and determine if my tab has exceeded six figures yet, as well as reserve and request books from anywhere in the country. What a convenience! If your library doesn't have this service, ask if any others locally do and sign up for it.

A Little Courtesy Goes a Long Way

One library in our area is particularly friendly to homeschoolers, and as such has become an informal waterhole for us. The staff has gone so far as to purchase resources from a wish list we compiled. This is likely when you go out of your way to serve your local library (volunteering to re-shelve books, for example) and manage your children's behavior while there.

They've Got the Very Best at an Unbeatable Price

This all leads to a bigger point: Your local public library is where you'll find the creative and motivating resources you need to individualize your program. The core of our studies for years was made up of children's literature and trade books (nonfiction) checked out of our library.

Books Kids Love

One of our targeted goals, you'll recall, was to raise children who love to learn. I wanted to put in their hands resources developed by folks with the same creative drive and passion for learning we're desiring to cultivate in them. These folks are not writing textbooks (subject to an array of artistic restraints); they are working where they have freedom to delve deeply into their subject and convey the essence of the material that so fascinates them.

As an example of this difference, compare these two presentations of the same Revolutionary battle:

> The fighting that had begun in New England spread to New York, New Jersey and other colonies. In December 1776, Washington and his army had to leave New Jersey. They crossed the Delaware River to Pennsylvania. On Christmas night the Americans recrossed the Delaware and attacked a camp of Hessians (hesh enz) at Trenton, New Jersey. The Hessians were soldiers from Germany who were hired to fight for the British. The American army captured 900 Hessians. This battle, known as the Battle of Trenton, was the first great victory for the Americans in the war.
>
> —Fifth-grade social studies textbook

What drama! What pathos! Don't stop reading, Mom. *NOT!* There wouldn't be any connection between why United States students can't remember the decade in which the Revolutionary War was fought and the vivid and compelling writing in their textbooks, now would there?

Here's how Joy Hakim describes the same event in her History of Us series:

> YOUR PUBLIC LIBRARY IS WHERE YOU'LL FIND THE CREATIVE AND MOTIVATING RESOURCES YOU NEED TO INDIVIDUALIZE YOUR PROGRAM.

127

Howe thought Washington and his army were done for and could be finished off in springtime. . . . But George Washington was no quitter. On Christmas Eve of 1776, in bitter cold, Washington got the Massachusetts fishermen to ferry his men across the Delaware River from Pennsylvania back to New Jersey. The river was clogged with huge chunks of ice. You had to be crazy, or coolly courageous, to go out into that dangerous water. While the Massachusetts boatmen were getting the army across, the Hessians, on the other side—at Trenton, New Jersey—were celebrating Christmas by getting drunk. Before the Germans could focus their eyes, the Americans captured 900 of them.

— *From Colony to Country*

Hakim was compelled to write her ten-book series of American history after seeing the insipid and dumbed-down textbooks her oldest daughter was required to read in school. Her enthusiasm for her subject is infectious. My daughter Kayte chose to continue reading through the series even during our summer break.

These Books Draw Us In

Why do you remember those favorite books from childhood? Because they were about people you came to care about. Children's literature and quality nonfiction employ the elements of good fiction. Their descriptive writing, vivid settings, realistic characters, and detailed action help us vicariously experience the drama ourselves.

One of the first books I read aloud with my kids was *The Sign of the Beaver* by Elizabeth George Speare. It is the story of ten-year-old Matt, who must survive alone on the frontier of Maine during the winter of 1721. Had he not been befriended by a young Indian brave who taught him to track and trap, he would never have made it. We can remember all the details of the harsh conditions colonists faced, the tensions between European and Native American cultures, and the historic events of the time because we cared about Matt, and these realistic details affected his life. That's just not true of material learned from a textbook—a sterile and impersonal presentation of fact upon fact upon irrelevant fact.

Why I Love Homeschooling

People ask me how I can enjoy homeschooling. The crux is right here: I love these books. I love the creative resources we used. Learning is fascinating when you are using materials created by folks who were fascinated with the subject themselves and want to light that spark of interest in their readers. I frequently read ahead in the books we were reading aloud to our kids. So did Kermit. Can't say I've ever been tempted to read ahead in a textbook, though.

More Advantages

1. Children's literature and trade books have the additional advantage of being specifically targeted to your child's interests and reading level. For example:

> ### Interest: Ben Franklin
> Reading level— second grade
> Choice: *Benjamin Franklin: A Man with Many Jobs* by Carole Greene
> Reading level— fourth grade
> Choice: *Benjamin Franklin: Young Printer* by Augusta Stevenson
> Reading level— junior high
> Choice: *Poor Richard* by James Daugherty
> Reading level—high school
> Choice: *The Autobiography of Benjamin Franklin*

Gabe was reading about George Washington a few years back. His specific interest, though, was his presidency—typically not covered at all in traditional history books. We found the perfect fit: *George and Martha Washington at Home in New York* by Beatrice Siegel, learning that the nation's capital was originally located in New York City.

2. Children's literature is easily adapted to multilevel teaching. Many of the books on the resource list beginning on page 131 can be used with all elementary-age children. And many are appropriate on higher levels as well.

Here's a sample of the books I used with my kids for a unit study centered around Colonial America:

- *Calico Captive,* Elizabeth George Speare (1973)
- *Can't You Make Them Behave, King George?* (1996) and others by Jean Fritz
- Childhood of Famous Americans biographies
- Cities of the Revolution series
- Colonial Craftsmen series, Leonard Fisher
- *Colonial Living,* Edward Tunis (1957)
- If You Were There series (Scholastic)
- Life in Colonial America series, James Knight
- *A Lion to Guard Us,* Clyde Robert Bulla (1989)
- *Sign of the Beaver,* Elizabeth George Speare (1983)
- *Steven Caney's Kids' America* (1978)
- *Witch of Blackbird Pond,* Elizabeth George Speare (1958)

3. Children's literature is integrated. That means the information is set in the full context of meaning. The Eyewitness book *Ancient Egypt* covers the history, geography, art, science, and chief players. When learned in this way, kids have a much easier time visualizing the implications of the information and understanding the concepts and principles rather than just memorizing facts that seem divorced from a meaningful context.

Here's Where I Start

When I set out to choose curriculum materials, I head to my local library. There I will find the resources that offer the greatest selection of choices for kids of all learning styles, readiness, and interests at the lowest price (usually free). If I am looking for resources to use consistently year-round, I review my options here first and then purchase the ones that fit best. But during my kids' elementary education, almost everything we did in history, literature, science, art, music, and geography came from books at

> CHILDREN'S LITERATURE IS EASILY ADAPTED TO MULTILEVEL TEACHING.

our library.

More Than 150 Titles Available at Your Local Library

I thought you might be interested in seeing some of the titles we've used. These titles are recommended on their artistic merit and adaptability to a home-education program. Our family has not found them offensive to our Christian worldview, but they are secular and may not all be suitable for your family.

- **"Young adult"** denotes language or situations that require parental guidance.
- **Authors in bold** are key writers in this subject area.
- **"OP"** means out of print but still available in better libraries.

Art and Architecture

Arnosky, Jim. *Drawing from Nature* (1982) and others. Use this with older children and *Come Out, Muskrats* (1989) with your little ones.

Bjork, Christina. *Linnea in Monet's Garden* (1987). A charming trip through Monet's life guided by a European "Ramona." Grade level: 2–5.

Brookes, Mona. *Drawing with Children* (1996). Buy this one. Grade level: K–6.

Brown, Marc, and Laurene Brown. *Visiting the Art Museum* (1986). Before you go to a museum, share this book. Grade level: 2–3.

Globok, Shirley. *The Art of Colonial America* (1970) and others. Integrate Globok's books into your history program. OP. Grade level: all.

Goldstein, Ernest. *Winslow Homer: The Gulf Stream* (1982) and others. From the Let's Get Lost in a Painting series. Learn to look at art in general as Goldstein draws your attention to the specific points of each masterpiece in this series. Grade level: 3–up.

Isaacson, Philip. *Round Buildings, Square Buildings and Buildings that Wiggle Like a Fish* (1988). A lawyer wrote this fascinating pictorial history of world architecture. Delicious writing. Grade level: 3–up.

Kohl, MaryAnn. *Mudworks: Creative Clay, Dough and Modeling Experiences* (1989) and others. Wonderful art projects for K–6. Recipes for every kind of goo you can think of. Grade level: elementary.

Macaulay, David. *Cathedral* (1973) and others. With meticulously drawn sketches, Macaulay shows us the process required to build the great churches of Europe. Grade level: 3–up.

Milord, Susan. *Adventures in Art* (1990). Activities and tidbits of art history. My art program came from here. Grade level: 2–8.

Nakano, Dokuohtei. *Easy Origami* (1985). This Reading Rainbow selection is the best one available for beginning folders. Grade level: K–6.

Parish, Peggy. *Let's Be Indians* (1962), and other Ready-to-Read Handbook titles. Grade level: 1–3.

Raboff, Ernest. *Michelangelo Buonarroti* (1969). Included in the Art for Children series. All titles are very worthwhile. Full-color reproductions in each. OP. Grade level: K–6.

Raczka, Bob. *Unlikely Pairs* (2006) and others in Bob Raczka's Art Adventures series.

Shachtman, Tom. *The President Builds a House* (1989). Photo essay about Jimmy Carter's work for Habitat for Humanity. Very moving.

Strickland, Carol. *The Annotated Mona Lisa: A Crash Course in Art History from Pre-Historic to Post-Modern* (2007). See also *The Annotated Arch: A Crash Course in the History of Architecture.* Strickland is the art critic for the Christian Science Monitor. All ages, though most fitting at the high school level. Strickland's layouts and explanations are superb.

Venezia, Mike. *Van Gogh* (1988). Getting to Know the World's Greatest Artists is a humorous, colorful new series for beginning readers. Grade level: 2–4.

Yenawine, Philip. *Colors* (1991) and others in the Childrens Book series from the Museum of Modern Art. Grade level: 2–up.

History/Geography—American

Alcott, Louisa M. *Little Women* (1947). Civil War era. Grade level: 5–up.

Armstrong, Jennifer. *Steal Away* (1992). Two friends escape to the North. Grade level: young adult.

Avi. *The True Confessions of Charlotte Doyle* (1990). We like the history titles Avi wrote during his earlier years. Grade level: 4–up.

Benchley, Nathaniel. *Sam the Minuteman* (1969). From the I Can Read series. There are other good history titles in the series as well. Grade level: 1–3.

Blos, Joan. *A Gathering of Days* (1979). New England in the 1830s. Grade level: 4–up.

Brink, Carol Ryrie. *Caddie Woodlawn* (1935). The Midwest in the 1860s. Grade level: 4–up.

Bulla, Clyde. *Squanto, Friend of the Pilgrims* (1990), *Pocahontas and the Strangers* (1987), and many others. Grade level: 2–4.

Caney, Steven. *Steven Caney's Kids' America* (1978). Instructions for re-creating colonial crafts intermingled with Americana folklore. Grade level: K–8.

Collier, Christopher, and James Collier. *My Brother Sam Is Dead* (1984). Some may find the earthy language and realistic descriptions in their books offensive, but the Collier brothers are unmatched in the authentic historic details of their fiction. Grade level: young adult.

Curtis, Christopher Paul. *The Watsons Go To Birmingham –1963* (2000). This hilarious yet deeply moving Newbery Honor winner blends the travels of a fictitious African-American family with the factual account of the bombing of the Birmingham church that killed four little girls.

Dalgliesh, Alice. *The Courage of Sarah Noble* (1954), *The Fourth of July Story* (1956), and others. Grade level: 2–4.

Daugherty, James. *Poor Richard* (1941), and others. Grade level: 5–8.

d'Aulaire, Ingri, and Edgar d'Aulaire. *Benjamin Franklin* (1950), *Abraham Lincoln* (1957), and many other biographies of early American leaders. Grade level: 2–4.

de Angeli, Marguerite. *Thee, Hannah!* (1940), *Yonie Wondernose* (1944). de Angeli may be the Pennsylvania Dutch country's most distinguished author. Grade level: 2–4.

Dear America titles, various authors. Grade level: 5–8.

DeFelice, Cynthia. *The Apprenticeship of Lucas Whitaker* (1996).

Edmonds, Walter. *The Matchlock Gun* (1941). The true tale of a boy's courage in the face of an Indian attack. Grade level: 2–4.

Fisher, Leonard. *The Blacksmiths* (1976). From the Colonial American Craftsmen series, includes *The Doctors, The Papermakers, and The Cabinetmakers.* Excellent wood engravings. OP. Grade level: all.

Forbes, Esther. *Johnny Tremain* (1960). Compare this book with modern author Avi's *The Fighting Ground*. Grade level: 5–up.

Foster, Genevieve. *1620: Year of the Pilgrims*. A favorite author—this title provides an overview of world history the year the Pilgrims landed; one of many world history books by this author. Her titles are being brought back into print by Beautiful Feet Books. Grade level: 3–8.

Freedman, Russell. *Lincoln: A Photobiography* (1987). The first nonfiction book to win the Newbery Award. A superb storyteller writing in the nonfiction genre. If you like Ken Burns's documentaries, you'll like Russell Freeman's writing. Grade level: 4–up.

Fritz, Jean. *And Then What Happened, Paul Revere?* (1973), *The Cabin Faced West* (1987), and many others. Don't miss this author! Grade level: 3–8.

Greene, Carol. *Benjamin Franklin: A Man with Many Jobs* (1988). A Rookie Biography book—a fine series for emerging readers. Lots of historic detail, illustrations, and photographs. Grade level: 1–3.

Giff, Patricia Reilly. *Lily's Crossing* (1999). Set during World War II. Grade level: 4–6.

Hall, Donald. *Ox-cart Man* (1979). Caldecott Medal. Grade level: K–2.

Henry, Marguerite. *Justin Morgan Had a Horse* (1954), *Benjamin West and His Cat Grimalkin* (1947). This beloved writer of horse stories also tells history in these. Grade level: 2–5.

Hesse, Karen. *Out of the Dust* (1999). Newbery Award. Set during the Dust Bowl and, amazingly, written as a cycle of poems. *Letters from Rifka* (1993), the story of a Jewish immigrant girl, is also noteworthy. Grade level: 4–9.

Holling, Holling C. *Paddle-to-the-Sea* (1941) and many others. A unique blend of geography and history. Grade level: 3–6.

Hunt, Irene. *Across Five Aprils* (1964). A Newbery Honor book set during the Civil War. Grade level: 5–up.

Keith, Harold. *Rifles for Watie* (1957). Newbery Award winner. Grade level: 5–up.

Kellogg, Steven. *Johnny Appleseed* (1988). This outstanding illustrator has told an entertaining tale for the 4–7 age group. Grade level: K–2.

Knight, James. *Jamestown* (1998) and others in the Adventures in Colonial America series. Grade level: 2–4.

Latham, Jean Lee. *Carry On, Mr. Bowditch* (1955). Lots of science and mathematics here. Grade level: 2–5.

Lenski, Lois. *Strawberry Girl* (1945). Lenski writes stories set in various regions of the United States. Grade level: 2–5.

Levine, Ellen. *If You Traveled on the Underground Railroad* (1993). From the unique series by Scholastic. Grade level: 1–4.

Loeper, John. *Going to School in 1776* (1973), *Going to School in 1886* (1984). Grade level: 3–6.

MacLachlan, Patricia. *Sarah, Plain and Tall* (1985). Newbery Award and Scott O'Dell Award. A simple story, but the writer's lyrical style and characterization are flawless. Grade level: 3–7.

Monjo, F. N. *The Drinking Gourd* (1993). I Can Read book about the Underground Railroad. Monjo has mastered the art of fine writing with a controlled vocabulary. Grade level: 1–3.

O'Dell, Scott. *Streams to the River, River to the Sea* (1986), and many others. This book follows the trail of Lewis and Clark. Don't miss this important author. Grade level: 4–8.

Peck, Robert. A *Day No Pigs Would Die* (1994). Based on Peck's boyhood growing up in a Shaker family in Vermont. He is also author of the delightful Soup books for younger children. Grade level: 6–8.

Perl, Lila. *Slumps, Grunts and Snickerdoodles: What Colonial America Ate and Why* (1975). Great recipes with historical notes. Grade level: elementary.

Roop, Peter, and Connie Roop. *Keep the Lights Burning, Abbie* (1985). Maine, 1856. Grade level: 2–4.

Ryan, Pam Muñoz. *Esperanza Rising* (2000). The story of a pampered Mexican girl who flees to America with her mother during the 1930s, where their only option is to become migrant workers.

Siegel, Beatrice. *George and Martha Washington at Home in New York* (1989). Grade level: 4–7.

Speare, Elizabeth George. *The Sign of the Beaver* (1983) and others. Winner of the Scott O'Dell Award. Grade level: 3–7.

Steele, William O. *The Perilous Road* (1990). A Civil War story. Also see *The Buffalo Knife* and others for a vivid portrayal of wilderness life. Grade level: 4–8.

Taylor, Mildred. *Roll of Thunder, Hear My Cry* (1997). First book in a trilogy of the Logans, a black family struggling against racism during the Depression. Grade level: 5–9.

Tunis, Edwin. *Frontier Living* (1961), *Indians* (1959), and many others. OP. Grade level: 5–up.

Turner, Ann. *Grasshopper Summer* (1989). Eighteenth-century prairie life. Grade level: 3–6.

Twain, Mark. *The Adventures of Huckleberry Finn,* and others. Grade level: 5–up.

Waters, Kate. *Sarah Morton's Day: A Day in the Life of a Pilgrim Girl.* A pictorial tour of Plimoth Plantation, a living history museum in Plymouth, Massachusetts. Grade level: 1–4.

We Were There series. Out of print but worth the search through interlibrary loan. Grade level: 5–8.

Wilder, Laura Ingalls. Little House on the Prairie series. Grade level: 2–5.

History/Geography—Other Lands

Alder, Elizabeth. *The King's Shadow* (1997). Set at the time of the Norman invasion, an excellent tale for understanding the evolution of the King's English. Grade level: 6–10.

Ballard, Robert. *The Lost Wreck of the Isis* (1990). Nonfiction that reads like high adventure. OP. Grade level: 3–6.

Carlson, Laurie. *Classical Kids: An Activity Guide to Life in Ancient Greece and Rome* (1998). Grade level: 1–5.

Ceserani, Gian Paolo. *Marco Polo* (1982). Grade level: 3–6.

Colum, Padraic. *The Children's Homer* (1918, 1948), *Children of Odin,* and *The Golden Fleece.* Best source of ancient mythology for elementary students. Grade level: 4–8.

Connolly, Peter. *The Ancient City: Life in Classical Athens & Rome* (1998). Author and illustrator of many titles on the classical world. Grade level: 5–8.

Corbishley, Mike. *The Middle Ages: Cultural Atlas for Young People* (1990). A great series to use for studies of Egypt, Greece, Rome, and the Bible world as well. Grade level: 7–12.

d'Aulaire, Ingri and Edgar. *D'Aulaires' Book of Greek Myths* (1992). Our favorite illustrations and stories of ancient mythology. Grade level: 3–8.

de Angeli, Marguerite. *The Door in the Wall* (1949). Medieval life. Grade level: 4–6.

de Jenkins, Lyll Becerra. *The Honorable Prison* (1989). Modern-day South America. Grade level: 5–8.

Foster, Genevieve. *Augustus Caesar's World* (1997). Grade level: 3–8.

Gaarder, Jostein. *Sophie's World* (1996). An ingenious novel about the history of philosophy. Great for worldview studies. Young Adults.

Grun, Bernard. *The Timetables of History* (1991). Reference tool.

Holman, Felice. *The Wild Children* (1985). Russia in the 1920s. Grade level: 5–8.

Hunter, Nigel. *The Expeditions of Cortes* (1990). One from the Great Journeys series. Grade level: 3–6.

James, Simon. *Ancient Rome* (1990). An Eyewitness book. All are highly recommended. Grade level: all.

Konigsberg, E. L. *The Second Mrs. Giaconda* (1998). The fictionalized account of Leonardo da Vinci and the *Mona Lisa*. Grade level: 5–8.

Krumgold, Joseph. *...and now Miguel* (1953). Newbery Award. Grade level: 4–6.

Lowry, Lois. *Number the Stars* (1990). Newbery Award. Set in Denmark during Nazi occupation. Grade level: 4–8.

McGraw, Eloise. *The Golden Goblet* (1986). Ancient Egypt. All of this author's books are the finest of historical fiction. Grade level: 4–8.

O'Dell, Scott. *The Hawk That Dare Not Hunt by Day* (1975). The story of William Tyndale. Grade level: 4–8.

Paterson, Katherine. *Rebels of the Heavenly Kingdom* (1983). One of my favorite authors. This story is set in China in the 1850s. Grade level: 4–8.

Pyle, Howard. *The Merry Adventures of Robin Hood* (1952). Grade level: 5–up.

Rius, Maria. Journey Through History series, including *The Middle Ages* and others (1988). This series includes a helpful parent-teacher guide. Grade level: 2–4.

Ryan, Peter. *Explorers and Mapmakers* (1990). Grade level: 3–6.

Speare, Elizabeth George. *The Bronze Bow* (1961). Palestine at the time of Christ. Grade level: 5–8.

Sperry, Armstrong. *Call It Courage* (1971). A South Seas Island boy must conquer his fear of the sea. Grade level: 3–6.

Stevenson, Robert Louis. *The Black Arrow*, illustrated by N.C. Wyeth (1944). The Wars of the Roses come to life in this master storyteller's hands. Grade level: 5–up.

Sutcliff, Rosemary. *Flame-Colored Taffeta* (1986), and others. Rich, detailed writings of English history. Grade level: 5–8.

Wright, David, and Jill Wright. *Facts on File Children's Atlas* (1993). Best atlas for the elementary level. Grade level: 2–6.

Mathematics

Anno, Mitsumasa. *Anno's Math Games* (1991), and many more. There is no one like Anno! Don't miss this inventive and brilliant author/illustrator. Grade level: 2–5.

Asimov, Isaac. *How Did We Find Out About Numbers?* (1973). OP. This leading science writer has authored scores of nonfiction titles for kids. Grade level: 2–4.

Burns, Marilyn. *The I Hate Mathematics! Book* (1975), and *The Book of Think* (1976). Both from the Brown Paper School book series—all worth your attention. Grade level: 3–8.

Dennis, Richard. *Fractions Are Parts of Things* (1971). OP. From the Young Math Book series, which teaches mathematical concepts through hands-on activities. Grade level: 1–3.

Froman, Robert. *Less Than Nothing Is Really Something* (1973). Introduction to negative numbers. Grade level: 1–4.

Gardner, Martin. *Aha!: Aha! Insight and Aha! Gotcha* (1978), and many more. Grade level: 5–up.

Ipsen, D.C. *Archimedes: Greatest Scientist of the Ancient World* (1988). Grade level: 5–up.

Macmillan, Bruce. *Eating Fractions* (1991). Grade level: Preschool.

Maybury, Richard. *Whatever Happened to Penny Candy?* (1993).

The best introduction to economics for young people. Grade level: 6–up.

Pappas, Theoni. *The Joy of Mathematics* (1989). Mathematics the way it ought to be learned! Many titles worth your time. Grade level: 4–12.

Schwartz, David, and Steven Kellogg, illustrator. *How Much Is a Million?* (1989), and *If You Made a Million* (1985). Lots of fun! Grade level: K–3.

Sitomer, Mindel, and Harry Sitomer. *Zero Is Not Nothing* (1978). Another Young Math Book. Grade level: 1–3.

Wyler, Rose, and Gerald Ames. *It's All Done with Numbers* (1979). "Magic" tricks performed with mathematics. Grade level: 2–5.

Science

Allison, Linda. *Blood and Guts: A Working Guide to Your Own Insides* (1976). Another excellent Brown Paper School Book author. Grade level: 3–8.

Berger, Melvin. *Quasars, Pulsars and Black Holes in Space* (1977) and others. Grade level: 4–up.

Beshore, George. *Science in Early Islamic Cultures* (1988). From a series that covers technological achievements of other cultures in other times. Grade level: 5–up.

Bourgeois, Paulette. *The Amazing Dirt Book* (1990). Activities for grades 2–5.

Caney, Steven. *Steven Caney's Invention Book* and others. Workman Publishing has many great titles for homeschoolers. Grade level: 2–6.

Cobb, Vickie. *Bet You Can't: Science Impossibilities to Fool You* (1985) and lots of others. Grade level: 4–8.

Cole, Joanna. *The Magic School Bus Inside the Earth* (1987) and others. All the titles in this series are wonderful—humorous with lots of detail. Grade level: K–3.

Durrell, Gerald. *Amateur Naturalist* (1986). Comprehensive, illustrated guide to collecting specimens from five environments. Grade level: 5–up.

Epstein, Sam, and Beryl Epstein. *Dr. Beaumont and the Man with a Hole in His Stomach* (1978). Don't miss this bizarre but true story from the 1820s. Grade level: 3–6.

Gallant, Roy. *National Geographic Picture Atlas of Our Universe*

(1986). *National Geographic* has done a few reference books for children, and they are superb. Grade level: 5–up.

Gardner, Robert. *The Whale Watchers' Guide* (1984). From a prolific science writer. Grade level: 4–6.

Grey, Vivian. *The Chemist Who Lost His Head: The Story of Antoine Lavoisier* (1982). Founder of the metric system. Grade level: 4–up.

Johnston, Tom. *Energy: Making It Work* (1988). Good activities to do at home from the Science in Action series. Grade level: 3–6.

Krupp, E. C. *The Big Dipper and You* (1989). A historical and scientific introduction to the night sky. Richly illustrated. Grade level: 2–4.

Lewis, James. *Rub-a-Dub-Dub Science in the Tub* (1989). For the two- to five-year-old set. Grade level: Pre-K–2.

Macaulay, David. *The New Way Things Work* (1988). Like Anno, Macaulay is in a class by himself. Grade level: all.

Milton, Joyce. *Whales: The Gentle Giants* (1989). From the Step into Reading series. Use this series to teach your child to read. It is great! Grade level: 1–3.

Ontario Science Center. *Scienceworks* and *Sportworks* (1984). Both OP. If you can't visit this outstanding hands-on museum, at least get their books. Grade level: elementary.

Provensen, Alice, and Martin Provensen. *The Glorious Flight* (1983). A Caldecott winner. Grade level: 1–3.

Quackenbush, Robert. *Ahoy! Ahoy! Are You There? A Story of Alexander Graham Bell* (1981). From a beginning-reader series that introduces kids to famous inventors. Grade level: 2–4.

Rey, H. A. *The Stars: A New Way to See Them* (1976). Surprise, surprise! Curious George's creator also liked astronomy. Grade level: 1–3.

Simon, Seymour. *The Moon* (1984) and many others. Clear, crisp writing and full-color NASA pictures make this series unbeatable. Grade level: 4–8.

Sussman, Susan, and Robert James. *Big Friend, Little Friend: A Book about Symbiosis* (1989). Grade level: 1–3.

Thompson, C. E. *Glow-in-the-Dark Constellations: A Field Guide for Young Stargazers* (1989). OP. Grade level: 3–6.

VanCleave, Janice. *Chemistry for Every Kid* (Wiley, 1989) and *Biology for Every Kid* (1990). Each book has 101 easy experiments. Grade level: 4–8.

Walpole, Brenda. *175 Science Experiments to Amuse and Amaze Your Friends* (1988). This book lives up to its title. Grade level: 4–8.

Williams, J. Alan. *The Interplanetary Toy Book* (1985). Use easy-to-get supplies to create space adventures. Grade level: 3–6.

Wyler, Rose. *What Happens If...?* (1974). We did every experiment in this book. Everything you need is on hand! My kind of science book. Grade level: 2–5.

Yolen, Jane, and John Schoenherr. *Owl Moon.* Caldecott Medal. Primarily listed here to draw your attention to Schoenherr, a naturalist/author/illustrator. Grade level: K–2.

Zubrowski, Bernie. *Bubbles* (1979). A Children's Museum Activity Book. Others in the series are good too. Grade level: 2–5.

Music

Athey, Margaret, and Gwen Hotchkiss. *Complete Handbook of Music Games and Activities for Early Childhood* (1982). A complete curriculum for K–3 within these pages.

Barber, David. *Bach, Beethoven and the Boys: Music History As It Ought to Be Taught* (1986) and other lighthearted but informative guides to the world of music.

Celenza, Anna Harwell. *Bach's Goldberg Variations* (2005). Celenza has a number of children's books that provide excellent background information about famous composers and their important composition, within the frame of a sometimes fictitious storyline. Grade level: K-3.

Fox, Dan. *Go In and Out the Window: An Illustrated Songbook for Young People.* Published by the Metropolitan Museum of Art (1987), this book integrates folk music and historical artifacts.

Langstaff, John, and Nancy Langstaff. *Jim Along, Josie: A Collection of Folk Songs and Singing Games for Young Children* (1970). Introduce your children to Langstaff's recordings of American folk songs too.

Rosenberg, Jane. *Sing Me a Story: The Metropolitan Opera's Book of Opera Stories for Children* (1989). Adults will find this a welcome source of explanation too.

Ventura, Piero. *Great Composers* (1989). Check out all of Ventura's books! They cover a wide spectrum of subjects. Grade level: elementary.

Wiseman, Ann. *Making Musical Things* (1979). Another Reading Rainbow selection. Kids can really make these very ingenious folk instruments. I used this to teach a music class to early-elementary students at our co-op. Grade level: K–4.

Language Arts and Reference

Becker, Barbara. *Free Things for Kids* (2007). Lots of places to request fun and educational things to receive by mail. Grade level: elementary.

Heller, Ruth. *A Cache of Jewels and Other Collective Nouns* (1987). This lavish Reading Rainbow selection is one of a series on parts of speech. Grade level: elementary.

Hirsch, E. D. *First Dictionary of Cultural Literacy* (1989). This makes interesting reading. Grade level: 1–3.

Kohl, Herbert. *A Book of Puzzlements: Play and Invention with Language* (1981). If you want some quickie games to play with your kids, here's a big book of ideas. Grade level: 4–8.

Macmillan Dictionary for Children. My favorite elementary dictionary.

Becoming a Connoisseur of Children's Literature

Children's publishing is enjoying unprecedented growth. The call for literacy, as well as the whole-language movement, has created a huge demand. Publishers are pouring millions of dollars into the industry and attracting better and better writers to it. Kids' books are bigger, brighter, and filled with impressive photography and graphic punch.

If you want to stay on top of the latest offerings or read reviews about the best books being released, here are sources to help you become an expert about children's literature:

Reference Tools at the Library

Books in Print. This massive database allows you to locate a book by subject, title, or author. Currently you must go to your local library to use it. Individual subscriptions are not available, but visit www.booksinprint.com for helpful information.

The Children's Catalog. An annotated listing of recommended books organized by subject area.

Fiction Index. Use this to locate historical fiction set in a specific time period or locale.

Associations and Periodicals

The Bulletin of the Center for Children's Books
501 E. Daniel Street, MC-493
Champaign, IL 61820-6211
217-244-0324; 217-224-3302 fax
bccb.lis.illinois.edu/

The Children's Book Council
12 W. 37th Street, 2nd Floor
New York, NY 10018
212-966-1990; 212-966-2073 fax
www.cbcbooks.org

The Horn Book Magazine
56 Roland Street, Suite 200
Boston, MA 02129
800-325-1170
www.hbook.com

International Reading Association
P.O. Box 8139
800 Barksdale Road
Newark, DE 19714-8139
800-336-7323
www.reading.org
Publishes *The Reading Teacher*

Parents' Choice Foundation
Suite 303
201 W. Padonia Road
Timonium, MD 21093
410-308-3858; 410-308-3877 fax
www.parents-choice.org
Parents' Choice awards for books, toys, and multimedia

Reading Rainbow
GPN Educational Media
1407 Fleet Street
Baltimore, MD 21231
800-228-4630
pbskids.org/readingrainbow

Scholastic Book Clubs
P.O. Box 1503
Jefferson City, MO 65102-9966
800-724-2424
www.scholastic.com

Books with Annotated Bibliographies

America As Story, Rosemary Coffey and Elizabeth Howard (1997)

American Historical Fiction: An Annotated Guide to Novels for Adults and Young Adults, Lynda Adamson (1998)—also has one available cataloging world historical fiction

Books Children Love, Elizabeth Wilson (2002)

Books to Build On: A Grade-by-Grade Resource Guide for Parents and Teachers, E.D. Hirsch Jr. (1996)

Eyeopeners II, Beverly Kobrin (1995)

Honey for a Child's Heart, Gladys Hunt (2002)

Honey for a Teen's Heart, Gladys Hunt (2002)

The Read-Aloud Handbook, Jim Trelease (2006)

Catalogs Specializing in Children's Literature

The Book Peddler
Order line: 800-928-1760
www.bookpeddler.us

Chinaberry
2780 Via Orange Way, Suite B
Spring Valley, CA 91978
888-481-6744
www.chinaberry.com

Greenleaf Press
3761 Highway 109 North
Lebanon, TN 37087
615-449-1617
www.greenleafpress.com

Lifetime Books and Gifts
18755 SW 272 Street
Homestead, FL 33031
305-248-1271
www.ShopLBG.com

Popular Programs Based on Children's Literature

All of these programs present material from a Christian perspective. More information on each can be found in the Resource Guide.

Beautiful Feet Books
1306 Mill Street
San Luis Obispo, CA 93401
800-889-1978
www.bfbooks.com
American history, world history, history of science, and geography units for primary, elementary, and high school

Five in a Row
P.O. Box 707
Grandview, MO 64030-0707
816-246-9252
www.fiveinarow.com
Integrated unit studies based upon one book. Units available for ages two through twelve

KONOS
P.O. Box 250
Anna, TX 75409
972-924-2712
www.konos.com
Integrated unit studies based upon a key character trait

My Father's World
P.O. Box 2140
Rolla, MO 65402
573-426-4600
www.mfwbooks.com
One of my favorite curricula; K–8 literature-based unit studies
integrated seamlessly with a biblical worldview

Sonlight Curriculum
8042 S. Grant Way
Littleton, CO 80122
303-730-6292
www.sonlight.com
Literature-based curriculum with a world missions focus

Tapestry of Grace
Lampstand Press
8077 Snouffer School Road
Gaithersburg, MD 20879
800-705-7487
www.tapestryofgrace.com
Emphasizing God's sovereign design in all of history; use this
classically-inspired, lush program in place of textbooks with
older students

Veritas Press
1829 William Penn Way
Lancaster, PA 17601
Toll-Free: 800-922-5082
In Lancaster: 717-519-1974
Fax: 717-519-1978
www.veritaspress.com

Publishes classical Christian curriculum built around children's books and their exceptional study guides

WinterPromise
10 Folsom Harbor Road
Grand Isle, VT 05458
802-372-9200
www.winterpromise.com
Literature-rich program, but with an equal dollop of hands-on activities to compliment the reading

CHAPTER 12
Surviving a Curriculum Fair

Now it's time to spend the money. What you can't find at your library, as well as resources that must be used longer than one month (or whatever your library's maximum lending time is), must be sought out and paid for.

And the best place to see all your options in the flesh is your state's curriculum fair.

These extravaganzas are not to be missed, especially if you are a new homeschooler. The chaos, the choices, the speakers, and the fellowship will rev your engines for this new venture—or run you quickly out of gas, depending on your temperament.

Here are some tips for maximizing your time:

Making the Most of Your Day

At my first curriculum fair I couldn't stand not buying anything and everything. That's the first impulse you have to resist—the temptation to overbuy.

I frequently take books *off* the piles accumulated by our customers at convention tables—I tell them they are getting more than they'll ever use. It may not seem like the wisest business practice, but I know helping folks make choices they won't regret will lead to loyal customers in the long run.

Keep these strategies in mind:

- **Do your homework before you come**
  Read reviews, visit websites, request catalogs, make a list. What goals and objectives do you have for next year? What core curriculum do you know you need for sure? What other products sound the most promising? How much can you afford to spend right now? Your best prices are usually at the fair, so it is wise to be prepared to buy.

- **Set realistic goals**
  Expect crowds and lines. Expect information overload

> THE FIRST IMPULSE YOU HAVE TO RESIST—THE TEMPTATION TO OVERBUY.

and feelings of confusion. It's the nature of the beast. If you come pressured to accomplish too much, you'll be frustrated and probably make bad purchasing decisions.

- **Prioritize**
  Come early and get your essential shopping out of the way. If there is a used curriculum section, visit that first. Attend the workshops highest on your list. If you tire out before you complete all you'd hoped to, at least the most important things are done. You can order the CDs from the workshops you missed and shop online at home.

- **Discuss your goals with your companion**
  People attend a curriculum fair for three reasons: to browse, to attend workshops, and to buy. If you go to the curriculum fair with a friend, discuss your goals for the fair before you arrive. If your companion has different goals, both of you are going to feel disappointed. Work separately to get the most done.

- **For new homeschoolers**
  It's better to get an education before you start buying. Go to the workshops. Talk with distributors and veteran homeschoolers first. You can always buy later. Information is what you need now. Bring a roll of address labels and use these to quickly add your name to mailing lists. By the time the next fair rolls around, you'll have received plenty of catalogs to review before going.

- **Say thank you to the volunteer coordinators**
  Hundreds of hours go into organizing a curriculum fair, and almost all the fairs are run by volunteers. These folks have sacrificed countless hours of family time to create this opportunity for you. They need to be appreciated.

Ten Questions to Ask Before You Buy

Is this product developed for homeschoolers? If not, is the product still designed for individualized instruction?
Homeschooling is more like tutoring than traditional schooling. Material intended for classroom or group instruction will have lots

THE MOST SUCCESSFUL RESOURCES WE'VE USED ARE THOSE RECOMMENDED BY OTHER HOMESCHOOLERS.

of stuff designed to keep everybody busy for a fifty-minute class period. You don't need to spend the extra money for a resource with heavy doses of busywork.

Is this a product that other homeschoolers I know are using? The most successful resources we've used are those recommended by other homeschoolers. Reviewers don't have time to use every product extensively before writing up their recommendations. And company representatives have a built-in bias.

Is this product compatible with my child's learning style, readiness, and reading level? You will find wide discrepancies among products labeled for a particular grade. You'll need to use the information provided about learning styles and readiness first and then check out the reading level. Generally the larger the print, the lower the reading level.

Does this product require a lot of teacher preparation? If so, will I conceivably have time for that throughout the year? The more kids you are homeschooling, the less time you can allocate to teacher preparation for individual subjects. If things never get fully used, it is usually for this reason. Self-instructional materials or those with everything planned out seem to work best when teaching more than one child.

Is this product consumable, or will I get years of use from it? This is an important consideration when evaluating the price. A DVD program that contains an entire year of high school algebra has a lot more return on the investment than a consumable reading program for the same amount of money.

What about the artistic merit? Are the student text and material colorful and artistically appealing? Does the layout draw the child into the pages? Is the writing lively, concrete, and specific? If this product is not inviting (especially a factor with younger children), what are you planning to do to engage your child's interest in the subject? Do you find this resource intellectually stimulating? If not, what attitude toward learning are you conveying to your kids?

Are there activities for the child to work on that involve higher-level thinking skills and move him or her away from the text and out into the world? If there is only one correct answer to chapter questions, then the text is only measuring memorization. Assessment tools that require more thoughtful responses, either in the form of an essay or research project, require students to work with the material on a deeper level.

Does the product have a resale value among homeschoolers? This is especially important if it is a big-ticket item and you hope to recoup some of that investment someday.

Does the material have a theological/philosophical slant that you can embrace? This should usually be evident in the introductory comments or the program overview. If not, ask the representatives. Some publishers believe learning is an avocation, and their materials are designed to cultivate this sense of wonder and joy. Others believe school is a child's job, and the material is designed to cultivate a work ethic.

Is the program complete, or must I buy supplemental materials? One expensive reading program I bought did not have readers. Some math programs require an additional purchase of manipulatives. Is the teacher's manual additional? And is it really necessary? Find out where the answers to the student assignments are printed. Make sure you ask these questions before you buy so you can accurately evaluate the cost of the resource.

Tips for Choosing a Vendor

As I alluded to in the last chapter, a number of homeschool suppliers have come and gone since the first edition of this book. While it has been my pleasure to buy great products from many wonderful and ethical businesses that emphasize customer service, our homeschool dollars are also attracting their share of fly-by-night operations. My hat is off to organizers in many states who now hold by-invitation-only conventions. This is an excellent way to provide a measure of consumer protection for attendees. Here are some further points to consider before surrendering your hard-earned dollars.

The consideration you give to each of these points will vary depending upon whether you are placing an order for materials to be shipped or are able to take the resources with you at the time of payment.

1. How well established is the company?

Has it been around a number of years? Does it have a place of business where you will be able to reach someone after the fair? Are they well known in the homeschool market, and do they have a good reputation with other homeschoolers you know?

2. What is the return policy?

Get it in writing. Make sure you get a proof of purchase at the convention if you anticipate making returns.

3. What level of customer support can you expect after you purchase the product?

A toll-free number? Website? E-mail? Does the company provide reliable hours of business when you can call or visit?

4. If paying by check, must the check clear first before the order is shipped?

If paying by credit card, will the card be charged immediately, or when the order is shipped? If the order is split-shipped, how will your card be charged?

5. What is the expected turnaround time for an order?

Is it guaranteed? (You will need to be understanding about shipping times during the height of the buying season. Most companies experience delays at that time of year.)

MAKE SURE YOU GET A PROOF OF PURCHASE AT THE CONVENTION IF YOU ANTICIPATE MAKING RETURNS.

PART 3

ORGANIZATION AND PLANNING

MAINTAIN CONTROL

PLAN

IN THIS SECTION

Setting Up a Learing Environment

Maintaining Control of Your Day

ORGANIZE

LEARNING ENVIRONMENTS

CHAPTER 13
Setting Up a Learning Environment

> **YOU WANT YOUR KIDS LIVING AND BREATHING IN AN ENVIRONMENT THAT NOT ONLY SUPPORTS LEARNING, BUT ALSO INVITES AND STIMULATES THEIR INQUIRY.**

A local newspaper featured our homeschool one year. The picture that ran with the article showed my kids composting with earthworms in the middle of our kitchen. I didn't realize how strange this would appear till several neighbors teased me about our health habits. (If you are interested, *Worms Eat My Garbage* by Mary Appelhof [wormwoman.com] will show you how to get started with this great science project. If you're squeamish, you don't have to maintain your worm farm in the kitchen.)

If you choose to homeschool, forget about being featured in *House Beautiful*. Creating a learning environment that invites invention, inquiry, and discovery is pretty much incompatible with clutter control. Most of the homeschooling houses I frequent have books, art projects, science apparatus, insect collections, etc. sharing space with all available seating. Good conversation is easily had, but standing-room-only is the standard.

What I can offer you here are suggestions for managing the mess but not for passing a white-glove inspection.

Swimming in Stimuli

Far more important than the actual lessons you may organize to present to your children is the environment in which they learn. Think in terms of "immersion." You want your kids living and breathing in an environment that not only supports learning, but also invites and stimulates their inquiry. Everywhere they turn as they move through daily life, they should find stuff for exploration at their fingertips.

Exploration

Long before you begin formal lessons in any subject area, your kids need a generous, leisurely time of informal exposure and investigation of the stuff they are going to be trained to use in a skillful way later.

If you want kids who read, immerse them in a print-rich environment. Put books and magazines in every room—some of my kids learned to read in the bathroom; we kept our Dr. Seuss collection in there.

If you want your kids to take an interest in science, they should be tripping over butterfly and insect collections, posters, magnifying glasses, binoculars, field guides, and other support material for scientific exploration at every turn.

 My favorite homeschooling household to visit is the home of Howard and Susan Richman, owners of Pennsylvania Homeschoolers. My kids voted it the top field trip one year. Instead of a house, imagine if you will a hands-on museum—or maybe the attic of a hands-on museum. The walls and ceilings of the Richmans' three-story farmhouse are papered with *National Geographic* maps. Computers (many assembled from spare parts), a bone museum, plant cuttings, musical instruments, drawings and art projects from every school year, science apparatus, and mathematical puzzles and games are spread throughout. Wasps' nests and origami projects suspend from the ceiling. Books, from very old to brand-new, rule the place. These tomes fill not only the makeshift bookcases and shelves but also rise in piles from the floor, sofa, and chairs. The Richmans' farmyard contains the same invitation to exploration.

The one thing missing—a television. (Well, there actually is a television in the attic, but without reception—they only used it for video instruction.)

The fruit of this environment: four kids who can't help but love to learn.

The Stuff You Need for the Elementary Levels

Here's a wish list for you to leave for Santa or the grandparents. Pass on faddish, plastic toys, and hold out for these old-fashioned and long-lasting favorites that require kids to use their imaginations. A lot of the educational resources sold at popular toy stores are very cheaply produced and will never outlast a passel of kids. I've included the source of durable goods that may cost a bit more but will last long enough to have on hand for your own grandkids.

Picture Books and Illustrated Classics

Some of our favorites:

Bedtime Hugs for Little Ones, Debby Boone and Gabriel
　　Ferrer
The Cat in the Hat and others, Dr. Seuss
Titles illustrated by Michael Hague, Jan Brett, Ruth Heller,
　　Eric Carle, and Tomie dePaola
The Princess and Curdie, George MacDonald
A Dangerous Journey: The Story of Pilgrim's Progress,
　　Oliver Hunkin
DK Eyewitness series
Goodnight Moon and *The Runaway Bunny,* Margaret Wise
　　Brown
St. George and the Dragon, Margaret Hodges
The Tale of Peter Rabbit and others, Beatrix Potter
The Way Things Work, David Macaulay
Usborne books

To find more suggestions for enduring children's books
you ought to own:

Books Children Love, Elizabeth Wilson
*The Book Tree: A Christian Reference for Children's
　　Literature,* Elizabeth and Jane Scott McCallum
EyeOpeners II, Beverly Kobrin
Honey for a Child's Heart, Gladys Hunt
Read-Aloud Handbook, Jim Trelease
Read for the Heart: Whole Books for WholeHearted Families,
　　Sarah Clarkson

Magazines

　　At various times during the elementary years, we found these
to be the most worthwhile subscriptions. I saved all copies, and
the kids used them over and over again for pictures and for
reports.

American Girl (608-836-4848), www.americangirl.com

Clubhouse (800-232-6459), www.clubhousemagazine.com
Clubhouse, Jr. (800-232-6459),
   www.clubhousemagazine.com/clubjr
Cobblestone (800-821-0115), www.cobblestonepub.com
Highlights for Children (800-255-9517),
   www.highlights.com
Kids Discover, kidsdiscover.com
National Geographic Explorer (800-647-5463),
   www.nationalgeographic.com
Ranger Rick (800-822-9919), www.nwf.org
Sports Illustrated for Kids (a super magazine for any kid but
   especially the reluctant reader) (800-992-0196),
   www.sikids.com
Your Big Backyard (800-822-9919), www.nwf.org

For stimulating imaginative and educational play:

Art supplies
Basic sports equipment
Big pencils
Binoculars, magnifying glass, microscope
Butterfly net
Calculator (Those made by Texas Instruments are best)
Computer
Easel
Field guides (Dorling Kindersley and Scholastic: First Field
   Series are recommended)
Flags of the world
Jump rope
Kitchen utensils
Large analog clock (the kind with minute and second
   hands—look for this at a farm supply store)
Lauri puzzles
LEGO sets
Magnetic numbers and letters, including lower case
Maps, globe
Math manipulatives such as Cuisenaire rods and
   Base Ten blocks
Puppets
Ravenburger puzzles

Stamps
Strategy games: checkers, chess, Abalone
Tools
Trunk of your old clothes for playing dress-up
Wooden and plastic figurines
Workbench

Materials for developing background knowledge and basic skills:

Desk
Musical instruments
Postcard prints of famous art masterpieces
Writing supplies

Music CDs:

American folk songs
Classical Kids series
French and Spanish folk songs
Judy Rogers Bible Songs (judyrogers.com)
Raffi
Sharon, Lois, and Bram
Wee Sing series

Audio recordings:

Focus on the Family Adventures in Odyssey episodes
Jim Weiss, Greathall Productions (www.greathall.com)
Your Story Hour (www.yourstoryhour.org)

A great source for these resources at discounted prices: Library and Educational Services (www.libraryanded.com)

Recommended sources of durable toys and art supplies:

Back to Basics Toys
800-356-5360
www.backtobasicstoys.com

Dick Blick Art Materials
P.O. Box 1267
Galesburg, IL 61402-1267
800-828-4548
800-621-8293 fax
www.dickblick.com

Discount School Supply
P.O. Box 6013
Carol Stream, IL 60197-6013
800-627-2829
800-879-3753 fax
www.discountschoolsupply.com

HearthSong
P.O. Box 1050
Madison, VA 22727
800-533-4397
www.hearthsong.com

Miller Pads and Paper
2840 Neff Road
Boscobel, WI 53805
608-375-2181
www.millerpadsandpaper.com

Montessori Services
11 W. 9th St.
Santa Rosa, CA 95401
888-513-3998
www.forsmallhands.com

Toys to Grow On
2695 E. Dominguez Street
Carson, CA 90895
800-874-4242
800-537-5403
www.toystogrowon.com

Make It Accessible

I erroneously tried to homeschool and keep all surfaces cleared at the same time. This is not possible. If you homeschool, it's hard to hide the evidence. Projects-in-progress cannot always be neatly put away at the end of the day.

I discouraged my kids' exploration by dragging home scores of books from the library and then shelving them neatly in the bookcase. Magazines were in dated order in the filing cabinet. Art supplies, science apparatus, and strategy games were packed away in their original boxes in cupboards with closed doors. My kids didn't touch them.

Then I tried an experiment. I took a few books off the shelf and set them on the coffee table. I left a crystal-growing kit on the kitchen table. I put the art easel up in the den. Guess what? My kids read those library books, took an interest in growing crystals, and started a major art project. Go figure.

Don't get the impression, though, that we let everything lie where it falls. I do require all entrances to be free and clear. And though I had to lower my expectations dramatically and learn to live with things a bit disheveled around the edges, I still believe Mom's organizational skills are the key to getting it all done.

> **MOM'S ORGANIZATIONAL SKILLS ARE THE KEY TO GETTING IT ALL DONE.**

Organizing It All

Where, exactly, will you hold school? This was really a dilemma when we first started. We kept migrating around the house the first few weeks—the kitchen, the living room, the kids' bedrooms. I realized I needed to make a decision, set up our learning area, and stay put. We settled on the kitchen table.

A Schoolroom Is Nice

I know quite a few families who have a schoolroom. It may be an extra bedroom or the basement. Lobbying heavily for our need for one of our own, I convinced my husband to build a new house a while back. But a month after we moved in, we were back where we started—at the kitchen table. This enabled me to work on my household chores while overseeing the kids' studies. (Once my kids reached high school, we had to create study areas for them in various corners of the house. But the kitchen table continued to serve as our discussion area.)

But the Kitchen Will Have to Do

So we had a kitchen that looked pretty odd. I kept a bookcase in the corner with the resources we used daily. We had maps and posters on the wall and art projects on the floor. We continuously cleared the table for meals and then for school. I got used to how it looked, but first-time visitors who didn't know we homeschool usually looked perplexed.

Hardware

You'll need a few items to create an organized learning space: For office supplies, we shop Sam's Club as well as Quill (800-982-3400). Shipping charges on furniture make Quill an impractical choice for bigger-ticket items. So we've bought most of our files, desks, and storage cabinets from a local home-office supplier, such as Office Max, which offers free delivery with a minimum order.

Also, search online with the keywords "Used Office Furniture." You may find a store is located in your area that may have just what you need at a fraction of the cost.

Setting Boundaries

At a seminar several years ago, I acquired an organizational strategy that became my saving grace. I used baskets, plastic tubs, containers, filing cabinets, storage chests, and such to *create boundaries for stuff*. For example, our math manipulatives were in one color-coded tub, our art supplies in another. I used stacking trays on the school shelf to separate graphing, construction, and handwriting paper. And each child had his or her own supply box for pencils, calculator, scissors, ruler, and such. I even used containers inside closets and drawers to keep everything clearly visible and easy to return to its rightful place. In my best moments these were all clearly labeled, and everyone knew what went where.

Every August when planning the next school year, I would de-junk the house and improve our organization. I bought a few more pieces of hardware to further help us manage the clutter.

One summer our project was moving Mike and Gabe to a bigger bedroom downstairs (on the ground rule they could not create a life of their own down there—we're still a family). We bought bunk beds, shelving, a bookcase, and a desk in order to better organize a study area for their changing needs. (They sprang for the stereo system they said enhanced their intellectual growth.) We couldn't make all the changes at once, but we prioritized our list and chipped away at it as we could.

Filing Cabinet

I kept files in every subject area. I stored any pamphlets, magazine articles, field-trip ideas, and teaching tips as I collected them. Then I pulled a file as I planned out a subject area for the year. It was one way to make sure all the good ideas I came across eventually got implemented into my program.

Of course, this was back in the olden days. You're probably thinking you'll store all this stuff online. Well, that certainly is now an option. I do have a scanner, in fact, and I like to turn important documents into PDF files just to prevent loss. My husband also uses Google (doc.google.com) to store his files online. Young children, however, still need to touch and feel things, so keep your online viewing to a minimum with them. And you will probably find it is simpler to review and organize your paperwork as hard copies. During the elementary years at least, you will likely still find filing cabinets a necessity.

So get something durable. I recommend a four-drawer, commercial-grade file cabinet with high sides for hanging folders.

Bookcases

I bought more every year and had our books shelved similarly to the library system so my kids could quickly see what we had on hand for research projects. The one in the kitchen was for current school subjects, but we lined a wall in the family room for our children's literature collection, and then of course there was the one in the living room, and some in all the bedrooms. There were none in the bathroom, but that's not a bad idea. Sauder is my favorite brand of ready-to-assemble furniture for quality, durability, and price (www.sauder.com). And for those of you who want budget storage with style, there is always Ikea, my adult children's furniture of choice.

> YOUNG CHILDREN NEED TO TOUCH AND FEEL THINGS, SO KEEP YOUR ONLINE VIEWING TO A MINIMUM WITH THEM.

Organization = Time

You get the picture, I'm sure. You can come up with your own systems for keeping things available but properly stored. Just remember: The more organized you are, the more time you will have. Any effort you invest in setting up and maintaining your learning environment will never be wasted.

Now on to the homeschool mom's greatest daily challenge . . .

> **JUST REMEMBER: THE MORE ORGANIZED YOU ARE, THE MORE TIME YOU WILL HAVE.**

CHAPTER 14
Maintaining Control of Your Day

A Method to the Madness

"Order brings peace," a spiritual mentor told me shortly after my conversion. And though I can't quote you a biblical chapter and verse, it's a life principle I'm convinced is true.

If there ever was a house in need of order, it was ours the weeks after we brought the twins home from the hospital. I couldn't believe the doctor had entrusted these babies to our care. They looked so fragile.

I needn't have worried. They may have been small, but Mike and Gabe had lungs of steel. And right away they started calling the shots. My salvation came from a book called *My First 300 Babies* by Gladys West Hendrick. Unfortunately now out of print, it is the best gift to hand a new mother. It was written by a nanny who, if you could afford her, moved in for six weeks with the new parents and whipped into shape not only that baby, but also the husband, household, and anyone else in her range of vision. (All you La Leche League members are cringing, aren't you?) Had I only brought home one child from the hospital, I wouldn't have been willing to make the efforts her program demanded. But as wimpy new parents of a pair who had obviously organized a coup in utero, we were ready for desperate measures.

I read Hendrick's book and announced to the twins, "This is the end of life on your own terms." Her strategy is simple. Baby is put on a daily schedule divided into fifteen-minute increments. This is followed no matter what the baby does: 10 a.m. bathtime, 10:15 singtime, 10:30 nap, 12:30 afternoon feeding, 7 p.m. bedtime, etc. I stuck to it—even awakening the boys if the schedule dictated and putting them to bed even when they weren't willing.

Did they complain? You bet. But a week later, they were synchronized and—here's the important part—contented. We were more flexible when Kayte and Kristen came along, but the principle of maintaining a consistent routine and structure was still applied. I am convinced order brings peace—and produces contented, secure kids.

Of course, we are no longer controlling our children's lives in fifteen-minute intervals. By high school my kids set their own routines, but that's the fruit. It is second nature to them to manage their time wisely and to structure their day and learning environment rather than take an undisciplined, chaotic approach to life.

Here are the strategies that will bring peace to your homeschool life by bringing order. They are simple and few. Complex systems that require too much time to maintain fail very quickly. These are the ones that have lasted at our house over the years.

> **COMPLEX SYSTEMS THAT REQUIRE TOO MUCH TIME TO MAINTAIN FAIL VERY QUICKLY.**

Strategy #1: Long-Range Planning

A peaceful and well-managed homeschool begins with a commitment to plan. You can't invest too much time at this end of the spectrum. Long-range planning and weekly goal setting will eliminate unnecessary day-to-day decision making and give you confidence. It will also give your children direction—if you take the time to clue them in on things (something I had to remind myself to do).

Summertime Is Planning Time

Some families find homeschooling year-round suits them. I tried that but found we did best taking a summer break long enough to miss school. I used this time to regroup and do my long-range planning. After soliciting feedback from my kids, I scoped out our year. First I focused on areas of weakness. I prioritized these and set goals for improvement. I would never correct all of them in a year's time, but I was determined to keep chipping away at the list.

Add Faith

Don't let unmet goals discourage you. You'll get more accomplished in life by setting goals and not meeting all of them than by not setting goals at all.

Bring faith to your planning. Treat your goals as a prayer list. Sometimes I felt as though we weren't getting anywhere or, worse, moving backward. But when I looked at my goals from previous years, I was encouraged by the gains that had been made. Often God brings special opportunities our way that allow us to meet our goals in unexpected ways. Just putting the goals on the list made me more conscious of God's commitment to our success and my awareness of His intercession on our behalf.

Foreign language was a big flop at our house. Everything we tried usually petered out by October. But I still put it on the list every year. Then finally, a missionary on furlough from France began teaching at CHESS. When the administrator told me about her application to teach, I felt God had answered my personal prayer unexpectedly.

Write Objectives

After tackling our weaknesses, I then wrote out objectives for every subject for each child. I first began doing this because it is required by Pennsylvania law, and these must be filed with our school district. The requirement is vague and could be done in a cursory manner, but I took the time to make it meaningful. I used this plan throughout the year as a yardstick for our progress.

Fortunately, our law doesn't require us to meet these objectives, so it is easy to adjust or change as the year progresses. Planning is the strategy that will help you hit those targets you are aiming at. But don't let it enslave you. Always be ready to adapt your program to the needs of your children.

At the end of each school year, I went into my objectives file on the computer and entered a brief paragraph indicating whether or not the objectives were *met, partially met*, or *not met* and then detailed evidence to support my evaluation. Again, this is not required by our law. I did it for my own benefit and accountability.

Below is my educational plan from Mike and Gabe's third-grade year, along with my end-of-the-year notes.

Before You Go Any Further

This is indeed what I did do with my sons in third grade over the course of an entire year. I counted summer activities as

> **TREAT YOUR GOALS AS A PRAYER LIST.**

> **ALWAYS BE READY TO ADAPT YOUR PROGRAM TO THE NEEDS OF YOUR CHILDREN.**

well. That they were reading independently helped significantly. However, read closely. A lot of what sounds intentional and time-consuming actually happened in the course of our daily lives, and much of it they were able to do on their own.

Truthfully, during the chaos of the school year it didn't really seem like much was being accomplished. Writing up what we did to meet these objectives at the end of the year was always a source of encouragement to me—it made me realize we had indeed made progress. I found the same thing to be true when I met to evaluate other homeschool families in my state at the end of their school year. I was able to help parents see they had in fact made gains and gotten an impressive amount of work done. So what follows is not intended to be intimidating (that's the feedback I've sometimes received on this section). It's meant to illustrate the benefits you will find if you take time to set objectives and then evaluate at the close of your year whether or not, by God's grace, you've made gains in meeting them.

Educational Plan
1991–1992 School Term

Students: Gabriel Joseph Bell   Michael Benjamin Bell

Grade: Third

Academic Objectives
(to include but not limited to the following):

English
(to include spelling, reading, and writing):

◎ *Will continue daily, literature-based, sustained silent reading program (thirty to sixty minutes/day).*
[End-of-year notes:] Michael and Gabriel continue to love reading and do so without encouragement. Typically we all read silently after lunch for at least an hour. This year they each read approximately sixty chapter books. They read well

above grade level with good comprehension and speed. For example, Gabriel's favorite book, *A Father's Promise*, is the novel that concludes Bob Jones University's sixth-grade reading course. Michael has been reading those titles in the *Chronicles of Narnia* series. Both have really enjoyed the *Childhood of Famous Americans* series.

◎ **Will continue reading widely from various genres: nonfiction, fiction, biography, poetry, etc.**

The boys willingly read biographies and historical fiction. I required them to read nonfiction titles as part of their Book-It goals this year. We read many nonfiction titles aloud, too, as part of our unit studies. They also regularly read the *New International Version Adventure Bible.* We read some poetry about sports this year, but I intend to increase their exposure to verse.

◎ **Will continue to master library and research skills. Will write their first research paper.**

We use the library at least two times a month. Michael and Gabriel know well how the library is organized, and they can find books independently on topics of interest and for their research. They also use the library computer system without assistance to locate titles by subject and author and are then able to request the books through interlibrary loan.

The boys successfully wrote their first research paper. I feel the final draft of the paper could have been better, but the time involved in the science fair project and paper became overwhelming. I was very pleased with the amount of reading and research they did on their topics. They sent away for information, ordered titles through interlibrary loan, read their books, met to discuss their projects with me, and then logged their notes and rough drafts in their journals and on the computer.

◎ **Will improve rate, expression, and enjoyment of oral reading.**

Mike and Gabe read aloud more frequently this year to me and to their sisters. Gabriel is particularly dramatic in his reading and enjoys entertaining his 4-year-old sister with a good book.

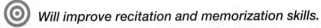 ***Will improve recitation and memorization skills.***

The boys portrayed several characters in a play our co-op produced, and they executed their lines flawlessly with good expression. Michael did especially well as the lead in *Ethan Allen and the Green Mountain Boys,* a character he was delighted to portray after reading a biography earlier in the year. They regularly memorized Scripture also.

Will continue to use contextual clues and phonics skills to expand reading comprehension and vocabulary. An emphasis will be placed on learning vocabulary across the curriculum.

Objective met. Vocabulary words were drawn primarily from the books we read together for history and science. They frequently ask me the meaning of words they run into while reading. I first ask for their ideas (which are usually close) and then precisely define it for them or refer them to the dictionary. We like to talk about words (or at least I do).

Will continue to improve spelling through reading critically and editing their work.

Objective met.

Will develop writer's voice through regular and sustained written composition.

I continue to be pleased with the writing that Michael and Gabriel do. They view themselves as writers. They did a wide variety of writing this year: science reports, history report, fiction, poetry, friendly letters, etc. They like to write letters and notes to friends. Their biggest frustration is in finding others who will write regularly to them. They prefer to use WordPerfect as opposed to longhand, and I do not blame them.

Will determine appropriate language, form, and content of written composition based upon analysis of audience and purpose.

Once again the boys participated in a writers group that I ran. We did several short lessons about the concerns of the writer. We've discussed these concerns at home mostly within the context of the letters they have written to friends and adults.

◎ *Will publish written compositions in a variety of forums.*
Michael and Gabriel were regular contributors to *The Learning Center Rag,* a student-run newspaper at our co-op. They made and sent many cards. They have submitted work to a couple of contests but have not been published yet.

◎ *Will develop editing skills.*
This objective was primarily met through the research paper they wrote and rewrote. They also jointly wrote a composition for a Mother's Day contest that went through many drafts (shown in the portfolio).

◎ *Will improve sentence structure, mechanics, punctuation, and word choice as dictated by the purpose of the written composition or oral communications.*
Objective met. The *Daily Grams* for third and fourth grade also provided exercises in these areas.

◎ *Will respond critically to the written work-in-progress of others.*
Objective met through the writers group they participated in and by reviewing each other's work.

◎ *Will develop listening skills through regular reading aloud.*
Objective met.

◎ *Will begin to develop their ability to respond critically to literature.*
Objective met. We read nonfiction and historical fiction this year for information, but I also drew the boys' attention to the writer behind the work. We informally discussed plot, conflict, tone, character development, and theme. They have very perceptive comments about why they do or do not like a particular book.

◎ *Will continue to improve and expand computer literacy and applications.*
Objective met. Boys learned to use the formatting and editing features of WordPerfect 5.1. They use the computer as a learning tool whenever I allow it.

Arithmetic

◎ *Will continue to recognize the importance and applications of mathematics and mathematical reasoning in daily life.*

Objective met. We seize opportunities to solve problems in daily life mathematically whenever possible, for example, determining the best buy, dividing items evenly between four children, scheduling our day, etc.

◎ *Will study the lives of famous mathematicians and their contributions.*

Not met.

◎ *Will review finding the sum or difference of three-digit and two-digit numbers when renaming is necessary.*

Objective met.

◎ *Will master the multiplication tables through 9x9=81 and division tables through 81÷9=9.*

Objective met.

◎ *Will begin to compute multiplication and division of two- and three-digit numbers by a single-digit number.*

Objective met and exceeded.

◎ *Will continue to use calculators effectively.*

Objective partially met. I intend to use some additional resources next year to expand their use of the calculator.

◎ *Will continue to develop multiple-step problem-solving strategies.*

Objective met, primarily through the Figure It Out workbook we used. The boys did not like this when we began it last year, but now they are feeling quite successful with it and enjoy the program.

◎ *Will continue to practice estimation skills with all problems.*

This is practiced in Saxon Math and in *Figure It Out*.

◎ *Will be able to identify order and place value of numbers through one million and explore those beyond.*

Objective met.

◎ *Will name, compare, and problem-solve with basic fractions.*

Objective met in Saxon and in making recipes. We typically double or even triple recipes.

◎ *Will use money to explore concept of decimal numbers such as tenths and hundredths.*

Objective met.

◎ *Will continue exploration of elementary geometry (polygons, angles, and parallel and perpendicular lines).*

Objective met.

◎ *Will work problems involving various standards of measurement (standard, metric, Celsius, Fahrenheit, etc.).*

Objective met.

◎ *Will continue to gather information from graphs, maps, charts, etc., as well as translate information into these forms.*

Objective met.

◎ *Will continue to discover symmetry and patterns in mathematics.*

Objective met, though it is their younger sister who loves this aspect of math and routinely points out patterns to them.

Science and Health

◎ *Will practice proper care of own body through diet, exercise, rest, and good hygiene.*

Objective met. Both Michael and Gabriel excel in this area. They eat a balanced diet, exercise daily, rest well, and practice healthy hygiene.

◎ *Will be introduced to human reproduction, birth, and growth.*

Objective met.

◎ *Will continue to study colonial craftsmen and methods of manufacturing goods.*

Objective met, primarily through visit to Valley Forge and

reading Leonard Fisher's Colonial Craftsmen series aloud.

◎ **Will study the history of science and the lives of famous scientists, especially during colonial America.**
Objective met. We mainly focused on colonial medicine because Michael had a great interest in that. We studied key doctors, the history of surgical methods, and the problems of caring for the wounded in times of war. Some of the scientists we covered include Benjamin Rush, Dr. Warren, Ben Franklin, Clara Barton, Florence Nightingale, George Washington Carver, Orville and Wilbur Wright, the Mayo brothers, Charles Goodyear, and Louis Pasteur.

◎ **Will study a science unit of weather, make weather instruments, and conduct numerous experiments related to this.**
Objective met. We studied this a good portion of the year. Michael reported to us frequently about his research for his science project.

◎ **Will study creationism and evolution.**
Objective met. A Bible scholar conducted classes at the science camp we participated in, and Michael and Gabriel attended a presentation at Hershey Evangelical Free Church. We read selections from a number of resources when we have questions in this area.

◎ **Will write a science research paper.**
Objective met. Michael wrote about measuring weather and Gabriel about the growing stages of the peanut.

◎ **Will participate in a science fair.**
Objective met.

◎ **Will do independent study into the life of a famous scientist of choice and present research orally to a group.**
Objective met. Michael reported on the Mayo brothers and Gabriel on George Washington Carver.

History of the United States and Pennsylvania; Geography and Civics

◎ *Will continue to deepen understanding of God's design for the family.*

Objective met through our discussions, primarily those following our regular Bible reading.

◎ *Will study Colonial America, the American Revolution, and the formation of a new nation.*

Objective met. This was our primary focus during the first semester. We read numerous books aloud and independently, and we listened to many tapes related to the topic. We also took field trips to Valley Forge and Philadelphia.

◎ *Will study geography within the context of Colonial America.*

Objective met. We used many maps during our studies. We also made our own maps.

◎ *Will study the history of types of government and the history of the political process in America.*

Objective met.

◎ *Will study current events and the effect they have upon our nation, community, and personal lives.*

Objective met. The boys both skim our daily newspaper (they devour the sports page) and listen to commentaries on the radio. They read a bimonthly current-events paper. We discuss events a lot.

◎ *Will continue to learn about and practice community service.*

Michael and Gabriel organized a youth group this year that raised money for Susquehanna Valley Pregnancy Center. They also helped to buy Thanksgiving turkeys for Bethesda Mission. We visited a nursing home. We value contributing to our community, and we discuss this value with them and strive to model it in our lives.

Our co-op also prepared care packages at Christmastime for Bethesda Mission and an orphanage in Romania.

◎ *Will study and appreciate people from different cultures in America and in the world.*

Objective met. Michael and Gabriel have been exposed to the customs and foods of other cultures through a variety of ways. We've done formal studies and several special projects at the Learning Center; for example, we had a special presentation about Romania by a woman who lived there. We've studied our own Arabic and Pennsylvania Dutch backgrounds.

◎ *Will continue to take an interest in other people, to practice hospitality, and to improve social etiquette.*

Objective met.

Physical Education

◎ *Will continue to value and demonstrate good sportsmanship.*

Objective met. Several of their coaches have commented on Mike and Gabe's encouragement to other players. Kermit emphasizes this quality over athletic ability. And our main purpose in involving the boys in organized sports is to enjoy the social benefits and learn cooperation.

◎ *Will continue to enjoy and appreciate the benefits of team sports as well as personal fitness.*

Michael and Gabriel exercise regularly. They worked toward the Presidential Fitness Challenge. Michael qualified for nationals, and Gabriel just missed (his "flexed arm hang" was a few seconds short). Michael and Gabriel were on soccer, wrestling, and baseball teams. They also are members at the community pool.

◎ *Will improve basic skills for soccer.*

Objective met.

◎ *Will participate in an advanced swimming course.*
Mike and Gabe passed the advanced beginners course.

◎ *Will improve wrestling skills and participate on a wrestling team.*
Objective met.

◎ *Will improve strength, speed, and coordination.*
Objective met.

◎ *Will participate in several track-and-field events.*
Objective met. We participated in the homeschoolers track-and-field day at Messiah College. More than 100 homeschooled students competed.

◎ *Will improve skills and knowledge of baseball.*
Objective met. I even enjoy baseball now. We have a *Sports Illustrated* video on baseball skills for kids, and that has helped a lot. Gabriel is doing well as a catcher for his team. Michael usually plays shortstop, but he is developing his pitching for next year. Both have been selected to play on the All-Stars team this summer.

Safety Education

◎ *Will practice water safety.*
Objective met.

◎ *Will practice bike safety.*
Objective met.

◎ *Will demonstrate understanding of the dangers and prevention of fires.*
Objective met. Attended a special presentation by the Elizabethtown Fire Department. We were interrupted by a fire alarm, and we had a real-life demonstration on the value of preparedness.

◎ *Will demonstrate cooking safety.*
Objective met. Michael and Gabriel enjoy cooking, and they made quite a number of recipes this year. At the beginning of the year we attended several 4-H cooking classes.

◎ *Will learn basic first aid.*
Objective met. We held a special class at the Learning Center.

Music

◎ *Will continue to develop the ability to sing on pitch with good tone quality.*
Objective met. My mother, a retired music teacher, gave the children some voice instruction over Christmas, and that helped a great deal. We sing a lot together, and the children sang with a children's choir several times this year.

◎ *Will continue to develop ability to hear and mimic rhythmic patterns.*
Objective met.

◎ *Will continue to learn to follow a conductor's directions.*
Objective met.

◎ *Will participate in regular group singing.*
Objective met. Mike and Gabe love to sing.

◎ *Will recognize types of music (jazz, folk, classical, hymns, contemporary).*
Partially met. Music is a big part of our family life, and we listen to a broad spectrum. They are beginning to recognize different styles.

◎ *Will study the lives of major composers, especially those who lived between 1492 and 1865, through their music and biographies.*
Partially met. We've read a few biographies but have done nothing formal. They have been exposed to the works of the major composers through the tapes we listen to.

◎ *Will begin instruction in the piano. Formal lessons are desired if an appropriate and affordable teacher can be found.*

Objective met. The boys studied with a talented music teacher this year and have done very well. They have progressed almost two levels. Plus, the opportunity to hear the other students (some of whom are quite advanced) sing and perform on piano at the recitals has exposed them to a diversity of styles.

Art

◎ *Will study the lives of famous painters, primarily during the period of 1492 through 1865, through their biographies and works.*

Partially met. We read a few biographies and looked at a special exhibit of paintings from this era at the state museum. I also used several library books with reproductions in them from the colonial period.

◎ *Will experiment with a variety of media (clay, tempera, pottery, etc.).*

Barely met. We did not get to several of the projects I had planned.

◎ *Will participate in a fine arts painting/drawing class.*

Partially met. Mike and Gabe had a few lessons in the fall, but we just didn't have the time to continue. I did subscribe to *Spark!* magazine, and we did several lessons from this.

◎ *Will complete several craft projects of own choosing.*

Objective met. The primary craft was the spinning, dyeing, and felting of wool. We also hand-dipped candles as well as made tin lanterns, an assemblage, and sand castings.

◎ *Will visit at least one art museum.*

Visited the collection at the state museum.

◎ *Will participate in an art/music appreciation class.*

Participated for two months during the fall semester.

Help with Objectives

Here are some sources of curriculum guidelines that are helpful in developing objectives. (I referred to these often but viewed them merely as a checklist for ensuring I didn't neglect an area Kermit and I thought was worthwhile in achieving our targeted goals.) My objectives for each child were primarily based upon his or her needs, readiness, and interests.

Scope and Sequence

A scope and sequence is the order in which various skills and subtopics of the major subject areas (social studies, language arts, science, and mathematics) are presented to grades K–12. You can request a scope and sequence from publishers such as Bob Jones University Press or Rod and Staff. Another helpful publication is *Kindergarten Through Grade Twelve: A Typical Course of Study*, available from World Book, Inc.

National and state standards have been developed in recent years, and curriculum suppliers wishing to make sales to public schools are aligning their materials with these. The beauty of homeschooling is we can use these lists as a framework for designing our own program, or we can pick and choose from what we like and disregard the rest. You can find standards listed by subject area and by state at www.education-world.com/ standards.

> MY OBJECTIVES FOR EACH CHILD WERE PRIMARILY BASED UPON HIS OR HER NEEDS, READINESS, AND INTERESTS.

 # Books with Objectives

Core Knowledge Outlines

Core Knowledge is the educational reform championed by E. D. Hirsch, professor emeritus at the University of Virginia. Hirsch has called for a return to a core curriculum as an essential component of a unified culture and prerequisite for socioeconomic advancement. In recent revisions, his books have integrated more subject matter from cultural traditions other than the classical Western view, though that is what predominates.

Hirsch's Core Knowledge series includes a book for every grade level—i.e., *What Your First Grader Needs to Know* and *What Your Second Grader Needs to Know*. Each title outlines objectives for each subject area and reading lists.

His original bestseller, *Cultural Literacy: What Every American Needs to Know*, is helpful in planning a high school–level curriculum.

Core Knowledge Sequence, a 200-page manuscript available from the Core Knowledge Foundation, gives you all the objectives for elementary school without the exposition found in the individual books. For $35, it is a worthwhile investment. Portions are available, along with lesson plans, at www.coreknowledge.org.

William Bennett, founder of *K12 Curriculum*, published the following hefty tome, also based heavily on Hirsch's model, *The Educated Child: A Parent's Guide from Preschool through Eighth Grade.*

Classical Christian Emphasis

This is a rapidly growing movement in the Christian schools and homeschool community. Essentially, the classical Christian model calls for a return to the great books of Western civilization and the study of church history as it emerged from within this culture. Its champion is Douglas Wilson, whose Reformed theology informs all his writings. While far too eclectic in my approach to adhere to any one system of core knowledge, the high school literature classes I teach at CHESS have been designed around this model. I have found the material spiritually enriching for me and for my students as well. Classical resources include:

The Well-Trained Mind: A Guide to Classical Education At Home, Jesse Wise and Susan Wise Bauer

Designing Your Own Classical Curriculum: A Guide to Catholic Home Education, Laura Berquist. Cindy McKeown, founding director of the CHESS family school, has found this book the best resource for designing an individualized program based upon a classical model. Evangelical readers can simply supplement or substitute the study of Catholic theology with their preferred material.

Charlotte Mason Approach

Charlotte Mason was a late nineteenth-century English educational reformer who established a network of very successful elementary schools. Her works have been reprinted and applied in varying degrees within the homeschool movement. The most popular principle of her reform is the use of "living books" (i.e., eschewing textbooks) and narration (the child orally retells the material in his or her own words to demonstrate understanding) as a form of instruction. First brought to public attention by Susan Schaeffer Macaulay in *For the Children's Sake*, the following titles outline a course of study for elementary grade levels:

> *Teaching Children: A Curriculum Guide to What Children Need to Know at Each Level Through Sixth Grade* by Diane Lopez was written by a longtime Christian school administrator. It is a fairly ambitious course of study and would be most helpful to those interested in following a rigorous curriculum.

> *A Charlotte Mason Companion* by Karen Andreola is a more laid-back approach than Lopez's. It emphasizes the use of "living books" in the curriculum but does favor a more hands-on approach.

Additional titles of interest here:

> *A Charlotte Mason Education,* Catherine Levinson

> *When Children Love to Learn: A Practical Application of Charlotte Mason's Philosophy For Today,* Elaine Cooper, editor

Other

Finally, I love the material developed by Kathryn Stout of Design-A-Study. Written specifically for homeschoolers, Kathryn's books include objectives, activities, and teaching strategies for K–8 in specific subject areas. Her most popular titles include:

> *Comprehensive Composition*

Guides to History Plus
Maximum Math
Natural Speller
Science Scope

Strategy #2: Weekly Planning

You aren't done yet. Planning is an ongoing discipline that allows you to maximize your time. Without it, you will waste time daily gathering resources, making decisions, and solving problems you didn't anticipate. Then you will feel frustrated and unsuccessful. Your children will sit around waiting for you to give direction, or more likely, they'll wander off. Carve two hours out of your schedule regularly to prepare for the coming school week.

Before my older children began managing their own time, I spent an afternoon every week at our local library working on our homeschool program. I used the time to anticipate problems and prepare for them, to gather books, and to script out my goals and schedule in my plan book.

Leaving the house was an essential part of being able to focus and get organized. And I deeply appreciated Kermit's commitment to seeing I had this time.

Remember: Time on task determines mastery of a skill or subject area. Plan so that your children can use their time wisely.

> **PLANNING IS AN ONGOING DISCIPLINE THAT ALLOWS YOU TO MAXIMIZE YOUR TIME.**

Your Schedule Will Be Uneven

When setting up your weekly schedule, don't shoot for even allotments of time across the board as they do in a traditional setting. This strategy does not help children achieve mastery in any area.

I look at the elementary years as one big chunk of time and the secondary years as another. Over the course of each, I had goals I intended to meet, but within the context of each school year our program had strengths and weaknesses. As we took time to focus on certain subject areas, I purposely neglected others. For example, we overdosed on American history for four years—we loved the field trips and the historical fiction that we could integrate into this subject area. Where was our program weaker as a result? Art and science. But then several classes in these areas were offered at CHESS and the Learning Center homeschool co-op. I seized the opportunity to focus there and neglected history in order to do so.

Some families do science first semester and history second. We found science once a week, with at least two or more hours devoted to experiments and study, worked well for us. As a rule of thumb: *Skill areas* are mastered through practice. Handwriting, spelling, mathematics, reading, etc., should be on your daily schedule. But *content areas* such as literature, history, and science, are better learned through fewer sessions in larger chunks of time. These also require more setup time on your part, so doing them once a week or for one semester is often better time management.

Plan for Toddlers

The best-laid plans of homeschool moms can quickly be blown to smithereens by our little ones who have no commitment to all those objectives we've so carefully crafted. Don't forget to anticipate your younger children's needs as you script out your weekly schedule. See chapter 30 for suggestions for occupying and integrating your toddlers into your plans for homeschooling older siblings.

Strategy #3: Establish Policies and Procedures

My best household management tips come from the business world, where profit is the bottom line and efficiency is key to maximum productivity. At home, at the office, and at the co-op, I am a manager, investing my time in developing organizational systems that allow everyone to know what his or her job is and how to do it without my constant oversight or direction. How does this translate into your home?

Make a Rut to Run In

Routines may get boring, but they still make things run smoothly. (If you can't take consistency, just cut a new rut periodically.)

What decisions do you currently make daily? Meals?

> ROUTINES MAY GET BORING, BUT THEY STILL MAKE THINGS RUN SMOOTHLY.

Chores? School assignments? Who sits where in the car? (Are we the only family with this squabble?) Plan these out at least a week at a time, if not by the month.

During the school year, kids should have a set bedtime and rising time. You should too. I began losing control of my day the minute we slept in. From there, maintain a loose routine for the day and week. Food was a pretty important motivator for my kids. I had minimum standards they had to reach before lunch and then before supper.

If I hadn't lost control by sleeping in, I surely did when I answered the phone.

Just Say No!

Remember the anti-drug slogan from a few years back? I used to have it hanging on my phone. Not because I was tempted to substance abuse but because I was tempted to say yes to anything anyone asked of me. My goals for the day would quickly go by the wayside as I let the phone calls control my day.

Get Voice Mail

I didn't have enough internal discipline to say no to people, so my first strategy was to stop answering the phone. I didn't have the discipline to resist this either, so I bought an answering machine. But I still went running to hear who might be calling and frequently picked up.

My kids made me realize how intrusive they found the phone one summer while discussing ways to improve our next school year. After that, I not only went to voice mail, but I also turned all the phones in the house off so I didn't even know when they rang. If someone wanted to reach me, they had to send a fax or e-mail.

I still don't answer the phone. My children don't either. From them, I've learned the efficiency of text messaging.

You probably have more self-control than all this, but minimally, controlling these kinds of intrusions will save you loads of time and prevent your day from slipping away from you with phone calls that turn into long conversations.

Strategy #4: Use Organizers

Pocket-Size

A personal organizer is an essential life-management tool. After reading Anne Ortlund's classic *Disciplines of the Beautiful Woman*, I purchased an inexpensive three-ring binder that was small enough to fit into my purse. I divided the notebook with tabs that categorized my life: meals, husband, children, house, prayer, Bible study, calendar, and a daily "to do" list. Over the years, the divisions have changed a lot. (Kermit still hasn't recovered from the fact that his tab has been replaced.) But the practice hasn't.

I've kept an organizer now for nearly thirty years. One homeschool student called it "my brain," and she is right. Without my organizer, I forget lots of commitments I've made and goals I've determined to reach. It's my peace of mind. Do intrusive thoughts often disrupt your concentration, usually during your quiet time? With my organizer beside me, I quickly jot them down and then forget them. Without it, I invest lots of time reminding myself over and over to remember not to forget to do whatever.

A few years ago, of course, the concept really caught on, and the market was flooded with trendy organizers for today's high-impact woman. My little black notebook looked pretty paltry next to them. I held a garage sale and squandered all the cash I earned on an updated deluxe model. But then I felt obligated to maintain all those sections—at least twenty of them. This became a major time commitment. Besides that, my new organizer was too big to fit in my purse. I kept forgetting to bring it with me. I started missing appointments because I was leaving "my brain" at home.

I finally sold my organizer at my next garage sale and purchased a little black notebook for $4.95 that fits in my purse. I'm functional again. (My grown children, of course, are carrying PDAs.)

The essential premise is this: Use an organizer (or techno-wonder) simple enough to take with you everywhere you go. Create a section for every area of life you currently need to manage. Include a monthly appointment calendar and a section for frequently used addresses. I've found an eighteen-month academic calendar is best for my needs.

Every morning I make a list of what I need to do that day

> **USE AN ORGANIZER SIMPLE ENOUGH TO TAKE WITH YOU EVERYWHERE YOU GO.**

and record it in my organizer. I prioritize this and check things off as they are completed. It takes no more than ten minutes because it is an ingrained habit. (I'm sure by the next edition of this book, all my organizational tools will be online. But for now, I still find I need the pleasure of physically crossing off my accomplishments.)

Central Calendar

Kermit and I were both good about maintaining our appointment books, but we started running into scheduling conflicts because we didn't know each other's commitments. Eventually, our four kids all had outside commitments of their own too. We kept a central calendar on the refrigerator, and everyone penciled in his or her appointments there as well.

This also helped my kids feel more in control of their lives. I'm a great one for planning things and not telling anyone else. As soon as I put up the new monthly calendar, my children hurried to see what was coming up and then transferred that information to their own daily organizers.

If your kids are old enough to be online safely, then you can accomplish this same goal by using Google's calendar or Cozi Central (www.cozi.com), which I like because everyone can add to a central shopping list as well. Both are free.

Teacher's Plan Book

A teacher's plan book is the only other organizational tool I use regularly. Quite a few that are designed for homeschooling are on the market, but my favorite is *The Homeschool Journal*, published by FERG N US Services. It's the simplest, that's why, and the most easily adapted to different families' needs. FERG N US also has a plan book for high school students, and my kids used this to record their assignments and weekly goals once they reached junior high.

For those of you who prefer to keep everything online where you know it is less likely to be misplaced, take a look at Homeschool Tracker and Edu-Track Home School as solutions. Also, Google Docs is fast becoming the place to store records safely on the Web at no cost.

Here are some other sources of good tips on organization and planning:

Confessions of a Happily Organized Family (contains a great chapter on "How to Organize Another Person!"), Deniece Schofield

Help for the Harried Homeschooler: A Practical Guide to Balancing Your Child's Education with the Rest of Your Life, Christine Field

Homeschooling at the Speed of Life: Balancing Home, School, and Family in the Real World, Marilyn Rockett

Is There Life After Housework? and other titles, Don Aslett

Once a Month Cooking (revised and expanded), Mimi Wilson and Mary Lagerborg

The website www.donnayoung.org is a stop not to miss. Donna has blogged her way through her homeschooling adventure, providing free of charge all kinds of organizational helps and lesson plans for you to download and use as your own.

Marla Cilley, author of *Sink Reflections*, is the "Fly Lady" (www.flylady.net). Her guide to getting your home and life organized starts with shining your sink. Sign up online to receive a daily e-mail that walks you through a fifteen-minute program for de-cluttering and cleaning your house. At the end of twenty-eight days, your home will be cleaned and your routines for maintaining this state established.

And this is as good a place as any to direct your attention to Susan Schaeffer Macaulay's book *For the Family's Sake: The Value of Home in Everyone's Life.* It isn't a manual of home-management tips, but a wonderful philosophical basis for creating a warm, nurturing, restful home through balance and routines.

PART 4
PREVENTING BURNOUT

IN THIS SECTION

CHAPTER 15
Burnout Buster #1:
Raise an Independent Learner

When it comes to the difference between surviving or thriving in homeschooling, raising an independent learner is the key. It's also in your child's best interest. Kids learn best when they take responsibility for their learning.

Lessons from a Toddler

Think back to your children's early years. They were remarkably independent little learners, weren't they? They spent the entire day exploring and investigating on their own—especially what you didn't want them to! They didn't need you to motivate them or organize their exploration.

School Days

But look what happens when these highly motivated, independent learners are packed off to school at age five. We make them *dependent* upon the teacher for their learning. Now she decides what will be taught, what projects will be tackled, and what schedule will be followed.

By junior high, many of these energetic grade school children have little motivation to initiate learning on their own, and the teachers have little discretion in selecting a curriculum that fits the needs and interests of each student.

Don't Repeat the Pattern

Unfortunately, we often repeat this same pattern in our home education programs. We wish our children would take more responsibility for their own learning, especially as they grow older. But we take our five-year-old independent learner and turn him into a dependent learner by following traditional teaching methods (refer back to the chart on page 87). And then we wish he would mysteriously turn back into a self-motivated student once again.

The solution? Don't make him a dependent learner in the first place. Here's how:

> KIDS LEARN BEST WHEN THEY TAKE RESPONSIBILITY FOR THEIR LEARNING.

#1. Give Him Control

When the twins were nine and Kayte was seven, I took steps to transfer responsibility for their learning from me to them. As is typical of my temperament, I make radical right turns in life, for which minor adjustments are then needed. The week I undertook to transfer this responsibility, I neglected to mention my plans to Kermit.

How Not to Start Out on the Right Foot

I met with each of my school-age kids separately for a Monday morning tutorial. Here I gave them a daily log in which they were to record the goals in each subject I wanted them to complete that week. It was up to them to manage their time as they chose.

I was surprised and offended when Mike asked, "What happens if we don't get done?"

Having not given any thought to this possibility, I hadn't considered any consequences. So I said the first thing that came to mind, "Well, you won't eat on Friday night till you are done."

"You can't do that," he replied. And the line was drawn in the sand.

Gabe and Kayte liked this new idea, and they went happily along with it. But come Friday night, Mike had three long lessons of Saxon Math uncompleted. I told him he could not have supper. Unfortunately, I was in the laundry room when Kermit arrived home from work, so Mike beat me to the door. Here he informed his father that I was forbidding him to have dinner just because he hadn't completed all his math that day. I heard Kermit say, "We'll see about this."

Hearing the tone in his voice, I knew I needed to talk fast. I asked Kermit to meet me in the bedroom for a private consultation and said, "Honey, I know I didn't tell you about this new plan I was using in school and I should have, and I should have thought through the consequences more objectively, but I need to win this one! If you don't back me, not only will Mike not think he has to get his schoolwork done, but everyone else will start revolting as well."

After reminding me (once again) to talk these major shifts

in policy over with him ahead of time, he went downstairs and informed Mike he could not have dinner till the Saxon was done.

Mike is my most emotionally controlled child, or rather I thought he was. We just hadn't pushed the right button before. Apparently food is pretty high up on his list of basic needs. This kid sat in the family room trying to do all this math, wailing, while the rest of us tried to have a family dinner. Have you ever had one of those dinners at your house? Pretty soon I could see Kayte's lower lip start to tremble, then Gabe's, and suddenly they were both sniveling in sympathy.

I was so relieved when Mike got his work done two hours later. I didn't even care if it was right; I made him a nice hot meal.

But you know what? Come Monday morning Mike was the first one up and at work on his weekly assignments. And I've never had anyone not complete his or her goals since (with the exception of Kristen, whom we will talk about later, in the reluctant learner chapter).

I learned some other interesting things about my kids when we started this plan. They all chose to manage their time differently. Mike, probably because of this childhood trauma inflicted by his mother, would get up early and complete his assignments as quickly as possible with a goal to have Fridays free. Kayte liked to do one subject a day—a week's worth of math on Monday, a week's worth of spelling the next, a week's worth of handwriting the next, and so forth. I found this amusing, but it was her time and I wanted her to have control. Gabe, like his mother, works best under pressure. He ran a pretty light schedule on Mondays and Tuesdays. By Wednesday he'd show some signs of life, and Thursdays and Fridays were heavy-duty workdays with lots of accompanying groans—especially since Mike was in the backyard kicking the football.

How It Evolved

The next thing I did was give Mike, Gabe, and Kayte control of the curriculum. They began to determine what their weekly goals would be. At first I thought they might lower the standards and begin to underachieve. But actually, once they were in control of not only their time but also what they studied, they accomplished *more* than I would have expected.

I did have parameters. This was not a free-for-all. I required each of them always to be reading something, writing something, and researching something. They had to meet the requirements of the Pennsylvania law and show progress in every subject area; they couldn't just cut geography from the schedule. We did still meet regularly for reading aloud or group projects and activities I had arranged. And I worked at building a vision in them for future opportunities, so they saw the value of studying subjects that merely required discipline. (*"You want to grow up and play football for Penn State, don't you? You can't get in without at least two years of a foreign language." "Okay, Mom, you win; we'll sign up for French."*)

Joining the CHESS family school changed the complexion of our schedule once again. They then received assignments from their teachers and had to give up a measure of control in their lives, which they didn't necessarily like. The first year I made the mistake of signing them up for the courses I didn't want responsibility for at home. Because they never had any input into this decision, they complained a lot throughout the year about their classes. The next year, I let them make all the choices. Mike and Gabe weren't entirely satisfied with their classes, so we talked about how they might want to choose differently next time. As much as possible, I wanted them to feel in control. I wanted them to see that it was their responsibility to learn, not my responsibility to teach. I wanted them to set their own future targets and then take responsibility for hitting them.

By the time they reached high school, all four of my children were ready to take full responsibility for managing their time and assignments. I helped them when they asked. I held them accountable where they needed it, but they typically self-checked and corrected their tests. I could trust them to do so, because they weren't doing the work to please me; they were doing it because they saw their work as relevant to the goals they had set for themselves. They had ownership in the process.

This strategy was also God's provision for me. He knew the future. During the elementary and junior high years, Kristen needed a lot of one-on-one time from me. If my older kids had likewise still been dependent, I would have been overwhelmed with the responsibility. It's crucial that those of us with a passel of kids focus more on equipping them to learn independently of us than on teaching them what they need to know—that is, if we want to survive long-term in homeschooling.

#2. Give Them Choices

Allow your children to initiate projects and writings of their own choosing. We all have more motivation when it is our baby. Instead of relying on the assignments in your curriculum or topics in the composition book, give your children the guidelines and tools necessary, but let them choose what to make or write. Then you assist them in accomplishing their goals.

WE ALL HAVE MORE MOTIVATION WHEN IT IS OUR BABY.

My ears perked up when one of my kids said, "Mom, you know what I'm really curious about?" My next stop was the library to get a book or find a DVD to view. I wanted my kids to see that their participation really mattered and that one reason we were home educating was so they could have a tailor-made education.

If your child is engaged in an intellectually stimulating activity such as staging a play, writing a letter, or building an invention, don't interrupt him for "school." Rather, use his expressed interest as a springboard for skills he needs to practice: Integrate handwriting with his letter writing or arithmetic with purchasing the materials for his invention. You don't want to stifle this independence; you will regret it later.

Let your children choose the books they read. If they get stuck in a genre, nudge them forward by requiring them to choose from a different category, such as Newbery Award winners or historical fiction. Be as broad in your requirements as you possibly can. Yes, require a science fair project, but let your child choose the area of interest. Allow your teens to participate in curriculum choices and courses of study. They should go to the conventions with you, attend workshops, and talk to vendors. If you give them choices, this will fuel their motivation.

#3. Wait Till They Are Ready

Do not start a subject of study or project until the child is ready to do the majority of the work. I've prematurely launched too many ventures that dissolved into my kids watching me paint the mural, organize the play, or make the recipe because I was too anxious and they weren't ready.

Kristen took an elementary French class at CHESS in third grade, and there was a lot of written work to complete. As one of the youngest members of the class, she just couldn't keep up. At first I let her dictate her answers to me, but as the work became more challenging even that didn't work. The day I found myself filling out her homework assignment while she was off playing somewhere else, I knew something was out of kilter. Kristen said she didn't want to drop the class because it was "cool" (the teacher used a lot of French songs and audiotapes that Kristen enjoyed). She just wasn't ready for the amount of homework. Assured that she still had a strong interest here, I arranged with her teacher for Kristen to "audit" the class. We saved the written work for another year.

#4. Let Them Do It

Before you do anything for your child, ask yourself, "Could she do this herself?" If so, let her. For example, in states like ours, parents must present a portfolio of their child's work at the end of the year for review. I know homeschool moms who spend days, even weeks, pulling these together. The kids should have responsibility for doing this. I've also seen moms, myself included, spend two hours making up a chapter test that takes a kid fifteen minutes to complete. When you see that kind of imbalance of time, you know you are creating a dependent learner. This is why I favor essay tests. It takes me fifteen minutes to design one; it takes the students forty minutes to an hour to complete it. The responsibility for demonstrating learning should be on the student, not the teacher.

> **THE RESPONSIBILITY FOR DEMONSTRATING LEARNING SHOULD BE ON THE STUDENT, NOT THE TEACHER.**

I taught *The Hawk That Dare Not Hunt by Day* by Scott O'Dell a few years back to a literature group at the Learning Center homeschool co-op. This is a wonderful novel based upon the life of William Tyndale. When I began preparing for the class, I realized there were a lot of historical references in the book that I knew nothing about—Sir Thomas More, the Holy Roman Empire, Charles V, and the black plague. I had never studied this period of English history, and I doubted most of the students had either. I realized we would need some background information before we could begin.

I was actually at the library, a pile of world history atlases spread before me, when I realized I was going about this all wrong. It was going to take me hours to prepare a forty-minute lecture on the historical backdrop for the novel. I put away the books, went home, created a list of all the historical references in the book, and passed out the list to the kids the first day of class. I told them we needed some background information before we could begin and I wanted each of them to choose a topic, research it, and report back to the class next time so we might better understand the storyline.

It went great. The kids got an education, and so did I, but with a lot shorter time commitment from me.

At the Learning Center, the kids write, cast, and direct our spring program. They run the lights, and they design and print the program. The moms comprise the stage crew. Our productions are not at all as polished as some of the teacher-run performances I've been in. But in which scenario do kids learn the most? You should see how thrilled the students are to have more than a hundred people attend an evening performance of a play they have written and produced. And while not polished, the opportunity motivates the kids to create the very best production they can.

#5. Focus on the Skills for Independent Learning

Most moms I talk to with a serious case of burnout are running a very demanding program and are burdened by the fear they will skip something.

Aghhh! I've Skipped Something!

Let's address this universal fear right now. You are going to skip something. Further, it will probably be something *really important.* We're in the midst of an information explosion. Much of what we learn today will be irrelevant tomorrow. How will you figure out what will be applicable? You won't. Here's the solution:

Instead of wasting one sleepless moment worrying about "skipping something," all you have to do is teach your child

> INSTEAD OF WASTING ONE SLEEPLESS MOMENT WORRYING ABOUT "SKIPPING SOMETHING," ALL YOU HAVE TO DO IS TEACH YOUR CHILD HOW TO LEARN.

how to learn. Just focus on that, and when your kid *inevitably* finds himself in a situation where he doesn't know how to do something, he is not rendered immobile . . . stunted for life . . . no longer employable . . . ultimately a panhandler on the corner . . . a sign around his neck begging "Please feed me. My mother homeschooled me." Your worst fear realized.

Reality Check

Wait a minute! Get a grip. You forget—your child has the skills of an independent learner! He heads right down to the local public library or jumps on the Internet, does a computer search, requests some books, and figures it out for himself, thus averting the major disaster in his life that you had envisioned.

How do you cultivate these skills? By building a program that allows plenty of opportunity for research that culminates in a paper or project that reflects what your child has discovered. Your job is to provide him with the tools necessary to complete his investigation: technology, books, trips to the library, time spent with an expert, etc., and then aid him in his investigation.

I often told my kids, "It's your job to learn, not my job to teach." I am a facilitator, a mentor, a fellow lifelong learner, a guidance counselor, a coach, and only occasionally the teacher.

That Base of Knowledge Is Fluid

Our knowledge base is rapidly changing anyway. *Peak Learning* by Ronald Gross points out that the average half-life for the information acquired in medical school (that is, the point at which 50 percent of the knowledge is outdated) is fifteen years. Do you want to choose a physician sixteen years past graduation who doesn't have the skills or motivation to learn independently?

It's the same with our children. To compete in the twenty-first century they need the skills of a lifelong learner. That's at the core of my husband's job. Most of his time is spent just trying to keep up with the latest technology so his company can stay current. He has frequently commented that it isn't that there aren't good jobs available; it's that there aren't any qualified applicants. His company is looking for folks who know how to learn.

> TO COMPETE IN THE TWENTY-FIRST CENTURY THEY NEED THE SKILLS OF A LIFELONG LEARNER.

Research Skills

Teach your child to use the library. You can foster this by skipping the workbooks and assigning lots of research papers and research projects. This will give your kids a meaningful reason for familiarizing themselves with the atlases, indices, periodicals, and other reference tools there.

Teach your child to use the Internet. We'll talk specifically about this in chapter 28, but don't let your children leave school without equipping them to retrieve and sort information quickly here as well.

Find an Expert

Reading isn't the only way a lifelong learner acquires knowledge. He is also a people person who seizes the opportunity to draw upon the expertise and experience of the people he meets. My husband's the one who models this for our family. He has met the most fascinating folks on airplanes, in shopping malls, and at the beach just because he never hesitates to strike up a conversation. This is a very simple but effective method for gaining a firsthand education. I've read about China and Australia, but none of the books gave me the same perspective as the information Kermit gleaned from a young Chinese immigrant and an Australian businessman he sat next to on a plane.

We attended a Civil War re-enactment at Gettysburg one summer. The battle was impressive, but our real education came from walking through the grounds and talking to the men and women encamped there. They put a human face to all the facts we had read about.

Along with your children, track down the resource people in your community with interesting hobbies or knowledge. Invite them to share with your group, or visit them as a family. At least for our children, I've noted how much they remember from the conversations we've had with the interesting people we have met.

Study Skills

When working with your child one-on-one, show him how to tutor himself. In helping Gabe get a grip on his algebra, I focused on explaining to him how I *prepared* to tutor him each day:

- I read the unit summary at the end so I knew what the big picture was for every chapter.

- I referenced unfamiliar terms in the index so I could understand each sentence.

- I replaced the variables with real numbers and worked several samples so I understood the equation.

- If I didn't understand how they got the solution in the text, I didn't assume it was a misprint (his strategy); I looked at the part of the equation I didn't get and asked myself, *Now, where did they get that "4" from?* I looked back over each step, working backward till I saw where the sign changed from negative to positive, breaking it apart until I could see the solution.

These are study habits researchers have found successful students use. Your kids can find more study skill tips in these books:

The Everything Study Book, Steven Frank

What Smart Students Know, Adam Robinson

#6. Take Time for Questions

In Howard and Susan Richman's book, *The Three R's at Home* (Pennsylvania Homeschoolers), Howard cites research that found that 96 percent of the questions generated in a classroom are asked by the teacher. Another study showed that teachers, on average, wait three seconds for a student response to a question. Is it a surprise, then, that another study found children typically stop asking questions in school by age seven? Compare that with the kinds of questions your four-year-old fires off to you all day, every day.

If we want our kids to take responsibility for their education and to stay actively engaged in the learning process, then we must value and solicit their questions.

If you don't know the answer, show them their questions are important by writing them down and then researching the answer together the next time you are at the library. Before you take a field trip, ask your children to have questions in mind to ask of the tour guide. Consciously model this strategy for them by asking questions yourself.

#7. Use Discovery Learning

Every professional educator worth his or her salt will tell you that discovery learning is the best way for children to learn. Unfortunately, the classroom teacher does not have the time to allow each child to discover underlying principles and solutions on his own. But homeschoolers do.

Let your child uncover the connections himself. Bite your tongue when you think the answer to a problem should be obvious. A thought-provoking question is a better strategy.

Quite a few years ago I bought a software program called the *Alpine Tram Ride* that requires deductive reasoning to solve problems. Given the choice of twenty-five different animals, the player must determine which animals in which order are hidden behind the four tram doors. After the boys had gone to bed one night, I loaded the game and started playing it myself. Within a few minutes, I was able to strategically eliminate enough of the choices to solve the puzzle. So the next day I loaded the game for Mike and Gabe, and they began to play. Standing behind them, I felt my frustration begin to build as time after time they continued to randomly choose. I was just about ready to jump in and show them how to figure this game out when I thought, *Wait a minute, Deb. You paid good money for this program to teach them just that. Let them figure it out!* But I found it excruciating to watch. I had to leave the room and close the door behind me in order to restrain myself.

By the end of the week, my sons were calling me to come into the computer room: "Hey, Mom, let us show you how to play this game. See, we know it isn't the giraffe in this car; then it must be the lion in number three and . . . Here, you try and we'll help you figure it out."

They were so proud of themselves for discovering the underlying strategies on their own. I still remember the expressions on their faces. And I almost shortchanged them. I almost missed an excellent opportunity to build confidence in their ability to learn.

EVERY PROFESSIONAL EDUCATOR WORTH HIS OR HER SALT WILL TELL YOU THAT DISCOVERY LEARNING IS THE BEST WAY FOR CHILDREN TO LEARN.

When we give kids the time they need to figure things out, they take ownership in their learning. They feel successful and confident, and are motivated to learn more.

Cultivate Confidence

In life, we invest time where we feel successful. We minimize our time in the areas where we don't. That's why your children's view of themselves as learners must be carefully cultivated. Give your children the time they need. Don't make them feel they are not figuring things out quickly enough. Make a big to-do about the special moments of discovery they have made on their own. You can then build upon this confidence in other areas that are more difficult for them to grasp.

#8. Let the Child Teach

In any given learning situation, it is the teacher who learns the most. Think about it: We homeschooling parents know more about the Civil War, parts of speech, and converting decimals to fractions than we ever did in school because we've had to explain them to our kids. So turn the tables and let your child do the teaching.

> IN ANY GIVEN LEARNING SITUATION, IT IS THE TEACHER WHO LEARNS THE MOST.

Managing a Passel of Kids

How do you teach multiples? Give your older kids some of the responsibility for teaching the younger ones. Kayte helped Kristen learn to read. When Kayte competed in Math Olympiad, Mike (the previous winner) showed her how to solve the problems. A teen in our group taught a chess class at the Learning Center. A friend's seventh-grade daughter taught health one year to her elementary-age brothers. The speeches and reports I assign for my kids and co-op students are for the purpose of educating the whole group, not for earning a grade from the teacher in the back of the room.

This is how moms who know nothing about a subject guide their children through a course of study in that area. The kids do the research, and Mom gets an education along with everyone else in the family. My kids were thrilled when they knew something I didn't know (and this began occurring many moons ago). They enjoyed telling me about their independent studies. My job was to be an interested audience.

#9. Model Independent Learning Yourself

Remember, *"a student is not above his teacher"* (Matthew 10:24, NIV). We need to model what we want our children to become. Our own attitude toward learning is the key influence on our children's view of education. If our children see us reading, investigating, and discussing new areas of inquiry as adults, they will come to value lifelong learning too.

I credit my parents with transferring a love for learning to me. I grew up in a home where everyone was always reading (and where everyone always had an opinion as well!) When I stayed with my grandmother every summer, she was always reading—well into the middle of the night at times. When I caught the glow of a flashlight under blankets at night, I was thrilled my kids couldn't stand to put down that book. When Gabe told me he couldn't wait for football practice to be over so he could finish *Blood of Heaven* (1996), a terrific read by our friend Bill Myers, I knew his priorities in life were still in place—and our family tradition had been passed on.

This chart is an oversimplification of our program, but it is representative of the skeleton upon which our daily activities hang.

> OUR OWN ATTITUDE TOWARD LEARNING IS THE KEY INFLUENCE ON OUR CHILDREN'S VIEW OF EDUCATION.

Academic Achievement

Necessary Skills	Key Activities	Success Demonstrated by
Research	Writing	Papers
Communication	Reading	Projects
Technical	Research	Performances

CHAPTER 16
Burnout Buster #2: Raise Responsible Kids

I believe in moms at home, but not so everyone else can leave their dirty laundry on the floor, dishes in the sink, or projects on the table. We are there to train our children into responsible adults, not to burn out prematurely trying to homeschool and keep the house clean simultaneously. We must learn to do what any good manager does: delegate.

The Fine Art of Delegation

Quite a few years ago our church showed a parenting video with Benny and Sheree Phillips (authors of *Raising Kids Who Hunger for God*). They are really the ones who inspired me to pass on household duties to my kids at an early age. They did an excellent job of laying out a step-by-step procedure for *gradually* transferring responsibilities onto the children. However, all I saw were eight-year-olds *and younger* who could do laundry, vacuum, clean bathrooms, and make simple meals. I thought, *Hot diggity-dog, the Allied troops have landed! It's liberation day at my house!*

Mike and Gabe were five, Kayte was three, and Kristen was just out of the oven. But I ran home, skipped all the procedures, and announced, "Effective immediately, household chores have been transferred to my subordinates! All right, troops, fall out!"

The boys immediately pushed a kitchen chair up to the washer and set the dials while perched on top of the machine. They were learning estimating skills in mathematics, so they practiced this with the laundry detergent, erring heavily on the more-than-enough side. I didn't know it at the time because I was upstairs hooking up the vacuum cleaner for Kayte, who was trying hard not to cry. A week later, with all the whites now tinted pink, the vacuum clogged, and dirty dishes stacked in the cupboard, I reviewed my notes. Seems I had skipped basic training.

Here's the sequence of events to walk your children through in every area as you transfer responsibility for a chore, duty, or school assignment:

1. You show him how to do it.

2. You do it with him.

3. You watch him do it.

4. He does it alone.

5. He decides when it needs to be done.

Depending upon the degree of complexity involved, this procedure can take anywhere from one to six weeks, or more. Kermit began training Mike and Gabe to mow the lawn when they were nine. By age ten, they were skilled enough to do it alone, but he still required that he be home while they were mowing. By age twelve, this was no longer necessary. They not only had taken full responsibility for maintaining the yard, but neighbors, who had watched them work, hired them as well.

I've shared this model with quite a few moms who just didn't feel they had the time to train their children completely. It was easier to keep doing it themselves or to transfer responsibility quickly and then get frustrated when things were not done well. I know sticking to this training model is a time commitment, but you will reap a terrific reward down the line. My kids are all self-reliant now, and they were before high school. They had full responsibility for their rooms, bath, and laundry by age fourteen. During their teen years, there were household duties I never had to think about because my children had full responsibility for them. In college, they were among the few who seemed to know how to cook, clean, change the oil, and sort their laundry (not to mention go to class and complete their assignments). They're not special; they've just been trained!

We perpetuate our children's immaturity by continuing to take on tasks that should be their responsibility. If they are old enough to get their toys out of the toy box, they are old enough to put them back in. If they are old enough to sleep in a bed, they are old enough to pull up their covers neatly when they get out. If they are old enough to get food out of the refrigerator, they are old enough to clean up the table and put everything away.

You can facilitate this by simplifying your maintenance. That's why I bought lots of sealable plastic tubs and labeled them. Everything had an assigned place. At one point I even had my pantry alphabetized (I'm not quite so compulsive anymore).

Invest time in determining the simplest procedure for completing a task, and then train your kids in that. (I've been a changed woman since we listened to *Cheaper by the Dozen* on audiotape—listen yourself and find out why.)

It Builds Their Esteem

The Phillipses were so right when they said giving our kids responsibility would increase their self-confidence and make them feel like members of the team. Sure, I met with resistance at first because we had not had this philosophy in place from the beginning. We had to retrain attitudes and sometimes apply biblical discipline. But I've found, not only in my own children but across the board with all the kids I've taught, that when they know you are not backing down and are committed to consistency, they will comply and even reach the point where they are obedient from the heart.

What About Compensation?

Well, yes, the pay helps, too.

We've never been convinced of the merits of an allowance. So kids learn to manage money. But money they haven't earned? To me, that isn't a practical preparation for real life.

We did pay our children wages, though. When they were younger, this was often not money. I had a compensation package in place that involved complicated charts, stickers, and graduated prizes—sort of an Amway-type model. "Clean this bathroom and win a trip to your vacation dreamland—Dairy Queen!" It became a lot simpler once they understood the value of cash. Some chores had a set payment no matter who completed them, but my teens typically got an hourly wage because they did so much around the house, including meal preparation, babysitting, laundry, major cleaning, and yardwork. This was a lot simpler to keep track of. Mike, Gabe, and Kayte also received an hourly wage for working regularly at the Home School Resource Center.

And they learned to manage their money. We expected our kids to help pay for clothing, shoes, sports equipment, and other non-essential items. Our biggest area of emphasis was their

> **INVEST TIME IN DETERMINING THE SIMPLEST PROCEDURE FOR COMPLETING A TASK, AND THEN TRAIN YOUR KIDS IN THAT.**

savings account. And as a result of a stock market class they took at our co-op in fifth grade, Mike and Gabe started investing their earnings. They were better money managers at fifteen than I was at twenty-five. (I'm sure Kermit would edit that last sentence to say than I am now.)

Raising them to be responsible has been a key factor in preventing my burnout, but it's really for a greater reason than that. Raising them to be responsible is in their best interest. Having this character strength in an age of irresponsibility will make them successful in family life and the future job market.

Here are some other good resources for instilling responsibility in your children:

> **RAISING THEM TO BE RESPONSIBLE IS IN THEIR BEST INTEREST.**

Choreganizers, Jennifer Steward. An excellent tool for assigning chores to your non-reading children.

Life Skills for Kids: Equipping Your Child for the Real World, Christine Field. A superb resource from an attorney-turned-homeschool mom. Chapters include people skills, homemaking and maintenance skills, life navigation skills, time organization, space organization, money skills, nutrition, and much more.

Managers of Their Chores: A Practical Guide to Children's Chores, Steve and Teri Maxwell. This book also includes a chore kit for up to four children.

Our 24 Family Ways, Clay Clarkson

Raising Self-Reliant Children in a Self-Indulgent World, H. Stephen Glenn and Jane Nelson

Raising Unselfish Children in a Self-Absorbed World, Jill Rigby

CHAPTER 17
Burnout Buster #3:
Fantastic Field Trips

My kids got grumpy when our homeschool life got too routine and too bookish. Their bad attitudes generally resulted in my discouragement. I didn't like investing so much time and receiving nothing but complaints in return.

A quick home remedy for this is to do something fun. For us that meant either reading a book aloud together or taking a field trip someplace new. Both of these remedies reinvigorated me because I wanted to do the things that make homeschooling unique—the flexibility, the hands-on learning, the firsthand experiences all motivated me. Re-creating an environment that can just as easily be produced in a traditional classroom does nothing for my sense of achievement. It feels like wasted time.

Fantastic Field Trips

Many of our best moments in homeschooling came during the field trips we took. The awe and enthusiasm on my kids' faces was a real burnout remedy for me.

But there's a right way and a wrong way to do this field trip thing. I've had quite a few that were so ill-planned and harried I collapsed in sheer exhaustion once I got back home. Here's a hassle-free guide to field trips that teach and refresh:

#1. Make Them an Extension of Subjects You've Already Studied at Home

The more background knowledge kids bring to the experience, the more they will get out of the trip, and vice versa. The more field trips you take, the more your kids will get out of their studies at home.

Prior to our visit to Williamsburg, Virginia, some years ago, we read books on Colonial life, Patrick Henry, and the Revolutionary War events that occurred there. We also checked out a video of the site from the library. Without this, my children would have been quickly bored by the endless tour of houses. Instead, the

> **THE MORE FIELD TRIPS YOU TAKE, THE MORE YOUR KIDS WILL GET OUT OF THEIR STUDIES AT HOME.**

kids excitedly ran toward the places they recognized and asked detailed questions of our tour guides. Mike impressed the senior citizens in our group (who had at first questioned why he wasn't in school) by being the only one to correctly identify for our guide the House of Burgesses and its purpose. "He's homeschooled," I whispered loudly.

I've found that site staff members will go out of their way for kids who show any degree of interest and understanding. I took my children and several of their friends to visit a National Oceanic and Atmospheric Administration weather station after a unit of study. The meteorologists were surprised by the degree of background knowledge the kids had and waxed quite eloquent once they realized they had an engaged audience. They even entrusted the kids with some of the high-tech instruments— something they emphatically said they never did. When our co-op went sailing on the Chesapeake Bay through the Living Classroom Foundation, the crew kept us out an hour longer at no charge, just because the kids were asking such intelligent questions and the crew was having a ball with them.

#2. Bring Closure

Wrap up the trip with more reading and a family discussion. Ask your children what they enjoyed most, what was not as they had expected, and what they would like to know more about, etc., just to ensure that you wring all the learning potential possible out of the trip. (By golly, if we're going to spend the money, I'm going to make sure they never forget a thing!)

#3. Call Ahead and Ask for a Guide

My father originally taught history. Growing up I saw lots of monuments, museums, and historic sites that glazed my eyes over. After I married Kermit, I found out too late he was a history buff as well. Once again I found myself staring solemnly at battlefields and monuments, wondering how anyone found this interesting. Then another couple invited us to visit Gettysburg with a retired tour guide. I reluctantly tagged along.

We spent hours staring solemnly once again at battlefields and monuments, but this time I couldn't tear myself away. What a difference a guide makes! I was fascinated as this elderly

209

gentleman recounted story after story of the human drama that occurred there. I even bought a stack of books so I could read more. Since then, I've loved going to Gettysburg. And I also arrange for a guide when possible for any field trip.

#4. Go in the Off-Season

Visiting attractions during the off-season may mean reduced staffing or fewer artisans and interpreters at historic sites, but it still gives your kids greater access to the displays. We typically found that the guides and curators spent a lot more time talking with us when the site wasn't busy.

I would call ahead to find out the best time to come, always asking if any school groups were scheduled for the same time. Quite a few trips turned into useless ventures when a busload of poorly supervised schoolchildren, thrilled to be released from confinement, came tearing through the place. (And while we are on it, the benefit these kids get from racing through a hands-on museum pushing every button and pulling every lever is minimal. This didn't make me a candidate for Mom of the Year with my children, but I required them to read the display before touching anything.)

We found September to be a good time to find the site at full staff but the number of school groups and summer tourists greatly reduced. You'll often find reduced-rate days during the fall lull. We visited the Carnegie Science Center in Pittsburgh (one of the top hands-on science museums in the United States) on a Monday in September for half price and were among a handful of visitors in the building. My kids spent hours at their favorite areas with no pressure from anyone to hurry up and move on.

#5. Keep the Tour Group Small

Field trips are a fun thing to do with one other family, but beyond that you start losing educational value. First, you have the administrative hassle. Once we planned to spend the day in our state capitol with friends, and we got separated at the beginning in a crowded parking garage. More time was spent riding up and down the elevators looking for each other while trying to keep the kids corralled than we spent at the sites.

If I wanted to further embarrass myself, I could tell you

about the twenty-family field trip I tried to execute with everyone following me sixty miles to a rural site I had never been to before. (Did I mention that I lack a sense of direction?) Have you ever tried to have twelve vans—the vehicle of choice for homeschoolers— turn around on a farm lane? (By the end of the day we were getting pretty good at that maneuver.) I also learned some physics from an irritated mom. If the lead van goes the speed limit (or perhaps just a tad over the speed limit), everyone following must drive progressively faster. This mom, who was last, was going eighty miles per hour. Isn't that interesting?

The point? Keep the group small. Besides the administrative hassle, too many kids distract each other and compete for time on the displays. When a site requires a minimum group size for a tour or class, I passed out maps to the families involved, then it was every van for himself. Otherwise we kept our field trips to eight kids or less.

#6. Make Sure It Is Age-Level Appropriate

I've taken my kids on one too many nature hikes or dragged them prematurely to sites that presented material too abstract or technical for their understanding. We visited the Corning Glass Center in Corning, New York, for our very first day of kindergarten back in 1988. I was enthralled by the research going on there in fiber optics and loved the antique glass collection, but my kids had more fun at the McDonald's playland at lunch. It's still one of my favorite sites ever, but the learning potential was lost on my children, who were not old enough to understand the technology discussed nor to appreciate the artistry involved in spinning glass.

#7. Keep It Short

Most kids max out after two hours, even in a visually stimulating environment. If you've paid a hefty admission price, it's easy to assume you'll be there dawn to dusk to get your money's worth, but most kids just can't focus that long— especially without food.

One strategy for museums and sites within driving range is to purchase an annual membership and then visit the site several times during the year, each time focusing on a new aspect. I

> MOST KIDS MAX OUT AFTER TWO HOURS, EVEN IN A VISUALLY STIMULATING ENVIRONMENT.

headed back to all the science museums and battlefields we had visited years ago because Kristen just wasn't old enough to benefit. And my older children were then ready to think through these experiences on a higher level as well.

#8. Give Guidance

A tour guide is not always possible, but you can provide this service with just a bit of preparation beforehand. I learned this from Kermit, a devoted reader of AAA travel guides. He always has interesting tidbits of information to pass along as we travel through cities.

You can extend your children's attention span by doing some reading beforehand and then giving direction to their learning while at the site. Point out areas of interest and guide them through the displays.

> **YOU CAN EXTEND YOUR CHILDREN'S ATTENTION SPAN BY DOING SOME READING BEFOREHAND AND THEN GIVING DIRECTION TO THEIR LEARNING WHILE AT THE SITE.**

What Constitutes a Field Trip?

Any site can be turned into a "field experience" if you take the time to provide background knowledge, direct children's attention while at the site, and engage the staff in conversation. Help young children understand how their community works by visiting the fire department, city hall, the post office, and local businesses.

Visit engineering projects, medical centers, and research facilities to help your teens see abstractions in math and science concretely applied to life.

Wherever possible, I look for a way to give kids field experience. When possible, I spend time talking with site staff members about our co-op kids' background experiences and suggest what we most hope to get out of our trip. This bit of investment goes a long way to better tailor the visit to our group's needs and interests.

Bring the Field Trip to You

Sometimes it's easier to bring the field experience to your homeschool support group than to take the kids there. We've done this by inviting hobbyists and senior citizens with areas of interest and expertise to visit us. In many cases, these folks are delighted to be asked to share. My favorite was Pastor Holman, who was close to ninety when we met him. He was an amateur geologist, but all the science centers we visited couldn't compare with the samples he had collected from his missionary trips around the world. And he was very generous in allowing the children to handle his treasures.

Where to Find Field Trip Ideas

These resources can help you find fantastic field trip sites in your area:

A Guide to Great Field Trips, Kathleen Carroll

Open the Door, Let's Explore More!: Field Trips of Discovery for Young Children, Rhoda Redleaf

Travel magazines geared toward senior citizens have lots of interesting suggestions. Raid your parents' magazine rack, as I have. Also, you might want to check out Michele and George Zavatsky's website and resources at www.kidslovetravel.com.

AAA membership has been well worth the investment for our family. It offers lots of free maps and pamphlets we can study even if we don't go. And road service is indispensable for a mom alone on a trip with a carload of kids.

Your local library and tourism bureau will also have free information on area attractions and community resources.

Use the Internet to search for more ideas at the sites maintained by your local Chamber of Commerce, parks and recreation department, or your state or city.

CHAPTER 18
Burnout Buster #4: Share the Load

Homeschooling shouldn't mean you are your children's only teacher. It just means you get to control who their teachers are: virtual or real.

Self-Instructional Resources

Mix into each child's program some resources that can be used independently. GeoSafari, software, online courses, and DVDs are engaging and complete. If you need one-on-one instructional time with a child, have his or her siblings involved with a meaningful activity like these—not busywork.

Educational Television: An Oxymoron?

When my kids were younger, we even included one television show a day in their program. Some of the shows we followed included *Reading Rainbow, 3-2-1 Contact*, and *Square One*. (My good friend Joanna, who homeschools young children, tells me *Liberty Kids!* and *Cyberchase* are current PBS shows with educational value.) This gave me a welcomed mid-morning break. It's always best to watch television with your children, but I admit I often used this time to get lunch started or catch up on laundry.

You can also take a load off your shoulders by becoming a member of the class and watching documentaries together. Take notes and hold follow-up discussions. Being avid sports fans, our family enjoyed Ken Burns's documentary on baseball a few years ago. We extended the experience into a history unit with our follow-up reading and discussions. The girls, Kermit, and I also watched Burns's documentary *The West* and marveled at how history has changed since we were kids. (I think the cowboys and Indians stereotypes we were raised with *needed* some revision.)

One year I used the PBS show *Newton's Apple* several times a week for science. Checking these out on video from the library enabled us to stop the program when someone had a question or to re-watch certain parts to reinforce our understanding.

We lived without a television for several years at the beginning of our marriage. When we finally bought one we quite virtuously watched only PBS and Penn State football games—and then my kids reached high school. This can be viewed as an erosion of our values, depending upon which member of our marriage you talk to, but we now have (gasp!) cable. There is some excellent educational broadcasting available. Educational television can ease the burden, if you can restrain yourself from otherwise wasting time in front of the tube—which we do find to be an issue.

> **THERE IS SOME EXCELLENT EDUCATIONAL BROADCASTING AVAILABLE.**

You can extend the value of educational television by printing out program notes and teaching activities from the following sites:

A&E (www.aetv.com)
Biography (www.biography.com)
The Discovery Channel (dsc.discovery.com)
The History Channel (www.history.com)
The Learning Channel (tlc.discovery.com)
PBS (www.pbs.org)
Reading Rainbow (pbskids.org/readingrainbow)

Cooperative Activities

Pool your teaching talents with other homeschool families. In most regions of the country you'll find support groups already in place that offer enrichment classes, special activities, or field trips that are open to new families. If not, then start your own. (Remember, initiative is one of the successful homeschool ingredients.)

The Benefits to Kids

We have involved ourselves in a wide array of cooperative groups. My teaching style probably explains why we do more than our share. But I also believe strongly in the benefits of cooperative experiences. Your children will be challenged to grow in character and intellect as they interact with kids and adults who look at the material differently.

Besides that, becoming a team player is an important skill in the workplace and the church. Without this training, it is easy to produce selfish children who don't understand that God has given them gifts and talents to use for the mutual benefit of the body of Christ, not for their own glory or self-gratification. (This is one reason I am hot on organized sports—with the right coach, kids learn that pooling their strengths and talents together for a common goal often results in success, while every-man-for-himself attitudes and self-seeking glory invariably lead to defeat.)

One year we participated in the Science-by-Mail program (now disbanded). It was very worthwhile educationally. But the greatest area of growth came in my sons' character, not their knowledge. I had two groups of kids working to solve the science challenge simultaneously. My guys were in a group with three of their friends—all terrific kids with a lot of intelligence and leadership. That was the problem. They were all used to being in charge and had underdeveloped teamwork skills. While Kayte and her friends effortlessly organized themselves and set out to attack the science problem, I spent most of my time helping this group of guys come to a consensus opinion.

When all was said and done, though, I was glad that I had put my sons in a situation where these character issues could come to the surface and I could help them deal with them while they were still under our supervision.

The Benefits for Mom

But let's focus on the benefits for Mom: You get to take entire subjects off your plate and put them onto someone else's. Art, physical education, science, chorus, weaving, sign language, health, and many more subjects have all been taught to my kids by others with far more knowledge and passion for the subjects than I could ever muster.

You'll have adult conversation on a regular basis too. I loved all the online opportunities my kids were able to access, but it never replaced our cooperative learning. I needed the encouragement and stimulation that came from weekly interaction with other homeschooling families.

How to Organize Your Co-op for Success

Our homeschool co-op, the Learning Center, is now twenty

years old. It includes twenty-nine families and more than one hundred kids, including twenty-three teens. It meets twice a month on Fridays from nine a.m. to twelve-thirty p.m. During that time we run three class periods. The younger grades take an art, gym, and unit study class; the older students sign up for a number of electives at the beginning of each semester.

I've advised a number of co-op leaders over the years and have unfortunately seen several groups disband, always for similar reasons. Here are some essential ingredients that will position your co-op for long-term survival and prevent leadership burnout.

#1. Clear, Recognized Leadership

The Learning Center was originally comprised of four families at my church. As other church members began homeschooling, they were invited to join. For a few years the co-op was small enough to be run by consensus. With a growth in membership, though, we inevitably hit an issue on which we could not agree. In our case it was balancing the needs of older students against those of younger ones. For other groups it has been such things as contemporary Christian music, membership qualifications, or managing children.

The issues are often different, but the problem is the same: How do you decide what to do when a consensus cannot be reached? In our case, we asked our pastors for help. For a number of reasons, they elected to disband the Learning Center as a ministry of our church and turned the future of the co-op over to me, making it clear to all members that I was free to discontinue it completely or reinvent it as I willed.

After some prayerful consideration, I held a meeting in which I presented the direction and organization of the co-op and invited previous members to rejoin. Everyone did. It may have seemed a little silly on the surface, but it was a crucial foundation to put in place.

For ten years, I continued to lead the Learning Center. Several years into it I appointed two other women to serve on a leadership team with me. I realized I was often arbitrary in my decision making (my big clue: people were mad at me). Adding others with complementary gifts and talents formalized the process but resulted in more thoughtful and equitable decisions, which keeps members happier—or at least spreads the dissatisfaction around a bit more. And when I stepped down from leadership in 2003, this tradition continued on.

Input is solicited regularly from members through summer meetings and semester evaluation forms. Open discussions are held on important issues, and the leaders strive to reach a consensus among members wherever possible. When it is not reached, time is taken to explain thoroughly the rationale for the direction chosen.

#2. A Commonly Held Vision

Every prospective member of the Learning Center receives a membership packet that clearly defines the targets we are aiming to hit. By now, you know how important I think a personal vision is. I also believe a common vision is the essential ingredient that holds any organization together, be it the family, the church, a nonprofit ministry, or a homeschool support group. People who aren't working toward the same goal cannot labor together. We can be friends, we can fellowship, but we can't pool our talents and build something successfully.

This packet includes membership qualifications and responsibilities, our teaching philosophy, the types of classes we offer, and expected standards of children's behavior. When a family signs our membership contract, they should have a pretty good idea what they are getting involved with and be ready to contribute to that end.

#3. Shared Responsibility

From past experience, I knew I would burn out if I didn't delegate responsibilities among others. The Learning Center works because every mom is contributing her share to the pot. Moms teach or help two out of the three scheduled classes. Exceptions are granted for extenuating circumstances—a new baby, for instance—but we try to keep these to a minimum. There are other duties, too, that are divvied up as evenly as possible. We have an administrator who doesn't help with any classes at all but contributes more than her share of time by handling all the scheduling, the newsletter, and the arrangements with the church.

Don't accept anyone into membership who is not in a position

> A COMMON VISION IS THE ESSENTIAL INGREDIENT THAT HOLDS ANY ORGANIZATION TOGETHER, BE IT THE FAMILY, THE CHURCH, A NONPROFIT MINISTRY, OR A HOMESCHOOL SUPPORT GROUP.

to contribute to the workload (even moms with extenuating circumstances find ways to help out). Stay small and only grow as you have interested families who come ready to contribute their gifts and talents. If you feel torn between this position and ministering to new or weaker families, then start a support group as well. But—and this is from a lot of experience—don't try to provide meaningful cooperative experiences for your kids and run a support group for needy families under the same umbrella; it is a conflicting vision and will not work.

#4. Deal with Offenses Biblically and Quickly

Every ministry or organization I know of that has failed did so because of personal conflicts that arose and went unresolved. It's our adversary's most potent tactic.

Besides adding members with a common vision, add only those who understand how to handle personal conflicts and are committed to dealing with them appropriately.

I delegated so much of my leadership responsibility in the Learning Center that I viewed dealing with relational rifts as my primary responsibility. Our co-op provides some fantastic experiences for children, and the friendships among the women are a crucial factor in their long-term survival in homeschooling. But we know that personal conflict is the one area that could do it all in quickly. I kept this at the forefront with our members. If you are offended and cannot extend grace in the situation, then you must go to the person directly—*not after discussing it with several other people.* If you cannot resolve the situation, then you must involve leaders. Our goal is to keep the conflict as small as possible. That's why dealing with it quickly is essential. I've learned the hard way that things don't go away with time; they fester, get bigger, and ultimately pollute others.

#5. Keep Things Fluid

The Learning Center has been going strong now for two decades—but we've also had to reinvent it a number of times to ensure its continued survival. In hindsight I now see the willingness to flex and change as a key component of success.

Our main challenge in the past few years has been keeping our teens meaningfully engaged at the co-op. Most take classes at CHESS family school or at a local college. With a heavy academic program, co-op days are easy to skip. This leaves moms who've taken time to prepare frustrated and disappointed. At first we tried having clubs and activities for the students instead of classes. Some were even student-led with elected officers, and this gave teens a source of extracurricular and leadership activities to mention on college applications. Some were quite successful; others weren't. So we canned the high school program and gave more attention to the elementary kids.

Besides losing our teens, we lost some long-term moms as well. Rumors circulated that the Learning Center might disband. My longtime administrator told me to make a speech of vision and passion. That did help, but better yet, some new families were sponsored for membership. (We have found adding members upon recommendation of current members the best way to find like-minded, committed families.) These women brought fresh ideas and enthusiasm to the co-op. One, a systems analyst, taught a number of science and computer classes; the other, a former district attorney, organized a forensic science course complete with a visit from the drug dog, forensic pathologist, and polygrapher. As one of my sons noted, "Just when we stopped coming, the Learning Center got awesome."

We still have high school programs running at the Learning Center—they're offering a debate club, a mock-trial competition, and an auto repair class this year. When my daughter Kayte and her friends reached this age, they really didn't want to drop out, as my sons had. But they had big plans for their moms—they wanted to do full-scale drama productions. At that pronouncement all of us wished we hadn't been preaching an educational philosophy that supports a child's interests and ambitions for years. Writing from the other side of five major productions, I can say it was worth the effort. That became the reason why I finally stepped down from leading the Learning Center. No, I didn't quit in exhaustion. I passed the baton on to moms with younger children and far more talent than I ever had.

But me? I ended up chairing the committee for the Learning Center Players. This eventually became such a major venture that it became its own separate organization: Encore! Home School Productions. (I only know how to go from complicated to more complicated.)

#6. Build Upon the Bonds of Friendship

Relational glue is what will keep your family invested in the effort even when the co-op doesn't completely meet your individual needs or vision. At the Learning Center, we have a moms' lounge where we can relax together and share our lives during our free period. And we try to plan activities that foster friendships among the kids as well: overnight camping trips, picnics, open gym, etc. All these gatherings give kids informal time to get to know one another better. More than anything else, friendship is the reason we're still going after all these years.

The Benefits Are Worth It

You may be thinking that organizing a learning co-op sounds like more work than it is worth. Anything that lasts— your homeschool, your co-op, your Christian service—does so because the foundations are secure. And laying those foundations requires time. But once they are in place, things can run smoothly for a long, long time. A shoddy foundation requires continuous shoring up.

The rewards are worth the effort! The friendships we maintain through the Learning Center are our most valued possession. And many of our best opportunities have been only possible in this context.

Co-ops require time and energy from us, but the synergy that comes from pooling our resources sure makes that effort worthwhile for our kids.

> CO-OPS REQUIRE TIME AND ENERGY FROM US, BUT THE SYNERGY THAT COMES FROM POOLING OUR RESOURCES SURE MAKES THAT EFFORT WORTHWHILE FOR OUR KIDS.

Recommended Resource

Homeschool Co-ops: How to Start Them, Run Them and Not Burn Out, Carol Topp

CHAPTER 19
Burnout Buster #5: Get Plugged In

Building a support team is yet another strategy for keeping burnout at bay. As I mentioned, the more multilayered this is, the more quickly you will overcome moments of discouragement. So here's how to find the homeschool community locally, nationally, and virtually.

Locally

Use the Resource Guide at the back of this book to locate the homeschool organizations in your state. These folks will have information on support groups in your area. Evangelical churches, the public library, and Christian bookstores may also have contacts for local groups. Make sure you go to any scheduled conventions or seminars as well. These often have a new homeschoolers workshop track and will get you pointed in the right direction.

In most areas, you will find that a number of groups have been organized. Some of these may limit their membership. Don't be discouraged by this. Getting plugged in may take some time. Here are some tips for finding and joining the group that best suits your family.

What Kind of Group Are You Looking For?

You're looking for families with a faith and educational philosophy that complement yours and with kids you want your children to be influenced by. This is one of my favorite advantages of homeschooling. From their earliest years, my children have been surrounded by older kids I want them to emulate: kids not ashamed of their faith, respectful of their parents, and not caught up in the latest fashion or jockeying for position in a popular clique. They are kind to their younger siblings and work hard academically. This is the kind of peer pressure I want, and it's made a big difference in my children's lives. They need to see that others also embrace our family values.

> **USE THE RESOURCE GUIDE TO LOCATE THE HOMESCHOOL ORGANIZATIONS IN YOUR STATE.**

What Kind of Person Are Support Groups Looking For?

They are also looking for folks with a faith and educational philosophy similar to theirs and with kids they want their children to be influenced by. But more importantly, they are praying for folks who will come to give, not get.

One reason I am writing this book is to give the harried local support group leader a tool to hand to the myriad new homeschoolers who call daily asking for help. Homeschool moms are nurturers to a fault. With the burgeoning of the movement, most support group leaders I've met around the country are on the verge of collapse. They are struggling to meet their families' needs plus help all the local newbies.

Many needy families are trying out homeschooling as a last-ditch effort to salvage their family life or to get their kids through school. In one state, school officials are actually encouraging families with incorrigible kids to try homeschooling. Along with their expulsion notice is the phone number for the local homeschool leader. These poor women feel obligated to try to salvage the situation but invariably end up overwhelmed by the needs of the family. All of our families have blemishes— some a lot more than others. That doesn't disqualify us from homeschooling, but assuming others should take responsibility for our needs does.

Come with Your Sleeves Rolled Up

When you find a group you'd like to join, approach the leadership with an offer to help out. Certainly, you are looking for support and advice. The balance is being sensitive to their other responsibilities and looking for opportunities to lighten their burdens, too, where you are able.

Watching children, preparing a meal for the freezer, doing a mailing, organizing a field trip—thoughtful gestures like these go far beyond the practicality of the service. If you bring a servant's heart to the group, a lot of special opportunities and friendships are going to open up, not only for you but for your kids as well.

> WHEN YOU FIND A GROUP YOU'D LIKE TO JOIN, APPROACH THE LEADERSHIP WITH AN OFFER TO HELP OUT.

Nationally

A number of organizations, magazines, and newsletters will keep you abreast of national trends and opportunities. In the Resource Guide you will find the addresses and phone numbers for those listed in this chapter as well as several others.

Here are the key contacts to keep you tied in with the homeschool network:

Home School Legal Defense Association

HSLDA (www.hslda.org) has engineered much of the legal freedom homeschoolers now enjoy in all states. Its premier team of lawyers tirelessly presents a compelling defense for homeschooling families to legislators, school administrators, and media. Membership dues of $115 per year (less if you register under a recognized support group) will give you free legal aid should the need arise. And HSLDA provides enough discounts and benefits that you can quickly recoup your membership costs.

It also serves as one of the best online information sources for homeschooling at the high school level and working with children with special needs. Through the Home School Foundation (www.homeschoolfoundation. org), HSLDA provides support to widows, single moms, and many other homeschoolers in difficult circumstances. The Foundation's mission is to provide assistance to homeschooling families in need.

Apologia Educational Ministries

In addition to its excellent science curricula, Apologia now offers a monthly e-newsletter, an annual homeschool moms conference, and many other practical and inspirational resources for homeschooling families (www.apologia.com).

Homeschooling Today

This is the magazine for lovers of classical studies and literature-based learning. An energetic, creative bunch of people are publishing *Homeschooling Today* as well as creating products for the homeschool market that support this philosophy of education. A special feature is a full-color reproduction of an art masterpiece in every issue with study notes (www.homeschooltoday.com).

Practical Homeschooling

Editors Bill and Mary Pride embody the pioneer spirit of the homeschool movement. They can be counted on to create and report on the latest innovations and opportunities available to homeschoolers. Articles representing a broad spectrum of educational philosophies are regularly featured as well as lots of product reviews and recommendations (www.home-school.com).

The Old Schoolhouse Magazine

The Old Schoolhouse Magazine began publishing quarterly in 2002 and is currently the largest magazine in the market, with more than 200 pages an issue filled with articles on everything from political activism to product review and advice from a cross-section of homeschool experts (www.thehomeschoolmagazine.com).

Virtually

The Internet has rapidly become the superhighway of the homeschool community at large. And as you can see throughout this book and especially in the Resource Guide, I've included hundreds of websites. Here are some of the best sites for keeping abreast of the homeschool movement:

Eclectic Homeschool Online Magazine (eclectichomeschool.org)
A novel idea and a great site, this online-only magazine for creative homeschoolers is edited by Beverly Krueger and friends and gives you well-organized access to articles, forums, and product reviews. In the short time since its launch, EHO has become the premier site for

information on Christian homeschooling on the web.

Home School Legal Defense Association
(www.hslda.org)
Your source for legal and national news, information on your state organizations and homeschool laws, selected news and announcements, FAQs, and research library.

Homeschool World (www.home-school.com)
This is the site maintained by Bill and Mary Pride (publishers of *Practical Homeschooling*) and their brood of ten children. Filled with Mary's pithy articles and wry observations, I can always count on her site to feature information I can't find anywhere else. You will also find very neatly organized forums on a variety of topics: homeschooling in the military, special needs, curriculum trades, etc.

Online Forums

If you can't find support locally, you can make connections here. Most of the popular curriculum suppliers like Apologia, Sonlight, KONOS, Well-Trained Mind, Tapestry of Grace, and Institute for Excellence in Writing, maintain active forums or Yahoo! Groups. This is a good way to quickly find like-minded folks with similar concerns. You will also find that many of the state organizations provide forums for their members as well.

Well, the foundation's been laid. The framework's been constructed. It's now time to get down to the brass tacks. It's eight a.m. on Monday. The kids are seated around the table, wild with anticipation (at least on Day One). *What in the world are you going to teach? When? And how?*

Be Active

Math

PART 5

WHAT TO TEACH –
WHEN AND HOW

The ARTS

ENGLish

FOREigN LaNguage

HISTORY

ScieNce

CHAPTER 20
Real Teachers Play Ball

This is an "amateur field guide" to teaching the core school subjects, and it comes more from experience, observation, and self-education than from formal training.

In case you want to likewise be self-educating, here's how I've acquired my opinions of what I teach and how I do it:

#1. I Read Research and Educational Journals

I do my homework—but I don't just run headlong with what I find there. I've got some filters in place: I recognize that, first, I don't need to figure out how "most" children learn best; I need to figure out how *my* kid learns best. Even though 80 percent of tested children learned successfully with a particular method, my kids could be in the other 20 percent. And second, the worldview held by the folks behind the research may not be compatible with mine. Biases exist in the purest of studies.

But I still find a lot to think about in my reading. And it gives me the appropriate lingo to sling around when I talk about homeschooling with professionals. Here are some sources I regularly scan (most can be found online or at a good city library):

> **I DON'T NEED TO FIGURE OUT HOW "MOST" CHILDREN LEARN BEST; I NEED TO FIGURE OUT HOW MY KID LEARNS BEST.**

Heinemann Publishers
P.O. Box 6926
Portsmouth, NH 03802-6926
800-225-5800
www.heinemann.com
Heinemann is a publisher of many helpful books for teachers based on the latest research and innovations in education.

Education World
www.education-world.com
This website will furnish you with extensive information in a variety of areas. You will find helpful information for all grade levels and subject areas, and free lesson plans and

recommended websites already screened for educational use.

ERIC (Education Resources Information Center) www.eric.ed.gov
This is a free online digital library of educational research and articles maintained by the U.S. Department of Education. If you want to know what works and with whom, then you can find out here.

The Mailbox magazine (theeducationcenter.com) focuses on creative teaching tips for elementary classrooms, with great ideas and resource suggestions for easy reading.

At the U.S. Department of Education (www.ed.gov) site, if you spend a few minutes searching (select "Parents" heading), you will find some worthwhile publications to download for free. You will also find government literature on No Child Left Behind—federal legislation with potential ramifications for the homeschooling community. The publications on early childhood development, reading, science, and mathematics are very informative.

The Reading Teacher (www.reading.org/General/Publications/ Journals/RT.aspx) focuses solely on the teaching of reading. Academic research is included, but you'll also find a lot of good book titles buried in these articles.

And then the homeschool movement has its own resident scholar in the area of learning theory. Dr. Ruth Beechick spent many years working in public and Christian education before bringing her considerable knowledge and experience to bear upon homeschooling. Before retiring, Dr. Beechick wrote regularly for *Homeschooling Today*. You will find the following titles by Dr. Beechick worth your while in gaining a better understanding of what research has found to be true about how children learn:

> *Dr. Beechick's Homeschool Answer Book*
>
> *The Language Wars and Other Writings for Homeschoolers*
>
> *The Three R's: Grades K–3*
>
> *You CAN Teach Your Child Successfully: Grades 4–8*

Available from many homeschool suppliers and:

> Mott Media
> 1130 Fenway Circle
> Fenton, MI 48430
> 800-421-6645
> www.mottmedia.com

#2. I Ask Myself, "What Skills in This Area Are Necessary in Adult Life?"

This might sound like a dumb idea, but I ask people with jobs in the field what skills they use, and then I make those the targets I try to hit in that subject area. (*Duh!*)

I was foolish enough to pose this question in an undergraduate course one time: "Exactly how might we teach transformational grammar in a high school English class, Professor Albert?"

"Fool, you would never cast these pearls before swine. Transformational grammar is only for the elite!"

He didn't exactly say it that way, but that's my "transformation" of what he did say, and in a deconstructionist's world, it's my word against his. Transformational grammar is, if you are interested (keeping in mind I was in a junior fog at the time), the psychoanalysis of the abusive childhoods of sentences. *Lie down here, Mr. Verb, while we write reams of paper on your deeply embedded intended meaning.*

But I digress . . .

#3. I Observe Kids

I've been teaching kids since 1977. From the classroom to Sunday school to homeschool co-op classes, I've worked with kids of all ages in most subject areas. I pay attention to what works and what doesn't. When are they motivated? When are they bored? When did they get it? When were they confused? I'm more interested in figuring out how kids tick than in making them fit into my presupposed model.

I recommend that parents trust their "field experience" more than anything else, and maybe someday researchers will be interested in knowing what homeschool parents have figured out.

PAY ATTENTION TO WHAT WORKS AND WHAT DOESN'T.

If you're with me, then, here's what I've observed and concluded:

Lessons from the Ball Field

> *Stand and Deliver,* a movie about teacher Jaime Escalante, is one worth seeing. Though others viewed the Latino students of Garfield Senior High as disadvantaged and limited in ability, his faith in them and his inspired teaching resulted in record numbers of students passing the grueling Advanced Placement calculus test.
>
> When Dr. Dobson asked Escalante to what he attributed his success in the classroom, he simply replied, "I'm just the coach."

Besides a long-held fascination with how children learn, I've always been interested in how to teach well. I enjoy reading about master teachers, admiring deeply Jaime Escalante, Marva Collins, and Guy Doud, but I found the most powerful model for the classroom in the least-expected place: the ball field.

What piqued my interest were the many actual-spontaneous learners I recognized on my sons' baseball teams—and the fact that they were often the better players. Why were these kids intensely focused here and excelling, when I knew they were distracted and failing in school? And why did other players, like Mike and Gabe, invest significant time and energy—without prodding—in their athletic success? Why not the same commitment to their academic studies as well?

Certainly our culture's preoccupation with sports and hero worship of athletes are factors. If we'd likewise admire scholars and feature them every seven minutes on TV commercials, we'd see a marked improvement in kids' school performance. But I think there is a lot more to it than that—kids also give themselves wholeheartedly to athletic competitions that have not captured the public imagination and have no national heroes. My daughters have played field hockey, which is not an event to pack a stadium by any stretch of the imagination. But those girls work just as hard as their male counterparts who dream of the big leagues.

I'm convinced sports is a powerful model for the classroom. The teacher's the coach; the kids are the players. Our job is to prepare our teams through practice and drill to play regularly scheduled games where the rewards are worth the work.

How do you translate that into academic endeavors?

It means the work you have your kids engaged in during school is *purposeful and immediate*, not irrelevant and distant. When the kids ask, "When will we ever have to use this?" the answer should be "tomorrow."

Instead kids hear, "Okay, we will be studying algebra this year because a few of you will use it at your future job ten years from now. We will be studying French because it is a prerequisite for college admissions." And we wonder why they aren't motivated?

Now try this scenario: "Listen up, kids, our MathCounts team needs to get ready for the competition in two months. We will compete against hundreds of students in the area at a local college and get our pictures in the paper if we win, plus trophies and prizes. Now let's drill on simplifying polynomials, and then we'll do a lightning round solving for x in less than ten seconds."

Or, "Kayte, let's work on French words related to school so you can explain to your French-speaking pen pal on the Internet what it is like being home educated. We better practice conjugating the verbs 'to learn' and 'to study' so she won't tease you about your grammar."

In which scenario do you picture kids energized and motivated to complete their assignments?

What do you do while they're having all this fun? You coach—*from the sidelines.* Applaud their success, stretch their achievement, and *look for a field to play on* (i.e., find an authentic application of the skills they are learning).

Then get out of the way. Let the kids do the stuff. We adults have a very bad habit of seizing the learning opportunities from children—"Here, Johnny, you don't want to do it that way. Let me show you the best way to build that bridge from toothpicks," or, "Okay, kids, we moms have organized a spring program. We'll be assigning you each a part." Who learns the most, the children above or the kid who figures out the best way to build a bridge by repeatedly experimenting and improving his design? Or how about the kids who actually write, direct, and cast the spring program?

A speaker once asked a group of teachers at a conference I attended, "Are you 'the Sage on the Stage' or 'the Guide on the Side'?" I wanted to be the latter, but that was hard to pull off with a classroom of thirty-two students. Lecturing was the only way to cover all the ground I was required to cover in forty minutes. But not so at home.

Mary, here's how you do this; now you try. Okay, try that again. All right, let's put all the skills we've been practicing together and play the game: Write a short story for our family newspaper. We want the next issue to be ready for our Christmas mailing.

PLAY BALL!

Learn computer skills by creating a family blog.

Learn economics by participating in The Stock Market Game or starting a family business.

Learn civics by getting involved in a local campaign.

Learn science by setting up a backyard habitat or joining a conservation troop or an amateur astronomy club.

Learn geography by orienteering.

Learn to write by sending a letter to the editor.

As you review the chapters in this section and plan activities for your children in the core subject areas, always think in terms of *playing the game.* What skills do we need to practice for real life? What material do we need to cover that will enable the kids to complete this composition or project for this scheduled event?

If you find yourself fumbling around for an answer to the question, "Why do we need to know this, Mom?" it's time to rethink your approach.

CHAPTER 21
Subject-by-Subject Guidelines

Your Framework

Make the overarching framework for your program this: During the elementary years your goal is *breadth.* Give your kids broad exposure to all subject areas through reading, field trips, and opportunities. The purpose is to bring to the surface their areas of talents and interests. This is so you can begin to discern God's calling upon each of their lives.

Then, during the high school years, your goal should be *depth.* Let your kids invest significantly more time in those areas identified as gifts and interests and less in those that seem unrelated to their future calling. I didn't believe God was going to tell us specifically that Mike was called to be an aerospace engineer, but I did have faith to believe He intended to reveal the areas of focus we should have during the high school years in order to maximize our time.

The traditional system does not allow for in-depth study and mastery, but kids are ready for this by the time they reach high school. By high school, Mike allocated more time to mathematics than the humanities. Along with a strong interest indicator, his test scores consistently indicated a high aptitude in math. Kayte became interested in languages in junior high. By allowing her the flexibility she needed, she was able to become fluent in French before she graduated from high school. She studied in France, did a couple of homestays, took a college-level course, and worked with a tutor in Paris over the Internet. For this to happen, we had to minimize her work in other areas. Gabe to this day has the broad-based interests of a conceptual-global learner. In high school, though, an internship with a conservative think tank germinated a passion for public policy and politics. He really cleared his schedule by his senior year to make room for a twenty-hour-a-week commitment to this organization. That, in turn, led to public policy work for a couple of other groups.

> **THE TRADITIONAL SYSTEM DOES NOT ALLOW FOR IN-DEPTH STUDY AND MASTERY, BUT KIDS ARE READY FOR THIS BY THE TIME THEY REACH HIGH SCHOOL.**

Allowing time for these areas of concentration allowed our children to cultivate early skills that opened doors to quite a few unique opportunities in college.

About This Section

After I determined what targets in each subject area I was preparing our children to hit in adult life, I worked backward to determine the steps we needed to take to get there.

This section is designed to help you do just that.

To keep things simple, I've broken down each area into three stages:

1. Primary (preschool–second grade)
2. Elementary (third–sixth)
3. Secondary (junior high and up)

Children are going to progress through these stages at faster or slower rates, but in most cases this is the sequence of events they will follow as they move from readiness to mastery of a skill or content area.

I've suggested resources I and many other homeschoolers have found helpful. And—just a reminder—resources that are especially recommended are set in bold type. Take a look at these, but don't skip the guidelines in Part 2 before investing in the materials you believe are best suited to the unique needs of your child.

For a complete list and reviews of resources available to the homeschool market, check out these helpful guides:

 100 Top Picks for Homeschool Curriculum: Choose the Right Curriculum and Approach for Your Child's Learning Style, Cathy Duffy. Cathy continues to review at cathyduffyreviews.com.

Mary Pride's Complete Guide to Getting Started in Homeschooling. Mary also continues to write her pithy reviews for *Practical Homeschooling* magazine.

Reading

Where Are We Headed?

"Leaders are readers," Kermit commented in conversation shortly after we'd met. I thought, *Now here's a man with possibilities,* as I calculated my next move. Though not yet open to home education, I did know I would be miserable married to someone who was not self-educating or who held no vision for making an impact in his sphere of influence.

Twenty-odd years later, we're set on producing these same ambitions in our children as well, and reading is the prerequisite. If our kids do not read fluently, they will be limited in their spiritual growth, career choices, and social influence. It's another reason homeschooling was so attractive to us: In our program our children had all the time they wanted to read. There wasn't irrelevant busywork to compete with that.

Reading is also the key to preventing homeschool burnout. Once you have an independent reader, you're one short step away from having an independent learner.

How Do We Get There?

Forests have been leveled churning out books and dissertations on how to teach children to read. Sometimes called "The Great Debate," it rivals only evolution and creationism in the emotions it stirs (and just edges out the PC-versus-Mac wars). The two opposing camps are those who advocate intensive phonics instruction and those who recommend a "whole-language" approach.

Whole-language in its purest form advocates the use of real books (not "reader" textbooks) in the classroom and involving children in authentic purposes for reading and writing, for example, publishing a school newspaper or writing to a favorite author. It de-emphasizes phonics and spelling instruction, instead believing children will acquire these skills intuitively in the course of their more holistic (and meaningful) language experiences.

Phonics is, of course, an essential tool for teaching children to *sound out* words, but it does not teach children to *comprehend* or

> ONCE YOU HAVE AN INDEPENDENT READER, YOU'RE ONE SHORT STEP AWAY FROM HAVING AN INDEPENDENT LEARNER.

to *construct* meaning—both things a child must do before he or she is *reading.*

Unfortunately, whole-language has unleashed parental concerns more by the misapplication of its tenets than by the foundational principles of the movement. The politically correct crowd will seize whatever educational reform is currently in vogue to foist their propaganda on schoolchildren.

I find I get myself in a lot less trouble if I say I advocate a literature-based program with a strong phonics base. A lover of good books, I could never bear to hand my children a basal reader or boil the art of reading down to intensive phonics drills.

If you'd like to learn more in this area, *Beginning to Read: Thinking and Learning About Print* by Marilyn Jager Adams is the major work that supports the position that the best reading programs combine phonics instruction with the use of real books and contextual reading.

Also, Dr. Beechick's books listed on page 229 contain sound advice on reading theory.

Now, Back to Where You Live

But let's take this discussion down to ground zero. You have a child who needs to learn to read, and you haven't a clue where to begin. I didn't either. I was taught to read in a wacky, experimental program that made every word in our readers look like the pronunciation key in the dictionary. It was short-lived, to say the least, but may be the reason I am a poor speller.

Nevertheless, having emerged battle-worn but victorious from potty training my children, I figured I could muster the faith to teach them to read. I read lots and lots of books on the subject— convinced by "experts" that this was *one* task that *did* take a rocket scientist.

When I no longer knew which end was up, I had a thought: *You know, they said childbirth was very complicated, and it was pretty simple; they said parenting was complicated, and that's pretty simple, too. Complex reading theories must be just another setup to keep those "experts" employed.*

So I boiled all the theories down to three components that previous generations would have called plain old common sense:

237

- Kids need to be able to sound out words and understand their meaning.
- Kids need to be given books they want to read.
- Kids need to be taught by someone who loves to read.

That's the three-part program: basic phonics instruction, books kids are interested in reading, and parents who love to read. Sooner or later you'll produce a reader every time. Even if your child has a legitimate learning disability, you will find that any professionally designed program will feature one-on-one instruction using kid-engaging materials.

What to Do When in Reading

Primary Years

Reading readiness includes letter and number recognition, being able to make consonant sounds, and having an ear for rhyme. Why rhyme? Readers ultimately decode new words by associating them with words they already know. A child meets the word *grouse* for the first time and realizes it looks similar to *house*. A proficient reader will decode it by rhyming it, not by attacking every letter individually. Dr. Seuss is the best author for encouraging a child to read by rhyming.

Reading readiness also includes lots of background knowledge. Research has shown that children who come to school with a breadth of experiences—travel, attendance at plays and musical performances, visits to historic sites and museums, and meeting a variety of people, etc.—learn to read more quickly than children with limited exposure outside their home or community.

What is the connection? We think in pictures and construct meaning from the words we read through the images formed in our minds. If your child has visited a log cabin or a museum featuring artifacts from pioneer life, she will be able to imagine *and understand* more readily the stories Laura Ingalls Wilder writes about in her Little House series.

If you've never been around computers or used technology, a computer manual is difficult reading. Pick that same manual up after hacking around with your new system for a while, and a lot more of it will make sense. Give your child the same immersion

READING READINESS INCLUDES LETTER AND NUMBER RECOGNITION, BEING ABLE TO MAKE CONSONANT SOUNDS, AND HAVING AN EAR FOR RHYME.

into the world he'll be reading about.

Strategies

- Read lots of poetry, nursery rhymes, and lyrical stories. Beatrix Potter and E. B. White are premier examples of writers for young children who use language beautifully.

- Run your finger under the words as you read aloud to teach left-to-right reading.

- Read aloud daily to your child from a wide, wide variety of genres: fairy tales, biographies, science series, realistic stories, Bible stories, etc.

- Seize every opportunity to expose your young children to the wider world in which we live. Explain what they are seeing.

- Play word games.

- Use magnetic letters or other concrete models to teach letter recognition and sounds. They're hard to find, but a set of lowercase letters is very useful. Use these to approximate the way words will look in print. (*The Ordinary Parent's Guide to Teaching Reading* by Jessie Wise comes with an optional set of magnetic lowercase letters.)

> **SEIZE EVERY OPPORTUNITY TO EXPOSE YOUR YOUNG CHILDREN TO THE WIDER WORLD IN WHICH WE LIVE.**

Elementary Years:

As soon as your child shows an interest in reading, begin phonics instruction. If he is young, move at his pace, stopping when he loses interest or shows frustration.

Discontinue phonics instruction as soon as your child is independently reading chapter books (for example, series such as Boxcar Children or Childhood of Famous Americans) and move into higher reading levels roughly every six months. If you stop formal phonics and your child levels off before reaching a fifth-grade reading level (see *The Sign of the Beaver* by Elizabeth George Speare or *Caddie Woodlawn* by Carol Ryrie Brink as samples), then return to phonics instruction until he is progressing in his independent reading once again.

To continue plodding through a phonics program when your child has obviously "gotten it" actually discourages kids from reading. I've known several children who "unlocked the code" without any phonics instruction and read independently before kindergarten. In those rare cases you can give God the glory and just skip formal phonics instruction—they've figured it out intuitively. The children I know who did this continue to be voracious readers.

Kayte, Mike, and Gabe needed six weeks of phonics instruction to take off independently. I didn't get much beyond beginning consonant blends (*br, sh, pl,* etc.) before they had wings. I returned briefly to practice syllabication with Mike when he got stuck (he'd decode the beginning and guess at the rest), but that was it for the others. Kristen, on the other hand, needed a much longer time of phonics instruction running concurrently with her independent reading to help her break into higher levels.

A mother of identical twin girls told me one daughter learned to read almost solely with a whole-language approach while the other needed an intensive phonics course. The components are the same: real books plus a phonics base in a unique mix for each kid.

> **COMBINE REAL BOOKS WITH A PHONICS BASE IN A UNIQUE MIX FOR EACH KID.**

Strategies

- Even within phonics instruction there are divergent camps. One teaches blending words left to right: "Bat" is taught as *ba - t*. Other words in that grouping would include "bag," "back," "ban." The other teaches word families: "bat" is taught as part of the "at" word family, with other members being "cat," "rat," "fat," etc. I prefer the second approach because it is based upon rhyming, the ultimate way we decode unknown words.

- Reading is a skill. That means consistency yields fruit. Daily, progressive practice with the phonics-based program of your choice is the key to success.

Recommendations for Elementary Years

Sing, Spell, Read and Write is multisensory, systematic, and not phonics overload—just thirty-six steps to independent reading. The readers are so well written, my kids have mistaken them for real stories and enjoyed them. It's a more expensive choice, $226, but with video instruction, CDs, workbooks, and games, there's little preparation on your part. However, there isn't much reinforcement work in SSR&W for the child who cannot master the lesson the first time around. This does leave the parent creating additional exercises or supplementing with one of the resources below.

Explode the Code. These inexpensive workbooks teach the phonograms (basic sounds) in a carefully sequenced program. They are all some children need to unlock the door to reading. For many others, these workbooks make great tools for reinforcement and drill. *Explode the Code* is also available online by subscription at a very reasonable fee. I'd go this route, as the site is highly interactive and colorful.

Alpha-Phonics was created by noted education reformer Samuel Blumenfeld. This is the classic, low-budget program that teaches phonics through a word-family approach. When I used it, I had to supplement with books to read, games, and daily lesson plans. You can order the book from Paradigm for $30 or find an old copy at your library.

Mommy, Teach Me to Read!: A Complete and Easy-To-Use Home Reading Program, Barbara Curtis. This mother of twelve and certified Montessori teacher has written a great handbook for creating a literature-rich environment that fosters a love for reading in your kids. Use this book in addition to whatever phonics instruction program you choose.

My Father's World is a complete curriculum for K–12 designed as unit studies. A phonics-based reading program is integrated into this. MFW is designed by Marie Hazell, who has twenty years' elementary teaching experience. If I had a young child, I would be using this program.

Ordinary Parent's Guide to Teaching Reading, Jessie Wise (2004). A straightforward, scripted approach to phonics instruction. This will feel more up to date than Engelmann's classic *Teach Your Child to Read in 100 Easy Lessons,* and Wise incorporates more multisensory activities for the child.

Teach Your Child to Read in 100 Easy Lessons, Siegfried Engelmann. This program designed for individual instruction is based upon the highly successful DISTAR reading system developed in the late '60s by Englemann at the University of Oregon. It has a tight structure and direct instruction (i.e., highly scripted), but it is effective, especially with children who may be second language learners or need extra learning support. However, the intensive approach may be tedious for a child who is ready to read and can move quickly through the lessons. Used versions of this popular book are widely available online and throughout the homeschool community ($22 new).

You Can Teach Someone to Read by Lorraine Peoples. This new title may be the simplest and least expensive way to teach a child to read. Peoples, a longtime reading teacher, has put together a phonics-based tutoring plan to be used at home or in literacy programs. The daily lesson plans are detailed and very easy to follow. More than fifty phonics rules are presented as a "silly story" with word lists to practice for each. This book also concludes with reading comprehension skills, including understanding punctuation and contextual clues. Had this book been available when I was teaching my four to read, at $22.95, I would have tried this plan first.

ETA/Cuisenaire Reading Rods and VersaTiles. The makers of the famous math manipulatives have extended their innovations to support reading and literacy skills. Here are two proven manipulative sets that will supplement any reading program for preschool though grade three.

> Steer clear of expensive reading programs that promise miracles in a short amount of time. Find out what program a homeschooler you respect has used, and bet on that before being seduced by multimillion-dollar advertising campaigns through the media.

Independent Reading

Concurrent with phonics instruction, hand your child books of interest that gently move him or her to higher and higher levels of independent reading.

Here is a sample list of books in ascending order of difficulty you might use to systematically move your child to full independence:

 Bob Books, Bobby Lynn Maslen (www.bobbooks.com)

Sonlight's *Fun Tales*

Bright and Early books by Dr. Seuss.

I Can Read It All By Myself Beginner Books by Dr. Seuss, such as:

> *Hop on Pop*
> *Green Eggs and Ham*
> *The Cat in the Hat*
> *The Cat in the Hat Came Back*

Ready . . . Set . . . Read! and *Ready . . . Set . . . Read —and Laugh!,* compiled by Joanna Cole and Stephanie Calmenson

Step into Reading series, levels 1–5, such as:
> *Happy Birthday, Thomas!,* W. Awdry
>
> *The Bravest Dog Ever: The True Story of Balto,* Natalie Standiford.

An "I Can Read" Book series, levels 1–3, such as:
> *Little Bear,* Else Holmelund Minarik
> *Frog and Toad Together,* Arnold Lobel
> *The Golly Sisters Go West,* Betsy Byars

Rookie Biographies, such as:
> *Amelia Earhart.* Wil Mara (2003)
>
> *Ben Franklin: A Man with Many Jobs,* Carole Greene

Jackie Robinson, Baseball's First Black Major Leaguer, Carole Greene.

The Boxcar Children series by Gertrude Chandler Warner

The Childhood of Famous Americans series, especially those by Augusta Stevenson

Accidental Detectives series by Sigmund Brouwer

American Girl series

Dear America series

Little House books by Laura Ingalls Wilder

Scholastic biographies

Caddie Woodlawn, Carol Ryrie Brink

Shiloh, Phyllis Reynolds Naylor

The Sign of the Beaver, Elizabeth George Speare

Sustained Silent Reading

We also maintained for years what the schools call SSR—sustained silent reading. This started out as ten minutes after lunch each day. Everyone, including Mom, must read—or take a nap if you are a non-reader (adds some extra motivation). When we first started, the twins would ask every few minutes if time was up yet. But I stuck to it, and pretty soon they were looking forward to their daily independent reading time. The ten minutes quickly stretched to twenty and then to an hour. From there, it became common for our kids to spend hours reading good books for pleasure. It was a habit.

Vary the Genre

Once your child is reading independently, don't let him get stuck in a particular genre such as Hardy Boys mysteries or Janette Oke romances. One mom I know prevented this by requiring her children to read one historical fiction, one Newbery Award winner, one Christian biography, one nonfiction, and one book for pleasure per month.

This Is a No-No!

Whatever you do, don't stoop to the level of R. L. Stine or the Babysitter Club series, thinking this will produce an intelligent reader. This formula fiction is as addictive as television and does nothing to whet kids' appetites for better fare—rather, it dulls their senses.

More strategies and suggested titles for growing a reader can be found in these highly recommended sources:

The Educated Child, William Bennett

Honey for a Child's Heart, Gladys Hunt

Read for the Heart: Whole Books for WholeHearted Families, Sarah Clarkson

Teach a Child to Read with Children's Books: Combining Story Reading, Phonics and Writing to Promote Reading Success, Mark Thogmartin

The Three R's: Grades K–3, Ruth Beechick

Secondary

The key here is *breadth*. Kids should now be gaining the majority of their knowledge in the content areas from their own independent reading. They should be reading widely across the disciplines to expand their comprehension and vocabulary. Many parents do not realize that the vocabulary sections of standardized tests and the college boards are drawn from science and social studies as well as literature. If your children are only reading fiction, they will not acquire the vocabulary skills they need

A helpful tool is *Reading Lists for College-Bound Students* by Arco (2000). This will prepare them for the SAT as well as the kind of reading they'll be expected to handle in college.

For pleasure reading, the very best suggestions can be found in *Honey for a Teen's Heart,* Gladys Hunt (2002). Written from a Christian perspective, the book is a guide to engaging and well-written fiction suitable for teens. Hunt includes a synopsis of the author's worldview to help you with discernment.

Finally, *Book Lover's Guide to Great Reading: A Guided Tour of Classic & Contemporary Literature,* Terry Glaspey, is the title

> **IF YOUR CHILDREN ARE ONLY READING FICTION, THEY WILL NOT ACQUIRE THE VOCABULARY SKILLS THEY NEED.**

I use for selecting literature for my high school–level courses at CHESS family school. These titles will not only raise your children's SAT scores but, more importantly, will connect them to their rich Christian heritage (which we neglect at our peril).

Reading Critically

Train your children to read critically and analyze literature by using the Progeny Press Bible-Based Study Guides or Veritas Press Comprehension Guides available for many classic children's books, Shakespearean plays, and major works of American letters. Total Language Plus's Literature Guides are another resource to use during the primary years. Kathryn Stout's guidebook *Critical Conditioning* (Design-A-Study) is full of reading strategies and exercises to use with any reading material to improve comprehension and analytical thinking.

Reading Aloud

Final strategy for your independent readers: Read aloud. So many of us abandon this practice once our children have taken off on their own. But sharing a book is a wonderful way to bind your family together as well as to involve your kids in the better literature they might otherwise avoid. When all their children were still at home, the McKeown and Gamon families gathered once a week to read scenes from Shakespeare aloud. They've held Shakespeare parties and attended performances together. Their kids love the Bard because he's been introduced in the context of family fun.

We're very fond of audiobooks. Long-distance trips were eagerly anticipated if I took the time to order a special book to listen to on the way. And it's just the ticket for drawing a child into a book he might otherwise avoid.

 Sources of audiobooks:

Audible.com
(Download audiobooks directly to your iPod or other media device)

> SHARING A BOOK IS A WONDERFUL WAY TO BIND YOUR FAMILY TOGETHER AS WELL AS TO INVOLVE YOUR KIDS IN THE BETTER LITERATURE THEY MIGHT OTHERWISE AVOID.

Blackstone Audio
P.O. Box 969
Ashland, OR 97520
800-729-2665
blackstoneaudio.com

Books on Tape
400 Hahn Road
Westminster, MD 21157
800-733-3000
booksontape.com

Recorded Books
270 Skipjack Road
Prince Frederick, MD 20678
800-638-1304
recordedbooks.com

AudioFile magazine reviews books on tape/CD, including the quality of the narration and the best deals available:

AudioFile
37 Silver Street, P.O. Box 109
Portland, ME 04112-0109
207-774-7563
www.audiofilemagazine.com

Reading Classics

At least on the secondary level, but preferably sooner, please expose your kids to the great works of Western literature and then other traditions as well. As with any artistic form of expression, we must cultivate an appreciation for it. Inundated with music, art, drama, and books of pop culture that are exceedingly shallow and effortlessly produced, most kids, my own included, must be trained to understand artistic expression that requires mature thinking and personal reflection. Fortunately, I've found that once a taste for high-quality literature has been acquired, my kids are no longer interested in the "popular" fare.

Instead of fighting with your kids over the music, movies, and books of their corrosive youth culture, ruin their taste for it by cultivating in your home a love for fine art, music, and literature. At least this strategy has worked in our family. My daughter Kayte began reading classics in fourth grade—and that is all she has ever really favored. Even when she tried some of the more popular fiction around the house, she complained of how predictable it was (so I was wise enough not to force it upon her). While Kristen was not ready to read challenging literature at such a young age (nor were Mike and Gabe, for that matter), I picked up on Kayte's lead and used audiobooks to help Kristen likewise acquire a taste for the classics.

My sons took all of my literature classes at CHESS family school. They and their buddies at first complained about the "boring" reading material. But even they too have acquired a taste for fine music (acoustic guitar or jazz), art, and literature. I recently finished teaching *The Scarlet Letter* in my online literature course, and I loved having so many students take the time to say how much they enjoyed the book. One young man commented that he had previously read the book and hated it, "but now that I understand why the book is considered a classic, I found I really enjoyed reading it."

Well, what do you use to help kids recognize the quality and substance of great works of literature? Here's what I use to prepare a lecture or design a course.

> **INSTEAD OF FIGHTING WITH YOUR KIDS OVER THE MUSIC, MOVIES, AND BOOKS OF THEIR CORROSIVE YOUTH CULTURE, RUIN THEIR TASTE FOR IT BY CULTIVATING IN YOUR HOME A LOVE FOR FINE ART, MUSIC, AND LITERATURE.**

Recommendations for Secondary Years

I'm probably the world's only English teacher who not only advises students to read the *Cliffs Notes* for a book but also gives credit for doing so. *Cliffs Notes* are an excellent resource if they are used to *prepare for* reading a work and not *instead of* reading it. Even with a master's degree in English and twenty-some years' experience, I can't read a classic and on my own recognize all the nuances and noteworthy facets of the book. I read the *Cliffs Notes* too. *Cliffs Notes* are now available online at no charge. Go to http://education.yahoo.com/homework_help/

Listen to a literature course from The Teaching Company. I've yet to order a course from these folks that I didn't thoroughly enjoy—and we've purchased at least twenty courses. Now, when the discussion is literature and we get up to modern times, the material can get pretty coarse fast, and so can the lecture (anything published after Freud is suspect). So you will need to preview material of this ilk before passing them on to your kids. But I've used excerpts from a number of these audio courses in my classes, and our teens listened to entire courses for several high school-level credits.

Reading Between the Lines: A Christian Guide to Literature by Gene Veith will give you an appreciation for the place of literature in the Christian life and show you how to understand various genres (i.e., poetry, drama, nonfiction, fiction, etc.). Veith, provost and professor of literature at Patrick Henry College, is a regular columnist for *World* magazine and the main reason I subscribe.

Literature: An Introduction to Fiction, Poetry, Drama, and Writing by X.J. Kennedy is the basis for all the lectures I've developed on understanding the classics. This is a good text to use for Advanced Placement English or for a two-year course of study in high school. It is available from Follett Educational Services, a seller of used and reconditioned textbooks. You will be just fine with an older, less expensive edition. I use the fifth, ISBN: 0-6735-2046-3.

My Secondary English Courses

Because I am asked so frequently, here are the core texts I recommend for the six English courses I designed for CHESS family school:

For introduction to composition, I use the *Write Source 2000* English handbook from Great Source. The students complete several of the writing models in the handbook, and we also participate in the Scholastic Writing Contest. This course is taken in seventh, eighth, or ninth grade.

For introduction to literature, I teach the elements of fiction using the Kennedy volume listed previously as the basis for my lectures and as the source for the selected poetry. We also read and discuss *The Giver* by Lois Lowry, *The Old Man and the Sea* by Ernest Hemingway, and *The Night Thoreau Spent in Jail* by Jerome Lawrence and Robert E. Lee. The last title is a drama and a bit outdated, but it introduces the students to Thoreau and

Emerson, whose influences are central to the study of American literature. This course is taken in seventh, eighth, or ninth grade.

For my American literature course at CHESS family school, I use the Bob Jones University Press eleventh-grade anthology. The teacher's guide is excellent, but I must supplement with important pieces that have been excluded, i.e., *The Tell-Tale Heart* by Edgar Allan Poe, *The Open Boat* by Stephen Crane, and *The Lottery* by Shirley Jackson. (Less representative, but I assume potentially less offensive, pieces by these authors have been selected for the BJU anthology.) I also teach *The Scarlet Letter, The Adventures of Huckleberry Finn,* and *The Great Gatsby* to complete the course. Recommended for ninth through twelfth grades.

For my British literature course, I use the British Tradition from *Prentice Hall Literature: Timeless Voices, Timeless Themes* (1999). There is a lot of stuff in here I skip. I make my own assignments and tests, essentially because I don't like anything that reduces great pieces of literature to the level of a sitcom — i.e., "Write your own commercial for the made-for-TV version of *Hamlet*." But the selections are superb, and so is the commentary; this anthology includes *Macbeth*. We also read *Hamlet* using the version published by Oxford University Press. Recommended for tenth through twelfth grades.

For advanced composition, I use *Writers INC* from Great Source and *On Writing Well* by William Zinsser. In the introduction to compositions my students learn to write reports. In my literature classes I teach the analytical paper, and in this advanced compositions course, students complete units in research (using primary and secondary sources), essays, journalism, and creative writing. Recommended for tenth through twelfth grades.

For my favorite course, Christian literature and the arts, I introduce students to as many great Christian writers as possible. I use *Reading Between the Lines: A Christian Guide to Literature* by Gene Veith to support our studies. The main literary selections include Augustine's *Confessions,* Dante's *Inferno,* and selections from *Paradiso*, Milton's *Paradise Lost,* the devotional poetry of John Donne and George Herbert, selections from *Pilgrim's Progress,* C. S. Lewis's *Perelandra* and *Till We Have Faces*, and works by modern writers such as Annie Dillard, Flannery O'Connor, and Walter Wangerin. Students develop their own artistic expression of their faith in response to the literature studied. It culminates with an evening performance of original works by the students. I love to teach this class. Recommended for eleventh and twelfth grades.

Language Arts

Perhaps a definition is in order: *Language arts* is the collective term used for composition, speech, reading or literature, spelling, vocabulary, and grammar.

Where Are We Headed?

If you recall the targets Kermit and I set for our children's education, then it will come as no surprise that we had heavy doses of language arts in our program. Here is where our children honed the communication skills they needed to confidently and competently articulate in speech and writing their faith and ideas.

My goal was that our kids would not shrink from opportunities to influence the world, but would pursue them. I knew that for them to do this, they needed to be confident in this area. So I made sure we practiced and played the game often.

Influential leadership aside, communication skills are also at the top of nearly every job qualification list I checked into. The information age is for the articulate. Don't send your kids out the door without a strong grasp of the English language.

> **COMMUNICATION SKILLS ARE AT THE TOP OF NEARLY EVERY JOB QUALIFICATION LIST I CHECKED INTO.**

How Do We Get There?

Employ two key strategies in your program:

1. **Kids need to write and speak *regularly* for an audience, K–12.** The operative words are *regularly* and *for an audience.* Before your kids hit the self-conscious stage of adolescence, they must be confident speaking in front of a group and sharing their written work with others. This happens through regular practice.

2. **Language arts skills should be practiced in the context in which they are used.** That means we don't

subdivide these six areas into separate subjects, i.e., spelling, vocabulary, grammar, etc.; instead we integrate them into authentic assignments such as creating stories for a family newspaper or preparing a speech for the Thanksgiving performance. Research has shown that kids who read avidly and write regularly acquire competency in grammar, vocabulary, and spelling. The converse has also been shown: Kids who practice grammar, vocabulary, and spelling skills divorced from regular reading and composing don't.

What to Do When in Language Arts

Primary

The first stories your child creates will be the pictures he draws. If encouraged, he will begin to experiment by adding letters to his pages. As he begins to acquire an understanding of phonics, he will approximate the spelling of words by approximating their sounds. Your child might produce "DRS" for "dress" or "YL" for "while." His vocabulary will expand or stagnate, depending upon the amount of "live language" he is exposed to and the level of its complexity. (Live language is conversation between family and friends and not speech overheard from radio or television.)

Primary Strategies

- Do not talk down to young children. Use English precisely and speak in complete sentences. Engage your child in discussion about the pictures she is creating. Call these "stories."

- Your child will be ready to compose complex stories long before she is able to print them. Let her dictate these to you. I wrote down stories for my children even through third grade. By then they had keyboarding skills that could keep up with their thinking.

- Most primary curricula I have seen require far too much handwriting of young children. Fine motor skills do not develop as rapidly in children as their thinking skills. Don't limit your child's progress by requiring her to do all this

> RESEARCH HAS SHOWN THAT KIDS WHO READ AVIDLY AND WRITE REGULARLY ACQUIRE COMPETENCY IN GRAMMAR, VOCABULARY, AND SPELLING.

writing. She can read, speak, and think far faster and deeper than she can print. So do some of the printing for her or do the required work orally. Better yet, see that she has a computer and a children's word processing program as early as possible. Take a look at *Canvastic*, an affordable desktop publishing program for K-8 (www.canvastic.com).

- Some of our favorite mementos are the books my children created during their primary years. You can do this by folding several sheets of eight-and-a-half-inch by eleven-inch paper in half. With a cross-stitch, sew along the folded edge with dental floss. Bind cardboard covers to the pages with packing tape.

- Occasionally provide an audience for your child's inventive play. Encourage her to perform a puppet show for you or act out a favorite Bible story. But don't take over. Children love to create secret worlds not populated by adults.

- Inventive play stimulates a child's mental development and creative thinking skills. Our children and their homeschooled friends engaged in this almost until adolescence. Elaborate battles between Narnia and the evil Calormenes raged back and forth for hours in the backyard while scores of stuffed animals were positioned to defend the bedrooms. Had they gone to school, I'm sure they would have been teased into stopping this. But I knew this was not immaturity on their part; rather, it was laying the groundwork for their future reading and writing skills.

- Don't start dumping money into resources yet. Delay structured learning and seatwork as long as possible. Young children may be anxious to "play school," but they are not really asking you to structure their time and require assignments of them. Rather, support their initiative in composing, inventing, and conversing.

 A regular rereading of *For the Children's Sake*, by Susan Schaeffer Macaulay and *The Power of Play*, by David Elkind will remind you of the benefits of a carefree, lingering time of childhood for your kids. Don't worry—the rat race will still be there when they must finally leave childhood behind.

Recommendations for the Primary Years

1-2-3 Reading and Writing by Jean Warren is a collection of easy-to-do readiness exercises for primary-level children. Jean's books are now out of print, but still widely available used at online sites such as Amazon. However, she has put most of her content up on her site (www.preschoolexpress. com), where you can now download it for free.

A Fresh Look at Writing, Donald Graves. This is a comprehensive overview of Graves' philosophy of teaching writing to young children. It is filled with practical suggestions and will serve you well as an ongoing reference in homeschooling.

Mommy, Teach Me: Preparing Your Preschool Child for a Lifetime of Learning, Barbara Curtis. This former homeschool mom, mother of twelve, and Montessori teacher gives you simple at-home activities to incorporate into your lifestyle that will lay a foundation for later, formal learning.

More Than Letters: Literacy Activities for Preschool, Kindergarten and First Grade, Sally Moomaw and Brenda Hieronymus. I'm recommending this series of early childhood activities by Moomaw and Hieronymus because they understand the importance of immersing young children in a natural, tactile environment with freedom to experiment and explore. Skip the workbooks and seatwork with this crowd. That's not how they are wired to learn.

Elementary:

By the time your child leaves his elementary years behind, his writing portfolio should include both creative and expository compositions. Within the context of regular writing, he should master the conventions of English in spelling, grammar, and punctuation.

> **BY THE TIME YOUR CHILD LEAVES HIS ELEMENTARY YEARS BEHIND, HIS WRITING PORTFOLIO SHOULD INCLUDE BOTH CREATIVE AND EXPOSITORY COMPOSITIONS.**

Spelling will progress naturally and with practice from (wildly) inventive to standard.

The audiences with whom he shares his work should be varied and informal: his peers, his relatives, and his family.

The child should have daily opportunities to speak and formulate his ideas into thoughtful responses.

Recommendations for the Elementary Years

Great Source publishes my favorite language arts curriculum, which includes the English handbooks *Writers Express* (elementary), *Write Source 2000* (middle school), and *Writers INC* (high school). This series integrates what research has shown works best in teaching children to compose, think, and learn.

While the Great Source program integrates language arts around composition, the Total Language Plus program, developed specifically for homeschoolers, integrates language arts effectively around the study of a particular novel—i.e., *My Side of the Mountain, The Cricket in Times Square, The Scarlet Pimpernel.*

Introduce parts of speech with these incredible feasts for the eyes written and illustrated by Ruth Heller:

> *Behind the Mask: A Book About Prepositions*
>
> *A Cache of Jewels and Other Collective Nouns*
>
> *Kites Sail High: A Book About Verbs*
>
> *Many Luscious Lollipops: A Book About Adjectives*
>
> *Merry-Go-Round: A Book About Nouns*
>
> *Up, Up and Away: A Book About Adverbs*

Elementary Composition

Kids can only write about what they know or have experienced. A wide breadth of studies and diverse experiences must precede composing. The topics they write about should be drawn from this.

Elementary Strategies

- Kids need a regular time they can count on to write. Keep composing on the schedule, and it will eventually be a habit.

> **KIDS CAN ONLY WRITE ABOUT WHAT THEY KNOW OR HAVE EXPERIENCED.**

> **KEEP COMPOSING ON THE SCHEDULE, AND IT WILL EVENTUALLY BE A HABIT.**

- Help your children discover what they want to write about and who their audience will be. Instead of specific assignments, I gave my kids parameters for their writing—for example, a research paper on a topic of interest or a short piece of historical fiction. My job was to brainstorm with them to discover the topic they wanted to write about or to give ideas for getting unstuck while the piece was in progress.

Michael was a very reluctant writer when younger. I had asked him to keep a daily journal in third grade. But he was stubbornly stuck despite my continuous list of suggested topics. I knew to be motivated he needed an audience and a purpose for his writing that he cared about. I finally punched the right button:

Kermit is the storyteller in our family. He often snuck into the children's bedrooms after hours and kept them up late telling stories from his own childhood. My kids just loved this, especially since the goal was to make sure Mom didn't find out. I suggested to Mike that he record his daily life and the current events going on in the world so he could someday share them with his own kids the way his dad did. That did it. Mike filled his pages very quickly that year.

- Teach writing as a process of planning, composing, revising, and editing. A good piece will go through this cycle several times. This process is how real writers write; let your children mimic it.

- The goal is fluency. Many ideas should be started in their daily journals, but choose only a few to polish up and finish. These should be presented to an audience.

- One way to find an audience is to join a writers group. These work best if they are small enough for all the children involved to share a portion of their work in progress each time the group gathers.

Organize a Young Writers' Institute

When my sons were eleven, I arranged for their favorite author, Sigmund Brouwer, to teach some creative writing workshops for our homeschool co-op. I was trying to impress my sons, but I was the one impressed—with how motivated all the kids were to write after they'd spent a couple of days in class with a real author who they thought was pretty cool. This only led to more Young Writers' Institutes around the country featuring several popular Christian authors. Now that our kids are grown, we are no longer organizing these events, but you can. The following authors have developed content-filled, creative, and motivating workshops especially designed for homeschooled kids. You won't be disappointed.

Sigmund Brouwer, author of the Accidental Detectives, CyberQuest, Mars Diaries, Bug's Eye View series and others (www.coolreading.com)

Bill Myers, author of the Wally MacDoogle, Secret Agent Dingledorf, Bloodhounds, McGee and Me series and others (www.billmyersbooks.com)

Nancy Rue, author of the Lily, Sophie, Christian Heritage series and more (www.nancyrue.com)

Robert Elmer, author of the Hyperlinkz, Young Underground, Promise of Zion series and others (www.robertelmerbooks.com)

- When you or others respond to a child's writing, focus first on the content and last on the mechanics. The goal is to raise kids who have something worthwhile to say, not who have merely mastered the conventions of the English language.

- The success of a piece of writing should be measured by the degree to which it fulfills its intended purpose and reaches its intended audience. When the kids at our co-op created picture books to read aloud to the preschoolers, their success was measured by the interest shown by the little guys. When my secondary students write a research paper, their success is based upon the degree to which their research supports their thesis.

In these books you'll find more terrific strategies for encouraging elementary students to write:

Any Child Can Write, Harvey Wiener

Comprehensive Composition, Kathryn Stout

Writing from Home, Susan Richman

Writer's Jungle: A Survivor's Guide to Writing with Kids, Julie Bogart. Much more than an instructional manual, this is a Charlotte Mason-inspired way of life.

Speaking

Discuss with your child the material he is studying. This will teach him to be an active thinker and to practice formulating his thoughts into articulate responses. Ask questions frequently. The burden for learning is on the student, not the teacher. Require your kids to interact with the material and to expect to talk about it.

Find increasingly larger and varied audiences for your kids—first family members and relatives, then retirement centers and peers. Formal performances such as recitals and plays should be annual events.

The first time I taught a class of sophomores, I was so nervous I completed the forty-minute lesson in ten minutes. I stood petrified with no clue what to do for a moment and then gave a study hall, which got my relationship with the students off on the right foot. More than a thousand classes later, I never run out of things to say. Practice is what made the difference. I've made a fool of myself quite a few times, too, but I have so many positive experiences to offset those, it doesn't hinder my confidence one bit. That's the goal with your kids. Give them so much practice and so many opportunities that their success

ASK QUESTIONS FREQUENTLY.

rate far outweighs their sense of failure, especially when they are young.

I didn't participate in piano recitals until I was in junior high. Then I flubbed up and lost my confidence. After that I avoided the situation and even switched my major from music to English when I realized semester recitals would be a big part of my grade. I didn't want the same scenario for my kids. They've been in piano recitals twice a year since age eight and numerous plays and performances since age five. They probably suffer from overconfidence far more than underconfidence. But by the time they are adults I want them to be polished, articulate public speakers.

 ### Recommendations for Elementary and Secondary Years

From Playpen to Podium, Jeff Myers

Secrets of Great Communicators, Jeff Myers. This curriculum for older students includes six DVDs and a student workbook.

National Christian Forensics and Communications Association. This well-run, competitive association, supported by HSLDA, provides formal speech and debate experiences for homeschooled teens. Students must be part of a team with a committed coach, but there are now local chapters throughout the country. My daughter Kayte has said repeatedly this is one experience she wishes she'd had in high school, because invariably the peers who impressed her most at college for their ability to quickly formulate and defend an argument turned out to be those who had been involved in formal debate during high school (www.ncfca.org)

Elementary Spelling

I write from the experience of a poor speller who still managed to become an English teacher. I had a lot of private theories about spelling that have been validated by Dr. Richard Gentry, himself a

> GIVE THEM SO MUCH PRACTICE AND SO MANY OPPORTUNITIES THAT THEIR SUCCESS RATE FAR OUTWEIGHS THEIR SENSE OF FAILURE, ESPECIALLY WHEN THEY ARE YOUNG.

259

poor speller, who got back at the system by earning a doctorate in teaching spelling. His books *Spel . . . Is a Four-Letter Word* and *Teaching Kids to Spell* are highly recommended.

First, spelling is a visual perception problem, not a linguistic one. Hence, you can have kids who score very high in reading and vocabulary and bottom out in this area. I'm convinced natural spellers, like natural artists, can visualize correctly spelled words in their mind. At least that's what they tell me.

Despite having parents who are both poor spellers, Mike and Gabe have always spelled well. I never used a spelling program with them. I did nothing except encourage them as readers and writers. Kayte, on the other hand, my most inventive child, had atrocious spelling. She didn't even attempt phonetic equivalency for years. I couldn't decipher her compositions, and she often couldn't either. Self-confident child that she is, we could tease her about this.

Her spelling greatly improved by age eleven, because she regularly used *Spell It Plus* (Knowledge Adventure), a software program, and she read and wrote all the time. The computer spell-checker helped her clean up her work before submission too.

Spelling Strategies

- An effective spelling program is multi-strategy—that means you use a variety of methods and games for teaching kids to spell. Be concrete wherever possible: I used crossword puzzles, magnetic letters, Scrabble tiles, and word games like Boggle to help my kids better visualize standard spelling.

- Don't limit your children to writing only what they can spell. Inventive spelling is okay. We don't prevent kids from playing baseball until they know all the rules and have mastered all the skills; rather, we use playing the game as the method for learning the rules and improving their skills. Encourage your children to self-correct. As Kayte matured, she first learned to recognize misspelled words in her writing and then finally to spell them correctly.

Spelling Recommendations

Choose a spelling program that groups spelling words according to a generalization—for example, *i before e except after c or when sounding like "a" as in neighbor and weigh*. Bob Jones University's spelling program does this, as does Kathryn Stout's The Natural Speller (Design-A-Study), but many other traditional programs group spelling words randomly.

> **DON'T LIMIT YOUR CHILDREN TO WRITING ONLY WHAT THEY CAN SPELL.**

Secondary

It's time to prod Junior out of the nest. The tools he's acquired in speech, composition, spelling, and vocabulary should now be used in a masterful way to accomplish real goals—academic, civic, employment, etc. The audience to whom he communicates his ideas orally and in writing must be to a growing degree beyond his family members.

Your student should be writing to learn across the curriculum. Creative writing should continue, but technical writing and research should be a weekly practice. Besides writing from his experience, a student should now be writing out of the knowledge base acquired from his reading. This must go beyond just the regurgitation of facts he's memorized to a thoughtful discussion of ideas and opinions he is now formulating.

An intuitive understanding of English grammar should be in place as a result of all the writing and reading done on the elementary level. It is now time for the college-bound student to learn the correct terminology for grammatical constructions, i.e., adverbial clauses, participial phrases, etc. This technical understanding of syntax will give him the tools he needs to better control his writing.

Strategies

- To keep writing purposeful, serious students should be encouraged to enter some of the academic compositions listed in the Resource Guide, especially those that require a written project. Some support groups publish a newsletter or yearbook produced by high school students; this is another excellent way to involve kids in meaningful communications.

- Group activities that are discussion-based will give students an informal setting for testing ideas, modifying opinions, and improving communication. Make sure to place a high premium on class participation to nudge more reticent students into taking risks and learning to contribute.

- Either organize a semester course in public speaking or see that your child gives a formal speech or oral presentation at least once a year. Many students I evaluate have found a forum for doing this in 4-H.

Recommendations for Secondary Years

The program I mentioned earlier, Great Source, does the best job I know of teaching this technical understanding with direct application to purposeful writing.

Help for High School, Julie Bogart. Julie has a unique and effective approach to teaching writing. Drawing upon her years as a professional writer, she works backward from what she has learned from her life among the pros. Since she is also a Charlotte Mason devotee, all the hallmarks of Miss Mason's advice are here: living books, narration, copy work, and keen observation of the natural world. *Brave Writer* is actually a homeschooling lifestyle built around an emphasis on children's writing. Julie supports her writing philosophy with online classes, forums, and newsletters. This is an excellent follow-up to *The Writer's Jungle* (the elementary program), with a focus on constructing the academic argument through the five-paragraph essay.

Another recommended program for older students is Andrew Pudewa's Institute for Excellence in Writing. Andrew is one of the best communicators you are likely to hear at a convention, so don't miss one of his sessions, and his company is constantly improving and expanding its line of products for teaching kids to write well. The writing students I have had who have used Andrew's courses have all been fundamentally sound and eager to continue their development as a writer. More than his passion for writing, I think Andrew's infectious enthusiasm for learning is his greatest gift to those who use his materials.

WriteAtHome offers online classes developed by my two favorite people to hang with at homeschooling conventions: Brian and Melanie Wasko. WriteAtHome has a number of semester-long or year-long writing courses suitable for sixth grade and up, and they are very well priced considering the personal attention each young writer receives. The genius to this model is the personal writing coaches who work with students individually as they move through the curriculum Brian has written. Writers need feedback in order to improve, and here is the best place I know of to get that.

The Young Writer's Guide to Getting Published, Kathy Henderson. This book provides information on contests, publishers, and magazines interested in publishing young people's original writing.

Increase vocabulary through systematic study in Greek and Latin roots. Vocabulary from Classical Roots is one program that will help you do this.

Vocabulary for Achievement is the course I've recommended to prepare kids in a systematic way for the vocabulary and reading comprehension sections of the college boards. The vocab is taught in the context of actual reading selections taken from a wide variety of subject matter—i.e., literature, medicine, journalism, history, etc.—available from debrabell.com.

Webster's New World Student Writing Handbook by Sharon Sorenson contains models and step-by-step instructions for composing all the types of writing secondary students are expected to do across the curriculum. This is a good high school and college reference tool.

Mathematics

Probably nowhere have the changes in the standard curriculum been greater since you were in school than in mathematics. You'd have to be Rip Van Winkle not to know that American students are well behind their international peers in mathematical competency and that the U.S. is not producing enough engineers yearly to keep up with global demands. China and India are happily filling that gap. While there is a legitimate debate about how dire the situation actually is, since 2000 there has been a significant uptick in the demands of the curriculum because the economic effects of all this are finally lighting a fire.

Now don't panic. What to do when during the early years is still very manageable, and I've got some great resources to recommend. Your kids are going to be at an advantage if you capitalize upon the innovations in the homeschool community.

What to do when at the high school level is a bit more daunting. Most college-bound kids need to complete Algebra I by the end of eighth grade (it isn't just for the honors track anymore) and to complete pre-calculus by the end of high school. Those heading into the math and science end of things need to complete minimally one year of calculus and four years of rigorous sciences that require mathematical problem-solving. Again, not to worry—Apologia Science, VideoText, Teaching Textbooks, and others have you covered.

I just want to give you the heads-up: Using our own school experience as a frame of reference for what our kids should be able to do mathematically is not a good idea. So, let's get started.

Since I did not know this, I'll assume some of my readers do not either: *Arithmetic* refers to problem solving using the basic operations of addition, subtraction, multiplication, and division when all the quantities are known. *Higher math* is what we use to solve problems with unknown quantities or variables, often represented by x's and y's. (For example, it takes arithmetic to balance my checkbook when the "debit" and "credit" columns all have known quantities written in; it takes higher math when various entries have been left blank ranging back to 1988 or filled with variables, such as an emphatic-looking ??? or !!!! left by Kermit.)

USING OUR OWN SCHOOL EXPERIENCE AS A FRAME OF REFERENCE FOR WHAT OUR KIDS SHOULD BE ABLE TO DO MATHEMATICALLY IS NOT A GOOD IDEA.

Where Are We Headed?

We need mathematics to solve problems and make decisions in life logically (as opposed to *intuitively*, my preferred method of reasoning, otherwise known by my husband as *randomly*).

The bigger the numbers, the more pieces that must be factored into the solution, the higher the math necessary. As science, engineering, and technology increasingly invade every aspect of our lives, more and more of us who've tried to avoid this will need to use higher-level math to make the decisions and perform the jobs required in our daily lives.

I thought this algebra, trigonometry, and calculus stuff was just for techies like Kermit, but as our modest-size family business grew, I came to see my need for higher-level math. Even though I still can't set up the problems necessary for good financial management, Kermit is at least encouraged that I recognize the decisions we need to make are essentially mathematical. Fortunately, my kids will enter the adult world better prepared, but that is solely to their father's credit and not mine.

Your goals for your children in this area should be to equip them to be good stewards of their finances. Wisely budgeting for groceries, purchasing a home, investing for the future, etc., all require a strong grasp of basic arithmetic. At one time this might have been enough. But for them to compete in the future job market as well as make full use of the technological opportunities in their daily lives, they will need a better understanding of higher-level math than we have probably found necessary.

Further, if we teach mathematics as a method of thinking, we will have trained our children to effectively make decisions and solve problems—even those not involving numerical operations.

How Do We Get There?

To be ready, then, to use mathematical skills in adult life, our kids must be taught to manipulate numbers and solve complex problems within the context of their real-life application. A *Newsweek* special issue on learning gave this insightful illustration:

Most middle school kids are proficient enough to divide 1,128 by 36—at least with their calculators. But when a national assessment test asked American high school students to solve this problem: "An Army bus holds 36 soldiers. If 1,128 soldiers are being bused to their training site, how many buses are needed?" only 70 percent performed the correct operation—dividing 1,128 by 36 to arrive at 31 with a remainder of 12 (or 31 1/3). But worse, of those who got that far, only one in three went on to draw the conclusion 32 buses were needed. The rest, accustomed to the sterile, self-referential world of school math courses, did not stop to question an answer involving 1/3 of a bus.[1]

Kids need to see at every bend that arithmetic and mathematics are the tools that enable us to think through real-life problems to logical conclusions. If I didn't teach mathematics within the context of solving authentic problems, my kids would have ended up trying to put 1,128 soldiers on 31 1/3 buses just as I certainly would have in high school.

What to Teach When in Mathematics

Primary

As with every other area of study, we want to begin by immersing kids in an environment of numbers and mathematical concepts. We encourage them to mess around with these abstractions by playing games using concrete objects. We build a base for mathematical understanding by using mathematical terms while conversing with our children.

- *Johnny, please get me a couple of apples from the bin. I need to add two more apples to this recipe.*

- *Amy, please share two of your stuffed animals with Johnny. You will still have three left to play with.*

- *This recipe makes enough macaroni and cheese for four people. Because we have eight people in our family, we must double all the ingredients.*

> WE BUILD A BASE FOR MATHEMATICAL UNDERSTANDING BY USING MATHEMATICAL TERMS WHILE CONVERSING WITH OUR CHILDREN.

Here are some of the mathematical concepts to talk about and illustrate during the primary years:

Counting	**Shapes**
Measuring	**Size**
Date and time	**Matching**
Money	**Finding patterns**
Adding	**Doubling**
Taking away	**Dividing in half**

Primary Strategies

- Concrete, concrete, concrete—everything you do to get your child ready for formal instruction needs to be within the confines of a hands-on model. It's not time to be holding up flashcards and memorizing math facts yet—in fact, that's the very approach that gets children thinking mathematics exists only in an abstract realm and is not the outgrowth of our need to solve problems in daily life.

- You need lots of things to count and sort:

    Have at least one hundred counters that are all the same: pennies, Popsicle sticks, etc.

    Have another collection that is easy to sort into groups: colored poker chips, marbles, etc.

    Have another collection that is diverse in shape, size, color, etc.—for example, buttons.

Orally, give your child word problems to solve with these manipulatives.

When Michael was three, I created an ongoing tale of battle and valor for his wooden soldier collection. I would instruct him to bring me five soldiers from the playroom to reinforce the troops in the living room. I'd then ask him to take the seven fatally wounded men back to the playroom hospital. His next instruction would be to add six more reinforcements and let me know how many

> **EVERYTHING YOU DO TO GET YOUR CHILD READY FOR FORMAL INSTRUCTION NEEDS TO BE WITHIN THE CONFINES OF A HANDS-ON MODEL.**

soldiers were now on the battlefield. The story became more and more complicated involving dividing the troops in half, dispatching them to different venues, doubling their numbers, etc.

Create your own game. The strategy is to let your child hear the need for mathematical reasoning in the context of live language.

LET YOUR CHILD HEAR THE NEED FOR MATHEMATICAL REASONING IN THE CONTEXT OF LIVE LANGUAGE.

- Wonderful books are now being produced for children that cultivate math literacy within the context of story. Check out books by Stephen Kellogg, Anno, Tana Hoban, and Bruce McMillan from your library.

- Draw your young children into your daily mathematical decision making. Discuss this with them as you prepare dinner, go to the grocery store, clip coupons, count change, or make a purchase. The point is not so much that they understand the concepts but that they begin to understand that adults make mathematical decisions as a regular part of their lives.

- Hunt for patterns and symmetry in nature.

- Use jigsaw puzzles to help young children develop early problem-solving skills.

- Sort clothes, coins, buttons, and blocks into various categories—i.e., colors, shapes, value, etc.

- Teach fractions by dividing apples, pizzas, or desserts into equal parts.

- Learn children's counting rhymes and songs. Teach skip counting (2, 4, 6, 8, . . . 5, 10, 15, 20, 25, 30, 35 . . .).

- Even though we're almost all digital now, kids still need to tell time from a face clock. Purchase a big one at a farm supply center. When ready, use this not just to teach telling time but also to teach fractions of an hour.

- Make or buy a blank calendar large enough for children to mark the days on.

- Hang an oversized thermometer outside a kitchen window and have your children track the daily temperature.

- Use a large scale for weighing. Purchase a balance scale

as well to teach the concept of "equal." (This concrete image can later be used to teach older children to "balance" both sides of an algebraic equation.)

- Spend a day measuring the house. Use a ruler, yardstick, and Daddy's heavy-duty retractable measuring tape.

Recommendations for the Primary Years

Grocery Cart Math (Common Sense Press) is a booklet of strategies for turning daily household chores, such as grocery shopping, into an applied math lesson.

1-2-3 Math by Jean Warren (www.preschoolexpress. com) will give you more readiness games to play with your primary-age children. Jean's books are now out of print, but still widely available (used) at online sites such as Amazon. However, she has put most of her content up on her site, where you can now download it for free.

Math Safari (Educational Insights) is an electronic game based upon national math standards that drills kids in basic operations. It's a good tool for children who are ready for arithmetic but aren't ready for all the printing involved. Kristen found this resource very motivational.

More Than Counting: Whole-Math Activities for Preschool and Kindergarten by Sally Moomaw and Brenda Hieronymus (1995) provides hands-on, simple activities to get your young learners ready foundationally for the more formal, abstract math to come. Don't skip these fundamental experiences.

Elementary

After a leisurely season of math fun and games, you are now ready to add to this strategy formal instruction in arithmetic. The National Council of Teachers of Mathematics issued new standards for mathematics education in 2000. These have been widely adopted and are reflected in the most recent revisions of standardized tests. Among other things, the new standards heavily emphasize mathematical reasoning and communicating mathematically. This means kids are working on problems that are more complex and often in written form. And rather than teacher-directed instruction, the focus is on kids talking about the processes they have used in solving the problem.

At the same time, critics warn that this emphasis on these standards is taking precious class time away from drill and practice that helps students increase speed and efficiency in mastering lots of problems. Critics also disparage the idea that all routes to solving a problem are equal in value.

It probably won't surprise you to learn that I once again straddle the fence on this debate, advocating instruction that includes:

- drill
- daily practice in basic arithmetic
- weekly word problem solving
- lots of math projects and games
- regular doses of competition and group work

Elementary Strategies

- Before kids move into higher mathematics, they should be able to rattle off basic facts without thought. This will enable them to move quickly to the more difficult reasoning aspects of the problems. Math facts are mastered through drill—give your kids timed tests, making it a game to improve their time. *Calculadders* is one source of graduated and timed math drills. For the child who doesn't like lots of printing, drill him or her in math facts with the *Learning Wrap-Ups* for arithmetic. The correct answers are indicated by wrapping a string of yarn correctly around a plastic, palm-size board.

- Use manipulatives to create concrete models of mathematical concepts and abstractions. We used Cuisenaire rods daily. These rods are color-coded and graduated in size to represent the values 1–10. Deceptively simple and inexpensive, they are indispensable for illustrating addition, subtraction, multiplication, division, fractions, equivalencies, ratios,

BEFORE KIDS MOVE INTO HIGHER MATHEMATICS. THEY SHOULD BE ABLE TO RATTLE OFF BASIC MATH FACTS WITHOUT THOUGHT.

and more. I needed to do a bit of reading to learn how to use them, but once I understood the basic concepts it was easy to make them integral to our program. They are a regular part of the Miquon Math elementary program I used with Kristen and Kayte, and I frequently got them out to help the boys visualize their algebra concepts as well.

- A treasure trove of kid-enticing manipulatives and other mathematical tools can also be ordered from Delta Education's *Hands-On Math* (www.delta-education.com).

- Have fun creating charts and graphs. Create surveys and analyze the data. Gabe got so interested in a project surveying his friends, he ended up simulating university-level research by collecting data from homeschooled kids across Pennsylvania, compiling his results, and "publishing" them in a ten-page report—when he was ten. It was later part of a story he sold to a regional magazine.

> **HAVE FUN CREATING CHARTS AND GRAPHS.**

- Familiarize kids with the tools a mathematician has at his disposal—for example, calculators, weights and measures, charts, graphs, spreadsheets, etc. The best math calculators are made by Texas Instruments, available from Delta Education as well. We used the TI-108 for early elementary (it has big keys for little fingers) and the Math Explorer Plus after that. (Kids will need a graphing calculator in high school.) Once my kids understood conceptually the process by which an algorithm is solved, I allowed them to use the calculator to solve or check their problems.

- To foster mathematical reasoning, practice estimating the answer before solving a problem. Ask kids if their answer makes sense as well to keep them focused on using logic. (This is now a skill tested on most standardized tests.)

- Let them earn money around the house and then develop responsibility for managing it wisely.

- Use strategy games: cards, dominoes, chess, Mancala, Twenty-Four, and Muggins, develop mathematical reasoning intuitively.

- Organize a Math Olympiad group. This is a super problem-solving competition for kids in fourth through eighth grades. A mathematically minded mom at CHESS runs a Math Olympiad group and a MathCounts team as a junior high class and uses this as a vehicle for teaching kids a repertoire of problem-solving strategies. If that's the focus, your kids will greatly benefit, no matter how successful they ultimately are at the meets.

- Music is essentially mathematical in structure. Studying an instrument and chord theory will also develop your child's mathematical thinking.

Recommendations for the Elementary Years

For developing mathematical reasoning and a concrete base, I recommend the following manipulative-based programs:

Math-U-See can rightly claim the title of "granddaddy" of manipulative-based, homeschool-friendly math programs. Developed by former math teacher and long-time homeschool dad Steve Demme, Math-U-See has been honed into a well-designed, educationally sound program best used to lay a sound foundation for the higher-level math of high school. The program includes engaging instructional DVDs and manipulatives that can be cleverly interlocked à la Legos. Several demonstration videos can be viewed online, and that's all you'll need to be convinced this is an exceptional program.

RightStart Math: I've been hearing rave reviews about this program from homeschool friends with young children. Developed by Joan Cotter who holds a Ph.D. in math education, the elementary-intermediate curriculum uses her innovative AL Abacus as the cornerstone of an elegant, manipulative-based program. The consistent comment I hear is that the program is easy to use, kids enjoy it, and moms can see real gains in their children's mathematical understanding (moms make gains, too).

Singapore Math: A number of my friends are very satisfied with their results from this import. I should mention that these happy users tend to be science- and mathematics-type people, and one friend candidly says her background makes using the program a lot easier than it probably would be for someone like me (she knows me too well). The company has a very helpful website with an active forum for getting support.

For drill work and daily practice in basic arithmetic operations, the King of the Hill:

Saxon Math: There is little to compete for ease of use and presentation with Saxon's middle elementary program.[2] This begins with Saxon 54 (indicates average fifth-grader, bright fourth; Saxon 65 means average sixth-grader, bright fifth, etc.). Kids who use Saxon Math often score markedly higher on those standardized tests that test traditional arithmetic skills. (It is, conversely, a disadvantage on tests modified to the new math standards.)

With Kristen, I used Horizon Math published by Alpha Omega. Unlike other programs, Kristen was able to write her answers in the workbooks through sixth grade. This meant the program was consumable and could not be re-sold, but it also saved me the time of writing out the exercises for her to solve. (My kids did much less math if *they* had to first copy the exercises from the textbook and then solve them.) You might want to take this factor into consideration when choosing a program—a lot of practice should be a priority.

For developing a repertoire of problem-solving strategies

Creative Problem Solving in School Mathematics, George Lenchner. By the founder of Math Olympiad and can be ordered through them. Use as a supplement or core text for students fourth grade or older.

Figure It Out: Levels 1–6 (roughly first through sixth) available from Curriculum Associates

For fun and games

Family Math, Jean Kerr Stenmark. Hands-on activities designed for parents to do at home with their children, K–8. Cindy McKeown used this with her sons in elementary school as her sole text, and they were then able to transition directly into Saxon 76 during middle school.

The I Hate Mathematics! Book and any others by Marilyn Burns, a leading educator in mathematics as well as a prolific writer. Read anything you can get your hands on by her, and you'll have all the ideas you need for a top-flight math program. (I know that copyright looks old, but Burns is still developing math resources today; and even with a 1975 imprint, her suggestions are still relevant).

Secondary

What course of study you follow in high school will be heavily influenced by the college and career goals your child is considering. If your daughter's talking medicine, you need three to four years of advanced mathematics; if your son is interested in starting his own business, you need to fulfill the basic algebra and geometry requirement and then focus on accounting and business math. But in today's climate, that still means he needs to be calculus-ready before college. So in this section, I'll limit myself to a general overview of high school mathematics and try to get you pointed in the right direction for scouring out your options.

The typical sequence of study at this level includes algebra 1 and geometry and then, for the college-bound, algebra 2, and trigonometry and precalculus, usually integrated into an advanced mathematics course. I also recommend squeezing in somewhere, through either a course of study or work experience, consumer math, financial management and investment, and computer science. These later skills are much more integral to real life than the trig will ever be.

> WHAT COURSE OF STUDY YOU FOLLOW IN HIGH SCHOOL WILL BE HEAVILY INFLUENCED BY THE COLLEGE AND CAREER GOALS YOUR CHILD IS CONSIDERING.

Secondary Strategies

- Expose your teen to as many occupations and fields

of study as possible to help determine early on if he is headed for the sciences or humanities at college or to a vocational or technical-training school—or if he is headed directly to the work force. Then you can hone in on the best sequence of mathematics to study during high school. Either visit places of employment or invite folks into your co-op to talk with the kids about their occupations.

- Use math tutors, video instruction, and software programs to cover the higher-level mathematics you are not up to.

- Expect your teens to earn and save money. If you require them to pay for all but their basic needs, you'll be able to mentor them in responsible money management while under your supervision.

> **EXPECT YOUR TEENS TO EARN AND SAVE MONEY.**

- Geometry is where I first learned the beauty and science of logical thinking—and that set me up for a *coup de grace* by C. S. Lewis, who proves in *Mere Christianity* that Christ is either who He says He is or a "lunatic—on a level with the man who says he is a poached egg—or else he would be the Devil of Hell." What he couldn't be, given his claims, is a "great moral teacher."[3] Deftly maneuvered into this course by Lewis's deductive reasoning, I was left without a comfortable choice. There was no syllogism for Christ as a good teacher or moral person, no overlapping circles where I could occupy the middle ground. Having dutifully practiced those geometric proofs in high school, I knew a conclusion, and only one, could be drawn. I had no recourse but to convert.

Geometry is the same tool I used to give my children a well-reasoned faith.

Recommendations for the Secondary Years

Basic texts

Chalk Dust Video Courses with Dana Mosely. This is

where I ended up in my uphill battle to challenge my sons with the higher-level math they were ready for but I had absolutely no interest in learning. For two years we used a math tutor, and together Mike, Gabe, and their tutor Carole worked through the Jacob's algebra and geometry text. But then we really puttered around for almost half a year while they struggled to complete daily lessons on their own in trigonometry. The weekly meeting with Carole just was not enough. Having used Dana's SAT Math Review video course with great results, they were willing to give this course a try. I had been balking because of the expense (more than $300 for the course, text, and solutions manual). But it was a lifesaver. Everyone who has previewed these videos, especially those with a math background, have concurred that Dana Mosely is one of the best math teachers you are ever likely to get in a high school or college classroom.

Keys to Algebra and Keys to Geometry. For the student who just wants to get this requirement out of the way and is highly unlikely to enter college, this simplified program is the most creative and least painful way to present the material. (This works well with accelerated elementary students who want a challenge too.)

Saxon Math. Algebra 1, algebra 2, advanced mathematics, calculus, and physics are the favored choices. The higher-level texts are challenging enough to prepare students for AP examinations. Some students find Saxon's repetitive presentation rather dry by this time; but for the homeschool mom, the lessons and step-by-step solutions manuals make it hard to pass up. This program also works well for tutoring. Saxon does little to demonstrate how this higher-level mathematics is applied, so you'll need to supplement through experience or other resources.

Teaching Textbooks. The Sabouri brothers have created a product with a true understanding of how homeschooling works. Their math programs are designed for students to use independently. The well-organized and engaging textbooks are supported with a multimedia presentation of the lesson on CD and then a step-by-step multimedia solution for each of the more than three thousand problems in the text. The solutions are on separate CDs, so you can make sure your teen works the problems on his own before checking his answers. Our daughter Kayte loved using these math programs for her summer tutoring jobs during college.

VideoText Interactive. Here is the best multimedia presentation of algebra (I and II) you will find on the market. It's worth the price, because your kids are going to retain the algebra they learn through Tom Clark's instruction. Cindy McKeown used this with her last child and raved about its ease of use and clarity of presentation. I believe its strength is in teaching kids to reason mathematically rather than just solving pre-designed problems. Dr. Jay Wile of Apologia Science recommends it for all his science students.

For financial management and applied math

Applied Math. More challenging than a consumer math program, focuses on business math and finance.

Consumer Math

Discovering God's Way of Handling Money, Howard Dayton. This is a course in money management that your teens can work through on their own, or you can organize as an elective at your local co-op. Support material for teachers is available.

Financial Peace for the Next Generation, Home School Edition, Dave Ramsey. Twelve dynamic lessons from Dave in his inimitable style and hip, multimedia presentation. Complete with lesson plans, quizzes, activities and tests.

For fun

The Joy of Mathematics and *More Joy of Mathematics,* Theoni Pappas. Integrate these wonderful problems and anecdotes into your weekly program to help foster a love and fascination for mathematics in your teens.

Science

It is tragic that the discipline designed by God to demonstrate His existence and character is avoided by Christians and worshiped by man. God has given us mathematics as a tool to reason rightly, and He has given us science to apprehend truth. It is the discipline whereby we discover natural law. And it all points to Him. As creation mirrors the Creator, so natural law is intended to mirror spiritual law.

As a young Christian I viewed science as a threat to my fledgling faith and avoided those courses in college, but as a mature believer who has pursued a better understanding of science with my children, it has become a powerful validation of our faith. When my kids and I studied the intricate microcosm of the atom and then saw that same intelligent design magnified in the structure of the universe, it defied all logic to conclude there is no Designer.

Instead of Christians retreating from these disciplines, they should be flooding these fields of study and using their discoveries to point folks homeward.

Where Are We Headed?

To serve us in our adult lives, what do we need to glean now from science? If we teach science with an emphasis on memorizing facts, then it's pretty difficult to make a list of essentials relevant for all of us. But if we teach science as a *process*, then we can use science to give our kids the skills they need to *analyze, synthesize,* and *evaluate* information—in any discipline.

Analysis is the process we use to take things apart—to subdivide, if you will, into components and categories. *Synthesis* is the process we use to put things together *in a new way*—it is the creative process that leads to new ideas, products, and

> GOD HAS GIVEN US MATHEMATICS AS A TOOL TO REASON RIGHTLY, AND HE HAS GIVEN US SCIENCE TO APPREHEND TRUTH.

procedures. And *evaluation* is the skill we use to draw conclusions and make judgments about all the choices we have.

In life, we use analysis, synthesis, and evaluation for three things:

- problem solving
- decision making
- invention

Are these necessary skills we want our children to have as adults? If so, then there is no better vehicle than science as a concrete model for practicing these processes with your kids.

How Do We Get There?

"Good science education is always discovered and never force fed."
—B. K. Hixson

My approach to science has been influenced by Bryce Hixson, science educator and developer of some of the coolest science labs I've seen. I was first exposed to Bryce's philosophy through the lab books he's produced for Wild Goose Science Company, a pretty off-the-wall science education company he founded.

Here's Bryce's advice for teaching science:

1. **It's got to be hands-on.** What we perform we remember, Bryce asserts, backing up his theory with neurological research that has mapped the human mind. Information kids learn through memorization shows up stored in one tiny depository. But information acquired while performing a task is found stored in numerous interconnected areas, creating, Bryce says, a 3-D hologram picture in our mind. Which approach enables us to retrieve and apply what we've learned to a variety of situations? Obviously, the one where kids get to *do*.

2. **It's got to be question-driven** — by the kids, that is. Your job is to ask open-ended questions. The kids' job is to find the answer. The criteria for the questions are:

   - The student is in charge of determining if her

279

answer is correct.

- Creativity, exploration, and inquisitiveness are required to answer the question.

- Failure is viewed as positive feedback.

3. **It's got to be fun.** Or, to quote Bryce accurately, *funny*. He's also collected a pile of research on the benefits of learning while laughing. Among other things, our bodies release a stimulus while laughing, making us more alert. If you see Bryce's stuff, you may suspect he merely searched for the research he needed to validate his personality. But I can't argue with the enthusiasm I saw in my kids after using his stuff at a Young Scientists' Institute we attended.

My reason for teaching science this way—or rather *facilitating* science opportunities for my kids with this kind of format—is the sense of wonder and discovery it evokes in kids. And that instills in them a reverence and awe for the One who is Creator.

We Now Interrupt Your Reading for This Theological Moment

Why did God create the universe? Have you ever answered that question for your kids? Another favorite proverb of mine:

"It is the glory of God to conceal a matter; But the glory of kings is to search out a matter."
—Proverbs 25:2

When Mike first started having quiet times years ago, he came downstairs quite frustrated one morning. "Why does God make the Bible so hard to understand?" he demanded.

I shared this proverb with him, saying, "Mike, this is what life is all about. God is not easy to know. He says He will only reveal Himself to those who diligently seek Him with all their hearts. But that's what makes life interesting. He deliberately conceals Himself and intends the pursuit of the knowledge of who He truly is to be a blessing in your life. It gives us purpose." (To quote Oswald Chambers one more time: "What we call the process, God calls

> YOUR JOB IS TO ASK OPEN-ENDED QUESTIONS. THE KIDS' JOB IS TO FIND THE ANSWER.

the end.")

I love the mystery of life. I love the discovery. That God made the world such a fascinating place and gave us the intelligence to apprehend it is evidence of His great love for us. That's the point of science: to give testimony to the nature of God.

And that's my beef with science textbooks—even Christian ones. They take the process of discovery out of it for the kids, settling rather for force-fed facts that defy the very reasons God created the universe in the first place—for our exploration.

Don't rob your kids of the opportunities to solve the mysteries of science themselves. There are eternal purposes at work in it.

What to Teach When in Science

The topics you introduce and the order in which you do so can really be driven by your child's interests. The goal is to use the area of exploration as a vehicle for developing process skills. Here are those listed by Bryce in *How to Turn Kids on to Science*:

- Creating

- Classifying (grouping things according to their similarities and differences)

- Experimenting (testing the hypothesis using the scientific method)

- Following directions

- Graphing

- Hypothesizing

- Inferring (drawing conclusions based on data collected)

- Measuring

- Observing

- Sequencing (placing things in logical order)

And what is the scientific method? Here are the official criteria we used for entry in a regional science and engineering fair. This procedure, of course, would be simplified for younger children.

1. The student poses a question that can be answered through experimentation. Example: "How does heat from below affect root development in house plants?"

2. He formulates a hypothesis predicting the results.

3. He sets up an experiment for testing the hypothesis and records the results.

4. He draws conclusions from these and then formulates a new hypothesis if necessary.

5. He repeats the experiment to validate the conclusions.

Primary

During the first few years of school, build a base of knowledge for your children to draw upon for more formal experimentation and laboratory work later on. The natural world (especially animals) and how things work are often of greatest interest to young children.

Primary Strategies

- Read to your child from science books. I recommend the A Closer Look series published by Dorling Kindersley, The Magic School Bus series by Joanne Cole, Let's-Read-And-Find-Out Science by Kathleen Weidner Zoehfeld, and those by Ruth Heller, Aliki, and others listed below.
- Collect things: insects, leaves, rocks, pictures of animals, etc.
- Grow things.
- Visit zoos, nature centers, and aquariums.
- Explore different ecosystems: a pond, a swamp, a forest, a meadow, the ocean.
- Set up your own ecosystem: a backyard habitat, an aquarium, a terrarium.
- Make recipes together; concoct your own.
- Observe birds, insects, changing seasons, weather patterns, etc.
- Play with construction toys: blocks, Legos, Erector sets, etc.

Recommendations for the Primary Years

Janice Van Cleave's Play and Find Out series. These activity

> THE NATURAL WORLD (ESPECIALLY ANIMALS) AND HOW THINGS WORK ARE OFTEN OF GREATEST INTEREST TO YOUNG CHILDREN.

books for the younger set provide a foundation of exploration in the sciences. Van Cleave has titles appropriate for students in preschool through high school.

More Than Magnets: Exploring the Wonders of Science in Preschool and Kindergarten, Sally Moomaw and Brenda Hieronymus. Hands-on, simple activities to get your young learners ready foundationally for the more formal, rigorous study of science to come. Don't skip these fundamental experiences.

Nature Friend Magazine (www.naturefriendmagazine). A monthly nature magazine which emphasizes the beauty and design of God's creation and our responsibility as Christians to steward this gift.

1-2-3 Science, Jean Warren (www.preschoolexpress.com). Hands-on readiness activities for young children. Jean's titles are out of print, but material is available free at the website.

Science Arts, MaryAnn Kohl. Fun art projects that illustrate a science concept.

Elementary

The following units of study are usually explored informally before kids move into the more technical aspects of science on the high school level:

- Rocks, minerals, and fossils
- Machines and motion
- Solar system
- Energy
- Human body, nutrition, and health
- Heat, light, and sound
- Weather
- Kitchen chemistry
- Nature and environment
- Creation
- Electricity and magnets

Elementary Strategies

- Have your child categorize his collections of rocks, plants, leaves, animals, etc.

- Begin acquiring lab equipment.

- Require your children to keep a lab notebook where questions, observations, experiments, data, conclusions, etc., are recorded.

- Using the list above, design units of study around experimentation and demonstrations.

- Bookmark www.sciencenewsforkids.org. This site archives articles from the magazine in seventeen categories. Your kids can read the articles (with full-color photos) and do the activities, while you can use the "teacher zone" to print off related worksheets to quiz their comprehension.

- Visit www.chemistry.org. (Once there, click on "Education," then "Science for Kids.") You will find all the cool stuff formerly published in their *Wonder Science* newsletter. You can do these experiments easily at home, and there is enough here to fill a year or two of rigorous elementary science.

HAVE YOUR CHILD CATEGORIZE HIS COLLECTIONS OF ROCKS, PLANTS, LEAVES, ANIMALS, ETC.

Recommendations for the Elementary Years

Organizing a day of science experiments does not come naturally to me. I'd rather administrate the group and find someone else to pull it off. So what I have listed here are those titles and sources I've found easy enough for me to pull off by my lonesome:

Apologia's Young Explorer series, Jeannie Fulbright. This is the absolute "must-do" science series for the elementary years. Jeannie is a lover of Charlotte Mason's educational philosophy, as am I, and her series integrates Mason's notebooking method beautifully into a thorough foundation for studying the sciences.

The Best of Wonder Science, two-volume set. More than 600 hands-on science activities compiled from the society's years of publishing *Wonder Science* for K–8 students. This mammoth, spiral-bound set shows parents and teachers how to pull off and explain simple experiments with materials around the home.

Biology for Every Kid and scores of other titles by Janice VanCleave. VanCleave's books are filled with simple, home-based experiments you can do with your kids, and titles are organized neatly into subject area, such as *Oceans, Human Body, Chemistry, Physics,* etc. VanCleave expresses her Christian faith in the foreword of a number of her titles, and I have not found any positions that conflict with our beliefs.

Blood and Guts, Linda Allison. Every title in this Brown Paper School series is a winner, but this is their bestseller.

Discovery Channel Young Scientist Challenge rewards middle school students (grades 5–8) who can organize an exceptional science project and write cogently about it. Students must first have science fair projects judged through a local or regional science and engineering fair recognized by Intel ISEF (International Science and Engineering Fair). Guidelines for affiliating are available at societyforscience.org.

Dorling Kindersley's Eyewitness books and multimedia such as David Macaulay's *The New Way Things Work* CD-ROM are attractively priced and eye-boggling.

History of Science is a unit study built around the lives of famous scientists and simple but content-rich experiments using items around the house.

Insect Lore (www.insectlore.com) is *the* coolest site for ordering all the life science kits, outdoor equipment, books and live insects, worms and frogs you need for your young explorers.

Lyrical Learning publishes both a life and earth science curriculum for elementary levels taught through song. Especially helpful for the auditory learner, but also an effective way for helping any child master the scientific knowledge necessary for preparing for high school-level courses later.

Science Olympiad is an elementary through high school competition that encourages homeschoolers' participation. Kids compete as individuals and teams at regional, state, and national tournaments. The projects are multidisciplinary, so kids get a broad exposure to all the core sciences. Homeschoolers are asked to contact their state chapter for registration requirements.

Tops Learning Systems are the resource of choice for creating appropriate laboratory experiences at home during high school. They have labs for children as young as third grade as well. They only provide the instructional manuals; you have to gather the supplies, but it's usually not too difficult.

Usborne books are also wildly popular with homeschoolers and their kids. You'll find many at the library or from the distributors listed in the Resource Guide.

The following companies specialize in science from a creationist or intelligent design perspective. They provide resources for a variety of ages and grades.

Apologia Educational Ministries
1106 Meridian Plaza, Suite 220
Anderson, IN 46016 US
Phone: 888-524-4724
Fax: 765-608-3290
www.apologia.com

Answers in Genesis
P.O. Box 510
Hebron, KY 41048
800-778-3390
www.answersingeneisis.org

Creation Ministries International
PO Box 350
Powder Springs, GA 30127-0350
770-439-9130
www.creation.com

Creation Resource Foundation
P.O. Box 570
El Dorado, CA 95623
866-225-5229
www.awesomeworks.com

Master Books
P.O. Box 726
Green Forest, AR 72638
800-999-3777
www.newleafpress.net

Order home lab kits, supplies, and books from the following places. The first three companies cater to homeschoolers.

Home Science Tools
665 Carbon Street
Billings, MT 59102
800-860-6272
www.homesciencetools.com
Home Science Tools is a unique company that has put together lab kits for homeschoolers that fit the science curriculum of major publisher—i.e., Bob Jones, A Beka, etc. They carry a broad range of science equipment as well.

Nature's Workshop Plus!
P.O. Box 425
Danville, IN 46122-0425
317-745-0443
www.workshopplus.com
Mennonite publication, reasonable pricing

Tobin's Lab
P.O. Box 725
Culpeper, VA 22701
540-829-6906
www.tobinslab.com
Tobin's Lab is a homeschool family business with a very helpful catalog organized in the order of creation and offering all the small quantities you need for lab sciences.

Carolina Biological Supply Company
2700 York Road
Burlington, NC 27215-3398
800-334-5551
www.carolina.com

Delta Education
P.O. Box 3000
Nashua, NH 03061-3000
800-442-5444
www.delta-education.com
Hands-On Science Catalog

Wild Goose Science
P.O. Box 35665
Greensboro, NC 27425
888-621-1040
www.wildgoosescience.com

Secondary

It's now time to acquire a rudimentary understanding of scientific formulas and the molecular structure of the universe without trying to kill all that science interest you cultivated in grade school. If I tell you the recommended sequence of courses often studied on this level, will you promise not to be legalistic about it? It's a springboard, folks, please!

> Seventh—life sciences
>
> Eighth—earth sciences
>
> Ninth—physical science
>
> Tenth—biology
>
> Eleventh—chemistry
>
> Twelfth—physics

Students heading into any kind of science or math-oriented field should complete this sequence one year sooner, and then add an additional advanced-level science in twelfth.

The laboratory experience is important at the high school level but perhaps the most challenging to facilitate at home, especially for the student headed toward a college major in this area. To maintain perspective, though, keep in mind that many public high schools have reduced their laboratory sciences to demonstrations because of the risks associated with allowing kids to use the equipment. So the challenge of providing laboratory experience is not a reason to give up homeschooling in high school.

Secondary Strategies

PARTICIPATE IN A SCIENCE FAIR THAT FOLLOWS THE INTEL INTERNATIONAL SCIENCE AND ENGINEERING FAIR GUIDELINES.

- At least once, participate in a science fair that follows the Intel International Science and Engineering Fair guidelines. It's a lot of work, and I did myself in by organizing one on the elementary level that all my kids entered projects in. You may want to try this with smaller numbers.

- If you want to try putting together your own curriculum for laboratory science at home, use the Tops Learning Systems, Wild Goose Press MegaLabs, or Castle Heights Press material and supplement with grade-level science reading.

- To keep my kids interested in scientific knowledge, I used the table of contents in a basic textbook to compile a reading list from the library of more interesting and better-written trade books.

- Here is where a course at the local community college or as part of a family school like CHESS really makes sense—Mike and Gabe took life sciences, biology, and physics at CHESS. They hated the pre-Apologia textbook we used, but they did thirty labs each year, including those with microscopes and dissection—not something I have the money or desire to complete in my kitchen.

- If those options are not available, consider a video course or software program. (See recommended sources on pages 322-325 and 327-328.)

- Finally, there is a vast body of information available on the Internet. Many websites are run by innovative college students and feature engaging graphical design and interactive capabilities that are ideal for high school. You can even find simulated labs to download. There is an unprecedented opportunity here. See websites listed in chapter 28.

Recommendations for the Secondary Years

Having tried a variety of science textbooks, all of which my three older kids detested, the Apologia Science courses developed by Jay Wile are the only texts I now advocate. When I first heard "Dr. Jay" speak at a convention many years ago, I realized he was a true teacher as well as a scientist, with a real heart to support the homeschool community. After that I switched to his materials, and science became a much more pleasant experience at our house.

All his texts have been written with the understanding that the student will likely not have a knowledgeable teacher who will "teach" the lesson on the other end. (This is a key point a lot of publishers trying to reach the homeschool market miss.) Assuming this, Dr. Jay's textbooks are almost twice as long as the average science textbook, Christian or secular, and are written in an engaging, conversational style — i.e., you get the information *plus* the teacher.

Under Dr. Jay's expert tutelage, you will fall in love with his materials as well as the subject matter. He's also conceived a way for you to complete the laboratory requirements at home with household supplies and minimal investment. Additionally, Apologia's science courses are also taught online at ApologiaAcademy with a qualified teacher.

The sequence of courses begins in seventh grade with general science, followed by physical science, biology, chemistry, and physics. Students should complete Algebra I before chemistry, and geometry and basic trigonometric functions *before* physics. Dr. Jay has also completed texts for advanced biology, chemistry, and physics. He highly recommends completing one of these during the senior year, especially if your child is interested in entering an engineering or medical field of study.

History

If the language arts prepare us to communicate our faith, math teaches us to reason rightly, and science helps us apprehend truth, then what do we study history for? To learn lessons from the past.

That's why God continuously reminded Israel to record events, make memorials, and observe feasts. These are still methods we need to use to ensure that the lessons are not forgotten.

To benefit from the study of history, we must teach it from this perspective.

Where Are We Headed?

Experience is the best teacher, the saying goes, but it's foolish to assume those experiences must always be our own and never gleaned from the experiences of others. I told my kids stories from my childhood in the hopes that they would learn from my mistakes and be spared the consequences of repeating them.

As adults, we must make decisions that direct our family, business, church, and civic life. Believing that God is calling us to raise leaders, I wanted to equip my kids to govern wisely the arenas of influence God opens up for them. And much of that equipping can be gleaned from studying people, civilizations, and events of the past.

How Do We Get There?

1. Focus on Individuals and Principles. We want to look to history for role models to emulate. We don't need to sanitize their lives or Christianize them to draw inspiration from them. The Bible is our guide here, and it does neither.

Rather, we can use books to prepare our children for the moral choices they may face in the future. I find historical fiction and biography to be ideal for this purpose.

> WE WANT TO LOOK TO HISTORY FOR ROLE MODELS TO EMULATE.

The recommended resources that follow will help you focus on principles, but you can easily do this yourself by choosing to talk with your children about the cause and effect of events in history, the character qualities of the main characters, and the biblical framework for making our choices in the same situation.

Though the books we read didn't intend this, we found much to discuss about the sovereignty of God in our study of Squanto. Captured and sold into slavery in Europe, there he was converted to Christianity. Upon his return to the New World, he found that every member of his tribe had been wiped out by disease. Now bilingual, he became an interpreter and friend to the pilgrims at Plymouth, teaching them to plant corn and smoothing relations between them and neighboring tribes.

We also saw the dramatic repercussion from missed opportunities. During another unit of study, we learned that the emperor of China had asked Marco Polo to bring priests to explain Christianity to him on Polo's return visit. But the missionaries who began the journey were frightened away by tales of marauders and Muslim Turks lying in wait along the Mideastern trading trail. Polo returned to China alone. Shortly after that, Buddhism appeared, the emperor converted to that religion, and Buddhism spread throughout the continent.

2. Tell History as a Story. This is what makes Ken Burns's documentaries so captivating. He researches the lives of representative individuals and then lets them tell their stories in their own words, drawing upon diaries, letters, and articles from the time. The Old Testament records history predominantly through story, and Jesus taught His followers through story. I think there's a pretty obvious principle here—we want to share our own recorded history with our children through a story format. Then they can identify with the characters and draw lessons from their lives.

What to Teach When in History

Primary

Working outward from your child's own history, begin to explore the past in greater and greater concentric circles. Storytelling is a powerful family tradition and one that should be recovered to give our children a greater sense of identity and purpose.

FOCUS ON BIOGRAPHY.

During this time our children acquire the broad strokes of our faith through the Bible stories we tell, as well. Look for resources that draw attention to the grand arch of God's redemptive activity in human history. Tapestry of Grace, for instance, makes this the heartbeat of its curriculum, whereas a lot of Christian material seems to focus on Bible stories as great adventures intended to entertain or as object lessons intended to elicit moral behavior. Neither approach points kids to their need for a Savior.

And finally, our primary-age children begin to acquire a base of understanding of our national history, primarily through the observance of holidays throughout the year.

Primary Strategies

- Make a family history book. Collect stories from

grandparents. This is a wonderful way to make them a part of your homeschool program—and maybe soften their concerns about your choice as well.

- Focus on biography. Read books and use resources that create a sense of character by coloring in the details of the studied individuals' lives.

- Dramatize stories from history.

- Make recipes and crafts from different time periods.

 ## Recommendations for the Primary Years

The Childhood of Famous Americans biographies are very popular books with emerging readers. These titles were first published in the 1940s, and many have now been reissued but not revised. Use interlibrary loan to find available copies of the more than 200 titles in the original line. Augusta Stevenson is the best author of the series.

Cooking Up U.S. History: Recipes and Research to Share with Children, Suzanne Barchers and Patricia Marden

Early Settler Activity Guide, Elizabeth Stenson

Greathall Productions. Storytelling at its finest by Jim Weiss. Jim has many selections from history.

Journey Through History series, Gloria Verges. Short, colorful guide books for young readers with helpful resource guide for parents and teachers in the appendices.

The Story of the World Activity Books, Susan Wise Bauer. The Story of the World series (coming up next in the elementary years) is a must-do sometime during the elementary years. I would hold off a bit with this age group unless you already have older kids and you want to do history together as a family. Then these activity books developed by Susan for grades 1-4 are just what you need to give busy hands something to do in order to make connections with the stories you are reading to them.

Your Story Hour tapes are very well produced and dramatize the lives of Bible characters, missionaries, and historical figures.

I've used historical coloring books from Bellerophon and Dover as inexpensive activities for young children to complete while studying a unit of time.

Elementary

You have a decision to make. Will you study American history or world history on the elementary level? It's a philosophical choice. Proponents of following the classical Christian tradition (e.g., Tapestry of Grace, Veritas Press, or The Well-Trained Mind) make a compelling case for teaching American history only after students have acquired a basic understanding of the roots of Western civilization. Their curriculum starts with the Old Testament, then ancient Egypt, ancient Greece, and so forth. And with the exceptional resources now available from these companies, it's hard to argue against following this model.

Developmentally, however, I'm not always sure this is the best place to start with young learners. I found in practice that it was easier to present American history on this level and then move to world history and cultures during adolescence. Why?

It's difficult for a young child to conceptualize "Ancient Egypt," where it is and when it happened. It's a lot easier to build a concrete base for understanding American history—family trips to Independence Mall in Philadelphia; Washington, D.C.; Plimoth Plantation; or local sites will help kids acquire a framework on which to hang these stories.

By high school they don't necessarily need these hands-on experiences to conceptualize ancient events.

Elementary Strategies

- Read historical fiction to better visualize the human drama and culture of the times. The catalogs produced by Veritas Press, Greenleaf Press, and Tapestry of

Grace organize historical fiction according to time periods. Bookmark their websites and use their recommendations to guide your choices.

- Use history as the focal point of unit studies that incorporate the sciences, music, art, and literature. This will help children better understand the cause and effect of historic events.

- Visit sites with interpreters and artisans. Draw them out to glean the stories from them.

- To avoid a revisionist view of history—i.e., recasting what really happened to suit our current political preferences—use primary source material in your program. This includes journals, diaries, and documents from the time period. The use of primary sources is being emphasized currently in the teaching of history, so more and more artifacts are being reprinted and made available. Jackdaw Publications is one example.

- Subscribe to *Cobblestone: The History Magazine for Young People* and *Calliope: World History for Young People* (800-821-0115).

- For current events from a Christian perspective, subscribe to God's World Publications (www.gwnews.com). These are bi-weekly newspapers geared to specific grade levels.

Recommendations for the Elementary Years

The Story of the World, Susan Wise Bauer. Susan is one of the most engaging writers working today, and this four-volume set covers world history from 5000 B.C.–A.D. 1994 Her materials have extended far beyond the homeschool community and achieved true best-seller status within the mainstream. Meticulously researched and crafted, even if you do not follow the Well-Trained Mind's scope and sequence and methodology, you most certainly want to find time to read this series aloud with your children during the elementary years.

> USE HISTORY AS THE FOCAL POINT OF UNIT STUDIES THAT INCORPORATE THE SCIENCES, MUSIC, ART, AND LITERATURE.

Tapestry of Grace. Marcia Somerville's curriculum is a work of art and inspiration. Why the accolades? Because Marcia knows the essential reason for all of human history—to put on display the redemptive and compelling grace of a sovereign, merciful God—and she has created a marvelous means for communicating that rich truth to future generations. Designed to be used by the whole family or in a co-op setting with multiple ages (although I find it most suitable for older students, especially if you do not have time to incorporate the hands-on activities for the younger ones), the curriculum is backed by an exceptionally well-run company you can count on to stay one step ahead of its customers' needs.

A History of Us, 3rd edition, by Joy Hakim is the best resource available to tell American history as a story. You won't agree with Hakim's biases at all times, but they certainly aren't enough to disregard these wonderful books.

Rea Berg's History Through Literature study guides will help you build a Christian framework around great historical fiction and children's trade books. Beautiful Feet has published units for world and American history as well as geography. This is a highly recommended company.

The World of . . . series, Genevieve Foster. If there is a title available by Foster for a time period we are studying, then I always make that the core resource. She sets the life of a historic figure in the context of world history (including progress in the arts and sciences)—for example, *The World of Augustus Caesar* and *The World of John Smith*.

Use Dorling Kindersley's Eyewitness books and multimedia such as *The History of the World* CD-ROM, as well as Usborne history titles.

For hands-on history activities

Time Travelers History Study Series. Amy Pak believes history for young children needs to be hands-on, and I agree. She has designed beautiful timelines, activity packs and unit studies primarily for American history, with other subjects under development. You can use her materials as your core program for American history, or you can use the timelines and other activities to supplement your history curriculum of choice.

Knowledge Quest. Terri Johnson has developed timelines, figures, and blackline maps to correlate with the top selling history programs—e.g. Story of the World, Tapestry of Grace, Sonlight, and others.

KONOS, Jessica Hulcy and Carole Thaxton. Called the "granddaddy of unit studies" by Michael Farris of HSLDA, this is an elementary curriculum that integrates the core subjects around a character quality. Each of the three volumes covers activities and reading for two years of study. Their new products, KONOS In-A-Bag and KONOS In-A-Box, are user-friendly, filled with teacher helps, and are designed to last nine to eighteen weeks.

Make It Work! History series from Two-Can Press. Crafts for various civilizations—i.e., ancient Rome, Japan, etc.

More Than Moccasins, and other activity books from Laurie Carlson.

For cultural studies that build a heart for missions in your family, the following are recommended courses of study

Kids of Courage newsletter (free)
Voice of the Martyrs
www.kidsofcourage.com
This organization will keep you in touch with the persecuted church. Its quarterly newsletter for students introduces kids to the geography, culture, history, and spiritual needs of various countries.

Operation World: The Day-to-Day Guide to Praying for the World, Patrick Johnstone. This wonderful resource for guiding your family prayers is now maintained online at www.operationworld.com. A 2005 print edition is still available, and the latest edition (2007) of the companion volume for young children, *Window on the World,* can be ordered from the website.

Sonlight Curriculum
8042 South Grant Way
Littleton, CO 80122
303-730-6292
www.sonlight.com
Window on the World: When We Pray God Works, Daphne Spraggett and Jill Johnstone). A child's version of *Operation World* with stunning photographs and a guide to prayer.

For geography

Rea Berg's *Geography: A Literature Approach* uses four popular books by Holling C. Hollings to present four major regions of the United States and the history of each.

A Child's Geography: Explore His Earth, Ann Voskam. In the inimitable style of V. M. Hillyer (*A Child's Geography of the World*, 1951), Voskam's series begins with an investigation of the planet on which we live and then moves to the countries and cultures now populating it. This first volume is equal parts science and geography, as we get our bearings on Planet Earth. Volume two covers the countries of the Holy Lands. There are more books to follow, and all the author's royalties benefit World Vision, a Christian relief ministry.

Geography for Life (National Council for Geography Education) is an elaboration of the new national standards for geography, K–12. This publication is now available online at www.ncge.org.

The Ultimate Geography and Timeline Guide, Maggie Hogan and Cindy Wiggers. Geography Matters is also your source for other resources and maps for studying geography. K-12.

Secondary

At this level, you'll either focus in on American history or zoom out to cover world history and cultures. There are so many well-written books and fascinating videos out there, it would be a shame to disintegrate to the textbook level for your studies here.

Secondary Strategies

- Focus on building a Christian worldview in your teens. There are many helpful resources you might use for this purpose. Summit Ministries, the longstanding source of worldview camps and materials, has developed *Thinking Like a Christian*, worldview curriculum designed with the homeschool community in mind—i.e., Mom and Dad may not know much about this topic either, so the teaching materials are thorough. I am also partial to books written by David Breese (*7 Men Who Rule the World From the Grave*), Nancy Pearcey (*Total Truth*), and Chuck Colson (*How Now Shall We Live?*).

- David Quine of the Cornerstone Curriculum Project has also finished his three-year, integrated high school course titled *World Views of the Western World*, based on the works of Francis Schaeffer. Subjects covered include philosophy, art, music, government, economics, science, and literature.

- Worldview Academy Leadership Camp is a weeklong course designed to equip teens with a Christian worldview. The camp focuses on three spheres: worldviews, apologetics (defense of the faith) and evangelism, and leadership. Mike and Gabe attended this camp in eighth grade, and they both had a great experience. I had to force them into the car to come home.

  Worldview Academy
  P.O. Box 2918
  Midland, TX 79702
  800-241-1123
  www.worldview.org

> **FOCUS ON BUILDING A CHRISTIAN WORLDVIEW IN YOUR TEENS.**

- Participate in the National History Day academic competition. Students may enter individually or as a team and may present a project or research paper. This is a very well-designed program.

Recommendations for the Secondary Years

A History of the American People. Paul Johnson. Also see *Modern Times*. Johnson, a British journalist, is an internationally respected *conservative* writer. You can often find his books as premiums offered by book clubs. Your teenagers should be exposed to his writings before heading to any college campus—Christian or otherwise. Johnson is a great admirer of democracy in America.

Social Studies School Services at socialstudies.com carries just about every resource you could ever want (excluding those from a Christian publisher) for teaching history, literature, and writing. It has a catalog just for Advanced Placement courses too. Get on the mailing list.

Western Civilization: A Brief History, Jackson Spielvogel. A comprehensive, college-level series used in many classical Christian schools. Kayte used this text for Advanced Placement European history in eleventh grade and enjoyed Spielvogel's style. She also completed an Annenberg/CPB video course titled *The Western Tradition* and listened to the Teaching Company's audiotapes on U.S. history (for Advanced Placement U.S. history in tenth grade). The Spielvogel text has a companion CD-ROM and interactive website.

For providential history that has not been sanitized or overly Christianized

The Story of Liberty (1997) and *Sweet Land of Liberty* (1993) by Charles Coffin were first authored in the early 1800s and are written as very engaging narratives of the spread of democracy, beginning with the battle of Hastings and culminating with the founding of the thirteen colonies. Reprints of Coffin's other titles are also planned.

What in the World Is Going On Here? A Judeo-Christian Primer of World History, Diana Waring. This includes a set of entertaining audiotapes by Diana that give an overview of world history, plus three study guides: *Ancient Civilizations and the Bible; Romans, Reformers and Revolutionaries*; and *World Empires, World Missions and World Wars.*

And, of course, I've already told you how much I like Tapestry of Grace, which is particularly strong as a college preparatory course of study.

For economics and civics

Whatever Happened to Penny Candy? and *Whatever Happened to Justice?* and others by Richard Maybury, a libertarian, use a fictionalized letter exchange between a young man and his Uncle Eric to simplify economics, civics, and government. Very lucid style.

Primary source documents

In Their Own Words series by Milton Meltzer—for example: *The Black Americans: A History in Their Own Words*

Cobblestone Publishing (800-821-0115) has several volumes of primary source documents with teaching activities, grouped according to historic period.

For Christian history: I know no better source than Christian History Institute, publisher of *Christian History* magazine. The staff has uploaded all the past issues of *Glimpses* bulletin inserts at the magazine's website (www.chitorch.org), and this is a terrific research center for teens. The contributors know how to make history interesting, with an engaging writing style and "human interest" format.

Leaders in Action is a line of biographies edited by George Grant that focuses on the moral leadership of great men of history. Recommended titles include:

Never Give In: The Extraordinary Character of Winston Churchill, Stephen Mansfield

Carry a Big Stick: The Uncommon Heroism of Theodore Roosevelt, George Grant

Art and Music

Though not considered core subjects, it's important that we not neglect study in these areas. Music and art as expressed through human history are the best ways for our children to understand the impact of philosophical ideas. These are concrete expressions of the abstract forces that shape a culture.

Further, it is important that our children learn to express themselves creatively. Our ability to create is a part of "being made in the image of God" and reflects the divine nature within us. God intends us to create for His glory and our own enjoyment in life.

Integrate art and music appreciation into your study of history and cultures, and cultivate your child's creative expression through art and music opportunities.

> IT IS IMPORTANT THAT OUR CHILDREN LEARN TO EXPRESS THEMSELVES CREATIVELY.

 ## Recommended Resources: Elementary

Adventures in Art, Susan Milord

Artistic Pursuits is a full-color, engaging curriculum for K-12 that allows kids to create their own art while studying the history of art through a study of great works. You can also buy discounted art supplies through their website.

Children of a Greater God, Terry Glaspey

Drawing with Children, Mona Brookes

Free (yes, you read that correctly) art lessons developed by professional artists are available online at www.homeschoolarts.com.

The Gift of Music, Jane Stuart Smith and Betty Carlson.

God & The History of Art kit, Barry Stebbing. Five-year curriculum with 250 lessons blending art history with hands-on instruction in drawing and painting.

The History of Classical Music, Rebecca Berg. A recent addition to these literature-based study guides, the core text is *Spiritual Lives of the Great Composers* by Patrick Kavanaugh and the Music Masters CDs. Best for grades 5-8.

Marsalis on Music. Wynton Marsalis introduces kids to the fundamentals of music in this four-part video series from Sony Music. You will find the DVDs, released in 2007, and the companion book online at Amazon.com.

Mudworks, MaryAnn Kohl

Music Masters CDs. This exceptional series integrates the lives of the composers with recordings of their most famous compositions. Produced by VOX, available at Amazon.com. Sample titles include *The Story of Bach in Words and Music* and *The Story of Mozart in Words and Music*.

Recommended Resources: Secondary

Adventures in Art, David Quine

How Should We Then Live? The Rise and Decline of Western Thought and Culture, Francis A. Schaeffer

Music and Moments with the Masters, David Quine

Final Note

The U.S. Department of Education has published a collection of booklets for parents on helping elementary children learn various school subjects. They are well worth your time. Many are now available online or by writing to:

Federal Citizen Information Center
Pueblo, CO 81009
www.pueblo.gsa.gov

"Education is what you have left over when you've forgotten everything that you've learned."
— Oscar Wilde

PART 6

HOMESCHOOLING TEENS

COLLEGE

TEENS

IN THIS SECTION

Should You Do It?

Planning a Course of Study

Navigating College Admissions Channels

College-at-Home

RighT FOR you?

Admissions

CHAPTER 22
Should You Do It?

The day I originally got the contract for this book, my sons, for the first time ever, announced they were thinking about going to school—public school! *Great timing, guys*, I thought, as my euphoria over the contract evaporated. And furthermore, their reasons were unbelievable: They wanted to be with their friends.

What had happened to their convictions? Where had Kermit and I gone wrong?

And this wasn't a momentary blip on the radar screen. They started bringing up the issue frequently.

It threw me into an emotional tailspin. I'd always been open to their participation in the decision—in theory—but I assumed this tactic would guarantee they'd always agree with me. I was outmaneuvered.

My first response was to begin forcefully going over all the reasons we had chosen to home educate them, cutting off their points, wildly gesticulating in the center of the living room while foolishly believing we were having a discussion. Michael would roll his eyes and mumble, "Another long lecture."

Kayte shrewdly played the tension to her advantage. She'd angelically slip through the room announcing, "I love being homeschooled, Mom," give me a hug, and return to her work.

Kermit, who had once been very lukewarm to the whole idea of homeschooling, would simply say, "They're not going!" then roll over and go to sleep. End of discussion. (How do men do that?)

I, of course, even debated telling you this. But I'm committed to writing from the reality of our experience—no revisionist history allowed. Once I finally got the bright idea I might want to turn to the Lord on this one, I realized our experience is right where many families choosing to homeschool teens live.

Homeschooling through high school feels like making that initial decision all over again. And in many ways it is, only the stakes are now higher. High school is the gateway to our children's future, and we're determining what résumé they'll be

> **HOMESCHOOLING THROUGH HIGH SCHOOL FEELS LIKE MAKING THAT INITIAL DECISION ALL OVER AGAIN.**

taking with them. Choosing a private/public school route means they'll have all the traditional documentation college admissions offices and employers are used to seeing. Home educating means we'll have a lot of explaining to do to get some of those future doors to open. And if we quit midstream, local school districts are not obligated to count the homeschooling years toward their high school graduation. We better be sure we're ready to go the distance before we bite off ninth grade!

The other issue is that our kids should now be more involved in the decision-making process. I still fall squarely in the "this is not a democracy" camp of family government, but I also know if teens don't have a personal conviction about home educating, they'll know how to make us miserable.

Wow. How do we decide? Biggies like this make me want to lie down and go to sleep. Wake me when it's over, but don't ask me to make the call.

Aren't you glad you're a Christian? Aren't decisions like this just why we know we weren't designed to figure life out by ourselves? We need a heavenly Father we can count on for the future. No matter how you educate your teenagers, it's a decision of faith.

At Cindy's House

I'm grateful I was able to watch my mentors, Cindy McKeown and Marie Gamon, walk through this season before I gave it a whirl. Every summer between Nate's four years of high school, Cindy struggled with the decision to continue homeschooling him. Nate's interest in medicine and a need for higher-level math and sciences really undermined her confidence. Cindy said repeatedly there wasn't a perfect choice; she and Cliff just needed to make the *best* choice and then work quite hard to make that choice work as well as possible.

What that meant was a continuous stretching on Cindy's part to match each program to each child.

Nate took classes his senior year at a community college as well as a distance education course through Penn State. His real passion in life was emergency medicine, so Cindy did the research necessary to find Nate an EMT course, which he passed at age sixteen. He then began riding regularly with the local ambulance crew and went on to get additional credits in rescue work and sports injuries before finishing high school.

Cindy's example as a facilitator wore off on Nate. Even though Nate received quite a bit of scholarship money and financial aid for college, he still had to pay for a substantial part of his education. He did this by joining the Army National Guard. His freshman summer he completed his medic specialist training, graduating with a number of honors. He also found time to occupy many leadership positions at school, including class president. So much for concerns about homeschoolers integrating well on campus!

Cindy's next son, Daniel, and Marie's oldest son, Tom, both had an interest in film. In eighth grade, Daniel bought his first video camera with his life's savings, and he and Tom made avant-garde video clips every spare moment during high school. All their extra change went toward more equipment. And what they couldn't afford, they improvised. I don't know what the neighbors thought the day they repeatedly dropped a dummy from their third-story window. Daniel and Tom received degrees in cinematography and film, respectively, at two respected schools in Manhattan. Both Daniel and Tom first completed as many courses as possible at a community college while living at home and saving money.

As with Nate during high school, Cindy set about facilitating opportunities for her son in his expressed area of interest. She called a friend from college who now owns his own video production company in the Washington, D.C., area. This friend not only agreed to set up an internship for Daniel and Tom but also invited them to spend the summer on location with his video crews. This opportunity gave Tom and Daniel valuable video experience and insight into the ups and downs of running a company.

After seeing his older brothers pursue unique areas, Cindy's youngest son, Joey, decided he needed to set goals at an early age as well. But rather than have me tell you about his high school life, Joey wants to speak for himself. (When you see how he flatters his English teacher, you'll know why I gave him the space.) Remember, this is the kid I talked about on page 29.

Okay, Joey, Here's Your Chance

"AAAAAAGH!"

The time was 1994, and I was sitting at my dining room table attempting to use the Pythagorean theorem to determine the amount of time a train had been traveling. My hands furiously flew through my dark blond hair in frustration. I let out a low moan and let my forehead rest on the table.

My mom, sitting across from me instructing my younger sister, Christi, looked up with sympathy. She tilted her head to one side, thinking. It was then she said something to me that would change my attitude toward school forever.

"Joey," she began, "there is one thing I really regret about my school experience when I was your age."

"Really? What's that?" I was mildly curious.

"I wish I would have taken my studies more seriously and not wasted my last few years of school. Now I realize how important they were, and I can't go back and change it."

The word "wasted" rang through my head all day, and the next and the next. I realized I wanted my life to be meaningful for myself, for others, and, above all, for God. Would I be looking back five years from now, frustrated that I had wasted time that should have been spent more wisely? I realized I wanted to look back on a life that had been productive, relevant, and filled with good memories.

I made a promise to myself and God. I would make the most of these important years, disciplining myself to perform my best in my studies. I would strive for excellence and give everything my best shot. I would find joy in learning by knowing it would help me now and later in life. I would develop better relationships with my family and friends. My attitude, which had only been defeating me, changed by God's divine power and grace.

Now I am in tenth grade. I have a beautiful wife, three lovely kids, a dog, just paid off our new home, and bought a new car . . . just kidding. Two years later, I no longer see schoolwork as daily torture I have to go through. I am involved in a lifelong, enjoyable pursuit of knowledge that I have chosen for myself. High school is more than four inconsequential years of my life. It is a

309

training ground, and I must treat it that way.

Studying still isn't always fun. I still get math problems wrong, science still confuses me, and my attitude stinks once in a while. I still have a lot of manicuring to do on myself, too. I still double-dip chips, leave the toilet seat up (an unpardonable sin in my mom's eyes), and burp at the dinner table. I'm not perfect, but I try to give it all I've got.

Last summer, I asked my friend Jeff, a fellow homeschooler, what subjects he would be studying this year. He laughed. "I don't know. My mom will tell me whenever I start."

I laughed with him, but I felt sorry for him because he is missing out on what I treasure most about homeschooling—drum roll, please—FREEDOM! (Wild clapping, general hoopla.) I value the chance to have an active role in determining my studies. I love that I can pick my subjects, my books, how I want to learn, when I want to learn, why I want to learn. My education is resting on my shoulders. The day-to-day operation of my schoolwork is my responsibility. I love it!

I have always admired people who can capture the emotions, actions, and speech of characters in a story. This is why I want to become a writer: to express a story with all the details of life, to make the reader visualize and feel the thoughts of my characters, their joys and sadness, laughter and tears (sniff, sniff). Okay, I just want to write well.

Which is why I am taking a writing class from the talented (and beautiful) Mrs. Bell. Last year I took a literature class from her, and I was turned on more than ever to the classics and writing. This year I've enrolled in her composition class at CHESS [Creative Home Educators' Support Services], and I hope this will be a turning point in my writing.

At four-thirty in the afternoon on a cool, fall day, Mom and I drive past the local high school where the soccer team is playing a game. My face pressed against the cold window, I see the biggest disadvantage to homeschooling: organized sports. Those two words bring back frustrating memories. All through elementary school I took soccer seriously. When I reached junior high, the community soccer clubs became a place where kids would fool around after their regular school practice. I wanted to practice harder with guys who were more competitive. I figured the coaches for the school team would be more strict and skilled. But my district wouldn't permit me to play.

My mom, God bless her, allowed me to consider going to school so I could play. But homeschooling has too many advantages for me to dismiss it. The soccer situation, though, was a big frustration until I found a small Christian school that would let me play. So far it has been a good experience. The attitudes of the guys are great, and they want to be there.

My future plans include women, living in the Bahamas eleven months out of the year (just kidding!), and some sort of writing—journalist, novelist, freelancer. I think college seems to be the best bet for my writing career. I am looking at Hillsdale College in Michigan and at St. John's in Annapolis, Maryland. Currently, my goal is to get published. Published and paid, that is. I am planning to enter a number of competitions.

Politics also interests me, and I am currently interning at Pennsylvania Family Institute, an affiliate of Focus on the Family. Here I hope to merge my interests in journalism and public policy—though right now I am stuffing envelopes.

God's plans for my future seem to be pressed against the pane of writing. I desire an open heart for whatever God has for me, as long as it doesn't involve mathematics.

—Joseph (Joey) McKeown, then fifteen

By Joseph's senior year, he had taken advantage of all the opportunities our family school, my English classes, and our homeschool community could offer. So for his final year of high school, Joseph set up his own course of study—a rigorous reading program that included Aristotle, Plato, Homer, Rousseau, Descartes, Hume, etc. And he began interviewing with colleges that had a great books program.[1] He had learned enough about himself to know that he did not want a traditional classroom situation. He prefers discussion, mentors, and personal reflection in writing as a method of learning. To culminate the independent course of study he had designed for his senior year, he worked evenings and weekends, saved his pennies, and then went to Europe *alone* while I held Cindy's hand back at home. He backpacked, stayed in youth hostels, slept on the train a lot (he had underestimated the number of pennies he would need), talked to strangers, went home with strangers (despite Cindy's e-mails in large caps), visited L'Abri, occasionally remembered to let his parents know where he was, had a great time, and came home with a serious case of wanderlust. After looking at a number of schools, he realized he didn't want to spend his money on an institution that did not evaluate ideas from a fixed point of reference—i.e., the Scriptures. In the fall of 1999, he entered Thomas Aquinas College, a Catholic great-books school in California.

Postscript: Today Nate is an emergency-room doctor, Daniel's a cinematographer, and Joseph (one thing that changed in college) is pursuing graduate studies.

Back on the Home Front

I'm sure you're wondering what happened at our house as well. I relaxed enough to listen to Mike and Gabe talk about their consideration of public school. I think they needed to know they could express their feelings and the lacks they sometimes felt in homeschooling without us overreacting. They had never been in a traditional setting (with the exception of a one-day field trip to a Christian school), and of course they were curious. It's easy to imagine a better life on the other side.

Through a series of events not orchestrated by Mom (believe it or not) they realized (1) the popularity they thought was awaiting them there could very well be fleeting (i.e., kids are fickle), (2) they would often be asked to compromise their faith to fit in, and (3) they had more opportunities through homeschooling.

Kermit and I, of course, never thought social life was a valid reason to send our kids to school—but I understood their growing desire to interact more with their agemates. I do think it is healthy for teenagers to move in wider and wider social circles. I desired for my children to be leaders and influencers in their generation, and if I wouldn't let them leave the nest, their impact would be nil. However, until Mike and Gabe's faith matured, I wanted those social circles to be ones that supported our family values. They weren't ready yet, we believed.

But I am a great believer in creative solutions. I don't want my children to view Christianity as limiting (my own misconception that kept me from seriously exploring the claims of Christ for years). I asked God to give us a plan.

Checkmate

As a result of the tension Cindy and I felt between providing rigorous academic standards during high school and giving our children wider social contacts, Cindy started Creative Home Educators' Support Services (CHESS), a family school that meets every Tuesday for thirty weeks during the school year. We rent the facilities of a church that once housed a Christian school. Classes are available for students in fifth through twelfth grades. Instructors are qualified more by their passion for teaching kids and love of their subject matter than by their credentials, though several have the accompanying piece of paper as well. Most instructors are homeschooling also, so they understand what parents are looking for.

Our goal, especially on the secondary level, is to provide a framework for a complete course of study. Parents are welcome to sit in on classes and are responsible for overseeing the completion of their children's work during the week. Cindy was deeply committed to retaining the foundational principles of home education:

> OUR GOAL, ESPECIALLY ON THE SECONDARY LEVEL, IS TO PROVIDE A FRAMEWORK FOR A COMPLETE COURSE OF STUDY.

- parental authority
- child-centered learning

Even though CHESS had to organize as a private school to satisfy state regulations, the last thing Cindy wanted to create was a traditional setting where parents have little input or control. We describe CHESS as a family school in order to better convey the level of parental involvement.

We've found CHESS supports our homeschooling families by providing:

- challenges for academic excellence and achievement
- outside evaluation and accountability
- deadlines
- group interaction and activities

In addition to the classes, CHESS hosts many events for the teens, including open gym twice a month, a volleyball tournament, graduation ceremony, and a yearbook. Enrollment doubled the second year, and many classes now have a waiting list. I believe family schools are the wave of the future.

One highly developed hybrid is UMS—the University-Model School, started in Arlington, Texas, at Grace Preparatory Academy. This parent-run high school holds classes three times a week. At this writing, twenty-five other UMS affiliates have opened to serve homeschoolers, and hundreds are in developmental stages. Here's where to find out more:

NAUMS
3610 W. Pioneer Parkway, Suite D
Arlington, TX 76013
866-760-9508
www.naums.net

And you can read more about CHESS family school at debrabell.com.

Advantages and Disadvantages of Homeschooling Teens

Drawbacks

1. It costs more money. To do it right, you're going to be spending money for DVD instruction, tutors, correspondence courses, textbooks, lab equipment, and technology. It does add up. Now's a good time to start expecting your kids to help pay for their education.

2. It will take more of your time. Not because you're teaching (they had better be learning independently if you hope to survive), but because you are going to be facilitating all the opportunities they need, like apprenticeships and mentors. If they are headed for college, that can be a pretty big deal depending upon how broad a scope you want to explore. Cindy spent hundreds of hours working on Nate's college admissions. Now we hope to save you some of that time by telling you what we've learned (notice how I take credit for Cindy's work). But still, you are the

> NOW'S A GOOD TIME TO START EXPECTING YOUR KIDS TO HELP PAY FOR THEIR EDUCATION.

guidance counselor in the homeschool equation. You will have lots of forms to fill out and lots of e-mails to send.

3. Loss of opportunities. By choosing to homeschool through high school, there are valid and worthwhile activities your child may have to forego—sports, journalism clubs, dramatic productions, a band, or orchestra. Unless you have time to find alternative sources for these opportunities or start them yourself, this needs to be part of counting the cost in making your decision.

One mom I know had a daughter graduate through homeschooling while a son graduated through a private school. She commented one day that it had been a challenge to demonstrate her daughter's leadership skills on college and scholarship applications—for her son, no problem. His involvement in many clubs and activities at school had been possible without much inconvenience to the family. Her daughter, on the other hand, hadn't had easy access to these conventional activities.

4. Loss of opportunities to influence others. It's debatable how much impact our elementary-level children might have on other kids. But our teens have the potential to make a real difference in other kids' lives—if they themselves are ready to withstand the peer pressure. I've seen many Christian kids do very poorly in public high school, but I've also seen Christian kids who've been a tremendous influence, not just on other kids, but on faculty and the entire school atmosphere as well. When I taught public school, a very large youth group met at my house. The kids came not because of the adults involved, but because of the Christian kids who invited them.

If I had thought my kids were called and ready to make that kind of impact, they'd have been there immediately. In fact, I prayed for it. I didn't want to push my kids out of the nest prematurely, but I didn't want to hold them back either. I believe our lives are solely for the sake of others. We are called to build strong families that demonstrate our faith with integrity to attract others to the gospel of Jesus Christ. Some of our most influential years as Christians are often during our teens and twenties. That's because those are the years our peers are most open to the

> SOME OF OUR MOST INFLUENTIAL YEARS AS CHRISTIANS ARE OFTEN DURING OUR TEENS AND TWENTIES.

gospel. They aren't set in their ways but rather are searching for answers and making decisions themselves. At least at our house, this was the biggest factor to weigh in deciding to continue on through high school.

Benefits

1. Your relationship with your teens. Kermit and I were jealous for the relationship we saw between many, many parents and their home-educated teenagers. It's hard not to conclude that homeschooling is a big factor in the trust and camaraderie evidenced there.

A good friend took her three boys out of Christian school several years ago and began to homeschool. When I asked her what benefits she had found in homeschooling, she nodded toward her fourteen-year-old son and said, "Debby, he talks to me." With young children at the time, I didn't understand her amazement. But it was clear to me that that was reason enough to her to stick with homeschooling.

Now I know what she meant. I am deeply grateful that my kids share their hearts with Kermit and me. We know what is going on in their lives. They covet our opinions and care deeply about our approval of them. They enjoy their friends a lot, too; but their peer group has never been their primary source of recognition and identity.

2. More opportunities. Homeschooling may close some doors of opportunity for our children, but it also opens other ones that may be more beneficial in the long run. Because of the flexibility of your schedule, your high-schooler can get a head start on the job market or make his high school résumé more attractive to colleges: college at home, courses online, apprenticeships, entrepreneurial ventures, travel, and mission projects are all more easily facilitated.

3. When you're done homeschooling through high school, you can go on *Jeopardy!* Yes, you can win thousands of dollars or turn your knowledge and life experiences into a college degree of your own. With a little ingenuity, you can broker all the mountains of knowledge you are accumulating into more profitable ventures. The homeschool moms I know are deadly in games of Trivial Pursuit. It's only one short step from there to a career on game shows, I'm sure.

Check out the chapter on college at home. All those strategies for your kids you can easily use yourself to complete a college degree or earn a new one. For instance, my good friend, Vicki Dincher, head of the science department at CHESS family school, completed her Master of Science Education degree through an accredited online program concurrently with finishing up her final years of homeschooling.

Here's insight into two families who've chosen to continue to homeschool through high school:

I'm convinced that the successful schooling of our children is directly related to successful parenting. And obviously, relationship is the core of that. One of our desires is to see our relationship with our children transition from parenting and coaching them to guiding them as they begin to walk on their own. I can't imagine doing that with them not home. Right now we—and their brothers and sisters—are the ones with whom they are developing their best friendships. And that positively influences their learning.

As far as pros and cons, I don't see any cons at this stage. Our children have always been homeschooled, so they haven't left an environment that they feel they are missing out on. As our son Tim will testify to anyone who'll listen, he loves the freedom homeschooling has afforded him. There are many experiences that he's been able to have because of the flexibility he's had in scheduling. And Jennifer, who is very involved as an athlete, appreciates this freedom too. Although I apply plenty of pressure to meet deadlines and require a good amount of work, she realizes her life is much less stressful than her friends' with whom she is competing.

We've been involved in work experiences and mission trips because the time constraint of school is removed. We've been able to focus on character and developing a work ethic because our goals are different from those of standard education. And we've been able to accelerate our children's learning because of the individualized attention they have. It's amazing how quickly our children can get things done. The older siblings are helping younger siblings. Our fourteen-year-old has almost completed high school. It was not our goal; it just happened.

—Karen, mother of ten

We have seven children, and our two oldest are grown. We've homeschooled off and on since 1979. This is our fourteenth year of steady homeschooling. Our oldest son went to public high school, and our second son went to a Christian high school, which we'd hope would be much better. To be honest, we were not at all satisfied with either.

The relationship that had been so important between us basically deteriorated as the boys were away. It happened with both of them. They were away all day, then they got involved with activities. And being teenagers, they ended up getting jobs. Pretty soon we were not seeing our children at all; at least that was our experience. We could have limited the school activities, but that was an important part of what we sent them to high school for.

We've been so satisfied with the results from homeschooling the rest of our children. We have a daughter who graduated last year, and we've been so blessed with her. We also have one son we had expected to have a lot of trouble with. He's always been very active and likes to get out around people. He is always running from one thing to another. He's a very high-energy person. But he has not been at all the problem we thought he would be. He's been a real blessing. He works. He raises exotic animals. He's usually doing some variety of home business, but in the midst of that we've seen a lot of growth in his character. He's still very active. He tends to grow into our family's beliefs a little more slowly than the girls, but he does grow into them. That hasn't happened with the ones who went to school.

I really don't see a downside to homeschooling in high school. All the reasons that apply in the early years apply just as much, if not more, in the older years. Peer pressure in school settings becomes so intense and so important. Quite honestly, a lot of the adults your children run across in a school situation tend to reinforce that idea. They believe all teenagers are supposed to be rebellious, questioning everything, dressing funny, seeking their own paths in a variety of ways. They don't expect to guide them—we learned that through a painful experience. So our children are left at the mercy of the influence of the other young people around them, an influence that may or may not be good.

—Vickie, mother of seven

CHAPTER 23
Planning a Course of Study

As with every other decision we've discussed in this book, planning a course of study for your high schoolers begins with listing the future targets they aim to hit:

- college
- trade or business school
- apprenticeship
- direct entrance into the job market

The avenues they might pursue in providing for themselves and future family must be foremost in determining the courses they take. Along with this, their targets may include preparation for marriage, leadership in the church or ministry, community service, and self-reliance skills. As they enter ninth grade, script out with your teens all the options you want to keep open. Plan your four-year curriculum so they are qualified to exercise any of these options upon leaving high school. As they narrow down their choices, you can more finely tune their program.

> **PLANNING A COURSE OF STUDY FOR YOUR HIGH SCHOOLERS BEGINS WITH LISTING THE FUTURE TARGETS THEY AIM TO HIT.**

Traditional Courses of Study

For students planning to follow high school with job training or college, here is an overview of the traditionally expected courses of study.

Trade and Technical School

A high school transcript that qualifies a student for a technical, trade, or business school includes:

- four years of English
- two to four years of mathematics
- one to three years of science
- two to four years of history and social sciences
- zero to two years of a foreign language

- coursework in technical areas of interest

Four-Year Degree

At the other end of the scale, a high school transcript that qualifies a student for admission to a four-year university will minimally include:

- four years of English
- two to four years of advanced mathematics (algebra, geometry, trigonometry, and calculus)
- two to four years of history and social science
- two to four years of laboratory science (biology, chemistry, physics)
- two to four years of the same foreign language
- one to two years of music and art
- computer skills

You will find the recommended high school prerequisites listed on the websites of any college you might consider for your children. Use their list and work backward in making a plan.

Direct Entry into the Job Market

If your teen's goals (such as self-employment) don't depend upon a traditional high school transcript, then the course of study you follow during high school can be much more flexible and fine-tuned with that end in mind. But don't be shortsighted. We don't want to close any doors our children might need open in the future.

Kermit and I certainly want our daughters to see marriage and motherhood as noble callings and as highly desirable. But studies show women, on average, must be self-supporting seven years of their lives either through singleness, widowhood, or late marriage. I don't want our daughters to be left stranded and unskilled should that situation be in their futures.

You Still Have Room to Maneuver

Keep in mind that the prerequisites listed earlier are merely the names of the courses your child is expected to take. You

> **DON'T BE SHORTSIGHTED.**

still have a great deal of flexibility in terms of the time devoted to each course and its content. Just because you use a traditional title does not mean you must use a traditional textbook or follow a traditional method of teaching. You can adapt the program to each child's readiness, interests, and learning style. For example, the introductory physics course Cindy designed for Joey focused on engineering—an interest of his—and used the Legos Dacta-Technic set to give him the hands-on activities he preferred.

My plan included lots of field experiences and projects. I assumed once my kids got to college, their learning would be predominantly lecture and textbook studies. This was my last chance to have them delve into material on a visceral level.

How to Do the Hard Stuff

Okay, you're saying, let's get to the bone of the matter when we're talking high school. What about physics, calculus, and foreign languages? How am I going to provide this on a high school level, especially a college preparatory one?

You Facilitate

You pool your resources within the homeschool community or seek out new ones. But you don't teach—unless you have the time and really want to learn the subject too. Pick the areas you do have an interest or background in and take responsibility there, but everything else you outsource. Here are your options:

#1. Video Courses

Say what you may about television, but when done correctly this medium can convey material better than any other. You just have to hunt pretty hard to find the few sources that have maximized the educational potential of video. The most dynamic science teacher cannot compete against Jeff Corwin or Bill Nye the Science Guy. She just wouldn't have the budget to pull together the models, real-life examples, experts, and experiments these shows use to illustrate scientific principles.

There are a growing number of companies providing complete courses of study on DVD. Here are three of the better produced sources.

> PICK THE AREAS YOU DO HAVE AN INTEREST OR BACKGROUND IN AND TAKE RESPONSIBILITY THERE.

PBS Video: This catalog offers not only PBS documentaries such as Ken Burns's *Civil War*, but also those from other top producers. And they do have a price schedule for home use that makes these resources affordable for most families. (The home-use rights are extended to a face-to-face teaching situation that is part of a systematic educational program. That means you can set up a class at your co-op and use them.) Additionally, many of the older programs can now be watched online at no charge.

Better, these series are often stocked by a good public library. Be bold. Find out which librarian does the ordering and ask her to consider purchasing the series of most interest to homeschoolers. There is, of course, lots of leftist-leaning fare, but *The American Experience, The Great War, Eyes on the Prize*, and all of Ken Burns's documentaries make for excellent resources in the high school curriculum.

PBS Video
P. O. Box 279
Melbourne, FL 32902-0279
800-344-3337
www.video.pbs.org

Annenberg Media: You don't want to miss this option because your teens can watch most of these online for free! Founded by TV Guide magnate Walter Annenberg, the Annenberg School is one of the leading schools of communication and technology in the country. These video courses offer a superb integration of instruction and visual illustration, and they were expensive when I originally purchased them. Annenberg Media has produced courses in physics, French, Spanish, algebra, statistics, the Western tradition, literature, ancient history, and more; most are now available to watch online at no charge through streaming video. Support material is available at no charge in many cases, so you can get by without even purchasing a textbook. Newer courses still must be purchased, but going this route—when you consider textbooks, teacher's manual, and tests—can really add up. And right now there is so much free material available on their website, I don't think this is really necessary. If there is a course you just have to have, it is worth contacting Annenberg to see if there is a home-use option that reduces the pricing. (There was when I was purchasing these, but currently I don't see it mentioned on their site.)

The other option for acquiring the newer courses for use in your co-op or watching on a screen larger than your computer is to sign up for the recording rights offered to teachers in your viewing area. You need to contact your local PBS affiliate to find out the details. This will allow you to record PBS series and Annenberg Media productions (frequently featured on PBS) for use in your homeschool. In my region it costs under $100 per year to secure this option.

Annenberg/Media
P. O. Box 55742
Indianapolis, IN 46205-0742
800-532-7637 (800-LEARNER)
www.learner.org

The Teaching Company: This company with a big vision has recruited the best classroom and college professors across the country and produced their lectures on video and audio. The material is affordable, but is not as captivating as the big-budget productions from Annenberg and PBS. The academically minded student will find these lectures fascinating. The teachers know their stuff and can explain it well. However, the kid who needs to be entertained will not be able to sit still for the direct lecture presentation.

Of special note for high schoolers at home are the algebra 2, chemistry, and geometry lectures, which are well presented and can be used as a support to any basic text. You will want to order the DVDs. Many of the other courses, though, are just as effective on audio, which is less expensive and can be conveniently listened to while traveling. In fact, the least expensive and fastest option is now to download these directly from the website as MP3 files.

When you see the universities from which these professors have been recruited, you will probably be concerned about the compatibility of their worldviews with Christian thinking. In an ideal world, a Christian publisher would produce a comparable program, but with that not being a choice, I have to say the presentations I reviewed were much more objective than expected. Every course offered by The Teaching Company will go on sale at least once a year—and this is when you want to buy it. Prices are slashed as much as 70 percent at that time.

The Teaching Company
4840 Westfields Blvd. Suite 500
Chantilly, VA 20151
800-832-2412 (800-TEACH-12)
www.teach12.com

Maximizing Video Instruction

The best way to use a video course is to view it as a family or group and follow up with discussion. One ambitious mom gathered a group of teens weekly at her home to watch the A Beka biology video course. She followed this up with simple labs, discussions, and tests. The videos themselves weren't that terrific; but in the larger context of discussion and interaction, the kids were motivated and the mom was able to cover a subject she knew little about beforehand.

In our house we have used video successfully to augment difficult subjects, such as Advanced Placement courses, chemistry, and world history. One of my sons in particular found he learned material best when it was presented in a number of different contexts—i.e., textbook, videos, hands-on activities, field

> THE BEST WAY TO USE A VIDEO COURSE IS TO VIEW IT AS A FAMILY OR GROUP AND FOLLOW UP WITH DISCUSSION.

trips, etc.—so we routinely ordered a set of videos to supplement most high school courses. And we also traveled to out-of-the-way libraries looking for the best video collection.

Sure-Fire Way to Do Your Kids In

Video is a great solution for one or two courses, but video schools are the pits. I've worked with several families who tried this route, and they all eventually varied their strategies to include more reading and field experiences. Nothing but video day in and day out will sap your kids of motivation, pronto.

#2. Tutors and Mentors

You will probably find a professional tutoring service a very expensive route. But you can find a qualified tutor or mentor for much less in many other ways. Tutors don't need degrees; they just need to know and love the subject. Perhaps a member of your church who uses the subject matter as part of his or her occupation is available. One gentleman in our church who does research in artificial intelligence mentored a homeschool student in computer programming (using C++, an advanced language). That student, later a National Merit Scholar, turned around and mentored a younger homeschooled student in the same area.

A member of Cindy and Marie's church tutored all of their children in advanced mathematics for several years, gratis. The kids found thoughtful ways to serve his family in return for his time. He wasn't a trained math teacher, but he loved math and attended math conventions for fun. The kids not only learned the material well, but often commented on how interesting he made their weekly tutoring sessions.

Another homeschool family found a senior math major at a local college to tutor their children. The student charged half the going hourly rate for the sessions. Elsewhere, a group of homeschoolers joined together to hire a furloughed missionary to teach a summer French course to their kids.

A local college requested that their student teachers be used at our co-op as part of fulfilling their practicum requirements. This was an absolutely free opportunity. Your homeschool group could initiate this suggestion and would likely find local colleges receptive to the idea. They need a variety of teaching situations for

> **TUTORS DON'T NEED DEGREES; THEY JUST NEED TO KNOW AND LOVE THE SUBJECT.**

their students.

You can also check with folks who provide services to school students during the evening hours; they will likely be interested in providing services to homeschoolers during the day. In our area, piano teachers, gymnastics clubs, and an ice skating rink all created special daytime classes for homeschoolers at reduced rates. They were eager to extend their services—their facilities were otherwise idle during these hours.

If your child's test scores identify him or her as academically talented, you may be interested in a program sponsored by Duke University. You must first find a qualified local mentor for your child and then register for the program. Duke supplies the text and course outline.

> Learn on Your Own
> Duke University Talent Identification Program
> 1121 W. Main Street
> Durham, NC 27701-2028
> 919-668-9100
> www.tip.duke.edu

Another idea is to approach the continuing-education department of a local college. They need to find new markets, and daytime classes are difficult to fill. A college-for-kids concept that traditionally runs only during the summer could be created during the school year for homeschool students.

Of course virtual tutors, mentors, and teachers are now available via the Internet, and I'll get to that life saver in just a moment.

#3. Software Programs

Most software courses have been developed to supplement a course of study, but there are a few that can be used as the core resource. Here are suggested titles to look into:

- A.D.A.M.: The Inside Story is a multi-award-winning program suitable for an anatomy unit (adameducation.com).

- Math Teacher (888-628-4525) provides step-by-step

instruction in pre-algebra through calculus. Visit www.mathkalusa.com to download a demo.

- Mathematica (800-441-6284) is a problem-solving program for math, science, and engineering.

- Rosetta Stone Language Learning Software (www.rosettastone.com) is *the* definitive product for language learning at home. Used by the Peace Corps and diplomatic community for years, Rosetta Stone is widely available in the homeschool market. We've tried all the popular products available, and this is the best if you must learn on your own. Audio and video clips of native speakers streaming via the Web make the difference.

- Switched-On Schoolhouse (800-622-3070) is a technologically enhanced version of Alpha Omega's LIFEPAC Gold curriculum. Each CD-ROM program includes five core courses—Bible, history and geography, language arts, math, and science—for a specific grade level from third through twelfth. Besides all the text you will find in their printed curriculum, Switched-On Schoolhouse makes use of Web links, e-mail, automatic grading, graphics, audio and video clips, slide shows, and interactive activities. It's not Encarta, but it is a pretty impressive step in the right direction for homeschoolers.

Just like video courses, this method can be overdone. Complete curriculum software packages are typically very heavy on text and very low on visual and interactive capabilities. One or two courses a day via technology will maximize their use; anything more and you'll soon have a diminishing return.

#4. Distance and Online Learning for High School

Another possible solution for a difficult subject is high school courses via correspondence or over the Internet. Because many courses completed through this method can also be converted to college credit, I'll devote a section to that in the next chapter. For now, let's look at several sources of high school courses via correspondence or online learning.

Here are a few things you should know before electing to

complete a course through this method:

1. Correspondence courses refer to those completed via the mail. I have listed a few below that have been around for quite some time and that cater to the needs of homeschoolers. However, this method is quickly being left in the dust by online technologies. I'm sure it is just a matter of time until these organizations convert solely to an online delivery system too. One savvy outfit, Keystone National High School, allows students to take courses either by correspondence or online or any mix of both.

2. This is one of the more expensive routes you can pursue. My survey showed full-year courses ranging from $250 to $600 each, plus student registration fees and books. When evaluating costs, determine how much teacher interaction you are purchasing. Some organizations merely keep track of student grades and prepare an official transcript for you. They may also be offering you an accredited diploma program. But the parent is still responsible for any teaching that occurs, or the student is expected to learn the material independently through his or her reading and completion of assignments. On the other end of the scale, the price of some courses includes a weekly or even bi-weekly online session with a tutor, plus limitless interaction with the tutor throughout the year.

3. Online courses can be delivered through a variety of methods. Make sure you have the technology to support a course before signing up. The simplest online courses merely interact with each student individually via e-mail. The more complex hold live video-conferencing sessions in which students and tutor can see one another as well as discuss material corporately. In between these extremes, you have the use of Internet chat rooms, bulletin boards, websites, audio feeds, and whiteboards to illustrate problems. For the more complex options you will need broadband Internet connectivity, video and audio capabilities, and an up-to-date operating system.

> **MAKE SURE YOU HAVE THE TECHNOLOGY TO SUPPORT A COURSE BEFORE SIGNING UP.**

4. Online courses can occur "live," requiring students to be online at a set time weekly for an hour or more, or they can be completed through methods such as e-mail and bulletin boards that allow students to be flexible with their schedules. Choose an option that will fit your lifestyle.

The Academy of Home Education
Bob Jones University
800-845-5731
www.bjup.com
This is the correspondence school for Bob Jones University. You use Bob Jones materials and submit your student's grades, and they keep track of your child's record, supply an official-looking transcript, and award a diploma upon completion. Consultation is available via their help line. BJU charges a modest fee for this service. The diploma is not accredited.

BJU Distance Learning (same as above)
Bob Jones University Press has now packaged its course content and live instruction in three convenient formats: You can subscribe to the whole nine-yards of content at all grade levels via satellite feed on a monthly basis, you can purchase individual courses on DVD, or you can get a full year of content on a hard drive you rent for thirteen months. BJU is at the vanguard of technological innovation, so even though this not yet interactive, the courses are up to date, graphically enhanced, and engaging.

Alpha Omega Academy
800-682-7396
www.aoacademy.com
This is a division of Alpha Omega, and the students use their Switched-On Schoolhouse software program for coursework. The software program automatically grades the student's work, but instead of your keeping track of the student's record and scores, they are automatically e-mailed to the proctor at Alpha Omega. Certified

teachers or teaching assistants do grade all subjective problems and reports and give personal feedback. Progress reports and report cards are issued to inform parents, and a permanent record and transcript for high school is provided. Students can receive an accredited diploma through this program. This is one of the few Christian organizations with an accredited diploma option.

American School of Correspondence
866-260-7221
www.americanschoolofcorr.com
This correspondence school has catered for decades to American diplomat families living abroad, and it offers a widely accepted accredited diploma. Secular texts, correspondence only.

ApologiaAcademy
888-524-4724
www.apologiaacademy.com
The folks at Apologia Educational Ministries now offer college-prep science, Bible, apologetics, and Christian worldview courses through a dynamic virtual-classroom experience. You can have your student participate in live online classes or download the sessions for convenient viewing. This is Christian-based curriculum taught by seasoned Christian teachers who are experts in their fields.

Christian Liberty Academy (CLASS)
800-348-0899
www.class-homeschools.org
This Christian correspondence school is a division of Christian Liberty Academy. It uses a mix of texts from various Christian (for the most part) publishers and provides transcripts and record keeping. Its diploma is not accredited. This is the largest satellite school program catering to the homeschool market and is very modestly priced. Because of its popularity, make sure you order materials far in advance.

Clonlara School Home Based Education Program
734-769-4511
clonlara.org
Nonsectarian. Student programs are individually designed and supported by a contact teacher. Some online classes are available via e-mail and Internet bulletin boards. An accredited diploma is available. Clonlara's fees are much higher than elsewhere, but this is the only place to obtain an accredited diploma while designing your own course of study. You'll have to decide if the accreditation is worth the cost.

Escondido Tutorial Service
www.gbt.org
This is the brainchild of Fritz Hinrichs, a graduate of St. John's College and a leading crusader for Christian classical education. One can see from his website that he's full of charm and verve and is dedicated to creating a learning community online. Even though Fritz's students are studying the ancients, they must have the latest technology to do so. Courses occur via video-conferencing on a weekly basis. Students are also encouraged to interact with one another, and attend special "live" events at Fritz's home in California for those who can make the journey. (Judging from the online photo album, many do.) Fritz has also gathered a consortium of tutors who are passionate about classical Christian education, so you will find an array of courses offered at his website, including some from Veritas Press.

Keystone National High School
School House Station
800-255-4937
www.keystonehighschool.com
Now here is a technologically savvy organization. Keystone's website is super slick and a breeze to navigate. (When you see how many folks on the faculty have degrees in instructional technology, you'll know

why.) You can choose between single courses or an accredited diploma program and also between snail mail or e-mail delivery. These folks will bend over backward to accommodate your needs. Traditional textbooks and a testing approach are used, but teachers do interact with students and encourage students to interact with one another. Driver's education, computer programming, and SAT test prep courses are available, too, and there's a toll-free help line.

The Potter's School is an online service (www.pottersschool.com) that uses state-of-the-art technology to offer a full range of core and elective courses for junior high and high school from a biblical worldview. But it is not a full-blown program with graduation requirements, transcript, or diploma program. You can complete all your high school classes here or pick and choose as needed. Classes meet once a week online for ninety minutes, and teachers make full use of voice, video, whiteboard, and chat capabilities. Jeff and Janna Gilbert, the directors, have a heart for homeschooling families on the mission field or in the military. This unique focus means classes consist of students from around the world, and this in itself makes checking out The Potter's School worthwhile. I've heard nothing but positive remarks from families that have completed these courses.

Schola Classical Tutorials (scholatutorials.org) is the vehicle through which well-known classical Christian education advocate Wes Callihan offers weekly group tutorials online in great books, Latin, and rhetoric. Families I know who have used Callihan's services have been quite enthusiastic.

Scholars Online
541-490-9353
www.scholarsonline.org
SOLA offers junior high and senior high courses in the classical Christian tradition. A complete course of study for high school, with a diploma, is available. A sister organization at the same site is available for Catholic homeschoolers.

School of Tomorrow
ACE Curriculum
1-800-925-7777
www.schooloftomorrow.com
The School of Tomorrow program allows each student to work on his or her specific achievement level in various subjects. The high school curriculum includes three levels of math, four levels of English, four levels of social studies, four levels of science, and one level of etymology, as well as twenty-five electives and fifteen advanced courses. Computer video interactive courses are available, and the diploma is accredited.

One final noteworthy course:

Constitutional Law for Christian Students Online
HSLDA
540-338-5600
conlaw.hslda.org/cms/
Taught by Michael Farris, president of Patrick Henry College. Students complete a text written by Farris and listen to eighteen prerecorded lectures delivered via the Internet using RealAudio. Farris holds live chats regularly with students and evaluates student work. Students can interact weekly with each other via a chat room.

Recommended sources of information on planning a high school course of study:

High School @ Home, Diana Johnson

Homeschoolers' College Admissions Handbook: Preparing Your 12- to 18-Year-Old for a Smooth Transition, Cafi Cohen and Linda Dobson

Homeschooling High School: Planning Ahead for College Admission, Jeanne Gowen Dennis

Homeschooling: The Teen Years: Your Complete Guide to Successfully Homeschooling the 13- to 18-Year Old, Cafi Cohen

Life Prep for Homeschooled Teenagers, Barbara Frank

CHAPTER 24
Navigating College Admissions Channels

Let's look now at the teen who plans to go directly from homeschooling to a four-year institution. His high school record is what you will use to gain that college admission. This chapter shows you what you may be asked to produce and how to go about doing that.

Preparing in High School for College Entrance

To prepare for college, you (and your child) can start taking steps when he or she is in eighth grade.

The Good News

Let me begin by putting your mind at ease. Homeschooled students are not having difficulties getting into college. It's a buyer's market, and colleges are pursuing nontraditional students in droves. The HSLDA website posts an online list of more than 500 colleges and universities with favorable guidelines for accepting homeschoolers, a dwindling list of those with entrance requirements they consider inequitable, and only one that still doesn't accept homeschoolers.

Further, homeschooled students already on campus have earned a reputation as highly motivated, responsible, independent learners. A study of 212 home-educated students at Oral Roberts University found that while they had virtually the same average ACT/SAT scores as the student body, they had statistically higher cumulative ORU grade-point averages. Of these students, 88 percent were involved in one or more outreach ministries, 80 percent in one or more campus clubs and organizations, and 90 percent in the intramural sports program. As a result of the study, ORU instituted a $2,000 scholarship for home-educated graduates.

Boston University wrote in a letter sent to homeschool leaders in Massachusetts, "[BU] welcomes applications from home-schooled students. We believe students educated at home possess the passion for knowledge, the independence, and the self-reliance that enable them to excel in our intellectually challenging programs of study."

A survey of more than sixty colleges and universities by the National Center for Home Education collected the following responses:

- Harvard University, which accepts approximately ten home-educated students per year, reported that "home-educated students have done very well. They usually are very motivated in what they do."

- Commenting on the fifty home-educated students at the University of Montana, officials responded, "The homeschoolers in this state seem to be up to date and well organized. We even have homeschoolers in the honors program . . . one [female student] . . . is one of our top students."

- "These homeschoolers write fabulous essays!" wrote Emory University. "Very creative!"

- "Our homeschoolers (about fifty) tend to be very bright, and have scored very high on standardized tests," responded the University of Kentucky.

- A Dartmouth College respondent said, "The [portfolio] applications I've come across are outstanding. Homeschoolers have a distinct advantage because of the individualized instruction they have received."

- Hillsdale College wrote of the seventy-five to ninety home-educated students there, "Homeschoolers are consistently among our top students; in fact, homeschoolers have won our distinct Honors Program the last three years in a row. We tend to look very favorably upon homeschoolers applying to our college."[1]

College reps, especially from Christian colleges, are now attending homeschool conventions and advertising in the homeschool marketplace. We are being courted, folks. You aren't going to have to bang down any doors.

On the Other Hand

Now the other side of the coin: You certainly will be able to find a college that will admit your child, but there are several things you need to do to facilitate your child's getting into the college of his *choice*—especially if it is a competitive school.

Repeatedly, college admissions officers have told me their dilemma is with homeschooled applicants who lack traditional documentation. They are used to seeing a diploma, a transcript, a grade-point average, and a class rank along with College Board scores. Many admissions departments are adapting to homeschoolers and setting up alternative methods of evaluation. I'm sure more will follow, but in the meantime it is not unreasonable of them to ask us to package our child's nontraditional education in traditional terms.

Start Talking to Admissions Departments Early

Before you finalize the course of study your teen will follow in high school, you need to talk with admissions officers at the colleges he or she may potentially attend. I realize that is difficult to anticipate in ninth grade, but you should at least know whether you will consider a public university, private institution, or Bible college. Talking to representatives from any that might be considered should give you a good idea of what other schools in the same category will want to see. (Many institutions feature a section for homeschool applicants on their websites; check there first.)

Tell the admissions office you anticipate home educating your child through high school, and ask what documentation and coursework the college will need in order to be considered for admission. In many cases you will need to indicate the child's areas of interest. In Cindy's case, Nate was interested in English and medicine. She focused on admissions requirements for the more competitive pre-med programs. Should Nate have changed his mind, his high school course of study to qualify for pre-med acceptance would certainly be ample qualification for a humanities department too.

Once you know what admissions offices will look for, you

> YOU SHOULD AT LEAST KNOW WHETHER YOU WILL CONSIDER A PUBLIC UNIVERSITY, PRIVATE INSTITUTION, OR BIBLE COLLEGE.

can either design a program that will meet their requirements or use the time between ninth and twelfth grade to negotiate for consideration of alternative documentation.

Diplomas: Do You Need Them?

Hurray! Since the first edition of this book a lot has changed. First, HSLDA succeeded in getting the military to change its policy regarding homeschoolers. A parent-issued high school diploma now qualifies them as Tier I applicants, to whom the best assignments go (previously they were lumped with Tier II applicants—high school dropouts).

Then in 2003, HSLDA successfully clarified U.S. Department of Education regulations regarding college admissions and federal financial aid requirements for homeschoolers. Your child does not need a state-recognized diploma (such as a GED) in order to receive federal financial aid, nor does the U.S. government require colleges to accept only applicants with state-recognized diplomas in order to qualify for federal funding. A parent-issued high school diploma will satisfy the standards.

However, this only has to do with federal funding. Organizations can set their own standards at will, so you will still find that colleges, potential employers, and scholarship committees may still want to see a state-recognized diploma from an accredited institution before they will consider your child.

So, onward with the options . . .

GED

Currently, if you need a state-recognized diploma, a GED is the only option most homeschoolers have. This, to me, is an unsatisfactory state of affairs (and I'm glad to see HSLDA also agrees and is doing something about it). The GED test is designed for only a tenth-grade general education. In fact, *GED* now stands for General Educational Development, not Graduation Equivalency Diploma as it once did and many assume still does. Institutions and employers that require a GED from a home educated student cheapen the quality of the education the student has likely received.

Secondly, many states do not allow students to take the GED exam until they reach the end of their state's compulsory school

> **CURRENTLY, IF YOU NEED A STATE-RECOGNIZED DIPLOMA, A GED IS THE ONLY OPTION MOST HOMESCHOOLERS HAVE.**

age (this can range from seventeen to nineteen), thus stymieing homeschooled students who finish their high school course of study early but are too young to take the test that a prospective employer or institution requires.

Local School District Diplomas

I am always surprised to find that many homeschoolers believe their local school district is obligated to issue a diploma to their children. That is not true, unless your homeschool is functioning under the umbrella of your local district. (This is possible in California, but the school district then sets the curriculum too.) A diploma signifies that you have met the requirements set for graduation by the institution issuing it. If you aren't meeting the requirements of its program, it is unreasonable to expect the school district to give you its diploma.

Satellite Programs and Correspondence Schools

Another avenue leading to a traditional-looking diploma from an accredited school is enrollment in a satellite program or correspondence school for the high school years.

Locally

There may be a local church or private school in your locale offering this service to homeschoolers through an umbrella program. However, this can mean paying close to full enrollment fees, following its course of study, using required materials, and submitting to student evaluations by its staff. The school may believe this is necessary to control the quality of its graduates. But in the process you may find yourself compromising the fundamental reasons you've chosen to home educate.

Furthermore, while the school may issue a diploma, if its program is not accredited by the state department of education, a GED may still be necessary for its graduates to meet admissions requirements.

Nationally

Quite a few correspondence schools and satellite programs now offer a high-school-at-home program with a diploma upon graduation. But when considering this avenue, you need to know if the program is *accredited* and *by whom*. There are a lot of accrediting agencies, and their beauty is only in the eyes of the beholder. You must find out if the institutions you want your child to be admitted to after high school *recognize* these diplomas. Again, working backward needs to be an essential part of your planning.

These programs still have many advantages to offer, but for the purposes of our discussion here, if you choose this route primarily to obtain a diploma, then you need to make sure up front that the school's diploma will open all the doors you want it to.

Homeschool Diploma Programs

Many state homeschool organizations issue their own diplomas and hold annual graduation ceremonies. I believe this is an important service to offer members. I support HSLDA's efforts to bring recognition to parent-issued diplomas, and these should be sufficient for financial aid. However, I find it understandable that institutions and employers weigh diplomas received from an outside agency more heavily than those issued by a parent. And I think it will be an uphill battle if we try to legislate this away. Scholarship committees do not have to reveal how awards are made; employers do not have to explain why one applicant is chosen over another. But it makes perfect sense that an applicant whose qualifications are verified by someone other than his mom would be viewed as more credible. (Now I know you would be objective, but think about your neighbor—is she objective when talking about her kid?)

So where should this outside validation come from? Your state association, for example, could set minimum requirements for graduation, and a simple system (that isn't intrusive) might be put in place to bring a higher level of credibility, accountability, and validation for what these kids have done. Your homeschool association, rather than a Christian school, is going to understand the unique needs of homeschoolers and design a program that is flexible yet respected.

In South Carolina, for example, the South Carolina Association of Independent Home Schools is given power by state law to approve homeschool programs. SCAIHS has a high school program that offers a wide variety of services to its members. (SCAIHS' services are not limited to homeschoolers in South

Carolina, but homeschoolers outside the state would need to make sure they complied with the requirements of their own state law.) In the ever-changing world of academia, the SCAIHS high school staff strives to remain on the cutting edge. Their dynamic program offers a wide range of services, including tracking and recording high school credits, issuing transcripts, providing curriculum counseling, informing parents about special extracurricular opportunities, providing guidance services, and hosting a formal graduation ceremony every year. Additionally, the SCAIHS staff has worked diligently for almost two decades to ensure that all homeschoolers in South Carolina are eligible for state scholarships and that in-state colleges accept the SCAIHS transcript.

In Pennsylvania, the state department of education recognizes homeschool diplomas issued through several homeschool programs (thus rendering them legally equivalent to a state-issued diploma). Some homeschoolers, including HSLDA, believe that states should not distinguish between a parent-issued diploma and those issued by an outside agency, even if it is a homeschool-run agency.

All my kids participated in one of our state-recognized homeschool diploma programs, and I could not care less that their diplomas were recognized by the state. Further, none of the colleges we applied to even asked about this. The outside validation was sufficient for them. What did delight me was *how much time I saved*. The wonderful folks at Pennsylvania Homeschoolers Accreditation Agency handled all the paperwork, issued an impressive-looking diploma, and sent an embossed, official-looking transcript from the PHAA offices quickly every time I asked (which was every time we filed a college or scholarship application anywhere).

My sons applied to an out-of-state school, which then turned around and sent me a long list of things I needed to compile because they were homeschooled applicants. It would have been hours of work. Essentially, they wanted me to submit a lot of paperwork signed by other people so they could validate my sons' work. I made a quick phone call explaining that we had a state-recognized diploma program in Pennsylvania and all my sons' records would be coming from them. I asked them if that would be sufficient in place of all this other stuff. They were surprised to hear of such a thing and said, "Why, yes, certainly. We won't need anything else then."

A Model Program

The program we participated in, PHAA, was the first one recognized in Pennsylvania, but since then, several other regional support groups have set up their own requirements for graduation and received recognition. Each group decides what they will require. I chose the one with the most stringent requirements because I wanted to position my kids for merit scholarships. (Kids coming from high schools with a higher academic ranking are more likely to receive merit scholarships than others; the same principle applies here.) At the same time, the program is flexible enough to allow parents to adapt their program to each child's needs—even special-needs kids. Parents award the credits, and an evaluator of the program approves them. Over the past ten years, thousands of homeschool graduates have received their diploma from PHAA, and it is highly regarded by the post–high school institutions in Pennsylvania. PHAA also holds graduation services, publishes a newsletter for its students and alumni, and collects and publicizes statistical research about its graduates. (For instance, 1 in 25 graduates is a National Merit semifinalist. The national norm is 1 in 200.)

The diploma programs in Pennsylvania are only open to Pennsylvania homeschoolers, but if you would like to encourage the same type of program in your state, information about PHAA and all the other homeschool diploma programs in Pennsylvania are available online or by writing:

Pennsylvania Homeschoolers
105 Richman Lane
Kittanning, PA 16201
724-783-6512
www.pahomeschoolers.com

Transcripts

A transcript is a record of your child's coursework and activities in high school. Traditionally it includes credits awarded, individual course grades, cumulative grade-point average, and class rank. This is another important document you need to prepare for your child if you homeschool through high school. The purpose, once again, is to communicate nontraditional education in the traditional terms outsiders will understand.

Reproducible transcript forms can be found in several homeschool publications, including *The Homeschooler's Guide to Portfolios and Transcripts* by Loretta Heuer. Software programs such as *Homeschool Tracker* and *Edu-Track* also include templates for creating a high school transcript. TranscriptPro Software (Version 4) by Inge Cannon of Education PLUS is designed to walk the homeschooling parent through all the steps necessary for creating a professional high school transcript.

Several websites show you how to make a transcript for a homeschool student. Visit google.com and type in "How to make a transcript."

Here are several places to get started:

www.teascript.com—Created by a homeschool graduate. For a modest fee, you can create and update your child's high school transcript online.

www.transcriptsmadeeasy.com—Created by Janice Campbell, long-time homeschooler, writer, and blogger.

www.hslda.org—Click on Homeschool Thru High School and then Transcripts. You will find blank, reproducible forms in Microsoft Word and PDF formats, along with several examples.

Computing Credits

There are various ways to award credits for your teen's coursework. Here are some choices. Choose the one that will be most meaningful to you and your child:

Most schools award one credit for completion of a full-year course and a half credit for a one-semester course. Sometimes honors and Advanced Placement courses are weighted to provide extra credits—usually 1.25 or 1.50 respectively.

In a traditional setting, core courses meet every day for thirty-six weeks for forty-minute classes. This is roughly equivalent to 120 hours of classroom instruction (traditionally called one Carnegie unit) and does not reflect outside assignment time. The college-bound student is expected to graduate with more than twenty credits.

The Pennsylvania Homeschoolers diploma program allows parents to award credit a number of different ways, one of which is for 120 hours of coursework. But given the amount of time so often wasted in a traditional classroom, your home-educated student will easily complete the same amount of work in far less time.

Other options for awarding credit can include number of days logged, completion of predetermined coursework, a score of 3 or higher on the appropriate Advanced Placement exam, or passage of a CLEP (College-Level Examination Program) test. We'll talk about the last two later. For the purposes of college admissions, you should be consistent in how you determine credit, though, and include an explanation of your criteria in an addendum to your transcript.

> **YOU SHOULD BE CONSISTENT IN HOW YOU DETERMINE CREDIT.**

Credit by Contract

I prefer contracts. Predetermine with your child what work he must accomplish for a course to be considered complete, and base his grade upon the level of his success in completing that work. Here is what I required to earn an A in my senior high American literature course at CHESS:

- Read the entire Bob Jones University eleventh-grade American literature anthology.
- Average 90 percent or higher on midterm and final exams as well as class quizzes.
- Score 90 percent or higher on ten-page (typed) research paper.
- Score 90 percent or higher on ten-minute speech.
- Score 90 percent or higher on three typed compositions (minimum length three pages).
- Read seven additional works of literary merit from the American literary canon.
- Contribute consistently and thoughtfully to class discussion and activities.

The reading requirements for this class are very ambitious, and I would support a parent's decision to list this as an honors English course and award 1.25 credits for completion.

Grades

Awarding grades to your high schooler for the purpose of the transcript is also the best way to communicate his or her level of success in understandable terms. As with credits, I suggest contracting with your child what work he or she must complete to receive an A, B, or C from you. Pass/fail grades are acceptable in non-academic courses but detrimental for core subjects.

A cumulative grade-point average can be computed by averaging all the grades for high school. Use the scale below (I assume you won't accept less than a C in a course):

$$
\frac{\begin{array}{l} 4 \times \text{number of A grades} \\ 3 \times \text{number of B grades} \\ + \ 2 \times \text{number of C grades} \end{array}}{\text{Total} \div \text{by number of courses} = \text{GPA}}
$$

Typically, Advanced Placement and honors courses are awarded five points for an A grade, four points for a B grade, and three points for a C grade. If you are proficient in Excel, then create your transcript in that program and use it to compute the GPA.

College Board Scores

While SAT and ACT scores have become less critical to a traditional student's acceptance at a four-year college, they are the most heavily factored documentation a homeschooled applicant will present. If your child scores exceptionally high on his college entrance exams, you will only need to provide minimal additional documentation (i.e., you don't have to be overly worried about all the paperwork I just covered). That score will vary for each program and school, but it is generally above 1200 combined critical reading and math score on the SAT (colleges evaluate the writing score separately) and 30 on the

ACT. If his scores, however, place him in the middle of the pack of applicants (1000—1200 on the SAT or 26 on the ACT), then your documentation needs to be designed to distinguish him from the competition.

Strategies to Maximize Board Scores

#1. Read

Students who score well on their college entrance exams are avid readers. The high school program you design should allow for ample opportunity to read widely across the curriculum and for pleasure. *Reading Lists for College-Bound Students* is a helpful resource that will give you an idea of the level of reading your teen should be reaching toward. This book compiles the freshman reading lists from more than 100 private and public colleges and universities.

> **STUDENTS WHO SCORE WELL ON THEIR COLLEGE ENTRANCE EXAMS ARE AVID READERS.**

#2. Study Vocabulary

Starting in junior high, use a vocabulary-builder program that focuses on the Greek and Latin roots of words. In addition, get your kids involved with the study of words. In my composition class, I ask students to create a vocabulary section in their writing portfolio consisting of words they like and words they've learned. Each entry includes the definition, part of speech, origin, source where they originally found the word (dictionary, newspaper, novel, conversation—it must vary), and an example of the word used in context. My purpose is to make the kids more aware of words and conscious of clues to their meaning.

Fun vocabulary builders:

Test of Time: A Novel Approach to the SAT and ACT, Charles Harrington Elster. Uses vocabulary from the SATs in the context of a mystery novel.

Word Smart Jr. and *Word Smart*

WordSmart software line (www.wordsmart.com)

#3. Complete Algebra 1 Through Trigonometry

The level of math on the SAT includes algebra, geometry, trigonometric function, and probability and statistics. The ACT

347

predominantly measures math competencies in algebra and geometry, but it too includes a small amount of trigonometry. Your best bet is to use test preparation unique to the college entrance exam your student is preparing to take.

This may be overkill on my part, but I supplemented our algebra 1 text with video courses from Annenberg Media and the Teaching Company. And I continuously impressed upon my kids the importance of not moving on to the next lesson in math if they did not understand conceptually what was going on. We didn't want to sacrifice understanding for the sake of completing a course in a year's time. Mike and Gabe worked on algebra I and II most of sixth through eighth grade. Later advanced math courses took far less time because we had laid a thorough understanding.

Another point to weigh: Saxon Math, a popular program among homeschoolers, does not provide a separate course in geometry. Rather, it is integrated throughout the program. I have had feedback from a number of kids who felt they were not sufficiently prepared for the geometry on the college boards as a result.

Geometry by Harold Jacobs has been used by college-bound students desiring concentrated study in this area. Most kids can cover what they need to know in less than a year.

Just prior to taking the PSAT and SAT tests, my three teens watched (and actually enjoyed) the SAT Math Review video series from Chalk Dust Company. This is a good investment and will give you a handle on just what kind of math you need to cover prior to taking these tests.

#4. Prepare

Test-preparation programs do result in higher scores. *Inside the SAT/ACT Deluxe* is an award-winning software program from Princeton Review. Study aids are also published by Princeton Review, Barron's, Gruber, and Dummies Guides. One student I evaluated who scored 1590 reviewed them all and recommended Gary Gruber's guide. Nate McKeown liked *Cracking the SAT* from Princeton Review—it had a more entertaining presentation than the others.

> **TEST-PREPARATION PROGRAMS DO RESULT IN HIGHER SCORES.**

Gruber's Complete Preparation for the New SAT, Gary Gruber

Cracking the New SAT with CD-ROM, Adam Robinson

The Rocket Review Revolution: The Ultimate Guide to the New SAT, Adam Robinson

#5. Practice

Taking tests is like learning to play baseball. The more you practice, the better you get. I don't like standardized tests as an evaluation tool, but because they are critical to college acceptance and academic scholarships, I have had my kids take all they can. I've even given them and other academically talented kids out-of-level tests (a standardized test one to four grade levels above their grade level) to sharpen their skills with a greater challenge. For students who typically score at the very top of the chart on a grade-level test, this strategy will give you a more accurate picture of your child's strengths and weaknesses.

A number of talent searches administer the SATs to seventh- and eighth-graders who score in the top 2 percent nationally on a standardized test. Johns Hopkins University's Center for Talented Youth is the most widely recognized. We weren't interested in (read "couldn't afford") the three-week summer residency program that qualifiers may participate in, but I wanted Mike and Gabe to have the experience—one they were pretty grumpy about ("Mom, it's our only day to sleep in!").

Incidentally, Mike and Gabe typically scored within a few points of each other on standardized tests, but in this situation the one who read through the test booklet and did the practice exercises did significantly better than the one who walked in cold. That convinced me they should use study aids to prepare when it really counted.

As an aside, participating in an academic talent search does look good on your child's résumé, and it gets your name on a lot of mailing lists for other worthwhile opportunities. So take advantage of the opportunity if your child qualifies. I've listed talent searches in the Resource Guide under Academic/Athletic Contests and Competitions.

The SATs are given numerous times throughout the school year. You register directly with the College Board for this test. (The fee is reduced if you register online.) Your child will need to provide student identification at the site. A driver's license or learner's permit is typical. If your child does not have this yet, most sites should accept your verification of your child's identity along with your driver's license. But set this up ahead of time. Some families obtain a passport or other official ID for their child for this purpose.

The ACT is not given as often as the SAT nor offered at as many sites, but it is still universally accepted as a college entrance exam. This test may better match the strengths of your student. The four sections of the test include English, math, reading, and science, and it measures achievement in these areas, not aptitude.

#6. Take the PSAT

The PSAT stands for Preliminary Scholastic Aptitude Test. It was originally intended to be a predictor of a student's future SAT scores. However, it is now used in a student's junior year as the qualifying test for National Merit Scholarship selection as well. Whereas the SAT is given numerous times throughout the year, the PSAT is given only once: a Wednesday or Saturday in October. Homeschool students must register through a local school, not through the College Board organization.

If you are in the hunt for top board scores, then have your teen take the PSAT in tenth grade for practice, preferably at the school where he or she will take it again as a junior. You should line up a test site in August or September. Don't be put off if a school turns you away. Private schools are usually most accommodating, but if a public school is the only available test site and says no, then contact the College Board for assistance. Ask the school to provide you with the test prep material sent from the College Board as well. (We have found that a change in guidance personnel can also mean a change in policy, so don't take no as a final answer.)

The maximum total score on the New SAT is now 2400. To predict future SAT scores from your child's PSAT scores, add a "zero" to each of the scores. For National Merit selection, the three PSAT scores are added together to generate an index

> IF YOU ARE IN THE HUNT FOR TOP BOARD SCORES, THEN HAVE YOUR TEEN TAKE THE PSAT IN TENTH GRADE FOR PRACTICE.

score. The possible total for this is 240. The score needed for National Merit varies from state to state (each state is guaranteed a quota of scholars). In most places, your child will need a score exceeding 200 to be considered.

You can use materials designed for the SAT to prepare for the PSAT. For the writing test, use the *Barron's How to Prepare for the SAT II Writing*. The same types of questions are asked on both.

Unlike the SAT, your child can obtain his actual test from the PSAT after the scoring has been completed. They will be returned to the test site, so make arrangements to pick up the test, as it will be the best help in preparing for the SAT.

Contact Information

ACT Registration
301 ACT Drive
P.O. Box 414
Iowa City, IA 52243-0414
319-337-1270
www.actstudent.org

The College Board
45 Columbus Avenue
New York, NY 10023-6917
866-630-9305
collegeboard.org (many test-preparation materials are available here)

National Merit Scholarship Corporation
1560 Sherman Avenue, Suite 200
Evanston, IL 60201-4897
847-866-5100
www.nationalmerit.org

PSAT/NMSQT
P.O. Box 6720
Princeton, NJ 08541-6720
888-477-7728
www.collegeboard.org

SAT Program
Educational Testing Services
Rosedale Road
Princeton, NJ 08541
609-921-9000
www.collegeboard.org

Online Princeton Review runs a very informative website filled with college, career, and financial information (www.princetonreview.com).

Also look at www.number2.com. This site offers free online test preparation for the SAT, ACT, and GRE (Graduate Record Exam). It wants your personal information, but will not share it unless you agree (it is supported through advertisers).

Your local school district's guidance department will also have information on all these tests.

Learning to Improve PSAT Scores

I took my first PSAT as a sophomore. My score was 1270 (560 verbal, 710 math). I then began efforts to raise my score—especially my verbal—by working through some PSAT/ SAT study books. I saw no improvement as I worked through the texts, so I disbanded the project.

When I took the test again in October 1994, my score was 1580 (780 verbal, 800 math). Even though I had not done a lot of work specifically aimed at raising my score, it had gone up. Without even considering my PSAT scores, I had decided that I wanted to become as knowledgeable as I possibly could on a wide range of subjects.

Between the two tests, I took a little over half of a year of Latin. This helped my vocabulary skills somewhat, but the largest contribution made by the Latin was that by doing it I became interested in reading about ancient Rome and the Roman poets featured in the program. Eventually, I began reading the works of other poets as well as continuing to read classic novels. In between the two tests, I covered many different types and styles of literature that I really had not read a lot of before. I also read through a set of encyclopedias, taking notes on important items in history, science, literature, and other academic areas. This gave me a lot of experience at grasping new facts and restating information in a more concise way. Also, due to the sheer volume of reading involved in my study, my vocabulary increased and my ability to interpret a word's meaning in context sharpened. With so much reading, it is easy to see why I also became faster at reading.

When I took the PSAT a second time, I was able to read through the comprehension sections more quickly and with a greater understanding of the author's point than I had the first time. The result was a 120-point rise in my verbal score.

My math score was already pretty good at 710, but I knew I could do better. I did a few math tests in an SAT practice book, and then I examined where my problems were. I found that some of the time I missed a problem simply by not thinking hard enough or by making a careless error that I should not have made. These were the same reasons I missed problems in my regular math class in homeschool (Saxon). I realized that if I eliminated these problems, I would be almost 100 percent accurate. I completely changed the way I did math. Instead of doing an entire problem set then checking my answers and trying to remember what I did wrong that caused me to miss a certain point, I began checking every problem immediately after doing it. This worked out very well because it enabled me to see where my problems were so that I could remedy them. I reached a point where I rarely missed a problem and was then able to return to the usual way of doing math. On my second PSAT, my math score improved to a perfect score of 800.

My advice to someone wanting to raise his or her PSAT/SAT score:

1. Stop wasting time and take responsibility for your education.
2. Pinpoint your problems and work to solve them.
3. Read, read, read your way to success.

—Rhett Smith, Pennsylvania

More from Rhett's Mom

Rhett makes many study aids for himself, including posters and wall charts of things like the periodic table for chemistry and formulas in calculus. He has over a thousand flashcards on author/written work, Latin/English translations, chemical structures/names. Some of the flashcards are stapled together into books now. In a loose-leaf notebook he also made an encyclopedia of his own about anything and everything he thought important. Rhett has done all this and become very organized on his own. His involvement in Quiz Bowls, an academic team program, encouraged him greatly.

—Audrey Smith, Rhett's mom[2]

My Two Cents

Audrey coached a homeschool Quiz Bowl team close to where my parents live. My dad regularly sent me features from the city papers about this team's success. They upset a local Catholic high school with a national reputation and made it to the nationals. I point this out to illustrate the level of motivation kids can achieve when their studies are purposeful and immediate. (Play ball!)

Additional Documentation That Looks Great on College Applications

#1. Advanced Placement or Other Advanced Courses

Advanced Placement courses are college-level studies completed in high school. Each May, then, students take an AP exam in various areas of study. A score of 3 or higher (5 being the top) is considered a passing grade. Most colleges award credit to incoming freshmen for AP tests passed in high school, though some may require higher than a 3 to qualify. It is possible to earn enough AP credits in high school to qualify for sophomore standing at leading universities (and save thousands of dollars in tuition).

Our sons were able to transfer in six credits through AP testing, and just this small head start, along with meticulous planning, allowed them to finish their first degrees in three and a

> ADVANCED PLACEMENT COURSES ARE COLLEGE-LEVEL STUDIES COMPLETED IN HIGH SCHOOL.

half years. Our son Gabe was so close to completing a second major in economics that he decided to stay one more semester. Our daughter Kathryn was even more intentional. She took five AP tests in the following order: U.S. History (tenth); European History (eleventh); and English Literature, French, and Psychology (twelfth). The University of Pittsburgh awarded her twenty-four credits and sophomore standing which allowed her to register right away for upper-level courses. Her high scores on these tests were also a contributing factor in her selection as a Presidential Scholar (five-year, full-tuition scholarship).

Currently, thirty-seven exams in twenty-two fields are available. The method of preparing for the test, though, is at your discretion. Barron's publishes AP test preparation books, and this is a good place to find help in designing a course.

The Advanced Placement Program also offers booklets available outlining the recommended course of study.

Advanced Placement Program
888-225-5427 (CALL-4-AP)
collegeboard.org/ap

Pennsylvania Homeschoolers began offering AP courses online in 1996. Visit their website for more information. I teach Advanced Placement English Language and Composition and AP Literature and Composition for this organization (pahomeschoolers.com).

> **ENCOURAGE YOUR TEEN TO TRY AN ADVANCED PLACEMENT COURSE IN HIS JUNIOR OR SENIOR YEAR.**

Encourage your teen to try an Advanced Placement course in his junior or senior year. Even if he does not pass the test or doesn't even take it at the conclusion of the course, it demonstrates to colleges that he has gone out of his way to challenge himself. This counts with admissions offices. They want to enroll students who will graduate, not quit midstream. Students who've taken challenging courses during high school have proven to be the better bet (even when they don't have the straight A's the kid with the lighter course load has).

Final note: As of 2007, courses cannot be labeled AP on a student's transcript unless the course has been approved through the College Board's audit process. The course syllabus must be aligned with the Board's course requirements. Ask an AP provider if the course is approved before enrolling your child. Individual homeschoolers may also submit a course they've designed to the College Board for approval. E-mail apcourseaudit@epiconline.org for further instructions.

#2. Outside Evaluations

College admissions offices will weigh heavily any recommendations or evaluations from non-family members who can give a knowledgeable assessment of your child's academic aptitude and achievement. Include with your application written recommendations from tutors, mentors, evaluators, or co-op teachers. These folks don't need to be credentialed as much as they need to be articulate. So look out for someone who can write a good letter, and get your kid under his or her tutelage for a season.

Most academic programs and scholarships require an outsider's evaluation in order for an applicant even to be considered for acceptance. The same is true for acceptance at a competitive college.

#3. Activities and Academic Honors

As erroneous as this is, many admissions offices will assume your kid has been living an isolated life and may not transition into the college experience well. (As a surprise, have Junior wear shoes to the interview.) They are wondering: *How will this kid handle the social life? How will he perform in a competitive environment?*

You can diffuse this issue quickly by including on the transcript the clubs, athletics, and organizations your teen has participated in during high school. Highlight any leadership, informal or formal, he has shown. Don't neglect to include church activities and cross-cultural experiences, such as mission trips. Long-term commitments are especially important to admissions offices. Has your teen been helping in children's ministry for several years? Has she been running her own babysitting or lawn-care business for two or three years? Get those facts down on paper.

Involvement and achievement in academic competitions are another real plus on the transcript. The Resource Guide includes a

> **LONG-TERM COMMITMENTS ARE ESPECIALLY IMPORTANT TO ADMISSIONS OFFICES.**

list of scholastic competitions that homeschoolers are welcome to participate in. Your child does not need to win, place, or show; it is the involvement that will count in the admissions officer's mind.

Remember, you are giving the admissions office concrete reasons not only for admitting your child but also for pursuing him or her with an attractive financial aid package. Everything you can think of that makes your kid noteworthy should be highlighted on the transcript or application. I've always been able to think of experiences overlooked by the students I've helped apply. Brainstorm with folks to make sure nothing has been forgotten.

#4. Junior or Community College Transcript

Many community colleges and two-year institutions have open enrollment. You don't need a diploma, a transcript, or College Board scores. Many also allow students to take courses while in high school. These can often be transferred to a four-year university as college credit. (If you intend to do this, make sure you talk to the college you wish to transfer credits to first.)

After Cindy McKeown worked with the admissions office at our local community college, they became very eager to accommodate homeschoolers, even to the point of accepting students as young as tenth grade. In fact, in the past few years, several area colleges have begun offering free and half-price courses to homeschoolers in the hopes of securing their full enrollment after graduation. Most of the college-bound seniors I know are taking courses for credit at local colleges.

The transcript record from a community college and the recommendations your child gathers from instructors may be all he needs to be considered for acceptance at a four-year institution.

And if cost-cutting is a goal, there is no better deal than completing the first two years of college at a community college and then transferring to a four-year institution. Your child's diploma will look the same as the one given to kids who paid a great deal more.

#5. SAT II Tests

The SAT II tests measure achievement in specific subject areas such as math, writing, biology, American history, etc. In the

> THERE IS NO BETTER DEAL THAN COMPLETING THE FIRST TWO YEARS OF COLLEGE AT A COMMUNITY COLLEGE AND THEN TRANSFERRING TO A FOUR-YEAR INSTITUTION.

absence of other documentation, many colleges are requiring a certain number of SAT II scores from homeschooled applicants. They believe this is an objective measurement of your child's level of mastery. HSLDA is working to eliminate this practice as discriminatory, and some schools have changed their policy or have required SAT II subject-area testing for all applicants. One student of mine, a National Merit Scholar, was required to take SAT II subject-area tests for admission at a couple of Christian colleges. I thought this was a bit ridiculous. They should have been grateful to be considered by a student of that caliber.

My kids have taken SAT II tests, and they are very similar to the Advanced Placement tests, but without essays. They aren't expensive (approximately $20 dollars each), take only an hour, and are one way to demonstrate mastery in an area. Prep books from Barron's are available that will help your child prepare well for these tests. It is best for your child to take the SAT II test for a specific subject as soon as he has completed the coursework. Don't wait until his senior year to find out a college is going to require it. Mike and Gabe took the SAT II for American history in ninth grade because that is when they took the course. They also took it to practice for the Advanced Placement test in that area. And it helped—they passed the AP exam.

SAT II subject tests may be an especially attractive route for the student who does not have impressive SAT or ACT scores. Taking an achievement test in a specific area of strength and scoring well should offset those board scores.

Financial Aid

Most families, no matter how well off, are looking for financial aid for college. This is also an area, then, you should start looking into early. There is plenty of financial aid out there, folks. Nobody pays full price for college, cars, or a night in a motel. However, there are always criteria your child must meet to qualify. That's why you need to have a plan in ninth grade that results in the right documentation at the end of the road.

The best source of information will be the financial aid offices of the colleges you are considering and the homeschoolers who have gone before you in this area.

> THERE IS PLENTY OF FINANCIAL AID OUT THERE.

First select the colleges you want to pursue based upon merit. Then work on the financial-aid package with their offices. Expensive private schools typically have big endowments, and it is not unusual to end up with a financial-aid package that actually comes in at less than the cost of a state-run institution.

What your child needs in order to qualify for competitive programs and scholarships:

- High SAT/ACT scores
- Honors and AP courses
- Strong written-communication skills
- Heavy course load in senior year—even if credits for graduation are already met
- Academic and avocational pursuits outside of school
- Leadership skills
- A *shtick*—being charming, unforgettable, and distinctive
- Great recommendation letters from credible folks outside your family

As the vast majority of financial aid and scholarship money out there is based upon need and not on merit, some strategizing is necessary on your part. Here is the best book for helping you out in that department:

Paying for College Without Going Broke (Princeton Review, latest edition). I plowed through this tome when Mike and Gabe entered ninth grade, and it is a good thing I did because the tips here have informed quite a few financial decisions we needed to make while they were in high school. For instance, it is better to hold funds for college under your account and not under your child's (his or her assets are assessed at a 35 percent rate, yours at 5.65 percent). I learned that I am also at a great disadvantage being self-employed. As many homeschool families are also entrepreneurs, it would be wise to take a look at the important strategies listed here before your child's junior year of high school (that is the year used to create a family financial profile on which financial aid is based.)

After reading Princeton Review's book, I asked a relative who is the dean of financial aid for a large university to evaluate our expected financial obligation. And his analysis proved Princeton Review's advice was indeed sound.

For more info:

And What About College?, Cafi Cohen. A well-written and personable book about Cafi's experience securing acceptance at the U.S. Air Force Academy and at a private college for two of her graduated teens. She offers lots of advice and resources that will ease your way through this process. The best place to get this book is used online (try Amazon.com).

College Planning for Dummies, Pat Ordovensky

Homeschoolers' College Admissions Handbook: Preparing Your 12- to 18-Year-Old for a Smooth Transition, Cafi Cohen

Homeschooling High School: Planning Ahead for College Admission, Jeanne Gowen Dennis

These are helpful guides for Christians considering what type of college environment is best for their spiritual health.

Choosing the Right College: The Whole Truth About America's Top Schools, John Zmirak

The Totally Usable Summit Ministries Guide to Choosing a College, Ronald Nash and J. F. Baldwin

Online there is a vast ocean of information. Make these stops first:

College Board (collegeboard.org). A search under "home schooling" at the College Board's website will pull up an entire area devoted to homeschoolers and college admissions. It's just another indication of how desirable our graduates have become.

Fastweb (fastweb.com). This is the best scholarship search engine on the Web. You'll have to give up personal information; but they not only let you search their massive database, they will also alert you via e-mail when new scholarships appear for which you might be eligible.

FinAid (finaid.com). This source provides free searches through massive databases for financial aid.

Christian College Mentor (www.christiancollegementor. org). Helpful advice for the Christian student in selecting a college, and a database that allows you to compare Christian institutions.

Home School Legal Defense Association (hslda.org). In its website's library, HSLDA maintains a list of colleges that have accepted homeschoolers. Additional archives provide information related to college admissions. HSLDA will also assist you if you should run into difficulties.

Learn in Freedom (www.learninfreedom.org). Karl Bunday is creator of the "School Is Dead. Learn in Freedom" website, one of the oldest and best maintained on the Internet. One of the most current lists of colleges that have admitted homeschoolers is published here. Bunday also has the latest admissions policies available for homeschoolers. This is a mammoth site with lots of other stuff of interest.

Peterson's Publishing (petersons.com). Peterson's online college and career center.

U.S. News & World Report (www.usnews.com). The education area of this site provides thousands of pages of comparative information on most colleges in the United States and Canada and includes sound advice about getting into college for homeschool students.

CHAPTER 25
College at Home
There wouldn't be a hassle-free, dirt-cheap route through college, now, would there?

Funny you should ask. Yes, Virginia, there is.

It's called distance learning, and it's another rapidly growing segment of the education market, along with homeschooling. We Americans may have big government, but we're still encoded with the independent spirit of our forefathers—rapscallions and ruffians that they were. Any system the government invents, we'll find a way to subvert.

How do you earn college credits or even a degree (called an external degree) without leaving home? Better, how can you maximize the high school years by earning dual credits with the same course? Through a number of strategies:

- Credit by examination
- Correspondence courses
- Online courses
- Life experience
- Independent study
- Portfolio assessment

Why Do I Want to Do This?

1. Your child gains the academic knowledge and skips the indoctrination. Again, my evolving opinions are Cindy's fault. After all that hard work she went through getting Nate into college, she's now gnashing her teeth over a lot of the twaddle and politically correct indoctrination he received. (Of course, spending his summers in the military did tend to offset the damages.) Cindy got me reading *The National Review College Guide* by Charles Sykes and Brad Miner. I know it's from a very conservative camp to begin with, but this review's criteria for recommendation have nothing to do with political leanings. This is a guide to "the few and the brave" institutions still offering a core curriculum in the

Western tradition. (If you need a persuasive defense for studying the Western tradition—no matter what your ethnic background—read E. D. Hirsch's *Cultural Literacy*.)

Sykes and Miner's research uncovered it is now possible to graduate from:

78% of the nation's colleges and universities without taking one course in the history of Western civilization

38% without taking any history course at all

45% without taking any course in American or English literature

41% without taking any mathematics

33% without studying natural or physical science[1]

You'll want to read *Illiberal Education* by Dinesh D'Souza as well. This impeccably researched but controversial book chronicles the massive revisionism of curricula taking place on most campuses today as well as the oppressive steps university administrations feel pressured to take to enforce political correctness.

Before you start shelling out tens of thousands of dollars on the presumption of giving your child an education, find out if the campus you're considering still upholds free speech and includes a few of the dead white guys—at least Shakespeare, Milton, and Homer.

2. **To save megabucks and complete a course of study at one's convenience.** The opportunities in distance education first evolved to accommodate working adults seeking a degree for advancement but unable to afford to leave work to become traditional students for a season. This still makes up the bulk of the students using these strategies, but at the second tier are homeschoolers. And institutions are beginning to heavily pitch their services directly to us, which means they are fine-tuning their programs to better meet our needs every day.

3. **To maximize your child's time and efforts in high school.** The credits earned through the following strategies can be used

to fulfill credits for high school graduation and converted into college credit as well.

In all cases, remember, it is the college to which you are applying that determines what credits, if any, it will award for these nontraditional strategies. However, the stigma once attached to correspondence courses and other distance learning options no longer holds true. Most universities and colleges accept credits earned through one or more of these methods.

THE STIGMA ONCE ATTACHED TO CORRESPONDENCE COURSES AND OTHER DISTANCE LEARNING OPTIONS NO LONGER HOLDS TRUE.

Strategy #1: Equivalency Exams

Advanced Placement tests mentioned earlier are the most prestigious equivalency exams, but they only allow students to opt out of general education courses and must be taken during high school. Credit for more advanced levels, as well as freshman courses, can be earned through other equivalency exam programs, and can be taken during college.

The most widely accepted are the CLEP (College-Level Examination Program) tests, available from the makers of Advanced Placement exams and the SAT. But college credit by exam is a growing industry, and there are several other sources of equivalency testing, among them the DSST program, Excelsior College Exams, the Thomas Edison College Examination Program, and CollegePlus (www.collegeplus.org).

After independent study, the student takes an equivalency exam that is representative of the knowledge typically acquired in that college-level course. More than three thousand universities and colleges award credit for CLEP exams, though each institution sets its own standards for what constitutes a passing grade. These exams cost about $72 and are often worth three to six college credits—not a bad exchange for the price.

At fourteen, a young lady in our co-op passed the biology I, American history I, and American history II CLEP exams after preparing with Bob Jones University's high school-level texts. Our sons "clepped out" of marketing during college by waiting to take the test during their junior year. With the knowledge they'd gained in other business courses, they didn't even need to study.

For information on CLEP exams:

College-Level Examination Program
P.O. Box 6600
Princeton, NJ 08541-6600
800-257-9558
www.collegeboard.org/clep

Study guides for the exams are available from the CLEP program. Also see:

> *Barron's How to Prepare for the CLEP*

> *CLEP Official Study Guide* (College Board, latest edition). Available at a discount from Amazon.com.

For information on other exams:

> DSST Program
> The Chauncey Group International
> 877-471-9860
> www.getcollegecredit.com

> Excelsior College Examinations
> 7 Columbia Circle
> Albany, NY 12203-5159
> 888-647-2388
> www.excelsior.edu

> Thomas Edison College Examination Program
> 101 W. State Street
> Trenton, NJ 08608-1176
> 888-442-8372
> www.tesc.edu

Strategy #2: Correspondence Courses

These differ from the distance and online learning courses listed in chapter 23 in that they award college credit for completion. And most of the ones you will find listed in the guides I recommend accept students while in high school. (Public schools are using university correspondence courses as an option for their gifted-and-talented track.) If you take advantage of this route, here's what I most recommend:

- Take a correspondence course affiliated with a nationally recognized university. These will be the most widely accepted. In many cases there will be no indication on your transcript from that college that the credits were earned via correspondence.

- Look for those that require more than fill-in-the blank assignments and multiple-choice tests. The courses we considered from Penn State University's distance learning program required extensive writing and essay tests. Credits earned through correspondence really save a lot of money, but I didn't want to compromise our main target of raising kids who love to learn. Much of the correspondence material out there is dry and academically under-challenging. Don't settle for just the credits; get an education.

Where to find listings of reputable correspondence courses that award college credit:

 Bear's Guide to Earning Degrees by Distance Learning, Mariah Bear

Strategy #3: Online Courses

There are now hundreds of courses available over the Internet, with new ones cropping up every day. Plus, most correspondence schools and distance-learning departments of universities are converting to online delivery faster than you can say "Bill Gates."

This technology will bring about revolutionary change to education, and in the not-too-distant future every traditional method of delivery—classroom, independent study, correspondence, etc.—will have an electronic component to it or be left in the dust. (I'm calling it right here, folks.)

Right now, the technology is in flux, and you can find all kinds of variations online. Some courses are conducted via e-mail, some are conducted real-time, and some are set up to allow live interaction back and forth between students and instructor. Technology that even allows for video and audio feed is now standard fare. You'll have to experiment to find which setup works best for your family. (If you can't type fast, forget about the live interaction format.)

Earn an External Degree from Two Big Ten Schools

Penn State University and the University of Iowa entered into a cooperative agreement in 1996 that enables students to earn a diploma in combination from these two highly regarded schools without leaving home and for less than $15,000. Students who complete an associate's degree through PSU's distance learning program are automatically accepted into Iowa's Bachelor of Liberal Arts distance learning program. The University of Iowa has found that 83 percent of its distance-learning graduates are accepted at the graduate school of their choice. And Penn State is very open to accepting homeschoolers still in high school into its distance-learning program.

Contact:

LionHawk Program
Penn State World Campus
128 Outreach Building
University Park, PA 16802
800-252-3592
www.worldcampus.psu.edu

University of Iowa
Division of Continuing Education
250 Continuing Education
   Facility
Iowa City, IA 52242-0907
319-335-2575
www.continuetolearn.uiowa.edu

A word of caution before you jump on this freight train, though: There are a lot of online scams from fly-by-night operations lurking on the Internet. Do your homework. Choose courses and degree programs from accredited universities. Check the credentials of the accrediting body; make sure *they* are legitimate and that those accredited by their organization are reputable. Before enrolling in an online course, call the administrative offices and ask questions, and talk to folks who've used their services. Find graduates of their program and ask for their recommendation. In order to not lose your money or end up with a worthless degree, you will need to do a bit more research than if you enroll in a traditional brick-and-mortar school.

Here are some resources where you can begin your search:

Lifelong Learning (educationonline.com). This site is sponsored by Peterson's Publishing Company. You'll find an excellent search engine for finding online courses in all areas.

World Wide Learn: The World's Premier Online Directory of Education (www.worldwidelearn.com). Or so it claims, but minimally, there's more selection here than you will have time to cull through. It is seamlessly organized with lots of helpful articles to get you oriented to this alternative world.

Yahoo! (yahoo.com/education/distance_learning)

Accelerated Distance Learning: The New Way to Earn Your College Degree in the Twenty-First Century, Brad Voeller.

Bear's Guide to Earning College Degrees by Mail & Internet, Mariah Bear

Peterson's Guide to Distance Learning Programs

Strategy #4: Life Experience, Independent Study, Portfolio Assessment

Has your child been overseas on a mission trip? Has he set up an extensive research project or completed substantial work in a particular subject area? These experiences can potentially be converted to college credit at a reputable institution.

You will find guidelines for doing so and the institutions that accept this in *Bear's Guide to College Degrees By Mail & Internet* and *Accelerated Distance Learning*, Brad Voeller.

College-at-Home Counseling Service

If you want help in developing a plan for earning college credits and a degree at home, Brad Voeller's Global Learning Strategies offers such a service to homeschoolers by donation. You can check out his website for more information or write:

Global Learning Strategies
5463 Road S SE
Warden, WA 98857
509-349-1995
www.globallearningstrategies.org

Apprenticeships and Careers

Just as homeschooling is an old idea making a big comeback, so are apprenticeships. For many careers, work experience and training are much more valuable than a college degree. Kermit recently found the graduate-level courses in computer science around our area to be a generation behind in technology. He realized he'd have to find another source of training. Institutions are just not equipped to adapt fast enough to the rapidly changing marketplace.

Finding a mentor who will train your child in his trade in exchange for the low-cost labor is an attractive opportunity for both parties.

If you pursue an apprenticeship, it is a good idea to talk through your expectations and those of the mentor before the apprenticeship begins. Then draw up a contract and a list of objectives that should be met during the experience. A written review from the mentor should be expected at the end of the program so you have the formal documentation to show. He will probably appreciate any evaluation forms you can provide him with as well.

> FOR MANY CAREERS, WORK EXPERIENCE AND TRAINING ARE MUCH MORE VALUABLE THAN A COLLEGE DEGREE.

Inge Cannon has fostered the resurgent interest in apprenticeships among the homeschool community. She conducts seminars on apprenticeships and career planning and has a helpful product available:

Education Plus
Mentoring Your Teen: Charting the Course to Successful Adulthood
317-222-1695
www.edplus.com

And for guidance in helping your child choose a career or course of study, I recommend the service from Crown Financial Ministries:

Crown Financial Ministries
P.O. Box 100
Gainesville, GA 30503-0100
800-722-1976
www.crown.org

Finally, let me draw your attention to Patrick Henry College, a four-year institution based upon the apprenticing model. Currently offering degrees in government, journalism, history, literature, and liberal arts, Patrick Henry has rapidly become the source of some of the most respected interns on Capitol Hill.

Patrick Henry College
1 Patrick Henry Circle
Purcellville, VA 20132
540-338-1776
www.phc.edu

PART 7

COMPUTERS IN THE HOMESCHOOL

Technology

good PROGRAMS

IN THIS SECTION

What Hardware Should I Buy?

What Software Should I Buy?

Navigating the Net

COMPUTERS

Which to Buy?

CHAPTER 26
What Hardware Should I Buy?

If the last 371 pages aren't enough possibilities to wade through, you've done gone and chosen to homeschool during the technological revolution, for pity's sake! Now you must grapple with all those choices as well.

It's a Great Time to Be Alive!

If you have my temperament style—easily bored—you'll love it. (On the other hand, if you still believe the computer is the mark of the beast, prepare to be terrorized.) I know our society is in decay and there's so much to be distressed about. But none of this pending disaster dampens my enthusiasm for the times in which we live. I find all this technology absolutely fascinating.

It wasn't always so. When we first married, my husband would rattle on and on about microprocessors, kilobytes, and RAM, and break into a cold sweat of anticipation every time IBM announced its latest PC. Me? I'd only feign interest if I couldn't fall asleep. "Honey, talk to me about computers," I'd say. Five minutes later my insomnia would be cured.

He watched me type my 150-page master's thesis on an old typewriter and clucked his tongue in pity. I couldn't see what word processing could buy me that correction fluid didn't already do. Such vision!

When the twins were five, Kermit bought me my first computer, a 286 AT. My response: I felt the same about the set of screwdrivers he gave me once for Christmas. Six months later, I was furious with him for not buying me one sooner.

We've bought two new cars in the last twenty-five years of marriage and twenty-some computers.

What You Need

I give up. In prior editions I've listed the minimum specs necessary to run all the cool educational software I mention in the next chapter. Well, that is an exercise in futility at this point. Technology is changing too rapidly. The specs I list today will be dated before this manuscript makes it to print. Besides, there are now three viable options for you to pursue: Mac, Windows and Linux-based systems. Open sourcing—the collaboration of professional and amateur developers around the world who make their work available free of charge—has gained ascendancy (Wikipedia being a prime example). What computer we use has become a highly personalized choice.

So I'll just give you a few rules of thumb:

1. For homeschooling purposes, you don't need to be among the early adopters of technology. You can be one or two generations behind and still be able to run the websites and software designed for educational purposes. Educational innovations are never at the vanguard; schools can't change to new technology that quickly.

2. Buy cheap laptops. Being able to compute on the go is worth the additional expense of a laptop. Teens especially will appreciate a low-end laptop over a stationary desktop. Wireless is available where we meet for co-op, and we make constant use of this in our classes. Many of my students now arrive with their laptops in tow. I say "cheap" because teens have a habit of spilling their lattes on keyboards or dropping their computers.

> **BUY CHEAP LAPTOPS.**

3. You're going to need more than one computer as your kids get older. Again, that's why I think low-end is the operative term: More computers with less power are better than one turbo-charged desktop with limited availability.

4. You need broadband. That's the standard presumed by Web designers. You need this to enjoy all the streaming video online and to download e-books and other large files of information.

If you are two left thumbs around computers, it is almost certain you will need technical support. The best support is twenty-four-hour, seven-day, and toll-free. Make sure a live person is available after normal business hours. (And when you do call, use a speaker phone so you can clean your house, make dinner, etc., while waiting your turn in the queue.) In the computer market, quality customer service needs to be a part of your buying decision. You'll need it.

Where to Get It

Here are the places my husband comparison-shops when buying a computer. In the past few years, we have found the best deals are back-to-school specials advertised in the Sunday papers. However, these specials are used to draw you into the store and then upgrade you. Only a handful of the advertised specials are actually in stock. So to snag one of these, we've found we must be there when the store opens that morning, which may mean getting to church late. We also stop at Costco first—they have the best return policy (ninety days, as of this writing, with no restocking fee). That's where I buy a computer if I need one in a hurry and do not have time to do much research. If it turns out not to be the best decision, I can take it back.

Best Buy (888-237-8289)
www.bestbuy.com

Dell (800-999-3355)
www.dell.com

Gateway 2000 (866-539-3901)
www.gateway.com

Circuit City (1-800-843-2489)
www.circuitcity.com

For peripherals:

Best Buy (888-237-8289)
www.bestbuy.com

Computer Discount Warehouse (800-850-4239)
www.cdw.com

PC Connection (888-800-0323)
www.pcconnection.com
Great service and competitive pricing

A very helpful website my husband uses for comparing and considering our next computer purchase is www.cnet.com. CNET includes customer comments and a comparative price list for e-commerce sites so you can quickly locate the computer you want at the best price available. My husband also consults *Consumer Reports.*

Do I Absolutely Need Technology?

No. But you're giving up a lot without it. Go back to that list of targets you're aiming to hit. Can you achieve them without technology? We couldn't. Your kids are headed for the future job market, and technical skills are essential. Even kids headed for Christian service will be equipped to make a greater impact with computer know-how.

Though a computer is not a replacement for you as teacher of your kids, there's no more powerful tool to aid you in your responsibilities.

EVEN KIDS HEADED FOR CHRISTIAN SERVICE WILL BE EQUIPPED TO MAKE A GREATER IMPACT WITH COMPUTER KNOW-HOW.

CHAPTER 27
What Software Should I Buy?

Enter Multimedia

It wasn't until the advent of CD-ROM that I became such an enthusiast for computers in our homeschool; prior educational software was pretty hokey and of limited value. Our greatest benefit came from word processing. (Don't expect your kids to do a lot of original writing without it.) We moved to CD-ROM when I realized we no longer had time for lots of runs to the library. I wanted my older kids involved in lots of research projects and papers, but without an encyclopedia set it was time consuming trying to find information in other sources.

What a deal—for less than $100 we got an entire set of encyclopedia on disk, plus sound and video enhancements, plus we can store it all in a small desktop case with scores of other research software. I would have spent more on just the set of bookshelves to hold a traditional encyclopedia set!

That was before Internet access. Now my kids not only have the encyclopedia at their fingertips, but they've also got the equivalent of the Library of Congress sitting on our desktop.

What to Look for in Software Packages

I'm going to name names in a minute, even though that's pretty risky. The software industry reinvents itself, it seems, every six months. What I mention here today may be woefully left in the dust by the time this book makes it into print (though the companies with cutting-edge programs today will most likely be the ones on the edge tomorrow). So, guarding against that inevitability, here are guidelines for evaluating software programs for your homeschool.

#1. How Much Educational Value Does It Have?

Unfortunately, this can be hard to determine. Most stuff

designed to sell on the mass market focuses on the game format, cartoon-like characters, frills, and thrills. Developers throw in just enough content to get away with slapping "educational" on the packaging to attract parents.

As a rule of thumb, software marked "edutainment" is probably twaddle. I've had a few programs, such as early versions of *Carmen Sandiego* and *Algeblasters*, that didn't require any problem solving or reading of information to play the game. Later versions became much more interactive and dependent upon the player acquiring knowledge.

Home versions of software initially designed for schools have a much higher chance of matching your needs.

#2. Does It Maximize the Technology?

Conversely, the designers who jam-pack their programs with educational substance often do a poor job of using the available technology. It's not unusual to find that an educational program (especially one for high school or college) is no more than the reading material for a course poured onto your hard drive. It's bad enough reading through a hard copy of a textbook; it's far worse trying to read all that information on-screen.

I want sound, video, interaction, and entertainment. Otherwise, I can get it from a book at a much cheaper price. The goal here is for Junior to use the software fairly independently of Mom. It's going to have to have some razzle-dazzle to do that.

Read the system requirements on the side of the packaging. Is a sound card required? Does the program feature full-color photos, video clips, and animation? Are there links to Internet sites, a reference library, or interactive modules? Any games and quizzes? These clues all indicate that a multisensory experience awaits you.

If it's boring packaging, it's a boring program. If they don't feature sample screens on the box, they've got nothing impressive to show you inside.

> IF IT'S BORING PACKAGING, IT'S A BORING PROGRAM.

Here's an Example of What You Want

A.D.A.M.: The Inside Story (Academic Superstore) will blow your socks off: 3-D fly-through animations right through the brain, down the spinal cord, into the heart. Voice pronunciation of more than twelve hundred anatomical structure names. One-button Internet access to top medical sites. Interactive quizzes. Animation. Dissection of over 100 layers of human anatomy. Identification of more than four thousand structures. Online Video Doctor. The ability to rotate and zoom in on visuals. Do I sound like I'm in sales? This is the kind of cool stuff I think will leave institutionalized learning in the dust. Once schools get wired, the days of boring lectures are over.

Recommendations

Here is a sample list of software that's popular at our house and with other homeschoolers. These programs are available from the software companies listed at the end of this section. These are all elementary programs. Software with an (S) can be used with ages twelve and above as well.

ART: *Kid Pix Deluxe 4* (Encore), *Digital Photo Activity Kit* (APTE), *Kidspiration* (Inspiration, Inc)

ENCYCLOPEDIA: *Microsoft Encarta Reference Library* (S) (Microsoft), *World Book* (S) (World Book)

GEOGRAPHY: *National Geographic Presents 3D Globe* (S) (National Geographic), *Eyewitness World Atlas* (S) (DK Interactive), *Crosscountry U.S.A.* (Didatech Software), *Where in the World Is Carmen Sandiego? Deluxe* (Broderbund), *Mission Possible World Geography* (S) (Edventure)

HISTORY: *Eyewitness History of the World* (S) (DK Interactive), *Liberty Kids* (Learning Company), *Where in Time Is Carmen Sandiego?* (Learning Company), *Oregon Trail* (S) (Learning Company), *World Explorer Deluxe* (DK Interactive)

LANGUAGE ARTS: *Hop! Writing* (S) (Cyberlude), *Grammar Made Easy / Punctuation Made Easy* (S) (DK Interactive), *Read, Write & Type* (The Learning Company), *Word Munchers* (Learning Company), *I Love Spelling* (DK Multimedia)

LOGIC AND PROBLEM-SOLVING: *Dr. Brain Action Reaction* (Knowledge Adventure), *Thinkin' Things* (Edmark)

MATH: *2Simple Math Games I* (2Simpleusa.com), *Math Munchers Deluxe* (Learning Company), *Quarter Mile Math* (S) (Barnum), *Mighty Math* (Edmark), *I Love Math* (DK Interactive), *Rainbow Rock, Vroot* and *Vroom* (Singapore Math)

MULTIDISCIPLINED: *Jump Start* series (Knowledge Adventure)

MUSIC: *Music Ace* (Harmonic Vision), *Adiboo: Discover Music, Melody & Rhyme* (Knowledge Adventure)

READING: *Phonics Based Reading* (Simply Media), *PhonicsTutor* (4:20 Communications), *Edmark Reading Program* (Edmark)

SCIENCE: *I Love Science* (DK Multimedia), Magic School Bus series (Microsoft), *Sammy's Science House* (Edmark), *The New Way Things Work* (S) (DK Interactive), *Eyewitness Encyclopedia of Science* (S) (DK Multimedia), *Encyclopedia of Nature* (DK Multimedia), *A.D.A.M.: The Inside Story* (S) (A.D.A.M. Software)

Software Reviews

You will find valuable reviews of educational software at The Discovery Channel's Parent's Corner: school.discoveryeducation.com/parents/reviewcorner.

And if you really believe in the educational value of new media, then subscribe to *Children's Technology Review*, available online at www.childrenssoftware.com.

Where to Buy Educational Software

You'll find best buys for popular programs at Sam's Club, Best Buy, and other vendors advertising in *PC World* and other computer magazines. For a wider selection and specialized attention:

Academic Superstore
2101 E. Saint Elmo Road
Suite 360
Austin, TX 78744
800-817-2347
www.academicsuperstore.com

Educational Resources (discount pricing)
1550 Executive Drive
P.O. Box 1900
Elgin, IL 60121-1900
800-860-7004
www.edresources.com

SoftwareOutlet.com
2431 S. Anne Street
Santa Ana, CA 92704
714-979-6161
www.softwareoutlet.com

CHAPTER 28
Navigating the Net

This Exit: Information Highway

The real fun and education begin when you venture beyond your desktop PC into cyberspace. This is where the education revolution is occurring and where home-educated kids have the opportunity to pioneer a world-class education online.

The Internet

What I Don't Like about the Internet

Just to give some balance to things, there are definitely disadvantages to cyberspace. Despite the fact our pages now load within the blink of an eye, the Internet is consuming gobs of our time that we likely should be investing elsewhere. And what our search retrieves needs to be evaluated. Anyone can now publish anything on the Web—there are no editorial gatekeepers providing some assurance that the facts have been checked for accuracy. We need to approach what we read on the Internet with a healthy dose of skepticism, and we need to take the time to teach our kids how to evaluate the reliability of a site and confirm their findings from a multitude of sources.

Kids still need plenty of time for reading real books and engaging in real human interactions.

> WE NEED TO TAKE THE TIME TO TEACH OUR KIDS HOW TO EVALUATE THE RELIABILITY OF A SITE.

Virtual Versus Reality

Learning is still better facilitated by group interaction and hands-on manipulation of material. Online learning is a great alternative when these options are not available or too expensive. But we need to be careful. Early reports are finding that time online is rewiring the way our brain works and eroding our attention span.[1]

When I talked with Cindy about the advantages and disadvantages of distance learning, she mentioned all the leadership skills college brought to the surface in Nate. She hadn't really seen this in him before because he had never been in a situation that created the opportunity. I think online courses are a serious option, but as with software and video instruction as well, I wouldn't want to use this for more than one or two courses at a time.

What I Do Like About the Internet

I like the incredible wealth of information conveniently available for practically nothing.

We used the Internet primarily to search for information on every topic imaginable and to get it at the earliest possible moment. We took classes online, got a jump-start on college with distance learning, and completed major research projects without leaving home. Quite honestly, it's one reason why homeschooling through high school makes sense. And it became even more important once my kids hit their respective college campuses.

We also shop on the net. I've always been a mail-order shopper—I hate to "go shopping." I don't like the time consumed. I don't like traffic, long checkout lines, or incompetent salespersons—I have a pretty long list of gripes. This method is even more convenient than mail, stores are always open, and the selection is vast. Protecting ourselves while online has become necessity as well as a growth industry; but it certainly is not reason enough to avoid the convenience and opportunities the Internet has opened up.

We also use the Internet to get connected to the virtual community beyond our locale—homeschoolers across the country, friends in other states, pen pals in other countries. We may all be cocooning, but virtually we're connected like never before.

> WE MAY ALL BE COCOONING, BUT VIRTUALLY WE'RE CONNECTED LIKE NEVER BEFORE.

Incredible Websites to Get You Started

I've tried to make your venture out into cyberspace less frustrating by scouring the Web for the best sites for virtual homeschooling.

GENERAL: Too Many Links to Categorize

About.com is a vast learning community with expert guides and links for all major subject areas. Good homeschooling forum. Check out the hands-on sites under arts and crafts (about.com/education or homeschooling.about.com).

Ask Jeeves for Kids is a "don't miss" site in my book. Excellent for your children's independent (and Internet-safe) research. Updated daily. Among other things, it offers a constantly changing exhibit of featured sites and virtual field trips (www.askkids.com; www.ask.com for adults and teens).

Global Schoolhouse Foundation works to create a worldwide educational community for kids online. This well-funded site primarily facilitates collaborative projects among classrooms around the world. Homeschoolers are welcome to participate in a project, such as building a virtual-field-trip site (globalschoolnet.org).

Net-Mom's Internet Safe Home is home to Jean Armour Polly, author of the *Internet Kids* and *Family Yellow Pages*. After six editions, Jean's books are out of print, but that's because the information is now maintained completely online at her site. Here you will find the latest educational places for kids to hang out or research on the Internet. Subscribe to her feed at the website to be notified of Jean's latest updates (www.netmom.com).

PBS Online offers lots of teacher support for programming as well as archives of past PBS shows (www.pbs.org).

B. J. Pinchbeck's Homework Helper has all the links you need for reference material in any subject. This site was started in 1996 by B. J., then age nine, and his dad.

The site has won more than 110 awards, and B. J. has been featured on many newscasts and on *Oprah!* For a number of years, B.J.'s site was part of the Discovery Channel's educational network; but now that he is a student at Drexel University in Philadelphia, he's struck out on his own, and the new site is slick and easy to navigate (www.bjpinchbeck.com).

LittleClickers.com: Brought to you by the people behind *The Children's Technology Review*, the site maintains "safe, fun Internet explorations for children." Each theme-based area is checked regularly for broken links; and the monthly collection is often taken from current events such as presidential elections, the Olympics, or snow.

Internet Public Library: This massive, well-organized site is maintained by a consortium of students at top universities around the country. It is especially useful because there is a section for elementary kids to do research and a section for teens to do research (www.ipl.org). In the fall of 2009, the site is scheduled to merge with the Librarians' Internet Index (according to an announcement on the site).

Education World: This site's tag line "The Educator's Best Friend" includes homeschool moms as well. You'll want to stop here first if you are gathering websites for a unit study or searching for online printable worksheets. Click on "Lesson Planning" to get to the heart of what this site has to offer (www.educationworld.com).

ART

ArtMuseum.net is sponsored by Intel. The changing exhibits at this site provide an interactive experience that extends a museum visit or exposes kids to a particular artist's work in an educational manner. It's won multiple awards (www.artmuseum.net).

Art History Resources on the Web: Maintained by Dr. Christopher Witcombe, professor of art history at Sweet Briar College in Virginia, this site is an index to all major periods and major cultures in art history. Best suited for older students, but not to missed (witcombe.sbc.edu/ARTHLinks.html).

Crayola is a commercial site, but nevertheless it's a place for kids to spend hours creating cyber-art (www.crayola.com).

A Lifetime of Color, maintained by Sanford, a competitor of Crayola, provides areas for those who wish to create art, study art, or teach art (www.alifetimeofcolor.com).

ENCYCLOPEDIAS

Wikipedia: Hurray for open sourcing and the rise of the rest! Wikipedia, the bane of academia, is at the vanguard of an end run around the establishment and all its gatekeeping. You'll still get skewered for citing this source, but it's where everyone goes first to begin research on anything (www.wikipedia.com).

GEOGRAPHY

The Greatest Places: Companion site for the Omnifilm by the same name, this graphically rich website takes kids on an educational journey to seven of the most geographically dynamic locations on Earth. Highly interactive with the opportunity for students to add a "greatest place" of their own (www.greatestplaces.org).

National Geographic Society operates a site for geography studies. Here you'll find maps, articles, photographs, and even a place to prep for the National Geography Bee. In particular, make sure you do not miss the "xpeditions" section (www.nationalgeographic.com).

Yahooligans Countries Index is the best jumping-off place for kids doing research on specific places (www. kids.yahoo.com/directory/Around-the-World/Countries).

HISTORY

Metropolitan Museum's Explore and Learn: This website section of one of the world's greatest museums will take students on a visual tour of the art world and ancient wonders. One of the best educational sites you will find. Visually stunning, elegantly organized (www.metmuseum. org > Explore & Learn).

Eyewitness to History: Presented by Ibis Communications, an educational software developer, this interactive site is highly navigable and filled with photos and video clips. The main content is first-person accounts of historical events and daily life from ancient times to modern day (www.eyewitnesstohistory.com).

Archiving Early America: Through newspapers, maps, magazines, and writings in primary-source documents, this site offers images, pictures, and text to help you learn about every aspect of early American history. For ages seven and up (www.earlyamerica.com).

Ben's Guide to U.S. Government: "Ben Franklin's" virtual tour for kids. It is neatly organized by grade level with interactive lesson plans explaining the history of our government and how it works today. Great for civics and history. A guide for parents and teachers shows you how to use the site with your kids (bensguide.gpo.gov).

Cobblestone Publishing is one of the few sites with history activities appropriate for elementary kids. It includes tips and lesson plans for using *Cobblestone* magazine in the classroom plus links to reviewed history sites (cobblestonepub.com).

History Channel is more interesting online than most of its TV shows. Click on Classroom for elementary-level information. See A&E, the parent site, as well, at www. aetv.com (history.com).

387

Library of Congress "American Memory" Project is part

of an otherwise dry site. It will capture kids' attention (memory.loc.gov/ammem/index.htm).

Perseus Digital Library has major corporate funding, which makes this *the* place to connect to the ancient classical world on the Web. It was designed by Tufts University's classics department (www.perseus.tufts.edu).

HOMESCHOOLING with SUBJECT LINKS

Some of the best sites with links of interest and help to homeschoolers have been designed by members of the homeschool community. Visit these sites, and e-mail a thank-you for all the hard work and service.

A to Z Home's Cool: One of the oldest homeschooling sites in cyberspace, Ann Zeise is still daily maintaining her emporium of everything homeschool. You will find a subject index here that is helpfully organized by age groupings (homeschooling.gomilpitas.com/index.htm).

Eclectic Homeschool Online: This takes you to a subject-by-subject listing of websites great for no-cost homeschooling online (eclectichomeschool.org > Resources > Weblinks).

Homeschool Central helps you locate subject-area links helpful to homeschoolers. Click on the subject resources (homeschoolcentral.com).

LANGUAGE ARTS

English Zone is designed primarily for English as a Second Language students, but you will find lots of printable worksheets in sequential order to use with your elementary students (english-zone.com).

Guide to Grammar and Writing is worth all the keystrokes it takes to get to this site designed by a college professor. You won't need to buy an English handbook. All the answers are here, plus more (grammar.ccc.commnet.edu/grammar).

Let's Get Creative! This site maintained by author/ illustrator Bruce Van Patter is filled with all kinds of story starters and lesson plans for encouraging your child's creativity and creative writing (www.brucevanpatter.com).

Literature and Writers' Resources. Found at Stardots. com—a search engine of reference tools and search resources on the Web. Lots of individual sites I use to teach my English classes are compiled here (www. stardots.com/reference/literature.shtml).

MATH

Cool Math is a "don't miss!" site designed for the pure enjoyment of math. The enthusiasm expressed here will make up for anything you lack in this area (www.coolmath.com).

Dr. Math is a tutoring area sponsored by the math students at Drexel University. It also includes lots of activities for kids and resources for teachers (www.mathforum.com/dr.math).

Mathcounts, the official site for the math competition for seventh and eighth graders, features a "problem of the week" and many other fun teaching resources (mathcounts.org).

Math Stories was developed by a frustrated father who felt his two daughters weren't getting enough analytical math problems to prepare them for the real world. He started this website for grade schools. You'll find well-conceived, fun word problems ready to print off as worksheets. New ones are added every week. With more than 2500 problems, you may not need to buy any math resources for several years (www.mathstories.com).

World of Math Online: This is the site my husband and my daughter Kayte, a math teacher, use first if they are answering a math question or helping the rest of us in the family with a math problem (www.math.com).

Mathscore.com: Developed by a MIT grad, this site provides math practice for students up through Algebra I. There is a monthly fee for this site, but it may be a better solution than paying a tutor to work with your child; and it is a good place to send an older student when you need time to work one-on-one with another child (www.mathscore.com).

MUSEUMS

Virtual Library Museums is a massive directory of museums around the world (www.icom.org/vlmp).

MUSIC

Energy in the Air: Sounds of the Orchestra is an award-winning *junior* site from the ThinkQuest competition. Make sure you have RealAudio so you can sample the sounds of all the instruments (library.thinkquest.org/5116).

Music Notes: An Online Interactive Musical Experience is yet another excellent site from the ThinkQuest kids. This one is devoted to teaching musical theory. With the sounds and the games, you won't find a better resource (library.thinkquest.org/15413).

PlayMusic.org is brought to you by the American Orchestra Symphony League. This is an interactive site that includes sounds of the orchestra but also many other games that bring kids into the world of classical music. Requires Shockwave (www.playmusic.org).

The Symphony: An Interactive Guide is another ThinkQuest winner (this one's in the senior division). After exploring the "Sounds of the Orchestra" site, listen to entire symphonies here while learning about the history and construction of the symphony (library.thinkquest.org/22673).

SCIENCE

Bill Nye the Science Guy: As you would expect, here is an interactive, state-of-the-art site that will keep you just as fascinated as your kids. Also requires Shockwave (www.billnye.com).

Discovery Online offers lots of areas to explore as well as activities to extend television programming. Includes sites for Animal Planet and The Learning Channel too (dsc.discovery.com).

Exploratorium is the website of the San Francisco Exploratorium, a museum of science, art, and human perception. It uses Webcasting, online exhibits, and other interactive technology to put together a state-of-the art website for young and old. Ten cool sites for science, art, and technology are featured every month. Check out the archives to link to more than 400 places featured in the past (www.exploratorium.edu).

Frog Dissection is one of the better virtual dissection sites on the Web. Select Dissection of the Frog in the Lesson Search box (educatus.com).

How Stuff Works was created by Marshall Brain, author of more than ten books, including *The Teenager's Guide to the Real World*, and former computer science professor at North Carolina State University. This award-winning site is updated daily, offering new links, new questions, and a well-organized archive of "how things work" for just about anything you can imagine (www.howstuffworks.com).

The Kinetic City Cyber Club, the American Association for the Advancement of Science website, drops your kids into the middle of a science mystery that changes monthly. It is designed to teach scientific concepts painlessly (kineticcity.com).

NASA operates one of the few inspiring sites designed by a government agency (most are pretty boring). Check out NASA Kids (www.nasa.gov).

Science Made Simple. Kids learn science the easy, hands-on way with Science Made Simple. Fun science projects and great experiments using household materials. Clear, detailed answers to children's science questions (www.sciencemadesimple.com).

Science NetLinks: This site is filled with lesson plans with embedded links to online sites that correlate with the national science standards by grade levels. This could ostensibly be your complete science curriculum K-12 (www.sciencenetlinks.com).

Hot Lists

Here are four places where you can find regularly updated "best of the Web" educational and interactive links for kids.

KidsOLR (Kids Online Resources): Homework help, education, fun, and games. Not all links are equal, but there is a lot here worth your while (www.kidsolr.com).

Eduhound.com: This is a subscription service for teachers, but there are plenty of free links in every subject area to follow.

Kathy Schrock's Guide for Educators: As the Discovery Channel's resident expert on educational websites, Kathy provides monthly theme-based studies and latest and greatest recommended websites (school. discoveryeducation.com/schrockguide).

Blue Web 'N: I don't know why in the world this cool site sponsored by AT&T has such a cumbersome URL, but don't let that stop you. Billed as a "library of blue ribbon learning sites on the Web," it has a great search engine and detailed information about all the sites it has selected to recommend (www.kn.pacbell.com/wired/bluewebn/index.cfm).

Search Engines

All the Web returns search results almost instantaneously. It will bring up international sites as well (alltheweb.com).

Google, far and away the winner in the search engine wars. If you don't yet own stock in Google.com, you should (google.com).

Metacrawler allows you to use all the major search engines at once (metacrawler.com).

Yahoo! I like the logical way categories are subdivided here (yahoo.com).

How to Stay on the Edge of Technology

These sources will help you acquire and maintain a cutting-edge understanding of technology.

Books

For Dummies series — i.e., *PCs for Dummies, The Internet for Dummies*, etc.

Teach Yourself Visually series

Magazines

These are the best magazines about surfing the Net and about technology in general — or at least these are the ones Kermit has piled around the bedroom that I am able to decipher.

PC Magazine (800-335-1195)
www.pcmag.com

PC World (800-825-7595)
www.pcworld.com

PART 8

CREATIVE SOLUTIONS

CHAPTER 29
Toddlers and Other Blessed Challenges

In a world that despises large families and routinely abuses or ignores little ones, the homeschool community should be a haven of welcome and adoration for our toddlers and babies. We need to make room for them in our lives, as well as support and revere parents of large families.

But that doesn't mean we let the tykes run the show. Toddlers are in desperate need of training if they are to grow up to bow their knee to the Lordship of Jesus Christ.

If you have toddlers, your homeschool program has to be designed with their needs in mind. Otherwise, you are going to be frustrated, and they will feel ignored. And the two-year-olds I know don't take being ignored lying down. They make you pay for it. Case in point: The day we moved into our new house, my daughter Kristen, just two, ate my contact lenses while I was consumed with unpacking. Fortunately, they were soft.

Despite all the challenges, it's possible for your older kids to get the education they need in an environment populated with assorted-size siblings. It may take an attitude adjustment though.

Tips:

1. Raise independent learners. Here's where the strategies in chapter 15 become essential. It is very easy to let our older kids drive the curriculum. But our younger children need our focus and attention to a greater extent. If we have designed a program that expects independence and self-government from our kids, our older kids should be able to complete their studies while we work in a more concentrated way with our young ones. Field trips, reading aloud, and hands-on experiences are essential building blocks for future academic success. You can't afford to shortchange them.

2. Maximize naptime. If you have maintained a consistent routine and schedule for your kids, then you should have an

> **IF YOU HAVE TODDLERS, YOUR HOMESCHOOL PROGRAM HAS TO BE DESIGNED WITH THEIR NEEDS IN MIND.**

afternoon nap to take advantage of regularly. This is when you haul out the science experiments and art projects that can't accommodate your toddlers' involvement. Kayte was never a nap-taker, but we still expected her to remain quietly in her room for an hour or more on weekday afternoons playing with her stuffed animals while I worked with the boys.

3. Allow older kids to teach younger siblings. While you tutor one child in algebra, assign another to complete an art project with or read aloud to your toddlers. Give your older child responsibility for designing the lesson. This will give her valuable experience and reinforce her understanding of the material.

4. Purchase special materials just for school time. Like the Velveteen Rabbit, your toddlers want to be real. Set up a school area for them and place special items in a box that may only be used during "school time." I used to rotate toys to extend my kids' interest in them. If Legos are always available and spewed everywhere, they are taken for granted. But if kept in a sealed container and only permitted out at certain times of the day, they keep most toddlers transfixed. Puzzles, quality art supplies, a colorful workbook, a tube of paste, construction paper, a pop-up book, and construction tools that are available on a limited basis will keep many kids occupied for the time you need to teach a brief lesson in history or grammar to other children.

5. Limit their range. Just as my kids did not have free access to all of their toys, they did not have free access to all of the house. I turned an unused pantry off the kitchen into a playroom. When they were toddlers, my kids spent their mornings there behind a safety gate while I did my chores or later taught school to the boys. Had they been there all day, they surely would have rebelled. But I periodically rotated their play area to other sections of the house. In a Montessori preschool, kids move from station to station throughout the day. The same principle, in a more informal way, can be practiced here with success. (At the Learning Center homeschool co-op, even though not necessary, we have the toddlers change classrooms throughout the morning just to keep them moving.)

More from moms who know:

- Have lots of hands-on items for your toddlers to do while you do lessons—for example, Play-Doh, felt books, erasable crayons and preschool workpages.

- Invest in several fun play sets such as Little People, Mr. Potato Head, a Fisher Price farm set, a tool set, or a Tonka truck, which are available only during school time.

- Spend time with your toddler ten to fifteen minutes of every hour. If toddlers are with a sibling too long, they get fussy.

- Use a hands-on curriculum, such as WinterPromise, with older ones so toddlers can participate as well.

> HAVE LOTS OF HANDS-ON ITEMS FOR YOUR TODDLERS TO DO WHILE YOU DO LESSONS.

CHAPTER 30
Transitioning from School to Home

The largest growth in the homeschool ranks is coming from families withdrawing children from a public or private school. If this is you, then you have a greater challenge than those of us whose children have never known anything else.

Your children have a very strong picture of what school is supposed to look like, plus they are conditioned to be with their peers for the better part of their day. Functioning apart from the crowd requires learning a whole new set of skills and cultivating new avenues of interest.

In some cases, it is the child who is asking to be homeschooled. He recognizes that he is becoming a casualty of the system and is asking for relief. These kids make the transition much easier than those whose parents decide to homeschool without their kids' full cooperation.

Setting Realistic Expectations

To give homeschooling the best shot in this situation, you'll need these strategies:

1. The Older the Child Is, the More Time It Will Take to Acclimate Him to Homeschooling

I've known several families who've homeschooled their younger children but have left their teenagers in school. They realized their teens were too entrenched to accept the decision well. In some cases, the older kids have asked to be homeschooled after seeing the benefits of homeschooling in their younger siblings.

If you decide to homeschool resistant children (and I would if I believed God was calling me to), invest significant time prior to the change to build faith for the venture in their hearts.

While I believed Kermit and I had full authority in our teenagers' lives, we were willing to talk through with them time and again our reasons for the limitations we place upon them. I wanted an open air of communication between us. I much preferred that they felt free to disagree (respectfully) with us than to create an authoritarian environment that provoked them into putting on an appearance of compliance while hiding the true intentions of their hearts.

Give your kids time to adjust. Look for small steps forward and thank God for them. As I've said earlier, parenting is a risk. There are no guarantees that we will always make the right decisions. But that's not what we put our faith in. We put our faith in God's commitment to work all things for the good. With that kind of promise, we have to go with our best instincts in a given situation and trust that nothing we do subverts God's will in our kids' lives.

> GIVE YOUR
> KIDS TIME TO
> ADJUST.

2. You Need Involvement in a Support Group or Co-op

Your kids are going to miss their friends at school—even feel as though they have lost their identity (which is probably something you want to replace anyway). They need a new network of friends. Start networking with the homeschool community right away; attend activities before your kids are even withdrawn from school.

3. Maximize the Opportunities Homeschooling Offers

If you merely re-create school at home, minus all the fun, your kids will likely be resentful. They need to see the benefits of homeschooling in a tangible way. One reason my sons concluded homeschooling was the best place for them was because of the opportunities they had.

If your kids only see the limitations, not the benefits (freedom to control their day, apprenticeships, field trips, travel, etc.), don't expect them to be grateful for your sacrifices here.

You may find that family schools or co-ops require families to complete one year of homeschooling before being considered for membership. This doesn't make the transition any easier for you, but many groups have found it is best that parents have fully assumed the responsibility for their children's education before

401

supplementing with other sources.

4. Be Confident; Be a Leader—Even if It Is a Bluff!

Having worked with and observed kids, including juvenile delinquents, in thousands of situations, I am convinced that strong leadership always brings out their best behavior. Once they perceive a lack of confidence, control quickly deteriorates.

The most humiliating job I've ever had was that of a substitute teacher. You have *no power* and *no penalty* to impose. There isn't a lot of backup for you, either. The administration is just hoping you survive the day, not teach.

I took this a little longer than my father would have—two days. Rather than let them mock and humiliate me for one more minute, I decided to call these brawny seventeen-year-olds' bluff—or die trying. Without any weapon but my tongue, I threw kids out of class, buzzed for the principal (who was not happy about that), or sent them to the office. I left detailed notes for the regular teacher. My husband even called some parents for me.

Instead of accepting the standard "Give them a study hall" instructions left by absent teachers, I brought in my own lesson plans, taught poetry, taught algebra (I was clueless—but they didn't know the difference), and generally acted like I was someone they wouldn't dare mess with. Pretty soon I didn't have any problems, and worse, I had far too many calls to substitute.

I sneak that story in just to say that if I can get high school seniors to treat a substitute teacher with respect (and you know what *you* did to substitutes when you were a senior), then you can get your own disgruntled teenagers to cooperate with you. You *have* power—you've got the food! Just act like you have no doubt they will do anything different.

CHAPTER 31
Motivating the Reluctant Learner

> **MOST OF US WILL HAVE SEASONS OF DIFFICULTIES WITH EACH OF OUR KIDS.**

Much of the time in most subject areas, my children were intrinsically motivated to learn. But there were definitely seasons in each of their lives when they routinely grumbled and complained. And there were subject areas they each just plain resisted learning. I responded to these situations by becoming mad, frustrated, discouraged, defeated, embarrassed, etc.

At first my kids' lack of enthusiasm threw me for a loop. From all the wonderful reports out there about homeschooled kids, I thought I was the only one with the problem. But the longer I've been at this, and the more I've traveled and talked with moms in the field, I've come to realize that most of us will have seasons of difficulties with each of our kids. Sometimes it's character issues; sometimes it's our strategies. Most times it is a combination of both.

Why Kids Can Be Reluctant

There are two possible explanations for children who are reluctant to learn, and these usually appear in combination:

1. their attitudes
2. their abilities

Both can be hampering their success. Let's look at them now and talk about possible creative solutions.

Character Flaws

"Foolishness is bound up in the heart of a child" (Proverbs 22:15)—not an honored premise of modern psychology, but nevertheless an unchanging truth of the universe. Any honest parent will have to conclude its reality from experience.

God's job description for us includes helping our kids replace that foolishness with wisdom. That's pretty difficult to do if we don't hold a biblical view of children or follow a biblical pattern of training them during their early years. But if you haven't, I can guarantee your homeschooling goals will soon be derailed by bad attitudes, rebellion, disrespect, slothfulness, disorganization, etc.

It's beyond the purpose of this book to cover parenting skills, but often the heartache we face with our reluctant learners is rooted in the unacknowledged sin in their lives.

When we discern that sin is the root of resistance, we don't serve our kids by sugarcoating the truth or dreaming up fun and games to entice them into cooperating. This is our opportunity to help them understand the heart of the matter and God's solution for their need: a Savior. Our parenting method should be to motivate by grace; our heart's desire should be to see them do well.

One evening I poured out my concerns about one of our children to Kermit. I carefully elaborated on all the areas of difficulty I was facing and also my fears. When I was through, Kermit said simply, "The problem is laziness." I had been expecting a more complicated explanation, but his succinctness had the piercing point of truth to it.

Prayerfully examine the areas of difficulty your child is having in school. What character flaws might be contributing to this? Kermit knew sin was a root problem in the situation we were dealing with because he saw this child's "reluctance" as a pervasive characteristic of his life. It wasn't just math that lost his interest; it was disinterest across the board in anything requiring exertion: piano, reading, chores, and getting up.

Ability to Learn

A child's ability to learn can be hampered. There are two factors to look at here:

1. Your child can be *internally* stalled because his learning style, readiness, or interests are not being respected.

2. He may be *externally* hampered by his learning environment. The lack of structure or routine, the resources you are using, or the approach you choose can all affect your child's ability to learn the material successfully.

I know that with my children, I didn't always honor their inner timetable for learning things. Despite knowing better, I compared them to each other or to other kids: "So-and-so was reading at this age," or "Mrs. G.'s son is doing this now; I think you should too." I expected my children to match the temperament and motivation of other kids I thought were doing well. And when they didn't, I'd use my frustration and my expectations to try and drive them forward. Some of my kids would pucker up and cry; others would dig in their heels and fight. But in either case, I was the one exasperating them (and the same scriptural injunctive for fathers can apply to mothers too).

Cultivating Their Motivation

I always want to get to the heart of a matter. And for reluctant learners, the root is almost always a lack of motivation. This lack can be caused by their attitudes and their abilities, as described above. Step one is to discern what factors in each of these categories may be a drain on their drive.

Once discerned, my focus is not, "How do I *teach* this child this stuff?" It is always, "How do I *motivate* this child to learn this stuff?"

When motivated, human beings can overcome tremendous obstacles. Think of the endurance and accomplishments of musicians Itzhak Perlman and Ray Charles; Miss America, Heather Whitestone; and Olympic gymnast Kerri Strug. All of them overcame great challenges but still managed to excel. They should inspire you to believe in your child's potential *once he is motivated*, even if he has been diagnosed as learning disabled.

So as you work with your reluctant learner, keep focused on the sole goal of motivating your child. Then let him take responsibility for his actual progress.

> **WHEN MOTIVATED, HUMAN BEINGS CAN OVERCOME TREMENDOUS OBSTACLES.**

Ten Motivating Strategies

#1. Build Faith in Your Child to Learn— Get Everyone on Board

Your child needs to believe he can learn. That confidence is engendered at an early age by what he hears his parents say about him.

You're the coach; tell him what to believe: "You are a learner." "God has given you the ability to learn this." "You are a reader."

"You are making progress." "Look how much farther you are than last week."

I tried to be attuned to our children's self-concept. I wanted to stay on top of what they believed to be true about themselves. I cringe when I hear parents introduce a toddler as "my little monster" or the kid "who drives me crazy." Those children are going to fulfill their parents' expectations.

When my toddlers disobeyed me, I often said, "I know you want to obey Mommy. You just need help again in this one area. I know you want to please me." I'd say it repeatedly to imprint that message on their brains: I obey Mommy. *Yes, I want to please my mommy. That's who I am.*

Even when the twins were teens, I frequently told them how trustworthy they were, how I *never* even worried about them doing *anything* behind my back. I knew it just *wasn't* in their hearts to do *such a thing*.

Some of you may think I stretch the truth a bit in these proclamations—I prefer to think that I have faith to believe in things yet unseen (see Hebrews 11) and a mother's love to believe the best of my kids (see 1 Corinthians 13).

Anyway, it appeared to work.

Protect your child from the hurtful comments of others. As your child grows older, he'll take more seriously the comments of his peers and siblings. I needed to remind my older kids to treat Kristen with respect and not discourage her progress. I reminded them to verbally encourage her and take an interest in her life. Because Kristen is the youngest, her older siblings frequently forget that she exists, or they only interact with her when she's done something annoying.

> **DO ALL THAT YOU CAN TO SHOW YOUR CONFIDENCE.**

It's very natural for young children to memorize a favorite story and say they are reading it. When Kayte began to do this with *Goodnight Moon*, her six-year-old brothers insisted, "You're not really reading that." I nipped that in the bud immediately. To read, a child needs to believe he can read. If your little one calls what Kayte was doing reading, support him in that. Do all you can to show your confidence in him.

#2. Adapt to His Learning Style

Go back to Part 2 and review the material on learning styles.

Do you have an actual-spontaneous learner you are expecting to do seatwork five hours a day? If your total program isn't designed around an understanding of how your child learns best, you are asking him to swim upstream from the get-go.

Since birth, Kristen has loved music and listening to audiotapes. We have the entire *Adventures in Odyssey* collection from Focus on the Family, and Kristen has many of the dramas memorized. She could probably start for Odyssey what Trekkies are for *Star Trek*.

Audiotapes were the only thing that interested her more than the television as a preschooler. And as with TV, it was frustrating me that that was all she was motivated to do with her time. It suddenly occurred to me one day (about six years and a hundred dollars in tapes later) that she was an *auditory* learner. I wondered if she would be willing to learn other material if it were presented on tape. I tried an experiment: I bought some American history stories on tape and some French tapes. She was just as happy to listen to those as well.

Since I was now investing more time in *observing* how my child learned best than in figuring out a way to make her adapt to my expectations, I also noticed how well she remembered material she had learned on tape. Our homeschool spent one field trip sailing the Chesapeake Bay on a replica Pungy schooner. As we sailed past Fort McHenry, the guide asked the students what had happened there. I was astounded when Kristen, then in second grade, shot up her hand. (I had not covered this with her. How could she possibly know? Do you know?)

Kristen not only answered correctly that Francis Scott Key had written our national anthem there, but she went into great detail about the War of 1812 between the British and the United States over water rights and how Key had been held captive during the night on a British warship. On the way home I asked her how in the world she had known all that stuff. "Mom," she said with a great deal of surprise. "Don't you remember? It was a story on *Odyssey*!"

Where does your reluctant learner give you the greatest resistance? The least? Is there a correlation between this and the points where your program honors his learning style to the greater degree? Use the suggested methods in Part 2 to better modify your program to his learning style.

#3. Re-Evaluate Your Methods

I am reminded of Tad, a fifth-grader I tested a few years ago. He didn't do as well as his parents had hoped, so I spent an evening discussing his scores with them. I mentioned that during the test their son had appeared stressed and hurried. From that comment, I learned that Tad gets very upset when he is being timed. This had been a favored technique in the private school he had previously attended. And his mom was now using a timer to keep Tad diligently focused on his schoolwork. Without this method, his parents felt Tad took excessive amounts of time on his work and often didn't even finish.

I suggested a compromise that now helps Tad to manage his time better and also gives him more control of his environment. His parents have given Tad the egg timer and allow him to set it. It has become a competition with himself to see if he can improve his score from day to day. It has worked. Now that he has control of the timer, he is not distracted or stressed by it. He can focus in on his studies.

I also re-tested Tad. Only this time I did not time the standardized test. I told him he could take as long as he liked. (I noted this deviation from the norms on the test report and the reason for doing so as well.) This time Tad scored above grade level in almost every area! I also noticed that he finished most tests in the allotted time. Removing this stressor from his environment freed Tad up to do his best.

#4. Re-Evaluate Your Resources

My kids have hated or loved a subject solely because of the resources we've used. Once I started using the *History of Us* series with Mike, Gabe, and Kayte, I didn't need to do anything else in that subject area. They loved Joy Hakim's fascinating style and read her books even when school was out. That resource alone made Mike name history as his favorite subject.

I switched my sons out of Saxon Math for the same reason. They repeatedly complained about math. I told them all homeschool kids love Saxon (I thought this was an inbred trait). It's a good program, and most kids I've tested who switch to

Saxon Math see a big jump in their standardized test scores. But I eventually accepted the fact that Mike and Gabe did not like the Saxon approach. We switched to *Elementary Algebra* by Harold Jacobs, and they did much better. Jacobs's text has personality and creativity injected into the approach. He has challenging puzzlers at the end of each unit for extra credit. For me, Saxon was the easier program to use, requiring much less time on my part. But for Mike and Gabe's sake, I stuck with Jacobs because it motivated them. (I tell parents who are faced with this decision, "If it ain't broke, don't fix it." If your kids are contented with Saxon's approach, stick to it.)

If you have a reluctant reader, make sure you are using books he or she is interested in reading. Mike and Gabe learned to read using sports biographies and the Childhood of Famous Americans series. Kayte read through all the Boxcar Children books the year she achieved independence, and Kristen's motivation finally kicked in when I purchased *The Beginner's Bible* for her.

Use some common sense. Ask yourself, *Would I be motivated to learn and retain this information if I were taught in this way?*

#5. Assess Your Learning Environment

Remember: Kids learn best where there are clear boundaries, structure, and expectations. The unschooling[1] approach only works when kids are intrinsically motivated. It's a disastrous decision for the reluctant learner. Make sure your child is clear about what he is expected to get done and when. Don't say, "Johnny, do your math"—better to say, "I want you to do ten problems, and I'll recheck your work before you break for lunch."

In his book *Strategies for Struggling Learners*, Dr. Joe Sutton tells of testing a young boy with learning difficulties. The evaluation showed that this young man needed a quiet, well-lighted place to learn as well as snacks for his high metabolism rate. An interview with the mom revealed that he was currently trying to do his studies at the kitchen table with his other siblings sharing the space. His mom also allowed no snacking in between meals. On Dr. Sutton's recommendation, she set up a private place in a separate room and supplied him with snacks she could live with: sliced vegetables and fruit. Her son was now ready to concentrate on his work.

> REMEMBER: KIDS LEARN BEST WHERE THERE ARE CLEAR BOUNDARIES, STRUCTURE, AND EXPECTATIONS.

#6. Make Sure There Is Timely Accountability

There needs to be a "day of reckoning"—a time when the project is due, the test is taken, or the paper is turned in. How high on your priority list are those things without deadlines or obligation to others? Not at the top, right? So too with kids. There needs to be a point at which an evaluation of the work is done.

Contracts are often helpful motivators with older children. I use these with the courses I teach for CHESS. I make it clear that I do not *give* grades; the students *earn* them. The first day of class, I pass out a syllabus detailing the due dates for all the major assignments. I also distribute a contract that states specifically what the student agrees to do to earn an A or a B. (I won't accept a student being satisfied with anything less.) Use this same strategy in your home on a weekly basis.

Give the student self-monitoring tools to mark his progress and keep him focused: a daily log, a checklist for marking off completed work, an evaluation sheet for self-checking and assessing his work. Give clear deadlines for major assignments and projects and then stick to them. If these deadlines are tied to something certain, such as a presentation at your writers club or a contest entry, you won't be tempted to change the deadline, and your child will be more focused on getting things done.

> GIVE THE STUDENT SELF-MONITORING TOOLS TO MARK HIS PROGRESS AND KEEP HIM FOCUSED.

#7. Use Outside Influences: Another Teacher, a Co-op Class, Peers

This is the value of a family school such as CHESS. Enrolling your reluctant learner in a class or a cooperative activity will often provide the accountability factor he needs. Parents have consistently commented that their children produce far more with less nagging for their CHESS classes. Older children especially need the extra incentive of an outside evaluation. They are naturally looking beyond Mom and Dad's approval for recognition.

I've also seen positive peer influence work well with reluctant learners. Among the homeschooled kids I know, doing well is valued and admired. This positive peer influence motivates the reluctant learner to do better to earn their fellow homeschoolers' respect.

#8. Introduce an Element of Competition

Competition is a powerful trigger for a child's motivation. Bring this element into play in your home program by using games or computer software that challenges him to continuously better his score. GeoSafari (Educational Insights) is a popular electronic game that the child can play with another person or against himself. Muggins math games and 24 are kid-enticing. Software like MathBlaster, WordMunchers, SpellIt Plus, and Dr. Brain require mastery of skills and academic content to win.

On a larger scale, you can also participate in one of the numerous academic contests now open to homeschoolers. We've been involved in quite a few of these: The National Geography Bee, Math Olympiad, MathCounts, Scholastic Writing, and Knowledge Open are some of our favorites. Check out the Resource Guide for more information on these and other competitions.

We usually didn't win, but that's not the point—at least for me. My kids invested lots of time they wouldn't have otherwise spent studying the subject areas for these contests. The weeks before the National Geography Bee, everyone was suddenly interested in the GeoSafari, following current events, or reading back issues of *National Geographic's World* magazine. Kayte read an entire atlas her first year of eligibility. The kids scoured the maps on the wall and quizzed each other at the dinner table—all things they don't do naturally.

Math Olympiad is a great competition for fifth and eighth graders. At each of five meets during the year, the students are given five problems to solve within thirty minutes, and all can be solved without using algebra.

The first time I saw a set of problems, I was stunned that elementary students could do these. Here is a set to try (answers appear at the end of this chapter):

> **1.** If 20 is added to one-third of a number, the result is the double of what number?
>
> **2.** Suppose five days before the day after tomorrow was Wednesday. What day of the week was yesterday?

> **3.** The product of two whole numbers is 10,000. If neither number contains a zero digit, what are the numbers?
>
> **4.** A woman spent two-thirds of her money. She lost two-thirds of the remainder and then had $4 left. With how much money did she start?
>
> **5.** A4273B is a six-digit number in which A and B are digits. If the number is divisible by 72 without a remainder, what values do A and B have?

The first year our group worked cooperatively without setting the timer. With moms and kids all helping out, we often got a few of the problems solved—but not without a great deal of frustration, and certainty there had to be typos in the problems or answers!

But we kept chipping away at these challenges at our weekly meetings. We studied the solutions and strategies given by George Lechner, the founder and problem designer. As our repertoire of strategies for solving mathematical problems grew, our scores improved.

The next year we participated competitively, and Michael won a gold pin by scoring in the top 2 percent nationally, Gabe a silver (top 10 percent nationally), and Kayte, as a fourth grader, a patch (top 50 percent). I even competed informally and would have earned a silver.

The better news is this: All their math work dramatically improved. Math Olympiad taught them how to tackle mathematical problems and to think things through logically. They all invested significant time in their math work—because they were motivated to do well in the mathematical competitions they were preparing for. No math curriculum would have ever produced this commitment.

If you are concerned about the negative effects of competition, these can be minimized by the tone that's set by organizers of the event. At the beginning, give everyone a pep talk on the purpose of the competition. Don't over-promote the winner, and recognize every child who participates—tell them that participation alone takes courage. Look for events that give lots of kids an opportunity for success. For instance, anyone who meets the standard can earn a Presidential Physical Fitness award. The National Geography Bee only recognizes one winner, but we added prizes on our own for the top five scores and a junior winner at the elementary level. And I found the Knowledge Open competition when my sons asked for a team event they could do *with* their friends rather than one where they competed *against* each other.

You don't even need these formal contests to have a competitive motivator, either. Create a team atmosphere on your own. When my friend Sue Geer taught a current events class at the Learning Center homeschool co-op, she created teams and posted their cumulative scores on weekly quizzes. This got everyone reading news magazines and daily papers in preparation.

I wanted to give the students in my CHESS English classes one more reason to delve deeply into the material we had covered that year. I was first intending an essay test, but I wanted an extra element of fun. So I broke the kids into teams and challenged them to create a puzzle, challenge, or quiz based on the course content to give to the opposing team to solve. The losers bought lunch. The actual event was chaotic and needed refining, but according to the parents, I achieved my goal: Those kids pored over their English notes all week and worked diligently together looking for a way to stump their opponents. In the process they thoroughly reviewed the course material.

#9. Use Rewards

Once again experience brought an adjustment to my strategies. I started out as a purist who wanted my children motivated to learn for learning's sake—no grades, no stickers, no hokey contests to get you to read or count or write a term paper.

The first concession came when I promised Kayte a trip to Friendly's for ice cream if she read ten books. Then someone organized a Pizza Hut Book-It program at the Learning Center co-op. We participated in that for several years, and I noted how many kids become independent readers during the five months of the program. The simple recognition of their names on a chart, a sticker for every monthly goal achieved, plus the pizza and the big party at the end are an irresistible combination. I admit it

> **CREATE A TEAM ATMOSPHERE ON YOUR OWN.**

now: Rewards work. And these incentive programs also motivate parents to consistently help their kids work toward their goals as well.

Just to let you know how far I've fallen, I've even paid Kristen for correct work. One day Kristen was getting every problem wrong on her math work. She couldn't even solve 6 + 1 = ___ or 3 + 1 = ___. I thought, *Wow, we may really have a problem here.*

I told her I'd pay her a nickel for every problem she got right and left her on her own. When I checked her work, she had nineteen out of twenty correct. The good news: She can do it when motivated. The bad news: She works for pay.

For some time, money continued to be one of the few extrinsic rewards that motivated Kristen. I had a big jar labeled "Kristen's Jar," and the pile of coins inside it grew. When I got it out, Kristen's success sharply increased. I'd rather not have paid her, but I wanted her to learn more, and this was a concession I learned to live with. To make the best of it, I used the money to teach her to count by fives and tens. I used it as manipulatives as well to illustrate fractions and decimals.

#10. Use Discipline

Discipline is also a motivator—one God uses with us, and one we as parents are commanded to apply if we love our children. When I have resistance from my kids in a given area, I first do a quick check of the list above. Am I honoring this child's learning style? Are the resources I'm using engaging? How about the methods? If I'm making a reasonable effort to give this kid his best shot at learning the stuff, I then look at the child's attitude. If that is the root of the problem, I need to bring restraints into his life through discipline.

Okay, here comes a controversial paragraph. Read it slowly so you don't miss any of the fences I've carefully constructed.

When our kids were younger, Kermit and I applied biblical discipline (that's spelled: s-p-a-n-k) in situations *where the boundaries were clearly defined and the consequences understood*. Biblical discipline was not applied out of anger, and forgiveness and restoration immediately followed.

As maligned as that method is, I have seen the fruit borne out. Our children, and the many children I know from homes where biblical discipline is understood and properly applied, are not repressed or violent. They don't lash out, hit others, or even sneak around behind their parents' backs. Sure, they still have a serious case of sin in their hearts and the final verdict is not in, but I see in these kids self-control, focus, and a responsive heart toward the Lord.

With older children, of course, this is no longer the proper route. The consequences that motivated my resistant kids to stay focused were chores or some other loss of privilege. Fortunately, with our teens, once genuine conversion had taken place in their lives, a heart-to-heart conversation was often all it took to see a change in attitude and an increase in effort.

It was very important to us that our children understood the boundaries we set and why they were God's boundaries, not just ones for our own convenience. This meant our parenting involved a lot of discussion and a lot of drawing our children out. In *Shepherding a Child's Heart*, Tedd Tripp does the best job I know of explaining the proper role of parental authority.

Let me close with the encouragement to bring the eyes of faith to these pockets of resistance and reluctance in our kids. A lot of times, God uses these circumstances to help our children see their need for a Savior. We all fall short of the glory of God, but it takes very specific moments where we can't or won't do what we know to be right to convince each of us individually that there is a big problem going on inside our hearts. My first impulse was to find a strategy to remove the roadblock and get on with our educational game plan. When I stopped to pray and ask God for His perspective, I almost always saw that something more significant was in play and I needed to align myself with His purposes—which usually meant more patience in the situation and a bigger view of what God was doing. It really wasn't about the way to succeed in math; it was about the opportunity for my children and me to deepen our dependency upon God's generous provisions in our lives.

Answers to Math Olympiad Problems
1. 12; 2. Friday; 3. 16,625; 4. $36; 5. A=5, B=6

PART 9

MEASURING YOUR SUCCESS

Assessments

Hitting
The
Mark

IN THIS SECTION

Are We on Target?

Methods of Assessment

Report Card: The Standardized Test

Pre-Game Pep Talk

Get
Excited

Standardized
Testing

CHAPTER 32
Are We on Target?

How well is your home-education program faring? You can't really answer that question if you don't have a method for assessment in place.

And how do we define success?

At our house, any assessment we use must measure our progress in achieving the goals we've set for our family:

- a love for learning
- a marketable set of skills
- an accurate understanding of the Christian faith
- a passion for reaching this generation with the gospel

The Annual Review

As I mentioned in chapter 14, I have an annual planning time each summer. Before I begin my planning, I first review and evaluate the previous year. I find it best to conduct this evaluation a couple of months *after* we've concluded our schooling. I need some distance before I can objectively assess things.

My first step in assessing our progress has to be an evaluation of the big picture. I am always fighting against absorption with the little things—for example, *Has Kristen's handwriting improved?*—versus neglect of the important things, such as *Has Kristen's love for learning deepened?* Or, *What is our superintendent going to say about these test scores?* versus *What is God going to say about our family focus?*

Prayerfully, I start by asking God to give me His perspective of our program and asking for the strategies for next year that will bring us closer to our targets.

Planning Retreats

On occasion Kermit and I have even gone away for the weekend in order to do this. It's very romantic. Kermit brings his briefcase and an agenda. We then work through a review of our marriage, family life, and homeschool program. He runs a great meeting and is very wise about setting realistic goals for improvement. I also find that husbands more naturally look at the big picture and can keep the family focused on what really matters.

It's been difficult to keep this up in recent years because of everyone's schedule, but I think this is the most effective way to conduct an annual assessment of family life.

Christianity 101: Conviction Versus Condemnation

Most of the homeschool moms I know have little problem with overrating their program. Rather, they labor frequently under the weight of condemnation. And because of this an annual review can seem intimidating. It's always helpful for me to remind myself of the following truths:

- Our family has an adversary working against our success. His most effective tool is condemnation.

- When the Holy Spirit convicts, He is always *specific* and always gives a *solution*.

If it isn't specific and there isn't a strategy for improvement, then I don't give in to discouragement.

Wise Counsel

I also solicit input from others. I have so much personally invested in my children's education and spiritual growth, I know it's unlikely that I'm objective in my thinking. Seeking out wise counsel is a biblical principle that further helps us see God's perspective. But what constitutes "wise counsel"?

One Special Adviser

Cindy's at the top of my list, first because she loves me and my family. She's demonstrated her commitment to our success in countless ways during the past twenty years of friendship. Second, she loves the Lord and consistently demonstrates this in her life. I know her to be a woman of spiritual wisdom and maturity. And finally, there's fruit in her life and family that I desire to see in mine. Those three factors—her love for me, her love for

> SEEKING OUT WISE COUNSEL IS A BIBLICAL PRINCIPLE THAT FURTHER HELPS US SEE GOD'S PERSPECTIVE.

419

the Lord, and the evidence of fruit—I believe constitute the biblical definition of wise counsel.

A Circle of Friends

I have three other women as well—Peggy, Colette, and Kathy—whom I can count on to speak the truth in love and to challenge and encourage me and who are involved enough with my children to have a helpful perspective. Beyond them, I have my support network at the Learning Center homeschool co-op.

Extend an Invitation

Wise counsel doesn't happen naturally. I have to invite this into my life, and if I want honesty, I must receive others' perspectives graciously, even when it illuminates a weakness or identifies sin. Humility doesn't come naturally to me, but I know it's a requirement for God's blessing in my life and my family.

I believe that these steps—an annual review and regular input from others of spiritual maturity—are God's method for assessing our program.

> **WISE COUNSEL DOESN'T HAPPEN NATURALLY.**

The Comparison Trap

Before we move on, it is also helpful to review what God's method of assessment is *not*.

Want to take a shot at identifying the Enemy's method for evaluating your program? You got it: measuring your success by comparing yourself to others.

It's a constant challenge the moms at the Learning Center face. Remember the prayer meeting we held at the start of school? Everyone was already struggling with feelings of failure and regret. We had not done enough in one area or another, our day was chaotic and disorganized, our household responsibilities were never done, one child or another was not getting the attention he needed, and somewhere in all we were trying to do, the spiritual qualities we had set out to foster were frequently put on the back burner.

But what was really doing us in was the belief that *everyone else* was doing a terrific job—from the families featured in the homeschool magazines to our circle of friends at the co-op. *I'm the only one who is making a mess of things!* was in everyone's mind. And that kept us from speaking up.

Comparing ourselves to others as a measurement of our success is a deadly trap. Sure, we can be spurred on by other homeschool families, we can gather resourceful and creative ideas, and we can pool our talents and give our children the broader benefits of the group. But we will burn out faster than a meteorite if we are constantly stacking our weaknesses up against others' perceived strengths.

That's why you need a family vision and a (short) list of targets from the Lord to measure your success against. Don't use someone else's measuring stick, especially when you can't see the whole picture of his or her life.

> **COMPARING OURSELVES TO OTHERS AS A MEASUREMENT OF OUR SUCCESS IS A DEADLY TRAP.**

CHAPTER 33
Methods of Assessment

Let's look now at the ongoing methods of assessment we can use with our children to measure their success in the core subject areas.

You may want to use one or all of these options in combination at different times during your child's school career. The mix is up to you. But here are two ingredients that are essential:

#1. You Need a Method of Evaluation in Place if You Expect Your Child to Stay Motivated

How long do you work at full tilt without evaluation or reward? If you have a long list of things to do, to which do you give priority? Those with a deadline and outside accountability, right? The older your child is, the more a moment of evaluation is essential.

#2. Your Child Needs to Know What the Standard of Evaluation Will Be Before Beginning His Work

The reason why grades, testing, and other traditional methods have fallen into disrepute is they are often subjective and arbitrary. Remember scoping out teachers ahead of time to find out their grading biases? Or the feeling of frustration when you were evaluated by a boss who never gave you a clue what qualities he had been judging your performance against?

Now compare this to the game of baseball, if you will indulge me once again. Aren't the standards of success clearly spelled out? Isn't that why rabid fans, such as yours truly, feel justified in jumping from their seats when the ump clearly violates the rulebook? Kids are motivated and focused in a game of baseball because the objectives are clear. Everyone knows what spells success.

Whatever method of evaluation you use, make sure the standards are clear to your kids from the beginning.

> WHATEVER METHOD OF EVALUATION YOU USE, MAKE SURE THE STANDARDS ARE CLEAR TO YOUR KIDS FROM THE BEGINNING.

To Grade or Not to Grade

Why do we grade a child's work in school? Most frequently because the classroom teacher cannot give every child as much time as he or she may want or need to complete or revise an assignment.

Mastery learning, on the other hand, says a child can study a particular subject area or practice a skill until he achieves competency. But without deadlines, kids often underachieve and procrastinate.

So we need to strike a balance in our homes.

Many homeschoolers do not give cumulative grades in a subject during the elementary years. Tests in arithmetic or spelling are certainly corrected and may be graded. But I find there is more benefit for my kids in reworking their problems or correcting their errors than in assigning a grade and moving on.

> **WITHOUT DEADLINES, KIDS OFTEN UNDERACHIEVE AND PROCRASTINATE.**

Self-Correcting

In fact, my kids used the teacher's book a lot to check their answers and figure out their own mistakes. In a traditional setting, this may be viewed as "cheating," but I find it to be a powerful learning strategy. Because my kids have a real purpose in their studies, they don't shortchange themselves by simply copying the answers. They understand why they need to master the material, and should they ever forget this noble cause, Mom's right there holding them accountable to their goals.

When Grades Work

Somewhere around junior high, though, many parents begin assigning grades to their children's work. If we have honored their learning styles and interests from the beginning, we should be pretty attuned to the amount of time they reasonably need to complete a project or paper well.

Create a Contract

If you grade, set objective standards of measurement ahead of time. This is why I use contracts with my students at CHESS (see page 345 for a sample). It's not possible for me to individualize these contracts in that setting, but at home, I suggest you *negotiate* the contract with your kids before beginning the course. Making your child a participant in setting expectations will give him

423

or her greater ownership and thus motivation.

Testing

Traditionally, a test is used to measure success in a skill or content area. But tests are often poorly designed and merely measure how skilled a child is at taking a test. Guessing is too big a factor on true/false, matching, or multiple-choice tests to give you an accurate picture of student achievement. A better test requires kids to recall the answers.

The Best Test

The best kind of test, as you know by now, is the essay test— especially if you wish to measure understanding and mastery in a content area such as literature or history.

Essay tests, with well-designed questions, require kids to think more deeply about the material and draw conclusions, make judgments, hunt for similarities, or highlight differences.

Here's an example of an essay test I designed for a literature discussion group at the Learning Center homeschool co-op:

> THE BEST KIND OF TEST IS THE ESSAY TEST.

FINAL

The Hawk That Dare Not Hunt by Day by Scott O'Dell

Name _____ Grade _____ Date _____

Directions:

The following essay questions are asking for your opinion, but you must support your position with evidence from the book. Write in paragraph form and use examples that show you understand the things we talked about and the book you read.

1. What direction do you imagine Tom's life may have taken as a result of the events in this story? Include how you think knowing William Tyndale influenced the outcome of the rest of Tom's life.

2. Do you agree with Tom's actions when he finally finds the traitor, Henry Phillips, at the end? What reasons do you think he would give for taking the actions he did here? Were you surprised? Was it the right decision in

---

your mind? What do you think you would have done?

3. If you had fifteen minutes to talk with Scott O'Dell about his book, what comments would you make? What did you like or dislike about his writing style, characters, plot, and setting? What questions would you like him to answer about this story?

4. Think about what you learned about life in Europe during the sixteenth century. What are some of the difficulties you think you would have faced if you had lived at that time? What are some aspects you think you would have enjoyed?

5. Choose a biblical figure that has similarities with each of these characters in Scott O'Dell's book. Give a short reason for your choices.

Tom Barton	Uncle Jack	Henry Phillips
William Tyndale	Herbert Belsey	King Henry VIII

The essay test has the extra benefit of being a learning tool as well. Kids can't write well if they can't think well about the material. This type of evaluation requires them to compose their thoughts and to practice articulating them coherently.

You can accomplish the same benefits with early elementary students by allowing them to give their answers orally or dictate them to you.

Alternative Methods of Evaluation

Even though I do give grades and tests to my kids and secondary students at CHESS, these are still not my primary methods of evaluation. Here are the ways I find kids can best demonstrate their mastery of material, have fun doing so, and learn a great deal in the process.

Projects, Papers, and Performances

I want my kids to more than memorize their history facts or grammar rules for a test. They will forget nearly everything learned using that method. That's why we focus on projects, papers, or performances to demonstrate what we have learned.

Here are some of the things we and other families have done that were not only learning experiences but doubled as a method of evaluation as well:

- An American history fair where every child displayed and explained the project he had made

- Several science fairs where younger children created models and older students were required to follow the scientific process. These projects were then evaluated by outside judges. The criteria used were given to the kids before they began their work.

- A world cultures night where each family designed a booth representing a different country and had games, food, music, or other activities planned for visitors

- Numerous research papers of varying length that were then presented orally to the group for the purpose of educating others (not securing a grade from the teacher)

- Historical fiction that was written and published in magazine form after studying *The Hawk That Dare Not Hunt by Day*

- Skits and plays written and produced by the kids for a family night

- Music and dance recitals

- A family newspaper with puzzles, cartoons, and articles about the American Revolution

Our list could go on and on. Nearly every major area of interest or study has culminated in a project, performance, or written report of some kind. These have been ultimately presented to an authentic audience, not a teacher for a grade, and my kids and their friends have been highly motivated to do their best.

If there's a downside, it's where to store this stuff. After all the work that's gone into these projects, it would be viewed as a sacrilege if I threw them out—further indication of the meaningfulness of the activity. (The one advantage of tests: No one cares if they are pitched.)

Written Evaluations

Another meaningful evaluation for your children is a written report from you or a tutor or mentor. Take a few minutes at the beginning of the year to write up what you hope to accomplish in each subject area. Go over this with your kids so they know what you are expecting, and then at the end, write up your review of the progress they have made. Add this to the permanent school record you are accumulating from each year. This little bit of formalization will give your kids an extra push in taking their work seriously.

Ask others who work with your children to do the same thing. You'll find your kids will pore over what anyone writes about them. And this will contribute significantly to how they view themselves as a learner.

At CHESS, teachers give each student a written progress report several times a year. After playing around with the format a bit I came up with this form for my literature and composition class. It doesn't take long to complete and it attempts to comment on the student's character, communication skills, and understanding of course material.

FINAL EVALUATION ENGLISH 301
(American Literature)

Name: Honoria Erudite   Grade: A

4 Leadership   **4** Ability to Communicate in Writing

3 Preparedness   **3** Ability to Communicate Orally

4 Participation   **4** Thoroughness of Assignments

5 Enthusiasm   **3** Ability to Analyze

5 Comprehension of Material

4 Outside Reading List

3 Timely Completion of Assignments

5 Final Project

Criteria:
5 (exceptional)   4 (above average)   3 (satisfactory)
2 (needs improvement)   1 (dismal)

Additional Comments:

I will always remember this first senior high CHESS class with a great deal of fondness. What a joy it is to have a student like Honoria who does her absolute best all the time and is so willing to receive direction and suggestions. Of special note is the exceptional job Honoria did on her research paper on Jonathan Edwards. This project went far beyond the requirements of the assignment and showed remarkably mature insight and well-supported conclusions.

I look forward to seeing Honoria continue to grow as a writer and to gain confidence in her ability to express her ideas orally and in writing. I encourage Honoria to pursue wider audiences for her work as well.

Debra A. Bell, M.A.

You will probably be more successful in obtaining written evaluations from mentors and tutors if you create a similar form that is quick and easy to fill out. (As someone who is asked to write lots of evaluations and recommendations, I really appreciate forms.)

Portfolio Assessment

In our state, home-educated students are required to present a portfolio of their progress at the end of the year to an evaluator who writes a progress report. Both are then submitted to the school district.

The portfolio is usually a three-ring binder (with a three- to five-inch spine) filled with pictures and work from the school year. I have a bookcase now filled with portfolios from every school year of each child's life. They were quite a time commitment to compile, but these are some of our family's most treasured possessions. Each is a scrapbook full of memories and a real pick-me-up when I was discouraged. I'd just pull one off the shelf and spend an afternoon reliving the special moments we had learning together. It's hard not to see progress in our homeschool program with this tangible evidence in the house.

Even if you are not required to maintain a portfolio, you may wish to consider it as an invaluable assessment tool. My kids put together their own. It took us about two weeks to pull them together—wiser women than I maintain theirs throughout the school year—but during that process my kids reviewed their year's work in every subject area and often edited a story one more time, finished an art project, or reworked some math problems. They knew their work was going to have an outside review, and they wanted to do their best. It was a great learning tool to reinforce our studies one more time.

The portfolio is divided into subject areas, and each is arranged chronologically so that it demonstrates academic progress. Here's a list of the kinds of documentation a family might include:

- written work from the student

- pictures of field trips and projects

- notes, outlines, rough drafts, and final papers

- tests and scores

- certificates from participation in National Geography Bee, Pizza Hut Book-It Program, etc.

- independent reading list with brief annotations—examples: award winner, nonfiction, biography, historical fiction, page length

- photocopied table of contents from text used, highlighting sections studied

- pamphlets from places visited

- list of resources referred to or read in each subject area

- list of objectives or units of study in each area

- pictures of learning environment—examples: computer, bookshelves, aquarium, educational video collection, outdoor gym equipment

- pictures of social experiences: favorite group of friends, co-op classes, volleyball tournament

- a narrative from Mom or older students explaining more about the pictures or projects included

Find an Audience Once Again

Once you've pulled your portfolios together, find an audience for your kids to share them with. My kids have relished the opportunity to explain each page in detail to their evaluator, grandma, or a reporter.

At our co-op, we had the students display theirs at the annual family night. I enjoy my role as an evaluator very much because I get to see all the great ideas and experiences other families have had. The same benefit can come from sharing our year's work through a display of projects, papers, and portfolios at a support group family night.

One-Subject Portfolio

If that sounds like too much work, you may want to compile a portfolio for just one subject. This is an excellent way for a high schooler to demonstrate the quality of his work to a college admissions office, for instance.

I require a writing portfolio for my junior and senior high composition classes at CHESS (I suggested a two-inch, three-ring binder.) When I teach a content area, such as American literature, I need to assess the students' mastery of a set body of knowledge. I use essay tests, quizzes, and papers to determine the grade. But composition is a skill. My goal here is to evaluate student progress. They are all at different places in their development as writers, and a lot of them have zero confidence in this area. I don't want my class to send that into the negative range. I want to encourage and inspire their growth as writers.

From the start I make it clear that their final grade is based upon their progress, and the writing portfolio is how they will demonstrate this. The first day, I take a writing sample (I compare this to taking blood). They choose from several topics and write cold for fifteen minutes. I also ask them to fill out a writer's inventory. This assesses their attitude toward writing, their previous writing history, and the process they currently go through when composing a paper.

Everything they do for class is to be kept in chronological order in the writing portfolio. Throughout the course I evaluate the progress demonstrated in the portfolio. At the end of the course, I take another writing sample and ask students to complete another writer's inventory. I trust I will see improvement in skill and confidence.

CHAPTER 34
Report Card: The Standardized Test

In many places homeschoolers are required—or choose—to have their children tested periodically with a standardized test. They are necessary here in Pennsylvania, and each year I test almost three hundred homeschooled kids at various sites around the state. Despite my assurances, it's still a traumatic event—for the moms. The kids do just fine.

And once the scores are mailed back, it's the one time of the year I get lots of phone calls from dads. "My son scored at the 70th percentile in spelling. What are we doing wrong?"

I can empathize. Despite all I know about the folly of standardized testing, when I opened my own children's return envelope, my palms were always sweaty as well. Those numbers look so exacting that it's hard not to give them credence.

The intent of the requirement is to evaluate our children. But the truth is, we parents feel we're the ones being measured. When I open my test site with prayer, I ask the kids to pray for their moms as well. They're the ones who need the assurance.

Here's a primer to help you keep testing in perspective and also some tips for using those scores to better your program.

What Exactly Is a Standardized Test?

#1. Most Standardized Tests Are Achievement Tests

> **A STANDARDIZED TEST IS NOT AN ABILITY OR AN APTITUDE TEST.**

That means they are designed to measure how well a student has mastered the material he has presumably been taught. A standardized test is not an ability or an aptitude test, as is the College Board's SAT, which is attempting to predict a student's future scholastic success.

Low scores on an achievement test may indicate the student has not mastered that material yet, or it could also mean he has not been *presented* that material yet. If your child is required to take an achievement test, do your best to find out what skills will actually be measured. Does the third-grade test include division? Does the eighth-grade test measure knowledge of Latin roots? The test scores will mean nothing to you if you don't know what material the test-makers had anticipated would be covered.

#2. Most Only Test in Language Arts and Mathematics

While other skill areas may also be included, language arts and math form the core. On the Iowa Test of Basic Skills (ITBS), the test I prefer to use, the basic battery includes vocabulary, reading comprehension, spelling, mathematical concepts (terminology), mathematical problem solving (word and number problems), and mathematical computation (speed and accuracy test).

The complete test, which I make optional, includes grammar, usage, punctuation, work study (library and map skills), science, and social studies. Those scores are not computed in the Basic Composite score but are part of the *Complete* Composite score.

If you are not giving the test yourself, ask the test administrator exactly what subtests will be given.

#3. Kids' Achievement Is Compared to a Sample Group

The scores your child receives are a comparison against the "norms" obtained from a sample group of children (usually tens of thousands) who took that same test at the same time of year. This is what is meant by "standardized." The average score of that sample group on each skill test translates into the 50th percentile. Your child's score at the 70th percentile in spelling means he did better on that test than 70 percent of the sample group of children who took that same test at that grade level.

The norms generated from this sample group are in use for several years. Test administrators can even choose between several sets of norms. For example, the 1998 norms on the ITBS were higher than the 1995 norms. So student scores normed against the '95 sample group were interpreted higher than the same achievement scores normed against the '98 group. A slight upward or downward swing across the board in scores for your child can simply mean different norms were used.

Norms also vary from test to test. The Stanford Achievement Test is the achievement test of choice in many private schools. Because those students are often part of the sample group, the norms for the Stanford are a bit higher than the norms on other tests.

Because of differences in norms and actual material tested, you get a more accurate picture of your child's achievement by using the same test year after year.

NORMS VARY FROM TEST TO TEST.

#4. Scores Are Reported a Number of Ways

Besides reporting your child's achievement in terms of percentile, the test report will probably include the following information:

- **Raw scores:** This is the actual number correct on a test. The percentile, grade equivalent, and stanine (explained below) are various ways of interpreting the meaning of this raw score when compared to the norms.

- **Grade equivalent:** This is usually the most misunderstood score. Your child's grade equivalent score of 79 on a fifth-grade reading test means he understood the reading material on that fifth-grade test the way we might expect an "average" seventh-grader in the ninth month of school to understand that same fifth-grade material. It does not mean you should advance him two grades or say he reads on a junior high level. You can accurately state that he is reading above grade level, which should have been already evident to you.

- **Stanine:** The stanine indicates which of nine groupings this child would fall into, with the fifth stanine representing the average group. The ninth stanine represents the group of children with the very highest achievement in this skill area, and the first stanine represents the group of children with the very lowest achievement in this skill area.
  I prefer to look at stanine when I am giving parents an interpretation of their child's test score. Stanines are a generalization of the child's achievement, and generalizations are all I believe you can accurately make when using a standardized test for evaluation. A lot of

factors can affect a child's performance on the test. Given the same test several times, his grade equivalency and percentile rankings will fluctuate. But his stanine will likely be consistent.

- **Composite score:** Composite scores are calculated by averaging the individual scores on the battery of tests. Read the report carefully to note exactly which test scores were averaged. Sometimes the composite score includes all tests; sometimes it includes just the basic battery in language arts and mathematics. This composite score is then interpreted in terms of percentile, grade equivalency, and stanine as well.

How Much Weight Should Be Given to Scores?

#1. Your Own Observation Is More Accurate

In a traditional setting, individual assessments of every child's achievement in all subject areas is not possible. That's why we have standardized tests. They are a stab at helping the classroom teacher determine who is having problems, who is doing just fine, and who may be ready for acceleration. They are a helpful but imperfect tool.

Lots of factors, other than lack of skill in a subject area, can affect a child's score: He may not feel well, he may not be comfortable with the testing environment, he may have incorrectly filled out his answer sheet, or he may not have effective test-taking strategies.

Your daily observation of your child's achievement at home is a *more accurate* assessment of his progress than the standardized test scores. In most cases, the test scores will affirm what you have already concluded from working with your child. When test scores are at odds with this, use caution in weighing them too heavily.

#2. There's a Growing Body of Research That Discredits Standardized Tests

The main problem with standardized tests is they report student achievement by comparing them to other students. That means the scoring always ensures some kids are not going to

> TEST SCORES WILL AFFIRM WHAT YOU HAVE ALREADY CONCLUDED FROM WORKING WITH YOUR CHILD.

pass muster. A more helpful report would measure how much a child has learned, without making comparisons. Additional problems of standardized tests include cultural biases.

Standardized testing is especially unfair to the homeschool parent, who is not allowed to see the test ahead of time. If you don't know what skills or content will be tested, how can you ensure that the material has been presented to your child? You can't. If a standardized test covers material never presented to your child, then how helpful are the scores? Not much.

 If you want to read more about standardized tests, check out these sources:

Parent's Guide to Standardized Tests for Grades 3–5, Drew Johnson. There are many more test and grade-specific titles in this series. Visit www.kaptest.com.

Also visit the National Center for Fair and Open Testing site at www.fairtest.org.

How to Benefit From a Standardized Test

Since I'm already leading the charge on a number of other issues, I'll have to pass for now on taking up arms against standardized tests. I accept them as a fact of life and give them to my children every chance I get so they can do their best when the scores count most.

And I'll grudgingly admit that they have been assuring and helpful over the years. Here are ways to make them work for you:

#1. If Possible, You Should Administer the Test to Your Child at Least Once

The sources that allow parents to administer the test are indicated at the end of this section. If you do this, you will learn a lot about the nature of a standardized test and about your child's strengths and weaknesses in taking tests. Does he race through the material? Does he recheck his work? Does he lose his place easily? Does he read all the choices before deciding? Does he manage his time wisely? You are now better able to prepare him for a group testing situation.

You may find, as I did, that it's a real feat to refrain from coaching him during the test or sending nonverbal cues when he is about to make a mistake. So although I do test each of my kids once in my home, all subsequent tests are given at my group test site or by someone else.

If you cannot administer the test, ask permission to observe your child being tested as the next best way to gather this information.

#2. If You Test, Test Annually with the Same Test

Because a child's performance on a test can be influenced by many different factors, it is more accurate to draw conclusions from the profile of your child's achievement that emerges over time. And this should be based upon the same test.

I frequently get calls from parents who have had their children tested with the CTBS (Comprehensive Test of Basic Skills) in the fall with another test service and who now wish to sign them up for the ITBS with me in the spring in order to see if their child has improved. When I know this, I discourage them from doing so. There is such a big difference between the two tests that the results cannot be accurately compared.

#3. Don't Put Much Stock in Early Test Results

The scores of early elementary children are very unreliable. My kids tested all over the board till fifth grade, when a consistent pattern began to emerge. I have seen this repeated time and time again with many children I have tested. I think states that require standardized tests of homeschool students before third grade are out to lunch. (Pardon my brashness.)

I've worked with kids who tested well below average during the early elementary years and who are now scoring well above average as teens. In the fall of fifth grade, my daughter Kayte's scores took a big jump. I thought it was a fluke (what faith) until I retested her in the spring and got the same dramatic jump. Something had kicked in (it's that inner timetable again), and my daughter suddenly became a very motivated and determined learner. It was a new twist to her formerly nonchalant self.

Don't let a test determine how you view your child's academic potential. I told my sons time and again (and prayed I was right) that the kids who were the best athletes in elementary school were often not the best athletes in high school. It's the kids who work hardest who end up on top when it matters.

I'm also convinced that is equally true of academic success. Kids with academic motivation will test the best when it counts. So don't give up on your child. Focus your energies on *keeping your child motivated to learn* by designing a program that honors his learning style and cultivates a love for learning.

> **DON'T LET A TEST DETERMINE HOW YOU VIEW YOUR CHILD'S ACADEMIC POTENTIAL.**

#4. Use a Test Service That Will Give You a Criterion-Referenced Report

Criterion-referenced sounds like a fancy word, but it's the information you need to really use the test scores. A criterion-referenced report will tell you exactly what skills were tested, how many of those problems in that category your child attempted on the test, and how many he got correct. Bob Jones University Testing Service, as well as my testing service, issues this kind of report.

When parents look at this report, they will be able to determine exactly where their child is having trouble and how to correct the problem.

Example 1:

Ellen scored at the 45th percentile on the fifth-grade math computation test. When we look at the report for this subtest, we see that she attempted all thirty-nine problems in this section. So we know she finished the test in the time allotted.

There were fifteen whole-number addition and subtraction problems, and she got thirteen correct. No problem there. But of the sixteen whole-number multiplication and division problems, she only got nine correct. Further practice in this area may be indicated. Plus, of the eight problems requiring addition and subtraction of decimals and fractions, she only got one correct. A discussion with Mom reveals that these types of problems have not yet been introduced in her math program. So her low score is understandable.

Let's look at another child.

Example 2:

William scored at the 53rd percentile on the fifth-grade reading comprehension test. His parents are a bit surprised. His independent reading at home had seemed to be above grade level. He had picked up *The Call of the Wild* that summer and had recently finished reading it. With a criterion-referenced report we can find the explanation for this apparent discrepancy.

Of the fifty-four reading comprehension questions on the test, William had only completed thirty-two, all of which were correct.

William had not finished the test in the time allotted. He isn't having any difficulties with reading comprehension—his high score on the vocabulary section is further indication of this—but he is a slower reader than "average."

My recommendation to his parents is to just keep William reading. His speed will increase the more he reads.

It's Easy to Draw the Wrong Conclusions

Without this criterion-referenced report, can you see how a parent might jump to erroneous conclusions? With just the percentile score, Ellen's mom may have decided Ellen needs to go back through all her math lessons this year to make sure she is really getting it this time. Or William's parents might have concluded that he is obviously not understanding these hard books he is reading and insist that he choose easier ones. It would all be for naught.

If you cannot get a criterion-referenced report for the test administered, the test is useless to you as an evaluation tool.

Tips for Helping Your Child Do Well on a Standardized Test

1. Use a test preparation program. Test-preparation programs such as Scoring High (available from debrabell.com) not only give practice with the content material typically found on the most widely used standardized tests but also teach your child test-taking strategies that prepare him to manage his time and make the best choices.

USE A TEST PREPARATION PROGRAM.

2. If possible, arrange to have him tested in a familiar setting by someone he knows.

3. Make sure he is well rested and has a nutritious breakfast high in protein and low in sugar the day of the test.

4. Send your child with a ruler to keep his place on the scoring sheet and a watch to manage his time wisely.

5. If it's allowed at the test site, he should also have a book to read if he finishes a test early and a high-protein snack for the breaks.

6. Don't drop your young child off at the test site; instead, be available at the breaks and lunchtime to encourage and affirm him.

7. Hide your own insecurities. The proper use of a standardized test is to give you a tool to better tune your program to your child's needs. It will help you know what he knows well and what he has not yet mastered. It should not be used to pass judgment on your homeschooling program.

National Testing Services

Bayside School Services
P.O. Box 250
Kill Devil Hills, NC 27948
800-723-3057
www.baysideschoolservices.com
Parents may administer the California Achievement Test (CAT/5) and CTBS/Terra Nova.

Bob Jones University
Greenville, SC 29614-0062
800-845-5731
www.bjupress.com/services/testing
The administrator may be a parent but must have a four-year degree; criterion-referenced report; Iowa (ITBS), Stanford (SAT), as well as many other types of tests.

Christian Liberty Academy
502 W. Euclid Avenue
Arlington Heights, IL 60004-5402
847-259-4444
www.homeschools.org
The administrator may be a parent; CAT; grade equivalency
report only.

Family Learning Organization
P.O. Box 1750
Mead, WA 99021-1750
800-405-8378
www.familylearning.org
Parents may administrator the CAT/5. Computerized
scoring report includes grade equivalencies and percentile
rankings.

Piedmont Education Services
1629 Turfwood Drive
Pfafftown, NC 27040
336-924-2494
www.pesdirect.com
A parent with a bachelor's degree may administer the ITBS
(latest edition) available from Piedmont to the student.

Seton Testing Services
1350 Progress Drive
Front Royal, VA 22630
800-542-1066
www.setontesting.com
Parents may administer the CAT-E (this is the survey
edition—i.e., it is shorter than the CAT/5).

Sycamore Tree
2179 Meyer Place
Costa Mesa, CA 92627
888-334-6711
www.sycamoretree.com
The administrator cannot be a parent; CTBS;
detailed report.

PRE-GAME
PEP
TALK

The Winning Strategies

1. Utterly rely upon the grace of God.

2. Keep a sharply focused vision in clear view.

3. Have faith in future fruit.

4. Give your kids control.

5. Give your kids a purpose that is immediate and relevant.

6. Enjoy the mystery of life.

7. Don't try this alone.

8. Be a learner.

9. Remember Oswald Chamber's comment: "What we call the *process*, God calls the *end.*"

10. Play ball!

PART 10

RESOURCE GUIDE

HOMESCHOOLING ORGANIZATIONS AND PUBLICATIONS

National Organizations

Home School Legal Defense Association (HSLDA)

P.O. Box 3000
Purcellville, VA 20134-9000
540-338-5600
540-338-2733 fax
hslda.org

HSLDA works on the national and state levels to advocate parental freedoms, especially the rights of parents to direct their children's education. It provides legal support to member families free of charge. It also publishes *The Court Report*, a recommended magazine of national and state news. There is an annual membership fee, with discount membership available through many state and local groups. With J. Michael Smith as president and a staff exceeding fifty, HSLDA provides a wide array of services to the homeschool community. Get on its mailing list and e-mail list and visit its website.

National Home Education Research Institute (NHERI)

P.O. Box 13939
Salem, OR 97309
503-364-1490
503-364-2827 fax
www.nheri.org

Brian Ray, Ph.D., heads this nonprofit research and educational foundation. NHERI is the definitive source of research conducted on homeschooling. It provides many helpful reports for use with legislators, media, and other public officials.

National Home Education Network (NHEN)
P.O. Box 1652
Hobe Sound, FL 33475-1652
413-581-1463 fax
www.nhen.com
NHEN is a nonsectarian organization that seeks to represent
the diversity of the homeschool movement. As such, they and
HSLDA, which is Christian in orientation, do not always agree on
some fundamental issues or the best political course of action.
Christian homeschoolers are welcome among this eclectic bunch,
and you will find interesting articles, resources, and methodologies
you will not find elsewhere.

National Alliance of Christian Home Education Leadership
www.beginninghomeschooling.com
The Alliance's primary purpose is to provide support to state
leaders. However, this site contains advice on getting started and
lists state contact information.

Home School Legal Defence Association of Canada
32B-980 Adelaide Street South
London, Ontario N6E 1R3
519-913-0318
www.hslda.ca

Canadian Home Based Learning Resource Page
www.flora.org/homeschool-ca
An extensive list of support groups, organizations, and suppliers
indexed by province.

State Organizations

You will find the most up-to-date information on state as well
as regional level organizations at the HSLDA website. HSLDA
also publishes state laws with explanations for compliance. Most
organizations published here are contact organizations for HSLDA
and adhere to an evangelical statement of faith. See the end of
this list for sources of inclusive, non-religious state organizations.

445

Please note: Most state organizations are staffed by volunteers. Please use the websites provided to obtain information, and most ask that you use e-mail before calling.

Alabama

Christian Home Education Fellowship of Alabama (CHEF of Alabama)
P.O. Box 20208
Montgomery, AL 36120
334-288-7229
www.chefofalabama.org

Alaska

Alaska Private and Home Educators Association
P.O. Box 141764
Anchorage, AK 99514
907-376-9382
www.aphea.org

Arizona

Arizona Families for Home Education (AFHE)
P.O. Box 2035
Chandler, AZ 85244-2035
602-235-2673 voice mail
www.afhe.org

Arkansas

Family Council
414 S. Pulaski, Suite 2
Little Rock, AR 72201
501-375-7000
www.familycouncil.org

California

Christian Home Educators Association of California (CHEA)

P.O. Box 2009

Norwalk, CA 90651-2009

562-864-2432

www.cheaofca.org

Colorado

Christian Home Educators of Colorado (CHEC)

10431 S. Parker Road

Parker, CO 80134

877-842-2432

www.chec.org

Connecticut

The Education Association of Christian Homeschoolers (TEACH)

10 Moosehorn Road

West Granby, CT 06090

860-435-2890

www.teachct.org

Delaware

Delaware Home Education Association (DHEA)

www.dheaonline.org

OutReach to Christian Homeschoolers in Delaware (ORCHID)

www.orchidde.com

District of Columbia

Christian Home Educators of DC, Inc. (CHEDC)

P.O. Box 29577

Washington, D.C. 20017

202-526-4108

Florida

Florida Parent-Educators Association (FPEA)
7682 Municipal Drive
Orlando, FL 32819
877-ASK-FPEA (275-3732)
www.fpea.com

Georgia

Georgia Home Education Association (GHEA)
258 Sandy Lake Circle
Fayetteville, GA 30214
770-461-3657
www.ghea.org

Hawaii

Christian Homeschoolers of Hawaii (CHOH)
www.christianhomeschoolersofhawaii.org

Idaho

Christian Homeschoolers of Idaho State (CHOIS)
P.O. Box 45062
Boise, ID 83711
208-424-6685
www.chois.org

Idaho Coalition of Home Educators
P.O. Box 878
Eagle, ID 83616
www.iche-idaho.org

Illinois

Christian Home Educators Coalition of Illinois (CHEC of IL)
2405 Essington Road
PMB 122
Joliet, IL 60435
815-341-8805
www.chec.cc

Illinois Christian Home Educators (ICHE)
P.O. Box 307
Russell, IL 60075-0307
847-603-1259
www.iche.org

Indiana

Indiana Association of Home Educators (IAHE)
320 E. Main Street
Greenfield, IN 46140
317-467-6244
www.inhomeeducators.org

Indiana Foundation for Home Schooling
P.O. Box 17385
Indianapolis, IN 46217
800-465-2505
www.indianahomeschooling.org

Iowa

The Network of Iowa Christian Home Educators (NICHE)
P.O. Box 158
Dexter, IA 50070
800-723-0438 or 515-830-1614
www.the-niche.org

Kansas

Christian Home Educators Confederation of Kansas (CHECK)
P.O. Box 1332
Topeka, KS 66601
913-599-0311
www.kansashomeschool.org

Teaching Parents Association (TPA)
P.O. Box 3968
Wichita, KS 67201-3968
www.wichitahomeschool.org

Kentucky

Christian Home Educators of Kentucky (CHEK)
P.O. Box 1288
Bardstown, KY 40004-1288
270-358-9270
www.chek.org

Kentucky Home Education Association (KHEA)
P.O. Box 51591
Bowling Green, KY 42102-5891
270-779-6574
www.khea.info

Louisiana

Christian Home Educators Fellowship of Louisiana (CHEF)
P.O. Box 226
Maurice, LA 70555
888-876-2433
www.chefofla.org

Maine

Homeschoolers of Maine
P.O. Box 159
Camden, ME 04843-0159
207-763-2880
www.homeschoolersofmaine.org

Maryland

Christian Home Educators Network (CHEN)
P.O. Box 2010
Ellicott City, MD 21043
www.chenmd.org

Maryland Association of Christian Home Educators (MACHE)
P.O. Box 417
Clarksburg, MD 20871
301-607-4284
www.machemd.org

Massachusetts

Massachusetts Homeschool Organization of Parent Educators (Mass HOPE)
46 South Road
Holden, MA 01520
508-829-0973
www.masshope.org

Michigan

Information Network for Christian Homes (INCH)
3721 W. Michigan Avenue, Suite 200
Lansing, MI 48917
517-481-5994
www.inch.org

Minnesota

Minnesota Association of Christian Home Educators (MACHE)
P.O. Box 32308
Fridley, MN 55432
866-717-9070
www.mache.org

Mississippi

Mississippi Home Educators Association (MHEA)
www.mhea.net

Missouri

Missouri Association of Teaching Christian Homes (MATCH)
2203 Rhonda Drive
West Plains, MO 65775-1615
www.match-inc.org

Families for Home Education
P.O. Box 742
Grandview, MO 64030
877-696-6343
www.fhe-mo.org

Montana
Montana Coalition of Home Educators
P.O. Box 43
Gallatin Gateway, MT 59730
www.mtche.org

Nebraska
Nebraska Christian Home Educators Association (NCHEA)
P.O. Box 57041
Lincoln, NE 68505-7041
402-423-4297
www.nchea.org

Nevada
Nevada Homeschool Network
P.O. Box 1212
Carson City, NV 89702
www.nevadahomeschoolnetwork.com

Northern Nevada Home Schools
P.O. Box 18652
Reno, NV 89511
775-852-6647
www.nnhs.org

New Hampshire
Christian Home Educators of New Hampshire (CHENH)
P.O. Box 961
Manchester, NH 03105
www.chenh.org

New Jersey

Education Network of Christian Homeschoolers of New
Jersey (ENOCH)
P.O. Box 308
Atlantic Highlands, NJ 07716
732-291-7800
www.enochnj.org

New Mexico

Christian Association of Parent Educators NM (CAPE-NM)
P.O. Box 3203
Moriarty, NM 87035
505-898-8548 voice mail
www.cape-nm.org

New York

Loving Education at Home (LEAH)
www.leah.org

North Carolina

North Carolinians for Home Education (NCHE)
4336-A Bland Road
Raleigh, NC 27609
919-790-1100
www.nche.com

North Dakota

North Dakota Home School Association (NDHSA)
701-263-3727
www.ndhsa.org

Ohio

Christian Home Educators of Ohio (CHEO)
616 Hebron Road, Suite E
Heath, OH 43056-1444
740-522-2460
www.cheohome.org

Oklahoma

Christian Home Educators Fellowship of Oklahoma (CHEF)
P.O. Box 471363
Tulsa, OK 74147-1363
918-583-7323
www.chefok.org

Oklahoma Christian Home Educators Consociation (OCHEC)
3801 NW 63rd Street, Building 3, Suite 236
Oklahoma City, OK 73116
405-810-0386
www.ochec.com

Oregon

Oregon Christian Home Education Association Network (OCEAN)
17985 Falls City Road
Dallas, OR 97338
503-288-1285
www.oceanetwork.org

Pennsylvania

Christian Home School Association of Pennsylvania (CHAP)
717-838-0980
www.chaponline.com

Pennsylvania Homeschoolers
105 Richman Lane
Kittanning, PA 16201
724-783-6512
pahomeschoolers.com

Rhode Island
The Rhode Island Guild of Home Teachers (RIGHT)
P.O. Box 432
Coventry, RI 02816
401-996-5991
www.rihomeschool.com

South Carolina
South Carolina Association of Independent Home Schools (SCAIHS)
930 Knox Abbott Drive
Cayce, SC 29033
803-454-0427
www.scaihs.org

South Carolina Home Educators Association (SCHEA)
P.O. Box 2707
Irmo, SC 29063
803-772-2330
www.schomeeducatorsassociation.org

South Dakota
South Dakota Christian Home Educators (SDCHE)
P.O. Box 9571
Rapid City, SD 57709
605-716-2090
www.sdche.org

Tennessee
Tennessee Home Education Association
P.O. Box 681652
Franklin, TN 37068
615-623-7899
www.tnhea.org

Texas

Christian Home Education Association of Central Texas
P.O. Box 141998
Austin, TX 78714-1998
512-450-0070
www.cheact.org

Family Educators Alliance of South Texas (FEAST)
25 Burwood Lane
San Antonio, TX 78216
210-342-4674
www.homeschoolfeast.com

North Texas Home Educators' Network (NTHEM)
P.O. Box 1071
Allen, TX 75013
214-495-9600
www.nthen.org

Southeast Texas Home School Association (SETHSA)
10592-A Fuqua #503
Houston, TX 77089
281-756-9792
www.sethsa.org

Texas Home School Coalition (THSC)
P.O. Box 6747
Lubbock, TX 79493
806-744-4441
www.thsc.org

Utah

Utah Christian Home School Association
P.O. Box 3942
Salt Lake City, UT 84110-3945
801-296-7198 voice mail
www.utch.org

Virginia
Home Educators Association of Virginia (HEAV)
2248 G Dabney Road
Richmond, VA 23230
804-278-9200
www.heav.org

Washington
Washington Association of Teaching Christian Homes (WATCH)
425-956-3282
www.watchhome.org

West Virginia
Christian Home Educators of West Virginia
P.O. Box 8770
South Charleston, WV 25303-0770
877-802-1773
www.chewv.org

Wisconsin
Wisconsin Christian Home Education Association
P.O. Box 320458
Franklin, WI 53132
414-425-6324
www.wisconsinchea.com

Wyoming
Homeschoolers of Wyoming (HOW)
4859 Palmer Canyon Road
Wheatland, WY 82201
307-322-3539
www.homeschoolersofwy.org

Local Organizations

To locate nonsectarian support groups in your area, visit Jon's Homeschool Resource Page at www.midnightbeach.com/hs.

Special-Interest Organizations

African-American

National Black Home Educators

13434 Plank Road, PMB 110

Baker, LA 70714

www.nbhe.net

Catholic

Catholic Homeschool Support

www.catholichomeschool.org

Keeping It Catholic

604 S. Main St.

Suite 224

Lapeer, MI 48446

www.keepingitcatholic.org

Love 2 Learn

Alicia Van Hecke, FRCH

P.O. Box 61

Hartland, WI 53029

www.love2learn.net

Classical Christian

Classical Christian Homeschooling website

www.classical-homeschooling.org

Christine Miller, webmaster

Trivium Pursuit

525 120th Avenue

New Boston, IL 61272

309-537-3641

www.triviumpursuit.com
Harvey and Laurie Bluedorn, owners
Magazine; online catalog, seminars, speech and debate,
discussion loop, links

The Well-Trained Mind
Peace Hill Farm
18021 The Glebe Lane
Charles City, VA 23030
www.welltrainedmind.com
www.peacehillpress.com
Susan Wise Bauer and Jessie Wise, editors
Book, newsletter, discussion groups, information, resources, links

Missionaries
Sonlight Curriculum
8042 South Grant Way
Littleton, CO 80122
303-730-6292
www.sonlight.com
John and Sarita Holzmann, owners
Literature-based curriculum created to provide homeschool
supplies to missionaries living abroad; mission emphasis to
curriculum, experienced in shipping overseas

South Carolina Association of Independent Home Schools
(SCAIHS)
930 Knox Abbott Drive
Cayce, SC 29033
803-454-0427
www.scaihs.org
SCAIHS staff does everything it can to work with missionaries on
the field; not limited to missionaries from South Carolina

LifeWork Forum
207-636-3792
www.lifeworkforum.org
Through her role as international consultant with the HSLDA, veteran homeschool mom Sandra Lovelace travels the globe encouraging missionaries and their families.

Special Needs

Almaden Valley Christian School
Sharon Hensley
16465 Carlson Drive
Morgan Hill, CA 95037
408-776-6691
www.almadenvalleychristianschool.com
Book, information packet, program planning

Child Diagnostics
Dianne Craft, MA, CNHP
6562 S. Cook Court
Littleton, CO 80121
303-694-0532
www.diannecraft.org
Seminars, private consultations, Right Brain Teaching Products

Exceptional Diagnostics
5 Jericho Court
Simpsonville, SC 29681
864-967-4729
www.edtesting.com
Dr. Joe Sutton, director
Strategies for Struggling Learners, testing service, evaluations

National Challenged Homeschoolers Associated Network (NATHHAN)
P.O. Box 310
Moyie Springs, ID 83845
208-267-6246
www.nathhan.com
Membership fee of $25 per year

Support organization for parents who are homeschooling special-needs children, publishes *Nathhan News* and a catalog of recommended resources, provides a network of ten thousand contact people in the homeschool community—some providing professional services to families

Timberdoodle
1510 E. Spencer Lake Road
Shelton, WA 98584
800-478-0672 or 360-426-0672
360-427-5625 fax
www.timberdoodle.com
Dan and Deb Diffinbaugh, owners
Homeschool supplier, in recent years beginning to specialize in support and educational resources for autistic children

Worldview Resources

Apologia Press
1106 Meridian Plaza, Suite 220
Anderson, IN 46016
888-524-4724
765-608-3290 fax
www.apologia.com
Publishers of the *What We Believe* series of textbooks, created in partnership with Summit Ministries. Also, ApologiaAcademy offers Internet courses on worldview, apologetics, and Bible.

Discovery Institute
208 Columbia Street
Seattle, WA 98104
206-292-0401
206-682-5320 fax
www.discovery.org
Intelligent design think tank; leading scientists and thinkers collaborate here

Probe Ministries
972-480-0240
www.probe.org
Kerby Anderson, president
Radio show, Mind Games, College Survival Seminar, resources, links

Stand to Reason
1438 East 33rd Street
Signal Hill, CA 90755
800-2-REASON
www.str.org
Resources to equip Christians to make an intelligent defense of the gospel, particularly on college campuses, and to graciously defend Christian values in the public square

Summit Ministries
P.O. Box 207
Manitou Springs, CO 80829
866-786-6483
www.summit.org
Creators of *Understanding the Times* video curriculum and summer leadership seminars

Worldview Academy
P.O. Box 2918
Midland, TX 79702
800-241-1123
www.worldview.org
Weekend seminars and camps for teens

Periodicals

God's World Publications
P.O. Box 20001
Asheville, NC 28802-8201
800-951-5437 subscription to *God's World* newspapers
800-951-6397 subscription to *World* magazine for teens/adults
www.gwnews.com
www.worldmag.com

Weekly news and current events publications for school-age
children through adults

Homeschooling Today
P.O. Box 244
Abingdon, VA 24212
866-804-4478
www.homeschooltoday.com
Classical Christian flavor, high school forum, understanding the
arts, ready-to-use lessons, worldview articles

The Old Schoolhouse Magazine
P.O. Box 8426
Gray, TN 37615
888-718-HOME
www.thehomeschoolmagazine.com
Biblical encouragement, a wide array of articles, "Laughable
Lines," product reviews, and more

Practical Homeschooling
Home Life
P.O. Box 1190
Fenton, MO 63026-1190
800-346-6322
www.home-school.com
Bill and Mary Pride, publishers

Homeschool Digest
Wisdom Gate
P.O. Box 374
Covert, MI 49043
269-764-1910
www.homeschooldigest.com

RECOMMENDED SUPPLIERS AND PRODUCTS

General Publishers and Suppliers

The companies listed below publish or supply homeschool products in many subject areas. A list of specialized publishers follows.

A Beka Books

P.O. Box 19100
Pensacola, FL 32523-9100
877-223-5226
www.abeka.com
Christian publisher of a traditional line of textbooks with a patriotic emphasis, online-secure ordering after an account is established

Apologia Educational Ministries

1106 Meridian Plaza, Suite 220
Anderson, IN 46016
888-524-4724
765-608-3290 fax
www.apologia.com
Known for its excellence in K-12 science curriculum for homeschoolers, Apologia is now branching out into other areas, including biblical worldview. Visit the website to find out the new product offerings, as well as information on its annual homeschool moms' conference and encouraging e-newsletter, its online catalog and secure ordering, and its scholarship programs for homeschool students in Indiana and North Carolina.

Alpha Omega Publications

804 N. Second Ave. E.
Rock Rapids, IA 51246

800-682-7391
www.aop.com
Christian publisher of inexpensive work texts and software
program; online catalog; secure ordering

American Home-School Publishing
P.O. Box 570
Cameron, MO 64429
800-684-2121
800-557-0234 fax
www.ahsp.com
Supplier with a classical emphasis offering an extensive selection
in all subject areas, especially good for high school, print catalog

Bob Jones University Press
Greenville, SC 29614-0062
800-845-5731
800-525-8398 fax
www.bjup.com
Christian publisher of traditional textbooks, including teacher's
manuals that are very helpful; online catalog and secure ordering
after an account is established

Book Peddler
www.bookpeddler.us
Supplier of primarily literature-based curriculum, well-designed
website, print and online catalog with secure ordering

Christian Book Distributors CBD
140 Summit Street
Peabody, MA 01960
800-247-4784
www.christianbook.com
Supplier of Christian products at a discount, including popular
homeschool titles; print and online catalog with secure ordering

Christian Liberty Press
502 W. Euclid Ave.
Arlington Heights, IL 60004
847-259-4444
www.christianlibertypress.com
Christian publisher and satellite school for homeschoolers; uses a mix of resources from various other Christian publishers as well; print and online catalog with secure ordering

Cornerstone Curriculum Project
2006 Flat Creek
Richardson, TX 75080
972-235-5149
www.cornerstonecurriculum.com
David and Shirley Quine, publishers
Popular, integrated, curriculum based on the work of Francis Schaeffer—math, science, music, art, literature; high school worldview course of study; online catalog

Debra Bell's Home School Resource Center
P.O. Box 67
Palmyra, PA 17078
717-473-8059 fax
www.debrabell.com
Scoring High test preparation program, Professor Wise's Discovery Corps Expedition Guides

Farm Country General Store
800-551-3276
www.homeschoolfcgs.com
Supplier, wide selection of resources, most at discount pricing; request catalog online

Library & Educational Services
P.O. Box 288
Berrien Springs, MI 49103
269-695-1800
269-695-8500 fax
www.libraryanded.com

School supplier and source of *Your Story Hour* tapes, great discounts on select items, primarily Christian fiction

Lifetime Books and Gifts
18755 SW 272 Street
Homestead, Fl 33031
305-248-1271
www.shoplbg.com
Gus and Shirley Solis, owners
Homeschool supplier emphasizing "living books," founded by Bob and Tina Farewell

Living Learning Books
110 Heather Ridge Drive
Pelham, AL 35124
205-620-3365
www.livinglearningbooks.com
Excellent source of curriculum guides paired with activity books and top-notch nonfiction for children, as well as award-winning science curriculum

Modern Curriculum Press
Pearson Learning
800-848-9500
www.pearsonschool.com

Mott Media
1130 Fenway Circle
Fenton, MI 48430
800-421-6645
www.mottmedia.com
Publisher and supplier, source of Ruth Beechick's titles, specializing in reprints of classic curricula such as *McGuffey's Readers* and *Harvey's Grammar*

My Father's World
P.O. Box 2140
Rolla, MO 65402
573-426-4600
www.mfwbooks.com
David and Marie Hazell, publishers
K–8 curriculum; distinctions include integrated Bible, phonics-based reading program, and literature-based unit studies; mission is to fund Bible translation projects around the world

Pennsylvania Homeschoolers
105 Richman Lane
Kittanning, PA 16201
724-783-6512
www.pahomeschoolers.com
Howard and Susan Richman, owners
Carries a select line of products you will not find elsewhere, including video courses for purchase or rental, used textbooks, and Advanced Placement and test-prep materials; specializes in high school resources; online catalog and secure ordering

Rainbow Resource Center
Route 1, Box 159A
Toulon, IL 61483
888-841-3456
www.rainbowresource.com
Supplier, discounts; online catalog and secure ordering

Rod and Staff Publishers
Box 3, Highway 172
Crockett, KY 41413
606-522-4348
800-643-1244 fax
www.rodstaff.com
Site operated by Anabaptist Bookstore, not by Rod and Staff Publishers of Anabaptist curriculum and readers popular with many homeschoolers

School Specialty Publishing
3195 Wilson Drive NW
Grand Rapids, MI 49534
800-417-3261
888-203-9361 fax
www.schoolspecialtypublishing.com
Primarily for the school market, but with a successful division
for homeschoolers; workbooks and reproducibles in every
subject area

Shekinah Curriculum Cellar
1815 Whittington Road
Kilgore, TX 75662
903-643-2760
903-643-2796 fax
www.shekinahcc.com
Supplier offering more than three thousand titles and guaranteed
low pricing; warehouse open to public

Sonlight Curriculum
8042 S. Grant Way
Littleton, CO 80122-2705
303-730-6292
www.sonlight.com
Publisher and supplier, source of international homeschool
curriculum that may be purchased complete or in parts; very
heavy concentration on reading excellent books

Sycamore Tree
2179 Meyer Place
Costa Mesa, CA 92627
888-334-6711 info
800-779-6750 orders
714-668-1344 fax
www.sycamoretree.com
Supplier offering an extensive line of resources in all subject areas;
school, online school, printed and online catalog, warehouse with
hours open to the public

Timberdoodle
1510 E. Spencer Lake Road
Shelton, WA 98584
800-478-0672 or 360-426-0672
360-427-5625 fax
www.timberdoodle.com
Dan and Deb Diffinbaugh, owners
Longtime supplier with unique selection of supplies, very informative catalog

WinterPromise
10 Folsom Harbor Road
Grand Isle, VT 05458
802-372-9200
www.winterpromise.com
Charlotte Mason-inspired curriculum with living books and activities

Specialized Publishers and Suppliers

Art
Artistic Pursuits
10142 W. 69th Avenue
Arvada, CO 80004
303-467-0504
208-567-4269 fax
www.artisticpursuits.com

How Great Thou Art
P.O. Box 48
McFarlan, NC 28102
800-982-3729
www.howgreatthouart.com
Christian program

Audio

Greathall Productions
Jim Weiss, storyteller
P.O. Box 5061
Charlottesville, VA 22905-5061
800-477-6234
www.greathall.com
Publisher of Jim Weiss's award-winning storytelling CDs; also an
excellent selection of children's classics and folklore

Sing 'n' Learn
2626 Club Meadow Drive
Garland, TX 75043
800-460-1973
www.singnlearn.com
Supplier, lots of audiotapes for your auditory learner

Your Story Hour
P.O. Box 15
Berrien Springs, MI 49103
269-471-3701
www.yourstoryhour.org

Catholic Suppliers

Bethlehem Books
10194 Garfield Street South
Bathgate, ND 58216
800-757-6831
www.bethlehembooks.com
Reprints of classic children's literature from the Catholic tradition,
many books of interest to homeschoolers

Catholic Heritage Curricula
P.O. Box 579090
Modesto, CA 95357
800-490-7713 orders
209-551-1781 fax
www.chcweb.com
Curriculum supplemented with additional resources

Ignatius Press
P.O. Box 1339
Fort Collins, CO 80522
800-651-1531
www.ignatius.com
Publisher of Catholic homeschooling books by Laura Berquist

Charlotte Mason

Charlotte Mason Research & Supply Company
P.O. Box 296
Quarryville, PA 17566
www.charlottemason.com
Dean and Karen Andreola, owners
Publishers of the *Charlotte Mason Companion* and articles on
Mason's philosophy

Queen Homeschool Supply
168 Plantz Ridge Road
New Freeport, PA 15352
888-695-2777
www.queenhomeschool.com
Specializes in the living books popular with a Charlotte Mason
approach.

WinterPromise
10 Folsom Harbor Road
Grand Isle, VT 05458
802-372-9200
www.winterpromise.com
Charlotte Mason-inspired curriculum with living books and
activities

Children's Books

Dorling Kindersley Family Learning
375 Hudson St
New York, NY 10014
800-788-6262 orders
www.dk.com

Publisher of informative and innovative books for adults and children; print and online catalog with secure ordering

Scholastic Book Clubs
800-724-6527
www.scholastic.com
Discounted software and children's books

Usborne Books at Home
Educational Development Co.
P.O. Box 470663
Tulsa, OK 74147-0663
800-475-4522
www.edcpub.com
Publisher of informative and lavishly illustrated books for children

Classical Christian
Canon Press & Book Service
P.O. Box 8729
Moscow, ID 83843
800-488-2034
www.canonpress.org
Publisher of curricula for classical schools, including books by Douglas Wilson; print and online catalog

Tapestry of Grace
Lampstand Press
8077 Snouffer School Road
Gaithersburg, MD 20879
800-705-7487
www.tapestryofgrace.com
Publishers of Marcia Somerville's hefty curriculum for high school; lovely integration of traditional curricula and the providential hand of God through time

Veritas Press
1829 William Penn Way
Lancaster, PA 17601
800-922-5082
717-519-1978 fax
www.veritaspress.com
Publisher and supplier of classical Christian resources and one of the most beautiful catalogs you are ever likely to see

Well Trained Mind
Peace Hill Press
18021 The Glebe Lane
Charles City, VA 23030
877-322-3445
www.welltrainedmind.com
www.peacehillpress.com

Coloring Books
Bellerophon
P.O. Box 21307
Santa Barbara, CA 93121-1307
800-253-9943
www.bellerophonbooks.com
Publisher of history-teaching coloring books, most using historical drawings

Dover Publications
www.doverpublications.com
Publisher of history-teaching coloring books with supporting text

Creation Science
Answers in Genesis
P.O. Box 510
Hebron, KY 41048
800-778-3390
www.answersingenesis.org

Apologia Educational Ministries
1106 Meridian Plaza, Suite 220
Anderson, IN 46016
888-524-4724
765-608-3290 fax
www.apologia.com
Christian publisher of excellent middle school and high school science curriculum written by Dr. Jay Wile, biblical worldview curriculum, and excellent elementary material using a Charlotte Mason approach; online catalog; secure ordering, and its scholarship programs for homeschool students in Indiana and North Carolina.

Media Angels
www.mediaangels.com
Felice Gerwitz and Jill Whitlock, publishers
Publisher of science study guides for geology, astronomy, and anatomy, primarily for elementary students; online catalog

Creative Writing
Brave Writer
7723 Tyler's Place Boulevard, #165
West Chester, OH 45069
513-307-1405
www.bravewriter.com
An approach to writing and homeschooling inspired by Charlotte Mason

Institute for Excellence in Writing
P.O. Box 6065
Atascadero CA 93423
800-856-5815
www.excellenceinwriting.com
Andrew Pudewa's brainchild for improving writing, spelling, and thinking

WriteAtHome
www.writeathome.com
Internet-based writing courses for teens directed by Brian Wasko, former high school teacher and homeschool father; all coaches are professional writers or educators

WriteGuide.com
43 Wood Road
Barrington, NH 03825
603-905-9039
www.writeguide.com
Online individualized writing courses for homeschoolers

Driver Education

National Driver Training Institute
4432 Austin Bluffs Parkway
Colorado Springs, CO 80918
800-942-2050
www.nationaldrivertraining.com
Publishers of a certified driver-training course that parents can conduct; accepted by many states and insurance companies; secure online registration

Educational Toys and Electronic Games

Back To Basics Toys
800-356-5360
www.backtobasicstoys.com

Educational Insights
152 W. Walnut Street, Suite 201
Gardena, CA 90248
888-591-9334
www.educationalinsights.com

Montessori Services
11 W. 9th Street
Santa Rosa, CA 95401
888-274-4003
www.forsmallhands.com

Geography
Bright Idea Press
P.O. Box 333
Cheswold, DE 19936
877-492-8081
www.brightideaspress.com
Maggie Hogan, proprietor
Specializing in geography; also publishes history curricula and timelines

Educational Insights
152 W. Walnut Street, Suite 201
Gardena, CA 90248
888-591-9334
www.educationalinsights.com
School supplier; distributor of *GeoSafari Electronic Game*

Geography Matters
P.O. Box 92
Nancy, KY 42544
800-426-4650
www.geomatters.com
Cindy and Josh Wiggers, owner
Publisher and supplier of geography curriculum, maps, other resources; great links for history and geography; online catalog

Knowledge Quest
P.O. Box 789
Boring, OR 97009
877-697-8611
www.knowledgequestmaps.com
Excellent geography program and blackline maps

477

National Council for Geographic Education
1710 16th Street NW
Washington, DC 20009-3198
202-360-4237
www.ncge.org
Publisher of *Geography for Life* national standards; online catalog; secure ordering

High School
Christian Home Education Press (CHEA)
P.O. Box 2009
Norwalk, CA 90651-2009
562-864-2432
www.cheaofca.org
State homeschool association and publisher of the *High School Handbook*; online catalog

College Board
45 Columbus Avenue
New York, NY 10023-6917
212-713-8000
www.collegeboard.com
Publisher of many books to assist students in preparing for College Board-administered tests and for college

Crown Financial Concepts
P.O. Box 100
Gainesville, GA 30503-0100
800-722-1976
www.crown.org
Money management and career exploration tools for teens; online catalog; secure ordering

Education Plus
9321 Brookville Road
Indianapolis, IN 46239
317-222-1695
www.edplus.com

Dr. Ronald and Inge Cannon, directors
Resources directed at parenting and equipping teens

Global Learning Strategies
5463 Road S SE
Warden, WA 98857
509-349-1995
www.globallearningstrategies.org
Publisher of *Accelerated Distance Learning* by Brad Voeller

Also see **Cornerstone Curriculum Project** in the General
Publishers and Suppliers listings.

**South Carolina Association of Independent Home Schools
(SCAIHS)**
930 Knox Abbott Drive
Cayce, SC 29033
803-454-0427
www.scaihs.org
Tracking and recording high school credits; issuing transcripts;
providing curriculum counseling; informing parents about special
extracurricular opportunities; providing guidance services; hosting
a formal graduation ceremony every year; membership not limited
to South Carolina families, but non-residents need to comply with
their state laws in addition to those of SCAIHS

History
Beautiful Feet Books
1306 Mill Street
San Luis Obispo, CA 93401
800-889-1978 orders
805-542-9847
www.bfbooks.com
Russ and Rea Berg, publishers
Also suppliers offering great study guides for history using classic
and quality children's literature

Christian History Institute

P.O. Box 540
Worcester, PA 19490
800-468-0458
www.chitorch.org
Publishers of excellent bulletin inserts on church history; many archived online

Cobblestone Publishing

30 Grove Street, Suite C
Peterborough, NH 03458
800-821-0115
603-924-7380 fax
www.cobblestonepub.com
Publishes several history and culture magazines, including *Cobblestone American* history magazine

Diana Waring Presents!

621 State Route 9 NE, PMB B-14
Lake Stevens, WA 98258
425-397-0631
www.dianawaring.com
Bill and Diana Waring, publishers and entertainers
Hilarious presentations; Diana is a popular speaker who has produced, among other things, a great history course; also a passionate Christian with a heart for missions; print and online catalog with secure ordering

Drive Thru History with Dave Stotts

Coldwater Media
P.O. Box 470
Palmer Lake, CO 80133
719-488-8670
www.coldwatermedia.com
Produces exceptional and entertaining DVDs on history and other topics

Greenleaf Press
3761 Highway 109 North
Lebanon, TN 37087
615-449-1617
www.greenleafpress.com
Rob and Cyndy Shearer, publishers
Also suppliers; beautiful catalog majoring in history resources and
the Greenleaf Press study guides

Home School in the Woods
3997 Roosevelt Highway
Holley, NY 14470
585-964-8188
www.homeschoolinthewoods.com
Specializes in timelines, timeline figures and unit studies

Jackdaw Publications
P.O. Box 503
Amawalk, NY 10501
800-789-0022
www.jackdaws.com
Hands-on primary sources for grades 5–12

Social Studies School Service
10200 Jefferson Boulevard, Box 802
Culver City, CA 90232
800-421-4246
800-944-5432 fax
socialstudies.com
School supplier offering a vast array of resources for high school
history, cultures, government, civics, and economics courses;
Advanced Placement resources as well

Veritas Press
1829 William Penn Way
Lancaster, PA 17601
800-922-5082
www.veritaspress.com
Publisher of an exquisite and history-based classical
Christian curriculum

481

Foreign Languages

Greek 'n' Stuff
P.O. Box 882
Moline, IL 61266-0882
309-796-2707
309-796-2706 fax
www.greeknstuff.com
Karen Mohs, owner
Latin and Greek curricula plus great links to the classical world; online catalog

Rosetta Stone
135 W. Market Street
Harrisonburg, VA 22801
800-767-3882
www.rosettastone.com
Excellent language courses used by the Peace Corps, the diplomatic community, and many homeschoolers

Language Arts

Easy Grammar Systems
P.O. Box 25970
Scottsdale, AZ 85255
800-641-6015
www.easygrammar.com
Publisher of *Easy Grammar* and *Daily Grams*; online catalog

Educators Publishing Service (EPS)
P.O. Box 9031
Cambridge, MA 02139-9031
800-225-5750
888-440-2665 fax
www.epsbooks.com
Publisher of *Explode the Code, Wordly Wise*, and other popular resources

Great Source Books
P.O. Box 7050
Wilmington, MA 01887
800-289-4490
www.greatsource.com
Source of *Write Source* curriculum

Total Language Plus
P.O. Box 12622
Olympia, WA 98508
360-754-3660
www.totallanguageplus.com
Publisher of a curriculum that teaches thinking and
communication skills using literature as a base

Literature

Five in a Row
P.O. Box 707
Grandview, MO 64030-0707
816-246-9252
www.fiveinarow.com
Literature-based unit study program for early elementary

Progeny Press
P.O. Box 100
Fall Creek, WI 54742
877-776-4369
715-877-9953 fax
www.progenypress.com
Bible-based study guides to the classics and popular children's
literature; online catalog

Math

ETA/Cuisenaire

500 Greenview Court
Vernon Hills, IL 60061
800-445-5985
800-875-9643 fax
www.etacuisenaire.com
Distributor of Cuisenaire products

Boxer Math

www.boxermath.com
Interactive and self-paced math tutorial for students in grades 3-12; lessons cover fundamentals of arithmetic through trigonometry

Chalk Dust Company

PMB 256, 16107 Kensington Drive
Sugar Land, TX 77479-4401
800-588-7564
www.chalkdust.com
Dana Mosely, instructor
DVD/video courses including algebra, algebra II, trigonometry, pre-calculus, calculus, and SAT review; online product descriptions

Common Sense Press

Educators Publishing Service
8786 Highway 21
Melrose, FL 32666
352-475-5757
www.commonsensepress.com
Publisher of *Grocery Cart Math*

Curriculum Associates

153 Rangeway Road
North Billerica, MA 01862
800-225-0248
www.curriculumassociates.com
Source of *Figure It Out* workbooks

Dale Seymour Publications / Pearson Learning
800-848-9500
www.pearsonlearning.com
School supplier of resources for elementary level; online catalog;
secure ordering

Equals
Lawrence Hall of Science
University of California Berkeley
Centennial Drive
Berkeley, CA 94720-5200
510-642-5132
www.lawrencehallofscience.org/equals
Publisher of *Family Math* and several other engaging programs for
children

Key Curriculum Press
1150 65th Street
Emeryville, CA 94608
800-995-6284
800-541-2442 fax
www.keycurriculumpress.com
Publishers of *Miquon Math* and the *Keys to . . .* series; online
catalog; secure ordering

Learning Wrap-Ups
1660 W. Gordon Avenue #4
Layton, UT 84041
800-992-4966
801-497-0063 fax
www.learningwrapups.com
Deftly simple and hand-held learning aid for teaching basic
arithmetic facts

Math-U-See
888-854-6284
www.mathusee.com
Innovative and hands-on math program by Steve Demme; must
be ordered through area representatives; ordering information
available online

Muggins Math
Old Fashioned Products
4860 Burnt Mountain Road
Ellijay, GA 30536
800-962-8849
706-635-7611 fax
www.mugginsmath.com
Math games; online catalog; secure ordering

Providence Project
14566 NW 110th Street
Whitewater, KS 67154
888-776-8776
www.providenceproject.com
Sequential drills; online catalog; secure ordering

RightStart Math
Activities for Learning
321 Hill Street
P.O. Box 468
Hazelton, ND 58544
888-272-3291
www.alabacus.com

Saxon Publishers
HMH Supplemental Publishers
181 Ballardvale Street
Wilmington, MA 01887
800-289-4490
800-289-3994 fax
www.saxonpub.com
Publisher of a traditional program widely available from
homeschool suppliers

Singapore Math
404 Beavercreek Road #225
Oregon City, OR 97045
503-557-8100 no phone orders
503-557-8103 fax

www.singaporemath.com
Import gaining broad appeal in the U.S. market against the face of declining math scores; K–12 program, emphasizing problem solving and concepts instead of rote learning; disciplines integrated and introduced much earlier than traditionally taught

Teaching Textbooks
P.O. Box 60529
Oklahoma City, OK 73146-0529
866-867-6284
405-525-3605 fax
www.teachingtextbooks.com
Curriculum for grades 4–7 and from pre-algebra through pre-calculus; companion CDs include a graphic demonstration of all lessons plus steps to correctly solve all problems; students can complete courses with little help from parents

Twenty-Four Math Game
Suntex International
3311 Fox Hill Road
Easton, PA 18045
610-253-5255
www.math24.com
Publisher of games that teach critical thinking using math facts and algebra

VideoText Interactive
800-254-3272
www.videotext.com
Lavishly produced video/DVD courses for algebra and geometry by master teacher Tom Clark, who is passionate about teaching math from a conceptual level, devoting ample time to the "why" undergirding the steps taken to solve a math problem; well-thought-out animations illustrate each lesson; program builds sequentially on students' prior knowledge

Wide World Publishing / Math Products Plus
P.O. Box 476
San Carlos, CA 94070
650-593-2839
650-595-0802 fax
www.mathproductsplus.com
Publisher of Theoni Pappas's excellent books; online catalog

Parenting Resources
Shepherd Press
800-338-1445
www.shepherdpress.com
Publisher of Tedd Tripp's *Shepherding a Child's Heart* and its
sequel on parenting teens, *Age of Opportunity* by Paul Tripp

Sovereign Grace Ministries
7505 Muncaster Mill Road
Gaithersburg, MD 20877
800-736-2202
www.sovereigngraceministries.com
Publisher of Bible studies and teaching recordings for families and
small groups; parent organization for Joshua Harris's teaching
ministry

Whole Heart Ministries
P.O. Box 3445
Monument, CO 80132
800-311-2146 orders
719-488-4466 info
www.wholeheart.org
Clay and Sally Clarkson, owners

Planners
Edu-Track Home School Software
ConTECH Solutions
5517 N. Farmer Branch Road, PMB 130
Ozark, MO 65721
866-682-3025

www.contechsolutions.net
High-tech solution to planning lessons and organizing records; customizable

Ferg N Us Services
P.O. Box 350
Richville, NY 13681
315-287-9131
www.fergnusservices.com
Publisher of the popular "Homeschool Journal" daily planners for moms and teens

Homeschool Tracker
TGHomeSoft
4521 Ross Lanier Lane
Kissimmee, FL 34758
www.homeschooltracker.com

Managers of Their Homes
1504 Santa Fe Street
Leavenworth, KS 66048-4141
913-772-0392
www.titus2.com
Publisher of *A Practical Guide to Daily Scheduling for Christian Home-School Families* by Steve and Teri Maxwell

Public Speaking
Myers Institute for Leadership & Communication
P.O. Box 7
Dayton, TN 37321
423-570-1000
www.myersinstitute.com
Jeff Myers, publisher of *From Playpen to Podium*

Puzzles

Lauri Puzzles
Patch Products
1400 E. Inman Parkway
Beloit, WI 53511
800-524-4263
608-362-8178 fax
www.lauritoys.com
Large selection of popular educational puzzles made of crepe foam rubber for preschool and elementary

Reading

4:20 Communications
P.O. Box 421027
Minneapolis, MN 55442-0027
888-420-7323
www.phonicstutor.com
Publisher of *PhonicsTutor* software; online catalog; secure ordering

Educators Publishing Service (EPS)
P.O. Box 9031
Cambridge, MA 02139-9031
800-435-7728
888-440-2665 fax
www.epsbooks.com
Publisher of *Explode the Code* and other phonics-based workbooks

Paradigm
208-322-4440
208-322-7781 fax
www.alpha-phonics.com
Samuel Blumenfeld, publisher of *Alpha-Phonics*.

Pearson Learning Group
800-526-9907
800-393-3156
www.pearsonlearning.com
Publisher of *Sing, Spell, Read and Write* and *Winning* reading programs

Teach 4 Mastery
800-745-8212
www.teach4mastery.com
Joyce Herzog's *Scaredy Cat Reading* program; use the website to find your area representative

Also see **My Father's World** under General Publishers and Suppliers.

Science
See also **Creation Science**

American Chemical Society
1155 Sixteenth Street NW
Washington, DC 20036
800-227-5558
www.chemistry.org > education
Publisher of *The Best of WonderScience*

Apologia Educational Ministries
1106 Meridian Plaza, Suite 220
Anderson, IN 46016
888-524-4724; 765-608-3290 fax
www.apologia.com
Christian publisher of excellent middle and high school science curriculum by Dr. Jay Wile and colorful elementary science texts by Jeannie Fulbright; online catalog; secure ordering; and its scholarship programs for homeschool students in Indiana and North Carolina.

Carolina Biological Supply
2700 York Road
Burlington, NC 27215-3398
800-334-5551
www.carolina.com
Large supplier of science resources, lab equipment, and supplies;
online catalog; secure ordering

Castle Heights Press
200 E. Iowa Avenue
Berthoud, CO 80513
970-532-2209
www.castleheightspress.com
Kathleen and Mark Julicher, publishers
Science programs for high school; online catalog

Delta Education
80 Northwest Blvd.
Nashua, NH 03061-3000
800-258-1302
www.delta-education.com
Hands-on manipulatives for science and math for grades K–8

Home Science Tools
665 Carbon Street
Billings, MT 59102
800-860-6272; 888-860-2344 fax
www.hometrainingtools.com
Supplier of science equipment and labs designed to match BJU,
A Beka, and other programs

Insect Lore
P.O. Box 1535
Shafter, CA 93263-1535
800-LIVE-BUG
www.insectlore.com
Source of exploratory kits and supplies for life sciences

Lyrical Life Science

8008 Cardwell Hill
Corvallis, OR 97330
800-761-0906
www.lyricallearning.com
Publishers of an excellent upper elementary/junior high science
program especially suited to auditory learners

National Wildlife Federation

11100 Wildlife Center Drive
Reston, VA 20190
800-822-9919
www.nwf.org
Publishers of *Your Big Backyard* and other nature magazines
for kids

Tobin's Lab

P.O. Box 725
Culpeper, VA 22701
540-829-6906
www.tobinslab.com
Homeschool supplier of science resources organized around the
six days of creation

Tops Learning Systems

10970 S. Mulino Road
Canby, OR 97013
503-266-5200 fax (preferred to calling for orders)
503-263-2040
www.topscience.org
Innovative, low-cost science—and now math — labs designed
for schools on small budgets; uses many household items for
excellent labs

Wild Goose Science Company

888-621-1040
www.carsondellosa.com
www.wildgoosescience.com

Scope and Sequence

Core Knowledge Foundation
801 E. High Street
Charlottesville, VA 22902
800-238-3233
www.coreknowledge.org
Source of "core knowledge sequence," the scope and sequence recommended in E. D. Hirsch's core knowledge books

World Book Educational Division
233 N. Michigan Avenue, Suite 2000
Chicago, IL 60601
312-729-5800
www.worldbook.com
Scope and sequence "Kindergarten Through Grade Twelve: A Typical Course of Study" is published free online

Software

4:20 COMMUNICATIONS
see Reading

Academic Superstore
2101 E. Saint Elmo Road, Suite 360
Austin, TX 787444
800-817-2347
www.academicsuperstore.com

Barnum Software
1910 Lyon Avenue
Belmont, CA 94002
800-553-9155
800-553-9156 fax
www.thequartermile.com

Broderbund/Edmark/Learning Company
800-395-0277
www.broderbund.com
Broderbund publishes a wide range of popular software;

Edmark specializes in software for remediation and reinforcement of skill areas; The Learning Company publishes the Carmen Sandiego software

Grammar Key
P.O. Box 33230
Tulsa, OK 74153
www.grammarkey.com

Harmonic Vision
210 S. 5th Street, Suite 12
Saint Charles, IL 60174
800-474-0903
www.harmonicvision.com
Publisher of Music Ace software

Knowledge Adventure School
800-871-2969
www.knowledgeadventureschool.com
Distributor of *Blaster*, *Jump Start*, Dr. Brain series, and *Spell It Deluxe* software

Standardized Tests
Bayside School Services
P.O. Box 250
Kill Devil Hills, NC 27948
800-723-3057
www.baysideschoolservices.com

Bob Jones University Press
Customer Service
1700 Wade Hampton Blvd.
Greenville, SC 29614-0062
800-845-5731
www.bjup.com/services/testing

Family Learning Organization
P.O. Box 1750
Mead, WA 99021-1750
800-405-8378
www.familylearning.org

Piedmont Education Services
1629 Turfwood Drive
Pfafftown, NC 27040
336-924-2494
www.pesdirect.com

Seton Testing Services
1350 Progress Drive
Front Royal, VA 22630
800-542-1066
www.setontesting.com
Parents may administer the CAT-E—survey edition, shorter than
the CAT/5

Sycamore Tree
2179 Meyer Place
Costa Mesa, CA 92627
800-779-6750
www.sycamoretree.com

Unit Studies

Amanda Bennett's Unit Study Adventures
423-243-4748
www.unitstudy.com

Design-A-Study
408 Victoria Avenue
Wilmington, DE 19804-2124
800-965-2719
www.designastudy.com
Kathryn and Richard Stout, publishers
Study guides for language arts, science, math, and social studies;
online catalog

KONOS
P.O. Box 250
Anna, TX 75409
972-924-2712
www.konos.com
Jessica and Wade Hulcy, publishers
One of the oldest unit-study programs, redesigned for easy use;
online catalog; secure ordering

Video Instruction

Annenberg Media
P.O. Box 55742
Indianapolis, IN 46205-0742
800-532-7637
317-579-0402 fax
www.learner.org
Distributor of high school- and college-level video courses; online
catalog; secure ordering

The Teaching Company
4840 Westfields Blvd., Suite 500
Chantilly, VA 20151
800-832-2412
703-378-3819 fax
www.teach12.com
Producer of audio and video courses featuring top-rated lecturers

Used-Curriculum Suppliers

The Back Pack
P.O. Box 125
Ernul, NC 28527
252-244-0728
www.thebackpack.com

Educator's Exchange
10755 Midlothian Turnpike, Suite 308
Richmond, VA 23235
804-794-6994 info
888-257-4159 orders
www.edexbooks.com
Jim and Glenda Chiarello, owners

Follett Educational Services
Home Education Division
1433 International Parkway
Woodbridge, IL 60517-4941
800-621-4272
800-638-4424 fax
www.fes.follett.com
Supplier of used and refurbished textbooks; good source of the Chicago Math [UCSMP] student texts, although support material must typically be purchased from the publisher

Homeschooler's Curriculum Swap
P.O. Box 645
The Dalles, OR 97058
www.theswap.com
Well-organized site with lots of other areas of interest, including moderated forums

Moore Expressions
6070 Indiana River Road, Suites 106-112
Virginia Beach, VA 23464
757-523-4965
www.mooreexpressions.com
Cherie Moore, owner
Store and mail-order business

ACADEMIC/ATHLETIC CONTESTS AND COMPETITIONS

24 Challenge Math Program
First in Math
Suntex International
3311 Fox Hill Road
Easton, PA 18045
610-253-5255
www.math24.com

Book-It! Program
Pizza Hut, Inc.
P.O. Box 2999
Wichita, KS 67201
800-426-6548
316-685-0977 fax
www.bookitprogram.com
Reading incentive program for grades K–6

Center for Talented Youth CTY Talent Search
Johns Hopkins University
McAuley Hall
5801 Smith Avenue, Suite 400
Baltimore, MD 21209
410-735-6277 or 6278
cty.jhu.edu
For second- through eighth-graders who score in the 97th percentile or above on standardized achievement test

Education Program for Gifted Youth EPGY

Ventura Hall
220 Panama Street
Stanford University
Stanford, CA 94305-4101
800-372-EPGY
http://epgy.stanford.edu
Expensive but prestigious courses online

Freedoms Foundation's National Awards Program for Youth

Freedoms Foundation at Valley Forge
P.O. Box 706
1601 Valley Forge Road
Valley Forge, PA 19482-0706
610-933-8825
www.ffvf.org

Future Problem Solving Program International

2015 Grant Place
Melbourne, FL 32901
800-256-1499
www.fpspi.org

Intel International Science and Engineering Fair

Society for Science & the Public
1719 N Street NW
Washington, DC 20036
202-785-2255
www.societyforscience.org/isef
National organization that sets standards for locally and regionally
juried science and engineering fairs

Invent America

www.inventamerica.org
Teaches creative problem-solving skills through inventions

Knowledge Open Academic Competition
Academic Hallmarks
P.O. Box 998
Durango, CO 81302
800-321-9218
www.greatauk.com
Competition comes on CD-ROM

Make a Difference Day
USA WEEKEND/Make a Difference Day
800-416-3824
www.makeadifferenceday.com
For all ages; group volunteer project

Math Olympiad
2154 Bellmore Avenue
Bellmore, NY 11710-5645
516-781-2400
www.moems.org
Registration deadline September 30
$75 per team of up to 35 students

Mathcounts
MathCounts Foundation
1420 King Street
Alexandria, VA 22314
703-299-9006
www.mathcounts.org

National Christian Forensics and Communications Association
NCFCA Corporate Office
P.O. Box 212
Mountlake Terrace, WA 98043-0212
505-516-5580
www.ncfca.org
HSLDA started a national debate tournament years ago to foster forensics. When the movement took off, this organization was formed to oversee the activities. Chapters are now located in most states.

National Energy Education Development Project (NEED)
The NEED Project
8408 Kao Circle
Manassas, VA 20110
703-257-1117; 703-257-0037 fax
www.need.org
K–12 group project

National Geography Bee
National Geographic Society
1145 17th Street NW
Washington, DC 20036-4688
www.nationalgeographic.com/geographybee

National History Day
0119 Cecil Hall
University of Maryland
College Park, MD 20742
301-314-9739
www.nationalhistoryday.org

National Spelling Bee
Scripps Howard National Spelling Bee
312 Walnut Street, 28th Floor
Cincinnati, OH 45202
513-977-3040
www.spellingbee.com

Odyssey of the Mind Program
c/o Creative Competitions, Inc.
406 Ganttown Road
Sewell, NJ 08080
856-256-2797
www.odysseyofthemind.org

Online Math League
269-795-9680
www.onlinemathleague.com

The President's Challenge
501 N. Morton, Suite 203
Bloomington, IN 47404
800-258-8146
www.presidentschallenge.com

Quill & Scroll Society
University of Iowa
School of Journalism and Mass Communication
100 Adler Journalism Building
Iowa City, IA 52242
319-335-3457
319-335-3989 fax
www.uiowa.edu/~quill-sc
Writing and photography contest

Scholastic Art and Writing Awards
Alliance for Young Artists & Writers
557 Broadway
New York, NY 10012
212-343-6100
www.scholastic.com/artandwritingawards

Science Olympiad
2 Trans Am Plaza Drive, Suite 415
Oakbrook Terrace, IL 60181
630-792-1251
630-792-1287 fax
www.soinc.org
Science tournaments for K–12 on regional, state, and national levels

The Stock Market Game
120 Broadway, 35th Floor
New York, NY 10271-0080
212-313-1350
212-313-1324 fax
www.smgww.org

Stone Soup Magazine
P.O. Box 83
Santa Cruz, CA 95063
800-447-4569
www.stonesoup.com
Publishes the creative work of children ages 8-13

ThinkQuest
www.thinkquest.org
Cooperative teams of students build websites related to
specified topic

Young America Horticulture Contests
National Junior Horticultural Association
15 Railroad Avenue
Homer City, PA 15748-1378
724-479-3254
www.njha.org
For ages 8-14; group/individual projects

Additional Sources of Academic Opportunities

American Society of Mechanical Engineers
www.asme.org/events/contests
Website maintains an up-to-date database of science competitions

National Association of Secondary School Principals
NASSP Contests and Activities Advisory List
1904 Association Drive
Reston, VA 20191-1537
703-860-0200
www.nassp.org
www.nhs.us/scaa/SCAA_List.cfm
National Honor Society lists the database, booklet of
recommended academic contests, updated regularly

The Young Writer's Guide to Getting Published, Kathy Henderson
Writer's Digest Books

NOTES

Introduction

1. Pennsylvania law requires periodic testing and an annual review of a home-educated student's work by a certified teacher contracted by the parents. In providing this service, I've had close examination of scores of kids from a broad spectrum of backgrounds and abilities.
2. In some states, parents are not required to report they are homeschooling to authorities; in states such as Pennsylvania, reporting is only required after a child turns eight. This accounts for the discrepancies between the U.S. Department of Education and Dr. Ray's findings.

Chapter 1. Determining Your Destination

1. "Classical education" refers to a course of study that focuses on the "great books" of Western civilization, beginning with the Greek and Roman manuscripts. This is also referred to as a "liberal" education or "the grand conversation." A classical, Christian education is enjoying a resurgence of interest fueled by Douglas Wilson's book *Recovering the Lost Tools of Learning: An Approach to a Distinctively Christian Education* (Crossway, 1991).

Chapter 2. The Advantages of Homeschooling

1. *What Works: Research about Teaching and Learning*, second edition,1987. The entire document is retrievable at www.eric.ed.gov.
2. *A Nation at Risk*, published by the National Commission on Excellence in Education, cited in Charles Sykes's *Dumbing Down Our Kids: Why American Children Feel Good About Themselves but Can't Read, Write, or Add* (New York: St. Martin's, 1995), 20.
3. Ibid., 16.
4. Ibid., 16.
5. Ibid., 16.
6. Ibid., 17.
7. Ibid., 19.
8. Ibid., 11–12.

9. A "great books" college is one that focuses on a classical education utilizing the great books of Western civilization, beginning with the Greek and Roman manuscripts.

Chapter 5. Single Parents, Special Needs, Careers, and Other FAQs

1. While I've seen many try, I've yet to see a family succeed at homeschooling in the evenings after putting in a full day at work. Both parent and child are usually too tired to care at that point.

2. *Fact Sheet III*, National Home Education Research Institute, 1995.

3. These conclusions are from National Home Education Research Institute's *Fact Sheet I*, 1994.

Chapter 9. Determining Your Child's Learning Style

1. For more information on Keirsey's work, see David Keirsey and Marilyn Bates, *Please Understand Me: Character and Temperament Types* (Del Mar, CA: Prometheus Nemesis, 1982).

2. The following information about learning styles is adapted from the work of Dr. Keith Golay, *Learning Patterns and Temperament Styles* (Manas Systems, 1982).

3. Golay, *Learning Patterns and Temperament Styles*, 30.

Chapter 21. Subject-by-Subject Guidelines

1. *Newsweek* (Fall/Winter Special Edition: Education, 1990), 18.

2. Saxon also has a K–3 program that is well designed and manipulative-based. However, it is fairly expensive and requires daily teacher-student tutorials. For this reason, I have not found it a practical choice for most families.

3. C. S. Lewis, *Mere Christianity* (New York: Macmillan, 1952), 56.

Chapter 22. Should You Do It?

1. A "great books" college is one that focuses on a classical education utilizing the great books of Western civilization, beginning with the Greek and Roman manuscripts.

Chapter 24. Navigating College Admissions Channels

1. "Survey of Admissions Policies, 1996," National Center for Home Education.
2. This article, reprinted with permission from the author, first appeared in the *Pennsylvania Homeschoolers* newsletter, issue 50. Rhett then attended college on a full academic scholarship.

Chapter 25. College at Home

1. Charles Sykes and Brad Miner, *The National Review College Guide* (New York: Simon and Schuster, 1993), 11–12.
2. Ibid., 16.

Chapter 28. Navigating the Net

1. Nicholas Carr, "Is Google Making Us Stoopid?" *Atlantic Monthly* (July/Aug 2008). Retrieved online at www.theatlantic.com, July 14, 2008.

Chapter 32. Motivating the Reluctant Learner

1. The "unschooling" approach gives children complete autonomy in choosing what they will study, when, and for how long.

INDEX

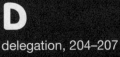

CONTACT THE AUTHOR

Debra Bell

Debra Bell's Home School Resource Center
P.O. Box 67
Palmyra, PA 17078
E-mail: debraabell@gmail.com
www.debrabell.com

Debra loves to travel and is available to speak at conventions and seminars. These are just a few of her most requested topics:

Twenty-First Century Homeschooling

Homeschooling from a Foundation of Grace

Cultivating a Love for Learning in our Homes

Motivating the Reluctant Learner

Raising an Independent Learner

Developing Creative and Critical Thinking Skills

Choosing and Using Children's Literature

Homeschooling Teens

Determining Your Child's Learning Style

Raising a Writer

Designing a College-Prep High School Program

For a description of these and many other seminar topics, visit www.debrabell.com.